DAILY LIFE IN

ANCIENT MESOPOTAMIA

Recent Titles in
The Greenwood Press "Daily Life Through History" Series

Daily Life in Elizabethan England
Jeffrey L. Singman

Daily Life in Chaucer's England
Jeffrey L. Singman and Will McLean

Daily Life in the Inca Empire
Michael A. Malpass

Daily Life in Maya Civilization
Robert J. Sharer

Daily Life in Victorian England
Sally Mitchell

Daily Life in the United States, 1960–1990: Decades of Discord
Myron A. Marty

Daily Life of the Aztecs: People of the Sun and Earth
David Carrasco with Scott Sessions

DAILY LIFE IN
ANCIENT MESOPOTAMIA

KAREN RHEA NEMET-NEJAT

The Greenwood Press "Daily Life Through History" Series

GREENWOOD PRESS
Westport, Connecticut • London

Library of Congress Cataloging-in-Publication Data

Nemet-Nejat, Karen Rhea.
   Daily life in ancient Mesopotamia / Karen Rhea Nemet-Nejat.
      p.   cm.—(Greenwood Press "Daily life through history"
series, ISSN 1080–4749)
   Includes bibliographical references and index.
   ISBN 0–313–29497–6 (alk. paper)
   1. Iraq—Civilization—To 634.   I. Title.   II. Series.
DS69.5.N5   1998
935—dc21   97–53110

British Library Cataloguing in Publication Data is available.

Library of Congress Catalog Card Number: 97–53110
ISBN: 0–313–29497–6
ISSN: 1080–4749

First published in 1998

Greenwood Press, 88 Post Road West, Westport, CT 06881
An imprint of Greenwood Publishing Group, Inc.

Printed in the United States of America

♾

The paper used in this book complies with the
Permanent Paper Standard issued by the National
Information Standards Organization (Z39.48–1984).

10 9 8 7 6 5 4 3 2 1

Copyright Acknowledgments

Excerpts from *The Sumerians: Their History, Culture and Character*, by S. N. Kramer.
Chicago: University of Chicago Press, 1963.

Excerpts from *Before the Muses: An Anthology of Akkadian Literature*, by Benjamin R.
Foster. Bethesda, MD: CDL Press, 1996

Excerpts from *Law Collections from Mesopotamia and Asia Minor*, by Martha T. Roth.
Atlanta: Scholars Press, 1995.

Every reasonable effort has been made to trace the owners of copyright materials in this
book, but in some instances this has proven to be impossible. The author and publisher
will be glad to receive information leading to more complete acknowledgments in subsequent printings of the book and in the meantime extend their apologies for any omissions.

To my beloved mother, Sarah R. Waldman,
who taught me a mantra since I was a child:
''When you grow up, you will get your B.A., your M.A.,
and your Ph.D.''
She was right!

Contents

Preface

The purpose of *Daily Life in Ancient Mesopotamia* is to examine original texts and artifacts in order to present a picture of life in ancient times. This book fills an important gap, since most of the "daily life" books were written thirty to forty years ago. Clearly, our knowledge of the area has expanded as new sites have been excavated, buildings and artifacts uncovered, and tablets deciphered.

Civilization began in the ancient Near East, with diverse ethnic groups occupying the region. Mesopotamia's size varied under the rule of different ethnic groups, such as the Sumerians, Babylonians, and Assyrians. Each people developed new kinds of government: city-states, nations, and empires.

This book briefly examines Mesopotamia beginning with the Paleolithic period and ending with the Persian domination. The focus of the book is historical Mesopotamia, the place where writing began ca. 3100 BC. Mesopotamia was rich in textual sources: literature, the "first dictionaries," "craft manuals," scientific and mathematical texts, legal documents, historical documents, official and personal correspondence, bureaucratic records, and magico-religious texts. These tablets have helped confirm, deny, or identify archaeological evidence.

All English translations of ancient texts have been attributed to various authors unless I have translated the text. Usually, I have used the translations of other scholars so that readers would be able to refer to the articles and books cited for further information. Because ancient documents often come to us in damaged condition, the following conventions have been used: parentheses ( ) to add words or explanations to make the text intelligible in English; brackets [ ] to restore words or parts of words restored or lost in damaged texts; and ellipses within brackets [. . .] to indicate a text that can no longer be restored. The endnotes contain both nonscholarly and scholarly references to aid the reader. The term "after" an author's name in the endnotes means that I have changed information or quotes in some way. The use of *apud* in the endnotes indicates that a specific citation can be found in a given book, easily accessible to the reader; that is, the citation is not the original source which is often found in obscure books available to scholars.

Terms from ancient languages, usually Akkadian, appear in italics, but Sumerian words are given in small capitals. I have tried not to burden the reader with a plethora of foreign words. However, ancient cultures have ancient concepts that are not easily translated, such as *muškēnum*, referring to a semi-free class of citizens. In ancient Mesopotamian words, the macron (‾) and circumflex (^) indicate a long vowel. Other symbols include š (for sh), ṣ (ts/ emphatic s), ṭ (emphatic t), ẖ (for kh) and ' (a throaty guttural for the letter "ayin"). For names familiar from modern literature such as Hammurabi or Sargon, the known forms are used. However, in all other texts Sh/sh is used for Š/š (as in Shamash), Kh/ kh for Ḫ/ẖ (as in Khumbaba). These adaptations have been used so that ancient names could be easily pronounced. To avoid unwieldy spellings, -ssh is used for -šš-, -kkh- for -ẖẖ-. The name "Aššur" referred to Assyria's god and its capital city. Here, Assur is used when referring to the god, and Asshur for the city.

Only two bibliographic abbreviations are used:

ANET³	J. B. Pritchard, ed., *The Ancient Near Eastern Texts Relating to the Old Testament*. 3rd ed. With supplement. (Princeton: Princeton University Press, 1969).
CANE	Jack M. Sasson, ed., *Civilizations of the Ancient Near East*, 4 vols. (New York: Charles Scribner's Sons, 1995).

Other abbreviations include:

CH	Code of Hammurabi
col.	column
obv.	obverse of a tablet
rev.	reverse of a tablet
ht.	height
w.	width

d.   depth
diam.   diameter
wt.   weight
l.   length

Weights and measures cannot be avoided when citing ancient tablets from Mesopotamia. The following brief table of metric equivalents may prove helpful:

Length	1 DANNA	*bēru*	"double hour"/ "double mile"	10.8 km
	1 GI	*qanû*	"reed"	ca. 3 m
	1 KÙŠ	*ammatu*	"cubit"	0.5 m
	1 ŠU.SI	*ubānu*	"finger"	ca. 0.17 m
	1 ŠE	*uṭṭetu*	"barleycorn"	ca. 0.28 cm
Area	1 BÙR		"bur"	ca. 6.5 ha
	1 IKU		"iku"	ca. 0.36 ha
	1 SAR	*mušaru*	"sar"	ca. 36 sq. m
Weight	1 GÙN	*biltu*	"talent"	30 kg
	1 MA.NA	*manû*	"mina"	500 g
	1 GÍN	*šiqlu*	"shekel"	8 g
	1 ŠE	*uṭṭetu*	"barleycorn"	ca. 0.05 g
Capacity	1 GUR	*kurru*	"kur"	300 liters
	1 BARIGA	*pānu*	"bariga"	60 liters
	1 BÁN	*sūtu*	"seah" or "ban"	10 liters
	1 SÌLA	*qû*	"sila"	1 liter

For chronology and dates, I have usually followed the four-volume *Civilizations of the Ancient Near East* (cited herein as *CANE*). Dating is hotly debated by scholars of the ancient Near East. *CANE* has followed a middle ground with which the author is comfortable (see Chapter 2 for issues of dating). BCE (before the common era) and CE (common era) have been used for BC and AD, respectively. The time line is based on both *CANE* and M. Roaf, *Cultural Atlas of Mesopotamia and the Ancient Near East* (New York: Facts on File, 1990), with additions and deletions based on my own way of presenting the material.

A time line and glossary have been included to guide the reader. In the notes to each chapter, I have tried as much as possible to point the reader to accessible sources in the Selected Bibliography as well as scholarly sources available in specialized libraries.

Acknowledgments

Writing this book has been an enjoyable journey for me through the archives and artifacts of ancient Mesopotamia. As one of the custodians of the history of the ancient Near East, I have been honored to write a book that students and educated lay people can enjoy—to open a window to the past for my readers. For this opportunity, I express my thanks to Professor William W. Hallo, Curator of the Babylonian Collection at Yale University, for introducing me to the publishers. Through the various stages of my career, he has always been there as a generous friend and mentor.

In addition, I would like to thank my editors, first Barbara Rader, Executive Editor, School and Public Library Reference, and then Emily Birch, Acquisitions Editor, School and Public Library Reference, for their advice, assistance, and understanding. They have truly epitomized the concept of the editor as friend. My other readers include my older son, Daniel ("the college student"), Rafael ("the high school student"), and, as always, my husband and friend, Mordechai ("the educated lay reader").

I would also like to thank Professors Ilene Nicholas and Wolfgang Heimpel for generously supplying photographs. Dr. Ron Wallenfels has always made himself available for identification of artifacts and seals as well as reading my manuscript to meet the book's deadline. Of course, all mistakes are my own. The Photographic Services of the Louvre, the British Museum, the Babylonian Collection at Yale University, the Oriental Institute of the University of Chicago, and the Art Source have also been most helpful in providing photographs at a speed not usually associated with institutions. In this regard, I would like to thank the Trustees of the British Museum, Mrs. H. Chang, Mr. Christopher Walker, and Dr. Irving Finkel at the British Museum, and, as always, Ulla Kasten, at the Babylonian Collection. The University of Chicago Press was also generous in allowing me to publish quotes from S. N. Kramer, *The Sumerians: Their History, Culture and Character* (1963).

Dr. Karen Rubinson did me a tremendous favor in referring me to Ms. Lauren Shulsky Orenstein, who has been a conscientious and excellent research assistant. She has been a truly wonderful detective in tracking down some difficult sources. Our telephone conversations have always been a pleasure. Other friends and colleagues who have been helpful are Professors Benjamin Foster, Jack Sasson, Martha Roth, Erle Leichty, Erica Reiner, Ellen Robbins, Laurie Pearce, and Yaakov Elman. My thanks to you all.

Time Line for Ancient Mesopotamia

archaeological periods approximate dates (BCE)	northern Mesopotamia	southern Mesopotamia	culture and technology
Paleolithic ("Stone Age") 12000			caves, open-air campsites small bands (200–300 people) hunting and gathering stone tools
Proto-Neolithic 9000	Aceramic (no pottery)		villages farming animal husbandry domesticated dog mud-brick weaving craft specialization long distance trade copper
Neolithic 6000	Hassuna Samarra Halaf		agricultural villages temples baked brick plow irrigation boats pottery stamp seals

4000	Ubaid Tepe Gawra Uruk	Ubaid Uruk Protoliterate	cities monumental architecture city walls wheel donkey cylinder seals writing
Early Bronze Age			
3000	Ninevite 5	Jemdet Nasr Early Dynastic (ca. 2900–2350)	Sumerian Civilization city-states fortified towns palaces tin bronze metal axes metal daggers developed cuneiform script
2500	Sargonic Dynasty of Akkad Hurrian movements Third Dynasty of Ur	Sargonic Dynasty of Akkad (ca. 2350–2193) Unification of Sumer and Akkad Gutian invasions Amorite movements Utu-khegal of Uruk Gudea of Lagash (ca. 2100) Third Dynasty of Ur Fall of Ur (ca. 2004)	empires ziggurats horses
Middle Bronze Age			

archaeological periods approximate dates (BCE)	northern Mesopotamia	southern Mesopotamia	culture and technology
2000	Amorite Dynasties Old Assyrian period Asshur and Old Assyrian trade (1900–1750) Mari archives (ca. 1810–1760) Shamshi-Adad I (ca. 1830–1776) Hammurabi annexed Mari (ca. 1760)	Isin-Larsa period Larsa Dynasty (ca. 2025–1763) First Dynasty of Isin (ca. 2017–1793) Old Babylonian Period First Dynasty of Babylon (ca. 1900–1595) Hammurabi (1792–1750) First Dynasty of the Sealand Babylon captured by the Hittites (1595)	nation-states chariots spoked wheels icehouses import of copper and luxury items Venus tablets
Late Bronze Age 1500	Mittani/Hurrian Empire Middle Assyrian period (ca. 1300–1100) The Dark Ages and the migrations of peoples (ca. 1250–1150) Assyrian raid on Babylon (ca. 1235)	Middle Babylonian Period (ca. 1595–1000) Kassite Dynasty (ca. 1595–1158) Amarna Archives (ca. 1350–1330) The Dark Ages and the migrations of peoples (ca. 1250–1150) Elamite raid on Babylonia (ca. 1158) Second Dynasty of Isin (ca. 1158–1027) Second Dynasty of the Sealand (ca. 1025–1005)	glass glazed pottery iron smelted horses for warfare chickens camels *kudurru*

Iron Age **1000**	Neo-Assyrian period (ca. 1000–612) Battle of Qarqar (853) Neo-Assyrian empire (744–612) /Sargonids Civil war in Mesopotamia between Assyrian and Babylonian empires (652–648) Esarhaddon's conquest of Egypt (673–671) Fall of Nineveh (612) Persian domination begins	Neo-Babylonian period (ca. 1000–539) Merodach-Baladan II (721–710) Assyrian domination Civil war in Mesopotamia between Assyrian and Babylonian empires (652–648) Neo-Babylonian Empire/ Chaldean Dynasty (625–539) Nebuchadnezzar II (604–562) Capture of Jerusalem (597) Cyrus invades Babylon (539) Persian domination begins	cavalry new Assyrian capital cities built large scale deportations and resettlements from conquered cities coins brass cotton Aramaic as lingua franca of the Ancient Near East Chaldean astronomy library of Assurbanipal museums of antiquities botanical gardens zoos Nebuchadnezzar's Babylon as an architectural marvel Hanging Gardens of Babylon city walls of Babylon
Persian Period **500**	Persian domination/Achaemenids (538–331)	Persian domination/Achaemenids (538–331)	

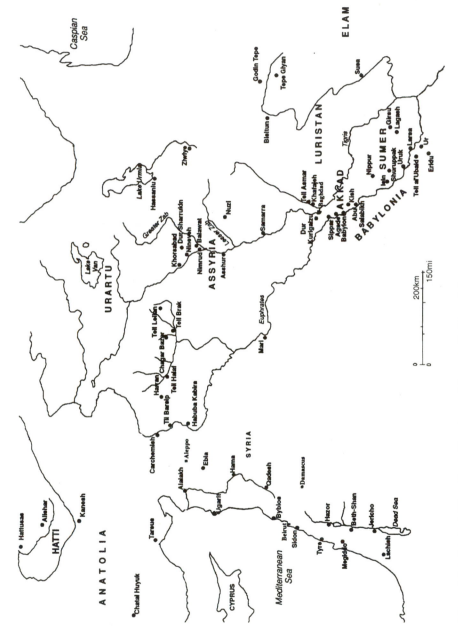

Map of the Ancient Near East. Courtesy of Lauren S. Orenstein.

1

Introduction

REDISCOVERY AND DECIPHERMENT

Mesopotamia, which occupied what is roughly modern-day Iraq, was the home of the Sumerians, Babylonians, and Assyrians, ancient peoples whose civilizations lay buried for centuries under mounds of earth called "tells" (Arabic for "hills"). Classical Greek historians such as Herodotus and Xenophon kept the memory of Babylonia and Assyria alive. The Old Testament also referred to these two civilizations. Their ancient capitals, Babylon and Nineveh, two of the largest mounds, were visited by European pilgrims, merchants, and adventurous travelers through the centuries. However, Sumer was not discovered until the nineteenth century.

Early Travelers' Reports

The first European traveler to the area known to us was in the twelfth century BCE—a rabbi from Spain, known as Benjamin of Tudela, son of Jonah, who visited Jewish communities in the Near East. While visiting the Jews of Mosul, he recorded: "It [Nineveh] is in ruins but within its ruins there are villages and communities. And the extent of Nineveh may be determined by its walls, about forty Persian miles, as far as the city Erbil."[1] Rabbi Benjamin correctly identified the nearby ruins as Nineveh, but he exaggerated the length of the city walls in his zeal to validate a Biblical passage in Jonah 3:3–4: "Jonah obeyed at once and went to Nineveh. He began by going a day's journey into the city, a vast city, three days' journey across." In the following centuries travelers continued to identify the ruins opposite Mosul as Nineveh.

In the first half of the seventeenth century, Pietro della Valle, a well educated Italian nobleman, traveled throughout the Near East, where he met and married a Nestorian Christian woman. He and his wife continued this journey as far as Iran. About two years after his marriage, his wife died. Wishing to continue his travels, but not able to part with her, della Valle had her embalmed and continued on his journey accompanied by her corpse for another ten years. Della Valle was one of the first travelers to describe the glories of Persepolis in Iran, where he copied the inscriptions carved on the palace doors in three versions of a wedge-shaped script. He brought back to Europe the first samples of this strange writing, which came to be known in 1700 as cuneiform (from the Latin *cuneus*, "wedge," denoting the shape of the writing). From the mounds in Hilla in Iraq, della Valle took with him inscribed bricks; he identified this site as Babylon and described its ruins.

As European powers competed for new trading opportunities, interest in the Near East grew. France, Great Britain, Denmark, and Germany tried to improve relations with the Ottoman empire, which had ruled Mesopotamia since the sixteenth century. The sultan was in Constantinople (modern-day Istanbul), a thousand miles away from Mesopotamia. Local officials were corrupt and uninterested in promoting law and order. Bandits, disease, and even wild animals awaited the early travelers. Ottoman rulers required visitors to sign a statement releasing authorities from responsibility for their safety. Numerous travelers came to northern Mesopotamia in the seventeenth century and especially in the eighteenth century, known as the Age of Enlightenment; they tried to identify and relate the ruins they saw to the Bible. Some even published copies of inscriptions they had drawn in their travel journals; others returned with souvenirs from antiquity. However, no scientific research was done until Claudius James Rich, while resident (ambassador) in Baghdad, was authorized by the East India Company there to do some archaeological research. Rich undertook the first scientific survey and crude excavations, which he published as *Memoir On the Ruins of Babylon* and *Second Memoir*, in 1813 and 1818, respectively. His memoirs caused a flurry of excitement in Europe.

In 1820 Rich investigated and mapped the site of Nineveh. He noted that the southernmost of the two main mounds of Nineveh, called Nebi Yunus (Arabic for "the prophet Jonah"), had a mosque on top of it and was regarded as a holy site by Muslims. Excavations are impossible even to this day at Nebi Yunus. He also collected many inscribed tablets, bricks, boundary stones, and cylinders, one belonging to Nebuchadnezzar.

In the eighteenth century the king of Denmark authorized an expedition under Carsten Niebuhr, a Danish
mathematician, who drew careful copies of the inscriptions at Persepolis. Niebuhr realized that the inscriptions
represented three distinct systems of writing. Today we
know that Persepolis was built by the Persian king Da-

**Decoding the
Inscriptions/
Digging Up
the Past**

rius, who had his inscriptions written in Babylonian, Elamite, and Old
Persian. Publication of Niebuhr's copies in 1772 led to the deciphering
of cuneiform.

Many European scholars worked on these inscriptions. The first to
succeed was Georg Friedrich Grotefend, a German high school teacher.
Using his knowledge of Greek historical texts, he was able to decode
about one-third of Old Persian, the language of ancient Iran from the
sixth to the fourth centuries BCE.

While scholars labored to decipher Old Persian, political relations between the European powers and the Ottomans were changing. The British established a consulate in Baghdad, which became a center for
archaeological and linguistic research in Mesopotamia.

The greatest of the nineteenth century scholars was Henry Creswicke
Rawlinson, an English soldier, diplomat, and linguist. While in Persia on
military duty, Rawlinson heard of rock carvings near the small town of
Behistun. More than three hundred feet above the ground up a sheer
cliff, the carvings portrayed the Persian king Darius standing in judgment over ten rebel kings with an inscription of about twelve hundred
lines recounting Darius's feats. Rawlinson could not use a telescope to
copy the inscription. So in the 1830s and 1840s he scaled the rock to
clean and copy the inscription. He became British resident to Baghdad
in 1843. There he worked on the copy of the inscription in his summer-
house while his pet lion cub rested under his chair. Rawlinson made
substantial progress in deciphering Babylonian, a language used by the
Semitic peoples who inhabited Mesopotamia along with the Sumerians
in the third millennium BCE. His studies identified many signs; he suggested that one sign could have more than one value.

Interest in Assyrian archaeology grew in Europe. Major excavations
started about 1840, twenty years after Rich's death. Two factors contributed to this turn of events: (1) the upper classes were interested in
antiquities and in collecting antiquities, and (2) European countries,
particularly France and Great Britain, were interested in increasing
their spheres of interest in Egypt, Mesopotamia, Persia, and India. In
the mid-nineteenth century, archaeology was used to forge ties in these
countries.

In 1842 Paul Emile Botta, an Arabist, doctor, and diplomat, was appointed the French consul in Mosul. The following year he began excavating at Khorsabad, the new Assyrian capital of Sargon II in the eighth century BCE. He uncovered limestone slabs carved with scenes in bas-relief and later bull-colossi which were sent down the Tigris by raft and on to a ship to France. Botta's success stirred up interest in Mesopotamia. In 1845–46 Austen Henry Layard, private secretary to the British ambassador in Constantinople, began digging at Nimrud, Biblical Calah, also built as a new capital for another Assyrian king in the ninth century BCE. Layard unearthed huge stone panels depicting scenes of war, lion hunts, and a hawk-headed deity, with some panels inscribed with cuneiform. Layard also dug at Nineveh (mound called Kuyunjik), where he found the library of Sargon's great-grandson; it contained 24,000 tablets with lexical, religious, and literary works of the Assyrians. In the ensuing months he found "no less than seventy-one halls, chambers and passages, whose walls, almost without exception, had been paneled with slabs of sculptured alabaster recording the wars, the triumphs, and the great deeds of the Assyrian king. By a rough calculation, about 9,880 feet, or nearly two miles, of bas-reliefs, with 27 portals, formed by colossal winged bulls and lion-sphinxes, were uncovered in that part alone of the building explored during my researches."[2]

Because of rivalry with Botta's successor, Layard also dug at six other sites in order to stake his claim for Great Britain. The rivalry continued between the French and the English as to who would be able to get the collection of Assyrian antiquities on display first. Botta won; he displayed his collection at the Louvre three months earlier than Layard did his at the British Museum. Because the first antiquities came from digs in Assyria, this new field was called Assyriology, a name still used today, even though we now are aware that Assyria was only a part of Mesopotamia. The large number of cuneiform inscriptions that came to Europe took about another ten years to decipher; the Babylonian-Assyrian script contained approximately six hundred signs, which represented syllables and/or entire words (ideograms). Each sign had multiple values.

Because multiple values were assigned to each Akkadian sign, the public was skeptical about the reliability of translations being published. In 1856–57 the Royal Asiatic Society asked four leading scholars to prepare independent translations of a newly discovered historical text without consulting each other. Copies of the inscription were sent to H. C. Rawlinson, an Irish parson and linguist named Edward Hincks, a mathematician, inventor, and amateur Orientalist, Fox Talbot, and the leading French Assyriologist, Jules Oppert. When the society's committee examined the sealed submissions six weeks later, it found them to be essentially the same. The legitimacy of the early decipherment was on firm

Massive winged lions with bearded human heads at the entrance to the shrine of Ninurta, which was built by Assurnasirpal II (ca. 865 BCE). Watercolor by F.C. Cooper, 1850, in A.H. Layard, *A Second Series of the Monuments of Nineveh* (London, 1853), plate 55b, 57 cm × 39 cm. © BRITISH MUSEUM, LONDON.

footing. Linguists quickly recognized the similarities between Akkadian and other Semitic languages such as Hebrew and Arabic.

Hincks later read a paper in which he suggested that the cuneiform system of writing was invented by a non-Semitic people who predated the Semites in Babylonia. Rawlinson confirmed this thesis, but the correct name of the Sumerians was discovered by Jules Oppert, based on the title "King of Sumer and Akkad," with Akkad referring to the Semitic peoples of Babylonia and Assyria, and Sumer to the non-Semitic peoples. Oppert even suggested that the Sumerian language bore close ties to the Turko-Altaic language family but this proved wrong. French excavations in southern Mesopotamia soon proved the existence of the Sumerians.

Rawlinson was authorized by the trustees of the British Museum to prepare a series of volumes of cuneiform texts, but the work was mostly done by others, in particular, George Smith. Smith had little formal education and had been apprenticed as a bank-note engraver. By the time he was twenty, he was a frequent visitor at the British Museum. Soon he became an assistant in the museum's Department of Oriental Antiquities, where he set to work cataloguing the collection of tablets. While working through a pile of tablets labeled "Mythology," he recognized the Akkadian version of the biblical Flood story. He was so excited that he ran around the room removing his clothes, much to the astonishment of his colleagues in the department. Smith's discovery was published in the *Daily Telegraph*. The owner of the newspaper decided to finance an expedition for Smith to go to Nineveh to find the rest of the tablet. After only five days of excavation, Smith found a fragment containing most of the missing lines. He returned later that year to Nineveh to find the rest of another important myth, the *Epic of Creation*. Smith died before he could carry out his plan to present a complete translation of the Genesis legends to the *Daily Telegraph* readers.

Throughout the nineteenth century the purpose of Assyriology was to authenticate the Bible. Translations of cuneiform inscriptions were published with notes referring to Biblical parallels. Charles Darwin's *Origin of Species* (1859) led people to question the literal truth of the Bible. Then in 1902 Friedrich Delitzsch, a German Assyriologist, presented a paper entitled "Babylon and Bible" to the German Oriental Society, with Kaiser Wilhelm II in the audience. Delitzsch argued that the Bible was preceded by literature from an earlier time period; it was not the world's oldest book. Delitzsch contended that the Old Testament could no longer be regarded as unique and divine revelation.

Excavations continued, and the Germans, under the patronage of the Kaiser, also began to dig in Mesopotamia. After World War I, the League of Nations gave the British (who had occupied most of Iraq) a temporary mandate over Iraq until it was considered ready for independence. During British rule, a Department of Antiquities was created, and an Antiquities Law was passed under the provisions of which the Iraqi Department of Antiquities received all unique finds made by foreign archaeological expeditions as well as one-half of the remaining finds from the excavations. In 1958 the Iraqi Antiquities Law was revised, denying foreign excavations half of all duplicate finds. It was Iraqi archaeologists who saved Nineveh from building speculators.

DATING THE PAST (RELATIVE DATING VS. ABSOLUTE DATING)

In today's world, we are used to knowing exactly when events occur. As we move further back in time, accurate dating of historical events becomes more and more difficult. Written records rarely provide a precise date. When such information does not exist, we rely on relative dating (approximate dating) rather than absolute dating (exact dating). Most archaeological research depends on relative dating; that is, artifacts (such as pottery, tools, jewelry, household objects, etc.), buildings, skeletal remains, layers of soil deposits, and even societies are deemed relatively earlier, later, or even contemporary by organizing them into sequences based on cumulative information. Absolute dating uses a fixed point in time for dating. Today, we have the Christian era which uses the birth of Christ as a point of reference. The ancient Greeks counted from the first Olympic Games (776 BCE according to our calendar), the Romans, from the establishment of Rome (753 BCE), and the Muslims, from the Prophet Mohammed's departure from Mecca (622 CE). Scientists who use radioactive methods wish to achieve a neutral international method of dating without reference to any calendars such as those mentioned above. Instead, scientists count years back from the present (BP), which refers to "before 1950," the year Willard Libby invented a method for radiocarbon dating. This method is most often used in prehistoric archaeology to describe dating in the thousands of years. Therefore, the discrepancy between 1950 and the current year is negligible.

In Ancient Mesopotamia towns were built of mud, since clay was the natural resource found everywhere. Houses **Archaeology** were made of clay, either piled up as mud (pisé) or masses of clay pressed together (adobe), or as (sun-dried) bricks mixed with organic material and held together with gypsum mortar. Kiln-fired bricks were used for palaces and temples. The houses required constant repair with new layers of clay due to winter rains. Also, garbage was thrown into the street; eventually the street level became higher than the floors of the houses, so rain and sewage seeped in. Then the floors had to be raised with more earth. Wars, floods, or disease might cause a town to be deserted, leaving the walls to cave in and seal off layers of settlement. After years of being deserted, the towns might become reoccupied. Rather than remove the ruins of the city, the new inhabitants leveled the walls to form the foundations for their town. This process could be repeated over the years as the city gradually grew above the plain. Eventually, most sites were deserted. Sand filled the remaining walls and streets, and rain smoothed the ruins so that a tell or mound of heaped-up layers of continuous occupation was formed over a long period of time.

For most prehistoric artifacts, dating is usually relative. However, absolute dates can be established by radiocarbon or carbon-14. Radiocarbon dating uses ratios of carbon isotopes to determine the age of anything that contained carbon. Plants and animals take in carbon-14 until they die. The isotope carbon-14, present in minute amounts, decays at a steady rate, expressed in terms of a half-life of 5,730 years. The age of a plant or animal can be calculated from the amount of radiocarbon remaining in the sample. The method can be used anywhere and can be used to date organic material as far back as 50,000–80,000 years. However, the technique is too inaccurate to be applied to the last 400 years.

Stratigraphy, the study of strata or layers of occupational debris lying

Different levels of occupation in Malyan, a modern village in Iran. COURTESY OF
ILENE M. NICHOLAS.

one above the other, provides a relative chronology from the bottom or
earliest layer to the top or most recent. The archaeologist organizes the
artifacts associated with each stratum and classifies them according to
similarities of style and type. Since change is usually gradual, typologies
can be developed.

Dendrochronology, or tree-ring dating, attributed to Leonardo da
Vinci, was developed as a modern technique in the twentieth century by
A. E. Douglass, an astronomer. Every year trees produce a ring of new
wood. Trees of the same species in the same area usually show the same
pattern of growth. Long master sequences have been developed for each
species. Dendrochronology is used to correct inaccuracies produced by
radiocarbon dating.

Chronology   Until scientific dating techniques were developed at the
beginning of the twentieth century, archaeologists and historians depended on correlating archaeological information
with chronologies and calendars used by people in ancient times.
Historical chronology is useful when many artifacts are found, sometimes even with dates or names of rulers who can be dated. A well-
established chronology for one country might be used to date events in
other countries whose events are referred to in another nation's records.

The ancient Mesopotamians kept long lists of year names, king lists,
historical chronicles, and other written accounts, some based on astro-

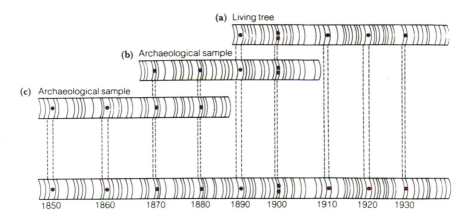

A reconstructed master sequence of dendrochronology (dating by tree rings). After B. Bannister, "Dendrochronology." In *Science in Archaeology*, 2nd ed., ed. D. Brothwell and E. S. Higgs (New York: Praeger, 1970), 191–205.

nomical observations, which aid in absolute dating. But accurate BCE dates are difficult to establish. Sources sometimes conflict; for example, they may record dynasties as being successive which were in fact contemporaneous or partly overlapping. The ancient Mesopotamians had no fixed system for dating until 311 BCE, when they adopted the Seleucid system. Until then, they referred to the years of their rulers' reigns in the following ways: (1) the years of the rule could be listed numerically, for example, the seventeenth year of Nebuchadnezzar, king of Babylon; (2) each year within a king's rule could be described by some important event, such as a victory, rebellion, construction of a temple, redigging a canal, and so on, or (3) each year after the first year of a king's rule could be named after an official (an Assyrian practice called *limmu*, "eponym," which dates to the second millennium BCE); the first full year of the king's reign was named for the king, for example, as in an extract of eponyms for the years before and after Tiglath-pileser III (744–727 BCE) came to power:

(744) In the eponym of Bel-dan,	(governor) of Calah	to Namri
(743) In the eponym of Tiglath-Pileser	King of Assyria	in Arpad, he defeated Urartu
(742) In the eponym of Nabu-danninanni	field marshal	to Arpad.[3]

These dating systems were only useful to the Mesopotamians because they had master lists of year names for each king, a list of kings of each dynasty and the length of their individual rules, and a list of successive dynasties. Some of these master lists have survived. These king lists could be restricted to one place and one dynasty or could include several dynasties that reigned in succession. Others, like the "Sumerian King List," encompassed long periods of time and dynasties of several kingdoms, including the mythical rulers "after the Flood" to second millennium BCE kings. Converting these chronologies into Christian era dates was made possible by Ptolemy, a second century CE Greek geographer from Alexandria. Ptolemy's Canon gives the length both of each king's reign and some of the outstanding astronomical events. The Assyrian *limmu* lists provide the main astronomical phenomena of the time between 747 and 631 BCE and coincide with Ptolemy's Canon, a list of the kings of Babylon and Persia from Nabonassar (747 BCE) through Cleopatra VII's reign (30 BCE).[4] Through the years, scholars continued working on Ptolemy's Canon to include Byzantine rulers up to the fifteenth century CE. One of the entries in the *limmu*-lists notes an eclipse of the sun, and astronomers can calculate the year this eclipse was visible in Assyria. With one year fixed, all 264 consecutive years of the Assyrian eponym lists can be precisely dated as far back as 910 BCE.

The Babylonian "Venus" tablets record the appearance and disappearance of the planet Venus during the twenty-one-year reign of King Ammi-saduqa (1646–1626 BCE), a ruler of the First Dynasty of Babylon. The tablets provide enough information for modern astronomers to calculate several alternative dates. Three chronologies, called high, middle, and low chronologies, have arisen for Babylonia during the second millennium BCE. We will use the middle chronology, which is the most commonly accepted practice among historians.

In Mesopotamia relative dating is reliable from the twenty-fourth century BCE down to the sixteenth century BCE. Earlier dates are usually estimated on the basis of archaeological evidence, a few radiocarbon dates that are not far back enough in time to be accurate, and paleography, that is, the changes in the cuneiform script through time (see Chapter 4).

2

General Information

THE GEOGRAPHICAL SETTING OF MESOPOTAMIA

Mesopotamia, a term coined by Greek historians in antiquity, means "(the land) between the rivers," referring to the **Between**
Euphrates and Tigris Rivers. Mesopotamia is a triangle that **the Rivers**
includes most of Iraq and parts of Syria, Turkey, and Iran.
The Euphrates (2780 km) and Tigris (1950 km) Rivers, also referred to
as the Twin Rivers, cut through this region. The sources of these two
rivers are in Armenia. In antiquity they were two distinct rivers, but
today they merge at Qurnah into the Shatt al-Arab and then reach the
Persian Gulf. In the north the Twin Rivers have altered their course very
little. But in the south the two valleys converge, forming a wide, flat
alluvial plain called the Mesopotamian delta; here the Twin Rivers wind
and form numerous affluents, which often overflow, creating a series of
lakes and swamps. Amazingly, the ancient Mesopotamians were able to
control their rivers; in fact, the two main branches of the Euphrates have
remained on the same course for nearly three thousand years. However,
we still find cities in southern Mesopotamia that are in ruins, the result
of the Euphrates or its branches changing course or overflowing. The
course of the Tigris in southern Mesopotamia was probably the same as
one of its branches today, the Shatt el-Gharraf.

The people who lived in Mesopotamia had no name for their country
as a whole; they used general terms such as "the land" or very specific
terms for its constituent parts such as Sumer, Akkad, Assyria, and Bab-

The Lower Euphrates with reed mat bunds and a coracle in the water. COURTESY OF W. J. HEIMPEL.

ylonia. Geographically, Babylonia refers to the southern part of modern-day Iraq, the area between Baghdad in the north and the Persian Gulf in the south. Historically, the term Babylonia explains the second millennium BCE unification of the northern and southern parts of this land, which were previously called Akkad and Sumer, respectively. To the north, in the upper Tigris valley around Mosul (ancient Nineveh) was the part of Mesopotamia known as Assyria. Assyria was constantly expanding and contracting; for a time it stretched from Egypt to Iran, and at other points was reduced to a small country no larger than the state of Connecticut.

Regional Variations There is great variety in the landscape, which includes desert, foothills, steppes, and marshes, with one common feature—lack of rainfall in the summer months. The climate and vegetation of Mesopotamia have probably not changed over the past ten thousand years. The desert zones had mild, dry winters and hot, dry summers, but there was no vegetation. In the foothills, the winters were mild, and summers were dry and warm. The vegetation included oak, pine, terebinth trees, grasses, barley, and wheat. The steppes also experienced mild, dry winters and hot, dry summers. The steppe lands were grasslands that were almost treeless. The climate of southern and central Iraq is very hot and dry, sometimes reaching 120°F in summer. The average rainfall is less than ten inches. The flood periods

The marshes of Iraq with reed huts and reed mats. COURTESY OF W. J. HEIMPEL.

of the Tigris and Euphrates are between April and June, useless for both winter and summer crops. Therefore, artificial irrigation became essential to agriculture.

THE PEOPLES AND THEIR LANGUAGES

The first settlers in Mesopotamia were not the Sumerians, but the study of the Sumerian language reveals the influence of the earlier inhabitants. That is, though the older languages no longer continued to be spoken, they left their mark on Sumerian as substrate languages. Substrate languages influence a more dominant language in vocabulary, grammar, and syntax. The names of the Twin Rivers, the Tigris and Euphrates, and the names of some of Sumer's most important cities are not Sumerian in origin.

Ancient Mesopotamia

We do not know with certainty the names of these early settlers who preceded the Sumerians. Historians and archaeologists refer to them as Proto-Euphrateans or Ubaidians (after the tell al-Ubaid, where their culture was first discovered); the Ubaidians established a number of agricultural villages and towns throughout Mesopotamia. Archaeological finds attest to their development of skilled crafts; the Ubaidians left behind hoes, adzes, knives, sickles, bricks, spindle whorls, loom weights, sculpture, and painted pottery. Temples, enlarged over time, have been found at their sites. The Sumerians borrowed from them the names for occupations such as farmer, herdsman, fisherman, potter, carpenter, metalworker, leather worker, mason, weaver, basket maker, merchant, and priest. Other non-Sumerian words include those for plow, furrow, palm, and date. Clearly, the development of these skills can be credited to these early settlers. The Subarians were the next early intrusive element probably coming from the north. Again, their language is known only from geographical names, vocabulary words, and people identified as Subarians.

The Sumerians appeared on the Mesopotamian scene about 3100 BCE. They may have been an indigenous population, or they may have migrated to Mesopotamia. According to their tradition, they came from the south, most probably via the Persian Gulf, and founded their first settlements in the south close to the Gulf. The Sumerians probably conquered the Subarians and any remaining Ubaidians. In fact, the word "Subarian" became a synonym for slave. The earliest names of Mesopotamian kings were Sumerian. The Sumerians turned an agricultural community into the first urban civilization in the world.

The Sumerian language is agglutinative; that is, verbs or nouns are expressed by a fixed syllable or root which can be modified by long chains of prefixes and postfixes, with each element signifying a specific grammatical meaning. Sumerian is not related to any language, living or dead. The dominance the Sumerian language achieved is unusual. History can offer few examples of intruders forcing their language upon the existing population; besides Sumerian, only Aramaic and Arabic have accomplished this. The Sumerians are credited with the invention of writing and a native vocabulary concerning writing, education, and law.

Semites immigrated to Mesopotamia from Arabia in the west not long after the Sumerians, about 2900 BCE. The presence of the Akkadian-speaking Semites has been well documented in early Sumerian texts. Akkadian words and names appear in archaic Sumerian texts. By 2350 BCE Semites ruled Mesopotamia from their capital city of Akkad, in northern Babylonia (its exact location in Iraq is not yet known). Their language, Akkadian, is a Semitic language, that expresses grammatical relationships both by changing the internal structure of words derived from a three-letter root and by adding prefixes and postfixes. From the Sumerian, Akkadians borrowed the cuneiform system of writing for their own language, and Akkadian culture mixed Semitic and Sumerian elements.

Sumerian was a living language in the third millennium BCE. Akkadian competed with and eventually replaced Sumerian, becoming the lingua franca of the entire ancient Near East during the second millennium BCE. The Akkadian language continued to be spoken in the second and first millennia BCE and included two dialects: Babylonian, spoken in southern Mesopotamia, and Assyrian, used in northern Mesopotamia. During the first millennium BCE, Aramaic gradually displaced Akkadian.

The ancient Mesopotamians distinguished between the urbanized Akkadians and the unassimilated Semites, calling the latter Amorites and their homeland Amurru. The Amorites originally came to Mesopotamia as soldiers and workers in the third millennium BCE but became politically dominant early in the second millennium BCE, even rising through military positions to become rulers in Mesopotamia. Their language, called Amorite, a West Semitic dialect, deferred to the Akkadian language of the country. All that remains of Amorite consists mostly of personal names.

According to the Mesopotamian view of their world, the four points of the compass were given ethnic labels: North (Subar), South (Sumer), West (Amurru), and East (Elam, discussed below), with Babylon at the center.[1]

3

Historical Overview

There were no villages anywhere in the world before 9,000 BCE. Human beings were rarely seen except, perhaps, while hunting, fishing, or gathering plants and fruit to eat. For the most part, they lived in bands and moved around without ties to any particular place. Early humans attempted limited forms of cultivation by leaving young animals and small fish undisturbed and by protecting selected species. The wild varieties of legumes, fruit, and nuts were nearly identical with their cultivated counterparts, though they all became bigger over time. The tools of early humans were made primarily of stone, hence the name "Stone Age." The long period of basic developments in stone tool technology called the Paleolithic (Old Stone) Age spanned from about 700,000 to about 9,000 BCE.

PERMANENT SETTLEMENT AND DOMESTICATION

The world's earliest known permanent settlements began with the Neolithic (New Stone) period in the ancient Near East ca. 9000 BCE and spread gradually to the rest of the world, as far as China, by about 4000 BCE. The Neolithic period marked the first attempts to obtain plant and animal food by cultivation and animal husbandry. Most sites showed evidence of a mixed economy based on hunting and gathering, herding of goats and sheep, fishing, and cultivation of wheat and barley. Neolithic settlements grew to ten hectares ($\approx$ 25 acres) or could have a population of a thousand or more. Trade activities soon developed, and more complex forms of social organization evolved.

THE BEGINNINGS OF CIVILIZATION: FROM FARMING VILLAGES TO CITIES

An ancient culture is named after the site where its artifacts and characteristic features were first identified. Three sites have given their names to distinctive cultures (ca. 6000–4000 BCE) that emerged in northern Mesopotamia: Hassuna, Samarra, and Halaf.

In the Hassuna period agricultural villages thrived. The presence of spindle whorls told of the production of cloth. Obsidian (dark, hard, sharp volcanic glass) and semiprecious stones provided evidence of long-distance trade. The concept of private property was clearly marked by the use of stamp seals to designate ownership.

The Samarra period was distinguished by its pottery, which was well fired and painted a chocolate brown color, often in striking patterns. At this time the buildings featured external buttresses at the wall junctions for added support.

In the Halaf period there were beehive-shaped structures built on stone foundations. The purpose of these buildings is unknown, and the building shape has been found in no other prehistoric culture. Arpachiyeh, a site dated to this period, even had cobbled streets and a workshop for potters, providing evidence of craft specialization.

In the Hassuna culture large collections of buildings were attached to one another, often with enclosed courtyards. At Umm Dabaghiyeh groups of families involved in preparing and trading animal hides lived in buildings clustered around a courtyard. There were also single, detached houses of different sizes dating to the Samarra and Halaf cultures. Variations in size may have indicated the social status or specialized economic activity of families or individuals. Some of the larger buildings were used for ceremonial or religious purposes.

During the Halaf period the tournette (a slowly rotating wheel) was introduced. The rotating work surface of the tournette turned as long as someone spun it. The invention of the potter's wheel with axle bearings soon followed in the Ubaid period (4000–3500 BCE). The potter's wheel has been associated with the division of labor, craft specialization, increased productivity, and a more uniform style of pottery.

The Ubaidians, the native substratum of Mesopotamia, were the oldest identifiable ethnic component. The Ubaid people settled in the south in small farming villages, which grew into large population centers. Isolated towns or cities have been found, such as Eridu (about 12 hectares), Ur (about 10 hectares), and Uruk (about 75 hectares). Near Eastern farming villages are the same size today.

The two halves of the country developed into distinct cultures, with Tepe Gawra giving its name to the northern cultures and Uruk to the southern cultures. In Tepe Gawra a carefully designed temple complex was constructed with three temple buildings close to each other in order to worship a pantheon of gods.

Uruk (Erech in the Bible, Warka today), located on the banks of the Euphrates in southernmost Mesopotamia, was a typical early urban site of the late fourth millennium BCE. It covered approximately twelve hectares and had an estimated population of 10,000. The monumental buildings of the Early Uruk period (3500–3200 BCE) suggests that a powerful elite controlled an organized, skilled labor force. In the Early Uruk period most settlements were located in northern Babylonia. But by the Late Uruk period, the number of sites in the south exceeded those in the north. High productivity combined with high population density led to a complex structuring of Babylonian civilization.

THE PERIOD OF CITY-STATES AND NATION-STATES: THE THIRD MILLENNIUM

The period of early high civilization (ca. 3200–2700 BCE) can be subdivided into three periods based on developments in architecture, pottery, seals, and writing: the Late Uruk (ca. 3200–3000 BCE), Jemdet Nasr (ca. 3000–2900 BCE), and Early Dynastic I (ca. 2900–2700 BCE) periods.

Sumer: The First City-states

In northern Mesopotamia, a derivative of the Late Uruk culture developed into the Ninevite 5 culture, so named after level 5 of the Prehistoric Pit at Nineveh. None of the sites dating to this period displayed any urban characteristics. During the Jemdet Nasr period the northern regions of Sumer, previously empty, became settled.

The term Protoliterate period (ca. 3200–2900 BCE) refers to the appearance of writing on clay tablets, mostly for accounting purposes. The invention of writing marked the end of the prehistoric period in ancient western Asia. Tablets of the Protoliterate period that have been deciphered were written in Sumerian. The Sumerians were probably present as early as the Ubaid period. By the third millennium BCE the predominant language spoken in southern Mesopotamia was certainly Sumerian, and it is proper to speak of these people as Sumerians.

The temple played the major social, economic, and political role in early Mesopotamian cities during the Protoliterate period. The temple controlled land ownership, employed both workers and craft specialists, managed long-distance trade, and exerted political authority over the city and its surroundings. At this time, bronze tools, weapons, and assorted implements were introduced on a large scale. Archaeologists have divided the periods of tool use into the Stone Age, the Bronze Age, and the Iron Age.

Each city and its surrounding area functioned as an irrigated island separated by stretches of desert and swamp. Many of these irrigated "islands" eventually developed into city-states, which functioned as trade centers and regional shrines. The citizens lived within the city walls and identified with the city.

In the third millennium BCE new political configurations arose and fell apart—decentralization (the city-states) alternated with the centralized rule of the monarchy, or nation-state. The chronology of the Early Dynastic period (2900–2350 BCE), based on archaeological data, can seldom be correlated with known political events.

The Sumerian King List, written early in the second millennium BCE, supplied the names of kings along with the lengths of their reigns, dynasty by dynasty, and concluded with the well-known rulers of the Third Dynasty of Ur and their successors at Isin. This chronological framework provided the barest outline of the political history of Sumer and Akkad after prehistoric times.[1] Kingship was considered an institution devised by gods for human life. Eridu was the most ancient of settlements inhabited continuously into Sumerian times and the oldest center of Sumerian civilization. The Sumerian King List treated overlapping and contemporaneous dynasties as successive.[2] Historically, no king extended his rule beyond his own city-state until the Akkadians came to power.

In the Sumerian King List, "before the Flood" referred to protohistoric time, and "after the Flood" to fully historic time. The antediluvian part of the Sumerian King List has often been equated with the Early Dynastic I period, the only source of information for this period. "After the Flood had swept (over the land) and kingship had descended from heaven, Kish became (the seat) of kingship."[3] Afterwards, kingship passed from Kish to Uruk. Some of the kings of Kish and Uruk listed in the Sumerian King List were also mentioned in Sumerian and Akkadian myths and legends, such as Enmerkar, Lugalbanda, Dumuzi, Gilgamesh, and Etana. The next dynasty in the Sumerian King List was Ur, under King Mesannepada (2560–2525 BCE), also identified from inscriptions. His father, Mes-kalamdug, king of Kish, left two inscriptions in graves in the Royal Cemetery at Ur.

Early Dynastic Sumer was a loose-knit confederation of small city-states whose relationships with one another varied from vassalage to equality, but never unity. There was no natural center; even Nippur, the religious (and geographical) center of Sumer and Akkad, exercised no political power.[4] Each city-state consisted of an urban center and the dependent populations of the undeveloped areas of land around it.

Each city-state was a politically independent unit with its own ruler. Sumer and Akkad each consisted of about a dozen city-states near each other along the branches of the Euphrates and Tigris. Early Dynastic inscriptions were full of references to battles between city-states. The

Plaque of Ur-Nanshe. This limestone plaque is perforated in the center and divided into two registers. In the top register King Ur-Nanshe of Lagash (ca. 2500 BCE) is carrying a basket on his head, symbolic of the king's duty to build the temple. Behind him is his cup bearer and before him a woman, probably his wife, and his four sons. In the bottom register Ur-Nanshe, seated, drinks from a cup, served by his cup bearer who stands behind him. An official and three of his sons stand before him. Ht. 40 cm. © LOUVRE MUSEUM, PARIS.

massive walls built by most Sumerian cities suggest a strong secular authority ready for military action.

Inscriptions from the Early Dynastic period have shown the Sumerian King List to be incomplete. The rulers of some city states, such as Lagash, were excluded. Even Mesilim (ca. 2550 BCE), the king of Kish, did not appear in the king list. Mesilim was famous for drawing the border between Umma and Lagash, a contentious point between these two cities. His decision, accepted by both parties, appeared to favor Lagash over Umma. The land later passed into the hands of the Ummaites until Eannatum of Lagash (ca. 2450 BCE) conquered them and made a new border treaty with the ENSI (city ruler) of Umma. To reduce future conflict between Umma and Lagash, he set a strip of fallow land on the Umma side of the boundary ditch as a no-man's land.

Eannatum conquered Elam and the southern cities of Sumer. He now felt powerful enough to assume the title "King of Kish," which implied rule over all of Sumer. Eannatum claimed to have defeated Umma, Uruk, Ur, Akshak, Mari, Susa, Elam, several districts probably in the Iranian Zagros, and Subartu in northern Mesopotamia. Umma, economically and militarily stronger than Lagash, was ordinarily the aggressor. Eventually, the ENSI of Umma liberated himself from provincial fixation with the Lagash boundary by concluding a nonaggression pact with Entemena (2404–2375 BCE) and establishing a kind of union over all of Sumer.

In Lagash, Entemena was succeeded by a series of short-lived rulers until Uru-inimgina (2351–2342 BCE) was chosen from 3,600 persons by Ningirsu, an ancient idiom used to mean that he was a usurper. Uru-inimgina was praised for his social and ethical reforms rather than his military exploits. During Uru-inimgina's reign, Lugalzagesi (ca. 2340 BCE), an ambitious ENSI from Umma, burned, plundered, and destroyed practically all the holy places of Lagash. Uru-inimgina offered little re-sistance. Lugalzagesi claimed that he unified Sumer and controlled the trade routes from the Mediterranean to the Persian Gulf. Lugalzagesi was soon defeated by Sargon (2334–2279 BCE), a Semite and founder of the powerful Dynasty of Akkad.

The Rise and Fall of the Akkadian Dynasty

Approximately 2900 BCE, large numbers of people with Semitic names settled in cities such as Kish in Akkad. Gradually this Semitic-speaking group, identified as Am-orites, adopted the urban lifestyle of the Sumerians, and eventually, the Amorites rose to positions of political power, including kingship.

Sargon the Great (2334–2279 BCE), as he is called by modern historians, was a brilliant military leader as well as an innovative administrator. Sargon was the first king to unite all of Mesopotamia under one ruler, and the Akkadian empire became a prototype for later kings.[5] Sargon began his career as a high official, cupbearer to a Sumerian king of Kish named Ur-Zababa. Lugalzagesi either dethroned or killed Ur-Zababa be-fore beginning a series of conquests. Sargon launched a surprise attack against Lugalzagesi's capital, Uruk, and destroyed its walls.

Sargon continued his conquests on the way to the Persian Gulf. On the way back, he completed his conquest of southern Sumer. Sargon then turned west and north and conquered the lands of Mari, Yarmuti, and Ebla up to the "Cedar Forest" (Amanus Mountains) and the "Silver Mountain" (Taurus Mountains), and in the east Elam and neighboring Barakhshi. When Sargon conquered city-states, he destroyed their walls so that potential rebels were deprived of strongholds. If the ENSI was willing to shift his allegiance, Sargon kept the old administration in of-

Bronze head of Sargon or Naram-Sin. Life-size bronze head, cast and then de-tailed with a chisel, was believed to be Sargon, founder of the Dynasty of Akkad, (2334–2279 BCE) or his grandson, Naram-Sin (2254–2218 BCE). His hair is carefully braided and tied in a bun, and his mustache and beard consist of rows of curls. His facial features show high-arched eyebrows, a prominent nose, and fleshy lips. Ht. 36 cm., Iraq Museum. © Baghdad, Iraq Museum. COURTESY OF SCALA/ART RESOURCE, NEW YORK.

fice; otherwise, he filled governorships with his own citizens. In this way, he encouraged the collapse of the old city-state system and moved toward centralized government. Sargon installed military garrisons at key positions to manage his vast empire and ensure the uninterrupted flow of tribute. He was the first king to have a standing army (see Chapter 10). Sargon built the capital city of Akkad, which soon became one of the wealthiest and most magnificent cities of the ancient world. Its exact location remains unknown, but Akkad gave its name to the dynasty and to the language.

Sargon was first succeeded by his son, Rimush (2278–2270 BCE), who inherited an empire torn by revolts. In battles involving tens of

Victory stele of Naram-Sin (2254–2218 BCE), commemorating his triumph over
the Lullubi in the Zagros mountains on the Iraq-Iran border. The king is the top
figure standing on the mountain pass. He is wearing a horned helmet of a god
and carrying a bow and arrow. He towers above the dead and wounded Lul-
lubians. Akkadian soldiers with spears and standards climb the wooded slopes.
Astral symbols appear at the top of the stele. Shutruk-Nakkhunte of Elam took
this monument when looting Sippar more than 1000 years later and carried it to
Susa. His inscription is carved on the mountain. Ht. 2 m. © LOUVRE MUSEUM,
PARIS.

thousands of troops, Rimush reconquered cities and countries of the empire. His inscriptions listed the total number of victims captured, killed, or massacred as 54,016. Rimush was followed by his older brother, perhaps his twin, Manishtushu (2269–2255 BCE), who followed a military and political plan similar to his brother's. Both were killed by members of their court. Manishtushu was succeeded by his son, Naram-Sin (2254–2218 BCE), whose military victories were numerous. To proclaim his conquests, Naram-Sin added "king of the four quarters" to his list of titles and even was deified as "the god of Akkad."[6]

Then disaster struck—the Gutians invaded. The Gutians were a ruthless, barbaric horde from the mountains to the east. The historiographic poem *The Curse of Agade: The Ekur Avenged* vividly depicted Akkad before and after its downfall. The destruction of Akkad was attributed to Naram-Sin's sacking of Nippur and desecration of Enlil's sanctuary. Famine descended on Sumer: "The great fields and meadows produced no grain; the fisheries produced no fish; and the watered gardens produced neither honey nor wine."[7] Famine led to rampant inflation. The situation was desperate. The gods cursed Akkad; the city would be abandoned forever:

> May your canalboat towpaths grow nothing but weeds,
> May your chariot roads grow nothing but the "wailing plant,"
> Moreover, on your canalboat towpaths and landings,
> May no human being walk because of the wild goats, vermin,
>   snakes, and mountain scorpions,
> May your plains where grew the heart-soothing plants,
> Grow nothing but the "reed of tears,"
> Agade, instead of your sweet-flowing water, may bitter water
>   flow,
> Who says "I would dwell in that city" will not find a good
>   dwelling place,
> Who says "I would lie down in Agade" will not find a good
>   sleeping place.[8]

The curse soon came to pass, so that "in not five days, not ten days,"[9] kingship left Akkad and the city became deserted. Naram-Sin's son, Shar-kali-sharri (2217–2193 BCE), tried to reverse some of his father's policies, but it was too late. The kingdom was reduced to the city of Akkad and the surrounding area. The Sumerian King List described his reign as followed by a period of anarchy: "Who was king? Who was not king?"[10]

Sargon's empire lasted just over a century. Its final collapse was prompted by the invasion of a people from the Zagros mountains who disrupted trade and ruined the irrigation system. But, all in all, its downfall was due to its intrinsic instability.

Little is known about the rulers of the various Uruk dynasties until the last one, Utu-khegal (2123–2113 BCE). He was appointed by Enlil, the chief god of Sumer, to rid the country of its barbaric oppressors, the Gutians. When a new Gutian king ascended the throne, Utu-khegal struck and was victorious. He restored southern Mesopotamia politically and economically from the state of almost complete paralysis caused by the Gutian invasions.

The Gutians, who conquered parts of southern Mesopotamia, became its nominal kings. Like many other conquerors of Mesopotamia, the Gutians assimilated completely, even honoring the local cults. The Gutian rulers became the dominant political group in the century following Shar-kali-sharri's death. Gudea (ca. 2144–2121 BCE), an ENSI of Lagash, came to power. His statues, some almost life-size, bore long inscriptions recording his religious activities in building and rebuilding Lagash's more important temples. He traded with almost the entire "civilized" world of antiquity.

The Neosumerian Renaissance: The Rise and Fall of the Third Dynasty of Ur
Despite a resounding victory, Utu-khegal's power over Sumer lasted only ten years. His throne was usurped by Ur-Nammu (2112–2095 BCE), one of his more ambitious governors. Ur-Nammu established the last important Sumerian dynasty, called the Third Dynasty of Ur (also called Ur III). Ur-Nammu was a talented military leader and an extraordinary administrator. He also promulgated the first law code in recorded history.

Ur-Nammu established an effective centralized administrative system in which the cities were managed by subservient provincial governors, ENSIS, appointed by the king. Ur-Nammu may have expanded his control over bordering lands, because "he straightened the highways from (the lands) below to (the lands) above."[11] Early in his reign he established a registry for ships trading with Magan in order to ensure their safety from marauders in the southern marshes.

Ur-Nammu died in battle with the Gutians, who continued to plague Sumer throughout the Third Dynasty of Ur. Death in battle was a rare fate for a Mesopotamian king, particularly a pious ruler. A hymn described the return of Ur-Nammu's body to Ur for an elaborate burial and gave details of the Sumerian view of the netherworld.

He was succeeded by his son, Shulgi (2094–2047 BCE), who started a major reorganization of the Ur III state and enlarged his empire. The king appointed military personnel to rule outlying provinces.

Near the end of Shulgi's reign, a new threat came from nomadic tribes in the west who attacked and looted. To defend the settled population, Shulgi built a defensive wall along the northwest border, called by di-

A statue of Gudea: the architect with the building plan. Gudea (ca. 2100 BCE) holds on his lap a plan of the Ningirsu temple, a calibrated measuring instrument and writing tool. The plan shows only the outer walls of the temple complex, pierced by six gates and protected by two projecting towers. © LOUVRE MUSEUM, PARIS.

verse names: "The wall in front of the mountains," "The wall of the land," and, after Shulgi's time, "Keeping Dedanum away."[12] But Shulgi was also motivated by economic concerns; he was anxious to expand the northeastern trade routes, which afforded access to lapis lazuli and tin (for the manufacture of bronze).

Shulgi was succeeded by two of his sons, Amar-Sin (2046–2038 BCE) and Shu-Sin (2037–2029 BCE); each was deified upon ascending the throne. Shulgi's son and successor, Amar-Sin, died of the "bite" of a shoe, probably a poisoned foot. During Shu-Sin's reign the Amorites

Inscribed brick of Ur-Nammu (2112–2095 BCE), founder of the Ur III Dynasty. Written in Sumerian is the following: "For Inanna, his lady, Ur-Nammu, the mighty man, king of Ur, king of Sumer and Akkad, has built her temple." 31.2 cm × 31.5 cm. © BRITISH MUSEUM, LONDON. See Walker 1987: 55.

from the Syrian and Arabian deserts made their first major raid. The king built a defensive wall.

In the twenty-first century BCE, during the Ur III period, texts from Umma and Lagash portrayed the Amorites as completely assimilated into Mesopotamian society by intermarrying, adopting the local dialect, and forsaking tribal customs. Neo-Sumerian literary texts painted a totally different picture of the Amorites as unassimilated foreigners. The Amorite was described as a tent-dweller of the mountain, unfamiliar with grain or cooked meat, with life in the city, or (worse yet) with death and burial in a proper grave—he was warlike, uncouth, and generally "foreign."[13]

Shu-Sin's inscriptions predicted the disasters that would befall his son and successor, Ibbi-Sin (2028–2004 BCE). The combined threat of invasions from the Amorites and Elamites proved the undoing of Ibbi-Sin and led to the collapse of the empire.

Though the Elamites besieged Ur, they could not capture it. As time passed, severe famine overtook Ur's defenders; in desperation, they unlocked the city gate. The Elamites brutally slaughtered everybody and ransacked homes and temples. *The Lamentation over the Destruction of Ur* recorded this tragedy:

> Dead men, not potsherds,
> Covered the approaches,
> The walls were gaping,
> the high gates, the roads,
> were piled with dead.
> In the side streets, where feasting crowds would gather,
> Scattered they lay.
> In all the streets and roadways bodies lay.
> In open fields that used to fill with dancers,
> they lay in heaps.
> The country's blood now filled its holes,
> like metal in a mold;
> Bodies dissolved—like fat left in the sun.[14]

The Third Dynasty of Ur lasted about a century (ca. 2111–2004 BCE). Once again Mesopotamia became divided into city-states under separate rulers; the empire was no longer centralized.

THE PERIOD OF NEW KINGDOMS: THE SECOND MILLENNIUM

In 2017 BCE Ishbi-Irra founded a new dynasty based at Isin that lasted more than two centuries. Isin's main rival was Larsa. The latest version of the Sumerian King List was created under Ishbi-Irra or his successors in order to validate Isin's claim: "Ur was smitten with weapons; its kingship was carried to Isin."[15]

The Isin-Larsa Period (ca. 2000–1800 BCE)

Lipit-Ishtar (1934–1924 BCE), the fourth king of the Isin dynasty, claimed the title "King of Sumer and Akkad." Early in his reign he promulgated a new Sumerian law code, which became the model for the famous code of Hammurabi. In the third year of Lipit-Ishtar's reign, an aggressive and dynamic leader, Gungunum (1932–1906 BCE), became king of Larsa.

The reign of Gungunum at Larsa marked the beginning of the first

Amorite dynasty in the south. Gungunum seized the old capital city of Ur. After that, a group of Amorite-dominated city-states competed for dominance in Babylonia. The Amorites consolidated power in new centers such as Larsa, Eshnunna, and Babylon, but ignored the prestigious Sumerian cities like Kish, Ur, and Uruk. Urban Amorites rose to prominent positions in Babylonia, including kingship in independent states. Sumerian was no longer spoken, and Akkadian became the language of daily life.

Continuous warfare promoted the rise of independent dynasties such as Uruk, Kish, and particularly Babylon. Rim-Sin (1822–1763 BCE), the last ruler of Larsa, invaded and captured Ur by defeating a confederation of armies. In the north, an exceptional Semitic ruler named Hammurabi (1792–1750 BCE) rose to power in Babylon. With Hammurabi, the history of Babylonia, a Semitic state built on a Sumerian foundation, began.

The Rise of Assyria The Old Assyrian civilization had two separate components: the independent city-state of Asshur, and a group of trading colonies and satellite depots in Anatolia and northern Syria, which the Assyrians managed.

Cappadocia is the classical name of central Anatolia (Asia Minor or Asiatic Turkey). More than ten thousand "Cappadocian" texts described Assyrian traders who came to Cappadocia. They made the long journey from Asshur to Kanesh on donkey-back via various routes to bring cloth from Asshur and tin from across the Tigris (to be made into bronze in Anatolia). In the early second millennium BCE Anatolia was divided into provincial city-states, each ruled by a prince; Kanesh was one of the most powerful city-states and the commercial center of at least nine colonies and ten or more subsidiary stations.

In the second half of the nineteenth century BCE, a complete break in Old Assyrian trade patterns occurred between Kanesh and Asshur, possibly due to conflicts between Hittites and the native (Hattic) rulers. By 1740 BCE the Hittites established a royal house of their own, and about one hundred years later the Old Hittite kingdom was founded to replace earlier centers of Anatolian power.

Both Hittite kings, Khattushili I (ca. 1650–1620 BCE), who took his name from the new capital, Khattusha, and his adopted son, Murshili I (ca. 1620–1595 BCE), fought with various great cities until the road to Babylon lay open. Hammurabi's dynasty came to an end, and the entire Asiatic Near East was plunged into a Dark Age of a hundred years (ca. 1600–1500 BCE).

According to the Assyrian King List, the king of Eshnunna ruled Assyria while Shamshi-Adad I waited in Babylonia. When the king of Eshnunna died, Shamshi-Adad captured Ekallatum and Asshur ca. 1808 BCE. Shamshi-Adad I (ca. 1830–1776 BCE) traced his genealogy back to the presumed ancestor, Puzur-Assur I, to legitimize his kingship at Assur.

Shamshi-Adad installed his elder son, the crown prince Ishme-Dagan, as governor at Ekallatum; he appointed his younger and less capable son, Yasmakh-Adad, at Mari. Shamshi-Adad chose Shubat-Enlil (the site of Tell Leilan in northeast Syria) further north as his own capital. From there Shamshi-Adad could rule the Khabur valley while watching his sons. Thus, the whole area between the middle Tigris and the middle Euphrates was consolidated under one Amorite family about 1800 BCE.

Shamshi-Adad I established a powerful Assyrian political and commercial state. His death shattered the unity of the northwest. Shamshi-Adad's son, Ishme-Dagan, maintained control over Assyria but lost the rest of the upper Euphrates region. Ishme-Dagan was overthrown, and Shubat-Enlil fell to the Elamites. At Mari, Zimri-Lim (1782–1759 BCE), son of a former king, reclaimed the throne from the unfit Yasmakh-Adad. Now, Zimri-Lim and Hammurabi exchanged letters and gifts regularly as signs of friendship and good relations. They also maintained foreign ambassadors at each other's courts.

By the end of the nineteenth century BCE, three powerful Amorite states arose in Babylonia: Eshnunna, Larsa, and Babylon. The future of smaller states depended on alliances with these three kingdoms. Hammurabi (1792–1750 BCE) was the sixth in a line of long-lived kings whose rule **The Old Babylonian Period** passed from father to son. When Hammurabi became king, Babylon was one of a number of small states. Contemporary records revealed a highly unstable political scene in which rival kingdoms joined in ever-changing alliances when power moved from one center to another.

Hammurabi's reign left a lasting impression on future generations of Babylonians, thus making him one of the major figures of Mesopotamian history. Hammurabi was never deified, and subsequent kings of Babylon followed this practice. Hammurabi's nation-state did not survive him, but he did make Babylon the recognized seat of kingship, a position that remained uncontested until the Greeks built Seleucia. Babylon even survived as a religious center until the first century CE.

Hammurabi's son and successor, Samsu-iluna (1749–1712 BCE), followed his father's policies, but soon the south revolted. Within ten years Samsu-iluna gave up most of the new empire. In 1738 BCE the south fell to Iliman, founder of the Sealand dynasty, who ruled Babylonia as far north as Nippur. The Sealanders had begun to move into the area shortly after Hammurabi's death. In the sixteenth century BCE the Sealanders occupied the Babylonian throne briefly, just long enough to entitle the Sealand dynasty to be included in the Babylonian King List, which chronicled the history of Babylonia.

The seventeenth to sixteenth centuries BCE marked a period of great political upheaval in western Asia. The Kassites were only one of a number of non–Semitic-speaking peoples, like the Hurrians and Hittites, who applied pressure from the north on the ever-weakening kingdom of Babylonia. In 1595 BCE the Hittites sacked Babylon. The Kassites united the country after recapturing the south from the Sealanders, and restored the Babylonian empire to the glory of Hammurabi's age.

The Kassite Dynasty
The origin of the Kassites remains unknown. Kassites first appeared in Babylonia as agricultural workers. But by the end of the seventeenth century BCE, the social standing of the Kassites grew. The number and order of the early Kassite kings is uncertain. The first king identified as ruling in Babylon was Agum II, who was credited with recovering the statues of the god Marduk and his wife after twenty-four years of Hittite captivity (ca. 1570 BCE). With Marduk reinstalled in Babylon, the Kassite kings were able to "take the hand of Marduk"—a symbolic gesture denoting dynastic legitimacy and respect for Babylonian traditions. The Kassites ruled more than four hundred years, longer than any other dynasty. They followed the social and religious customs of the Babylonians, and they even used the Akkadian language.

During the early second millennium BCE Hurrians (or kings with Hurrian names) controlled the states around the northern frontier of Mesopotamia. The Hurrians traded with Assyrian merchants in Anatolia, and their deities were even accepted by other nations. During the fifteenth and fourteenth centuries BCE, Mitanni, a Hurrian kingdom, extended from the Mediterranean Sea to Assyria. The capital, Washukanni, has not yet been found. The Hurrians followed many of the earlier Babylonian traditions and played a crucial role in transmitting them beyond Babylonia to Assyria, ancient Israel, and Phoenicia, and, indirectly, to Greece. Their most significant impact was on Hittite culture, which revealed a strong Hurrian influence.

Letters to and from Kassite kings (ca. 1350 BCE on) were found at Amarna in Egypt. State correspondence revealed that the Kassite and Egyptian royal families exchanged ambassadors, intermarried, and traded precious goods. Gradually relations declined between Babylon and Egypt. In their letters, Kassite kings complained of the poor treatment of their messengers and the cruelty of the pharaoh.

The Middle Assyrian Period
In the middle of the fourteenth century BCE, Mitannian power began to fail, and the Assyrians entered the scene for what has been called the Middle Assyrian period. Assur-uballit I (ca. 1366–1330 BCE) has been credited with establishing the Assyrian kingdom. He was the first ruler to take the title "king of the land of Assyria." Assur-uballit I changed the tradition of fraternal succession and replaced it with the usual succession of father to son.

Assyria rid itself of the Hurrian overlordship of Mitanni and rejected Kassite Babylonia's claims to power. The Assyrians negotiated on equal terms with all the great powers of the time. Throughout the fourteenth to the early twelfth centuries BCE, relations between Kassite Babylonia and Assyria were generally stable.

Near the end of the fourteenth century BCE Ramesses' army met the Hittites at Qadesh on the Orontes in northern Syria (1287 BCE) in one of the most famous battles in antiquity. According to his account, he defeated the troops of the Hittites and their allies, but according to the more believable Hittite version, the Egyptians were defeated and withdrew. In 1287 BCE the Hittite ruler signed a nonaggression pact with Egypt, later insured by the marriage of Khattushili's daughter to Ramesses II. The original agreement, sent to Ramesses, was a silver tablet with the impressions of the stamp seals of Khattushili and his wife. A copy of the Hittite text was kept in the archives at Khattusha.

Little was known of Babylon until the mighty Assyrian king Tukulti-Ninurta I (1244–1208 BCE) attacked Babylonia and plundered the capital in 1235 BCE. The reasons for the war are not clear. Under military pressure from the Assyrians and Elamites, the Kassite dynasty finally collapsed in 1158 BCE.

Tukulti-Ninurta's military achievements distinguished him—he fought in the east, north, and west, where he claimed to have crossed the Euphrates, taking 28,800 Hittite prisoners. In Assyria he assumed the title "King of Karduniash (Babylonia), King of Sumer and Akkad, King of Sippar and Babylon, King of Dilmun and Melukkha, King of the Upper (Mediterranean Sea) and Lower Seas (Persian Gulf)."

He undertook an extensive building program at his capital, Asshur. Three kilometers north of Asshur on the opposite side of the Tigris, he founded a new capital city, which he named after himself, Kar-Tukulti-Ninurta ("Quay of Tukulti-Ninurta"). The lavishness of his new capital may have caused increasing hostility. Local dissidents, led by Tukulti-Ninurta's own son and heir, locked the king in his new palace and burned it to the ground.

Tukulti-Ninurta's fame was preserved in garbled accounts of his reign in both Biblical and Greek literature. Genesis 10 noted his prowess as conqueror and hunter in the name of Nimrod; Greek legends recalled "King Ninos," and the building of his new capital, "the city of Ninos," and the fiery death of Sardanapolos there.

The "Dark Ages" described the period of time for which we lack information for both Babylonia and Assyria. The king lists for these dynasties provide only tentative information for this time period. Traditional theories, accounting for the crisis of the twelfth century BCE, referred to natural disasters such as earthquakes, famine, or climatic change. The shift from the Bronze Age to the Iron Age should, however, be viewed in terms of man's role.

"The Dark Ages" and the Migrations of Peoples

[Handwritten marginal note:] For some reason female historians 'garble' Nimrod with Tulkuti even though Tulkuti lived over 1000 years after Naram-Sin/Nimrod! How does Nimrod live in the 1200's as this writer contends when the bible says he lived 5-7 generations before Abraham, who lived in 2000 BC! Susan Bauer also does this, rewrites history. Thanks gals!

The Late Bronze Age was characterized by a continuous shift in the balance of power among a half-dozen major states, each ruled by different ethnic groups. By the end of the Bronze Age more ethnic groups appeared, and a wave of migrations transformed the political character of the entire Near East. Perhaps the major cause of these upheavals was the fall of Troy ca. 1250 BCE and the ensuing collapse of the Mycenaean cities of the Greek mainland. The survivors of these disasters fled along the coasts to find new lands to conquer and settle. The Hittite kingdom, Ugarit, and many of the cities of the Levant fell.

Shutruk-Nakkhunte (ca. 1165 BCE) became king of Elam and, in an age of weak kingdoms, made the Elamites a major power. He invaded Mesopotamia and seized seven hundred towns, exacting heavy tribute from them. When Kutir-Nakkhunte, his son, ascended the throne, he invaded Babylonia and brought the Kassite dynasty to an end. He carried off to Elam the statue of the god Marduk from Babylon and the statue of the goddess Inanna from Uruk. For these sacrilegious acts, Kutir-Nakkhunte was forever hated in the memory and poetic tradition of the Babylonians.

The Post-Kassite Period When the last Kassite king died, Babylon entered a long period of political unrest. Until the period of Assyrian supremacy in the ninth century BCE, the country was governed by six politically insignificant dynasties. In Syria and northern Mesopotamia, neo-Hittite and Aramaean newcomers clashed over control of the area. In Babylonia, the various dynasties after the Kassites had moderate success in handling the Aramaean influx. Assyria was the one major power in western Asia that survived the tumult at the end of the Bronze Age. Tiglath-pileser I (1115–1077 BCE) extended the boundaries of the Assyrian empire further than ever before, even into Lebanon.

Native Babylonians rose to power in a dynasty associated with the city of Isin and recorded in the king list as the Second Dynasty of Isin. Its most important king was the first Babylonian ruler named Nebuchadnezzar I (1126–1105 BCE). A *kudurru* described a grueling march to Susa, across the desert where today's summer temperatures often exceed 50°C (105°F): "The axes in the soldiers' hands burnt like fire and the road-surfaces scorched like flame. In the wells there was no water . . . the strength of the powerful horses gave out, and the legs of even the strongest warrior weakened."[16] The Babylonians looted Susa and took back the statue of the god Marduk.

While Tiglath-pileser I was busy with foreign conquests, Nebuchadnezzar's younger brother and successor, Marduk-nadin-akhe I (1099–1082 BCE), attacked Ekallatum, an Assyrian city near Asshur. Tiglath-pileser I retaliated by raiding northern Babylonia; Dur-Kurigalzu, Sippar, Opis, and Babylon were seized, and the royal palaces burnt. The Babylonian king remained in power until his eighteenth year, when a horrible famine struck the cities of Babylonia and the citizens were reduced to cannibalism. According to the Assyrian chronicle, Marduk-apla-iddina "disappeared."[17]

Both Babylonia and Assyria then experienced a period of national decline. The Aramaeans established local kingdoms along the Mediterranean coast, in northern Syria, and in Babylonia. Their language, Aramaic, a Semitic language written in an alphabetic script, eventually replaced Akkadian, lasting until the Arab conquest.

The rulers of the Eighth Dynasty of Babylon were usually grouped together with five others as members of "Dynasty E." This dynasty governed for about two hundred years, at the time when Assyria emerged as the greatest power in the ancient Near East.

EMPIRES IN MESOPOTAMIA: THE FIRST MILLENNIUM

The tendency in Mesopotamian history toward direct, centralized rule reached its height under the Assyrians in the first millennium BCE. They left extensive records of their military successes; Assyrian victories were recorded, but Assyrian defeats were either ignored or described as victories. Other versions of the same events have been found in the Bible and Babylonian chronicles.

The Rise of the Assyrian Empire

During the eleventh and tenth centuries BCE, Assyria's authority was confined to its original boundaries. But by the ninth century BCE, conditions stabilized and paved the way for renewed Assyrian expansion westward. Assyria became the major world power.

Adad-nirari II (911–891 BCE) needed six annual campaigns to defeat the Aramaeans, who tried to declare their independence. He conquered Babylonia in the south and then, in a series of campaigns, seized control of the Khabur region.

His son, Tukulti-Ninurta II (890–884 BCE), consolidated his father's military accomplishments. Aramaean communities along the Tigris, Euphrates, and Khabur paid tribute rather than endure Assyrian vassaldom.

Under Tukulti-Ninurta II's son, Assurnasirpal II (883–859 BCE), and grandson, Shalmaneser III (858–823 BCE), expansion continued. The Assyrian annals recorded that between 881 and 815 BCE, 193,000 people were deported to Assyria, of whom 139,000 were Aramaeans. Control of the whole area entailed several campaigns and the establishment of two new cities—"Assurnasirpal's Quay" and "Assur's Crossing Place," which regulated crossing of the Euphrates. Assurnasirpal II reached the Mediterranean and accepted tribute from Tyre (in modern Lebanon), but did not bother Israel. Assurnasirpal II and his successors continued their

Statue of King Assurnasirpal II (883–859 BCE), who is identified by an inscription bearing his name, title and deeds, carved below his beard. The statue originally stood on a block of red limestone. Ht. 1.06 m. © BRITISH MUSEUM, LONDON.

campaigns north and east into Anatolia and Iran, and south toward Babylonia. Their campaigns became annual events. The towns and cities along the way understood that they either had to pay the tribute demanded or face attack by the Assyrian military.

The expanding empire needed a northern capital. Assurnasirpal II built Nimrud (Calah). His new capital boasted a canal, magnificent buildings, a sewage system, and orchards filled with trees and plants gathered from his campaigns. He settled captives from all parts of his empire here.

Shalmaneser III's campaigns bore the characteristics of a grand plan. Assyrian annexations and deportations induced the western states to form defensive coalitions. In 853 BCE Shalmaneser III led his armies against a coalition of kings that was led by Hadad-ezer, king of Damascus. The forces met at Qarqar on the Orontes River. Shalmaneser claimed complete victory, declaring that 14,000 of 60,000 of the enemy were killed. Despite his reports, the Syrian coalition was effective, so Shalmaneser had to campaign again in 849, 848, 845, and 841 BCE, until the western states finally submitted. Later, the Assyrian empire swallowed up ancient Israel, and King Jehu was depicted on a monument bowing down before the Assyrian king. The final years of Shalmaneser III's long rule were characterized by revolt and civil war, until the old king died.

His son Shamshi-Adad V (823–811 BCE) put down the rebellion, which had spread throughout Assyria, with the help of the Babylonian king Marduk-zakir-shumi (854–? BCE). Shamshi-Adad V's wife was one of the few Orientals remembered by the Greeks. Her name was Sammuramat; she entered Greek legend as the beautiful, cruel Queen Semiramis. Five years after Shamshi-Adad V's death, Semiramis ruled on behalf of her minor son, Adad-Nirari III (810–783 BCE). She wielded real authority. She rebuilt Babylon and many cities in Mesopotamia and beyond.

During the next sixty years Assyria was rather weak. The king's authority fluctuated according to the amount of power the provisional governors usurped.

In 746 BCE a revolt led to the assassination of the royal family. Tiglath-pileser III (744–727 BCE; Pulu of the Old Testament), an Assyrian general, ascended the throne. He became Assyria's most capable monarch for more than a century and the founder of the Neo-Assyrian empire. Tiglath-pileser III led Assyria in regaining and consolidating its position as the supreme military power in the ancient Near East. Tiglath-pileser III led his armies south, defeating the Aramaean tribes who inhabited northern and eastern Babylonia. He

The Expansion and Downfall of the Neo-Assyrian Empire

appointed a eunuch as governor over the cities of Babylonia and took the title "King of Sumer and Akkad." Eunuchs were appointed as a means of curtailing the power of the nobles, because they had no off-spring, and therefore they were more likely to remain loyal to the king. But Tiglath-pileser III permitted Nabonassar, the king of Babylon (747–734 BCE), to remain on the throne.

For Assyria, the main problem was Urartu. Both Urartu and Assyria vied for control of Syrian routes crucial to Assyria for timber, metals, and horses. In 743 BCE Tiglath-pileser III attacked Arpad, which was held by Urartian forces. The Assyrians even paid Urartian spies for intelligence. After two more years of siege, he captured Arpad and received tribute. Tiglath-pileser's victory brought twenty-nine towns under Assyrian rule. He resettled the region with deportees from other conquered territories.

At this point records became fragmentary. Menakhem of Israel paid tribute: "Pul (Tiglath- pileser III), king of Assyria, invaded the land, and Menakhem gave him a thousand talents of silver to help him strengthen his hold on the kingdom . . . The king of Assyria turned back and did not remain in the land" (2 Kings 15:19–20). Tiglath-pileser III placed the coast of ancient Israel under Assyrian rule. The Assyrians also put an embargo on the export of timber from Lebanon to Egypt. The Egyptians tried to organize an anti-Assyrian operation in ancient Israel and south Syria, but to no avail. The Bible described the invasion and annexation of the kingdom of Israel, but each victory was short-lived, despite the attempts by three successive kings, Tiglath-pileser III, Shalmaneser V, and Sargon II.

Tiglath-pileser III also faced problems with the Chaldeans in Babylonia. In 734 BCE Mukin-zeri, the chief of one of the Chaldean tribes, occupied Babylon and became king. Tiglath-pileser III sent military forces, which were welcomed by most of the population of Babylonia. The Chaldean position was so strong that it took Tiglath-pileser three years to capture Babylonia. Mukin-zeri escaped to his own tribal capital in the southern marshes. The Assyrian army followed him, destroying his territory and that of his tribal allies. Tiglath-pileser III was formally granted kingship over Babylonia, an office no Assyrian king had held for more than four hundred years.

When Tiglath-pileser III died, Assyria was an empire that stretched from the Persian Gulf to the Egyptian borders and then up through north Syria into Cilicia and Anatolia. The Assyrians controlled Babylonia until 626 BCE, but the ties between the two can best be described as a love-hate relationship. The Babylonians wanted cultural dominance, and the Assyrians, military supremacy. Tiglath-pileser III established a dual monarchy, a practice followed by most of his successors for the next century. Tiglath-pileser III and his son and successor, Shalmaneser V

(726–722 BCE), were known in Babylonia as Pulu and Ululayu, respectively, and also in Biblical and Greek sources.

Shalmaneser V was replaced as king of Assyria by Sargon II (721–705 BCE). Under Sargon II and his successors Sennacherib, Esarhaddon, and Assurbanipal, called the Sargonids, Assyria methodically defeated and annexed many western Asiatic kingdoms. Eventually the Sargonid empire encompassed almost the whole civilized world: Syria, Phoenicia, Israel, Urartu, and Babylonia.

Sargon II became king after a revolt by the people of Asshur against his predecessor. The revolt began in Assyria and spread to other parts of the empire, and soon Sargon II was faced with trouble in Babylonia. At the beginning of Sargon's reign, Marduk-apla-iddina II (known as Merodach Baladan in the Bible) allied with Elam, and became king of Babylonia in 721 BCE.

Letters from provincial administrators to the king were full of references to clashes with Urartu and the use of Urartian spies. Sargon II finally raided Urartu, a dangerous operation due to the mountainous terrain and a string of fortresses. Sargon led his main army in a furious charge, attacking the Urartian coalition. The Urartian general directed his own army to a disciplined retreat, but his allies were in a state of anarchy and escaped to the mountains, where many died of exposure. Rusa, the Urartian king, abandoned his capital and fled to the mountains, where, according to Sargon II, he finally either died of grief or committed suicide by "stabbing himself with his own iron dagger like a pig."[18] The entire campaign was chronicled, and the Assyrian casualties listed only one charioteer, one cavalryman, and three foot soldiers. Thus, Urartu was disabled, and Sargon could turn his attention to Babylonia.

Sargon II drove a wedge between Marduk-apla-iddina II and his Elamite allies by seizing control of the entire length of the river between them. Sargon II had the support of north Babylonian cities, including the capital, and was formally acknowledged as legitimate ruler of Babylon. More than 108,000 Aramaeans and Chaldeans were deported from Babylon. Marduk-apla-iddina II fled from Babylon to the southern marshes, where he was besieged in his tribal capital. He paid Sargon II a hefty tribute to be allowed to retain control of his tribal territory.

In the eighth century BCE, the Cimmerians (Gomer of the Bible), a new wave of Indo-Europeans, entered Anatolia from the north and raided Assyria. Sargon II led his army against the Cimmerians, so the Cimmerians moved into the interior of Asia Minor. Sargon II's adversary was King Midas of Phrygia, who, in Greek legend, had a golden touch and grew ass' ears. Midas' capital was Gordion, named for Midas' father, Gordias, who may have founded the city. Crowded between Assyria and Phrygia, the rulers of this region had no choice but to submit and "polish the sandals of the Assyrian governor with their beards."[19]

In 705 BCE Sargon II was killed on the battlefield, an unusual death for a Mesopotamian king. His body was lost in battle, so he could not be buried in his palace—a terrible blow to Assyrian morale.

To separate himself from Sargon II's fate, Sennacherib (704–681 BCE) had his father's name eliminated from inscriptions and moved the capital to the ancient city of Nineveh, the natural geographic and religious center of Assyria. Nineveh became a symbol of the power, prestige, and wealth of the vast Assyrian empire—the last and most magnificent of Assyria's capitals. Nineveh was home to the last three monarchs of the Assyrian empire: Sennacherib, Esarhaddon, and Assurbanipal.

Babylonia remained a problem throughout Sennacherib's reign. Sennacherib took part in a religious ceremony that formally made him king of Babylonia, but instead of ruling the area himself, Sennacherib installed a Babylonian puppet governor, who was ousted by Marduk-apla-iddina II. Sennacherib led his army south, seized Kuthah, Marduk-apla-iddina's main base, and entered Babylon. Sennacherib claimed to have seized 75 of the Babylonian king's strong-walled cities and 420 smaller towns. Assyrian officials now ruled Chaldean tribal areas.

Marduk-apla-iddina tried to distract the Assyrians by fomenting rebellion among Sennacherib's vassals in ancient Israel. But, ancient Israel joined a coalition of coastal cities in a revolt that was backed by Egypt. Sennacherib's army invaded ancient Israel. He dealt with the coastal cities and repulsed the Egyptians. Then Sennacherib stormed Judah and placed Hezekiah's capital, Jerusalem, under siege. Hezekiah paid tribute and Jerusalem was spared, miraculously according to the Bible. The Assyrian army returned to Mesopotamia because of the deteriorating situation in Babylonia.

In 691 BCE, an alliance of Elamites, Chaldeans, and their supporters met Sennacherib's army on the Tigris, north of Babylon. In the bloody battle, Sennacherib's army succeeded in pummeling the Elamite-Chaldean coalition so severely that they could not proceed. Sennacherib proclaimed victory, but his army returned home. By the summer of 690 BCE, the Assyrians were back in Babylonia. The next year the Elamite king was "stricken by paralysis and his mouth was so affected that he could not speak,"[20] so Babylon lost its powerful Elamite ally. The Chaldean forces in Babylon held out but eventually succumbed to famine and disease. Babylon fell to Sennacherib's army. The Babylonian king fled but was quickly captured and killed; his captor received the dead king's weight in silver from Sennacherib. Sennacherib died in Babylon in 681 BCE, murdered by two of his sons, according to the Bible (2 Kings 19:37).

Esarhaddon (680–669 BCE) was designated by Sennacherib as his successor. Since the heir apparent resided in a special palace, the royal plans for the succession were clear. Succession was by appointment, so the firstborn male did not automatically become king. Despite Sennacherib's plans, Esarhaddon had to fight for his succession.

Esarhaddon changed his father's policy toward Babylon early in his reign. He directed the rebuilding of Babylon and its temples. He repatriated the citizens who had fled and restored their lands to them. By 676 BCE Esarhaddon used Babylonia as a base for his campaign far into Persia.

Esarhaddon tried to invade Egypt, a kingdom long coveted by the kings of Assyria. The attacks on Egypt began in 679 BCE, particularly from 673 BCE on. The next year he set out again to conquer a rebellious Egypt, still ruled by Taharqa. Esarhaddon died en route, and the expedition was abandoned. He named his sons to succeed him; Assurbanipal became King of Assyria and Shamash-shum-ukin, king of Babylonia.

Assurbanipal's (669–627 BCE) main problem was the unfinished conquest of Egypt. Despite successful campaigns, Assyria continued to face trouble in Egypt. Psammetichus, a prince of north Egypt and an administrator for Assyria, claimed national independence by expelling the Assyrian garrisons remaining in the cities of Egypt with Lydia's help. Assurbanipal formally cursed the ungrateful King Gyges of Lydia and proclaimed that Assyria no longer would aid him. The Cimmerians now felt free to invade the Lydian kingdom.

Assyria's troubles multiplied. It could no longer afford the considerable resources necessary to maintain forces in Egypt. The Elamite king took advantage of Assyria's preoccupation with Egypt to attack Babylon in 664 BCE. Assurbanipal sent an army south to repel the Elamites. Shamash-shum-ukin's kingship of Babylonia clearly depended on Assurbanipal for its defense.

Te'umman ascended the throne in Elam upon the sudden death of his predecessor. Assurbanipal grew to hate him as a result of their constant conflicts. In 653 BCE, Assurbanipal was at Erbil, where he received word of the mobilization of Te'umman's army against him. Assurbanipal's army entered Elam. Te'umman withdrew to his capital, Susa, and then tried to escape. He was caught and beheaded. His head was brought to Assurbanipal, who unleashed his loathing by slashing the dead face and spitting on it. A bas-relief depicted Assurbanipal and his wife enjoying a victory dinner in the garden while Te'umman's head hung from a tree.

In 652 BCE civil war erupted, and the two brothers, Assurbanipal and Shamash-shum-ukin, fought for four years. The Babylonians were supported by the Elamites, Arabs, and southern tribes. But by the summer of 650 BCE, Shamash-shum-ukin was besieged in Babylon. He defended the city until forced to surrender in 648 BCE; due to famine the inhabitants "ate the flesh of their sons and daughters."[21] Shamash-shum-ukin died in his palace when the city was set on fire. At the end of 648 BCE, Assurbanipal regained control of Babylonia. Shamash-shum-ukin's successor, Kandalanu, ruled Babylonia in peace for twenty-one years, acting as a proxy for direct Assyrian rule.

Elam suffered from civil unrest and from tensions produced by the Persians, who were new peoples from the north. The chaotic situation in Elam threatened Assurbanipal, because Elam could serve as a strategic base for Chaldean tribes who were hoping for independence in Babylonia. Assurbanipal ransacked Elam, looting its major cities, destroying temples, taking gods, defiling the graves, and mutilating the statues of its kings.

Assyria's resources were depleted by constant conflicts with Babylonia and campaigns to control distant provinces that supplied essential imports and many luxuries. Assyria had overextended itself. Upon Assurbanipal's death, his son succeeded him as king until 612 BCE, when the Assyrian empire collapsed.

The Rise and Fall of the Neo-Babylonian Empire

With the accession of Nabonassar in 747 BCE, a new era began in Babylonian history. Accurate records of historical events and astronomical observations were methodically kept.

In the ensuing confusion after the death of Shalmaneser V, Marduk-apla-iddina II, a Chaldean sheikh of the powerful Bit-Yakin tribe, seized the throne in Babylon. According to the king list, he was the only man to become king on two occasions (721–710 and 703 BCE).

The Assyrians recognized Marduk-apla-iddina II as the most important of the Chaldean sheikhs, and his reign was well documented. Marduk-apla-iddina II repaired major shrines and respected the ancestral privileges of the ancient cities of Akkad. He used the wealth of his tribe, Bit-Yakin, to pay for the services of the Elamite army in a campaign against Assyria. Marduk-apla-iddina II saw himself as the savior of the country.

In 710 BCE Sargon II marched against the Chaldeans while their Elamite allies were at home. According to the Assyrian account, Marduk-apla-iddina escaped to the marshes, where his Sealand territory was overrun and his principal fortress razed to the ground. Assyrian governors were appointed throughout Babylonia, and Sargon II assumed the kingship of Babylon (709–705 BCE). Later Sargon reinstated Marduk-apla-iddina II as king.

When Assurbanipal died in 627 BCE, revolts erupted. The struggle for power focused first on Babylonia. Kandalanu (647–627 BCE), king of Babylonia, was removed from power. Assur-etel-ilani, Assurbanipal's son, tried to supervise Babylonia through a loyal general whom he appointed king. In the same year, Sin-shar-ishkun (possibly Assur-etel-ilani's twin) rebelled with support from the main Assyrian garrisons in Babylon. Sin-shar-ishkun became king of Babylonia and then replaced his brother as king of Assyria.

Nabopolassar (625–605 BCE), who referred to himself as "the son of a nobody,"[22] founded the Neo-Babylonian Dynasty. He steadily extended his hold on Babylonia and tried to win allies abroad. Within ten years Nabopolassar controlled Babylonia, which he defended against Assyrian invasion.

In 614 BCE Median forces attacked Assyria and raided Nineveh. Nabopolassar, wishing to be present at the final moment, marched north, but he arrived after Asshur had already fallen. Near the ruins of the city he and Cyaxares, king of the Medes, met. They drew up a formal treaty, confirming their alliance by a marriage between Nebuchadnezzar, Nabopolassar's son, and Amyitis, a granddaughter of the Median king. The Medes returned home and directed their attention to Armenia and the rest of Asia Minor.

The Assyrian empire soon disappeared, its cities raided and its people enslaved. There is no information about the Assyrian empire after 612 BCE. The remnants of the Assyrian state were defeated in battles at Haran in 610 BCE and at Carchemish in 605 BCE. In the spring of 605 BCE Crown Prince Nebuchadnezzar II attacked the Egyptian army at Carchemish. Both sides suffered heavy casualties, but the morale of the Egyptian army was destroyed. Both Syria and ancient Israel fell to Nebuchadnezzar II. The Neo-Babylonian kings acquired the Assyrian empire, which had collapsed. Upon learning of Nabopolassar's death, Nebuchadnezzar II (604–562 BCE) and a few supporters hurried to the capital city of Babylon to lay claim to the throne.

In 601 BCE Nebuchadnezzar II advanced against Egypt. Both sides suffered heavy losses in a battle near the Egyptian frontier and retreated. Reports of Babylonian casualties encouraged Judah, an Egyptian ally, to stop paying tribute to Babylon. As punishment for non-payment Judah became a Babylonian province, and some of the population was captured and taken to Babylon.

Egyptian activity began once again in ancient Israel. Nebuchadnezzar II immediately sent a powerful army, and the Egyptians retreated. The Babylonians reclaimed many towns and besieged Jerusalem. After eighteen months there was severe famine in the city, and the Babylonians breached the walls (586 BCE). Zedekiah, the king, fled but was captured and delivered to Nebuchadnezzar II's headquarters. Zedekiah's sons were slain before his eyes, and then he was blinded and taken captive to Babylon. Jerusalem was ransacked, its walls torn down, and both the temple and palace were set on fire. Many of the survivors were deported to Babylonia.

Babylonia's association with the Medes continued to be friendly. But before the end of his reign, Nebuchadnezzar became distrustful of Median plans. He built a great defensive wall north of Babylon, called the Median Wall, which extended from Sippar to Opis, to keep out barbarian tribes and to block invasions from the north.

Nebuchadnezzar II's death in 562 BCE was followed by the brief reigns of three minor kings, the last one ruling only three months before being overthrown. Nabonidus (555–539 BCE), already in his sixties, ascended the throne after many years of service to Nebuchadnezzar II. The new ruler was the last of the Neo-Babylonian dynasts. He was not a member of Nebuchadnezzar II's family: "I am Nabonidus who has not the honor of being a somebody—kingship is not within me."[23]

At the beginning of his reign Nabonidus had a dream in which Marduk ordered him to rebuild the Temple of Sin in Haran, which had lain desolate for fifty-four years. Nabonidus rebuilt the temple and rededicated it to the god Sin. Nabonidus also gave special attention to other centers of moon worship at Ur and at the oasis of Teima in Arabia. His growing devotion to Sin was a religious change which caused friction with conservative factions in Babylonia. Nabonidus' mother, Adad-guppi, was devoted to this god at Haran. According to her biography, Adad-guppi lived 104 years; her life spanned the entire Neo-Babylonian period.

Despite the great agricultural wealth of its temples, the Neo-Babylonian empire suffered severe economic constraints. The military and building campaigns of both Nabopolassar and Nebuchadnezzar had taken their toll. Some of Babylonia's major trade routes fell to Median control. Inflation was rampant, with prices rising by 50 percent. Babylonia also suffered from plague and famine. Nabonidus tried to explain the famine as a result of the impiety of the Babylonian people.

After ten years in Teima, at the age of seventy, Nabonidus returned. The reasons for the king's return to Babylon are as baffling as those for his leaving for ten years. During his absence he left his son, Belshazzar, in charge as ruler of Babylon. But the balance of power in the Near East had shifted. In 539 BCE the Persian army, led by its king, Cyrus, invaded Babylon. Cyrus' troops surrounded the Temple of Marduk. They were told that religious services were being held and did not interrupt the citizens at prayer. The Marduk priesthood led a revolt in Babylon and gave the city to Cyrus. He was regarded as a liberator who freed the people from the oppression of Nabonidus.

The fate of both Nabonidus and Belshazzar remains unknown—either exile or death. Cyrus named a Persian governor but maintained Babylon's religious institutions and civil administration.

Cyrus II (538–530 BCE) continued to subdue all of Asia Minor. He permitted religious freedom among his subjects and levied reasonable taxes.

His capital, Pasargadae, was simple compared to the elaborate buildings of the Babylonian and Assyrian kings.

In the summer of 530 BCE, Cyrus died and was interred in a gabled stone tomb at Pasargadae. The immense Persian empire passed peacefully to his son, Cambyses (529–522 BCE). The Babylonians and the Assyrians had ceased to exist as great powers in western Asia.

4

Writing, Education, and Literature

ORIGINS OF WRITING

The invention of writing is credited to the Mesopotamians and is dated to the end of the fourth millennium BCE. At this time geographical and environmental conditions made settlement possible. We see the development of cities, which required a more complex social organization. The invention of writing was triggered by economic necessity—to keep a reliable record of grain, sheep, and cattle entering and leaving the warehouses and farms that belonged to the palaces and temples. Once developed, writing was the most efficient and comprehensive solution for recording information.

Factors Contributing to the Emergence of Writing

Writing was invented in Mesopotamia about 3100 BCE. But writing was not the first method developed by humans to keep track of information. Early lists of accounting devices note wooden sticks, a loom, and even an abacus. In the "Debate between the Sheep and the Grain," a second millennium text, we find early recording devices alongside writing:

Development of Writing

> Every day an account of you (the sheep) is made,
> The tally sticks are planted in the ground;
> Your shepherd tells the owner, how many ewes and how many
>   little lambs.
> How many goats and how many little kids there are.[1]

Jemdet Nasr tablet with pictograms and cuneiform (ca. 3000–2900 BCE). Each column concerns the issue of commodities as rations for a particular day. Each day number is given at the bottom of each column, day 1–day 5, with five different commodities issued. © BRITISH MUSEUM, LONDON.

Among the earliest forerunners to actual writing were clay tokens or counters, called "stones." The tokens were mostly made of clay and were usually the size of small marbles. They came in a variety of shapes: spheres, discs, cones, and rods. The token system can be dated to approximately 10,000 BCE. Initially, tokens were used for simple household and market bookkeeping. However, later, with the development of cities, the token system evolved, displaying a proliferation of markings in order to record numbers as well as an increasing variety of goods—a kind of ancient three-dimensional writing system. The technical word in Sumerian for token was "stone," a term that continued to be used into the second millennium BCE. Among the early forerunners of writing (fourth millennium BCE) are numerical tablets; these are small, sealed tablets with numbers whose values still remain undeciphered.

The earliest writing is found at Uruk in Mesopotamia. Slightly later examples of writing systems using similar signs have been excavated at sites from Syria to Iran. The early Uruk tablets contained both numerals and pictographs (drawings of objects). The tablets included approximately twelve hundred signs. Some of these signs may have had their origin in clay tokens, but most were pictographs, from which cuneiform signs later developed. For example, the drawing of an ox's head (sometimes even the whole ox) is used as the sign for ox, and an ear of barley is used as the sign for barley. The Uruk tablets were also authenticated by sealing. Approximately 85 percent of the tablets recorded goods, food, or animals delivered either by individuals or by the city's temples. The other 15 percent of the tablets are lexical (word) lists of officials, commodities, and animals. The same lists are still found six hundred years later, showing the continuity of a tradition.

Even in the early stages of writing, Uruk scribes began to systematize the script. They drew up lists of signs which were accepted throughout southern Mesopotamia. The language of the Uruk early writers remains uncertain. In a script denoting numerals and commodities (pictograms), the signs can be read in any language. For example, a pictogram of wheat can be read as "wheat" in English, "le blé" in French, "der Weizen" in German, and so on. In the early periods few grammatical elements appeared. That is, writing did not have a one-to-one correspondence with language.

The first texts we can read are from the first half of the third millennium—they were written in Sumerian. At this point the scribes used grammatical elements that clearly indicate that the language was Sumerian. The scribes achieved this by assigning phonetic values to signs which were ideograms. This happened in two ways. First, ideograms (symbols used to represent words) were extended to include a constellation of meanings by association; for example, the sign for foot also meant "stand" or "walk." Second, the range of sounds for ideograms was extended by punning, much the way the sign for "sun" could be extended to "son." Thus, a collection of syllabic signs was created, and scribes were able to indicate grammatical elements so that the script corresponded to the language. Sumerian is an agglutinative language. Each idea, whether nominal or verbal, was expressed by a single unchanging syllable (or polysyllable). This fixed syllable or root could be modified by long chains of prefixes and postfixes, signifying specific grammatical elements.

By the middle of the third millennium the Akkadians used the writing

Pictographic form (ca. 3100 BCE)	Early cuneiform representation (ca. 2400 BCE)	Late Assyrian form (ca. 650 BCE)	Sumerian equivalent and meaning
			MUŠEN bird
			GU$_4$ ox
			SAG head
			GIN/GUB walk/stand
			ÁB cow
			A water
			KU$_6$ fish

Evolution of signs.

system developed by the Sumerians. Akkadian was an inflected language, relying on the addition of prefixes, infixes, and suffixes to form a single word. Therefore, a single cuneiform sign could not convey the meaning of an Akkadian word. So, for the most part, Akkadian scribes wrote words out phonetically, even though they continued to use Sumerian ideograms to express some Akkadian words. In addition, in order to adapt Sumerian writing to the Akkadian language, the Akkadian scribes increased homophony (using the same value for several signs) and polyphony (asssigning many values to each sign). Even though Sumerian was superseded by Akkadian in the second millennium BCE, Sumerian continued to be used as a kind of shorthand for words or expressions. Thus, the practice of signs being used as either ideograms or syllables continued as long as cuneiform was used.

Other writing systems were influenced by Mesopotamia's cuneiform system and developed soon after. They include Egyptian hieroglyphics, proto-Elamite from Iran (which remains undeciphered), the Indus valley script from Pakistan and India (also undeciphered), Minoan Linear A from Crete (still undeciphered), Hittite hieroglyphics (used in central Asiatic Turkey), and Chinese writing. Each nation put its own unique stamp on the writing system that came from Mesopotamia.

With so many values for each sign as well as the same value for several signs, how did the ancient scribe manage to choose the correct value or meaning for each sign? Scribes used determinatives, that is, signs used either before or after a word as classifiers to indicate the category of objects to which the word belongs, for example, wood, deity, human being (male or female), river, city, fish, bird, and so on. Other aids to reading were provided by context, by signs preceding and following, and sometimes by variant writings which clarified the possibilities of reading the sign. Also, a scribe did not use all the theoretical possibilities of the sign in writing texts.

In the second millennium, as writing spread to other areas within Mesopotamia's cultural (and political) sphere of influence, certain problems arose because the scribes often spoke another language and were not as well trained as scribes from Mesopotamia. But records of transactions were still needed in the international community. As a solution, the district scribes simplified the script, either by giving it a quasi-alphabetic character or by eliminating duplication of phonetic values by reducing the number of signs. Also, cuneiform was adopted in simplified form to write other languages.

Numbers were written in all categories of cuneiform texts, from the earliest, ca. 3100 BCE, to the last datable text in 75 CE. Like the rest of the cuneiform script, the method of writing numbers also evolved. Initially, numbers were formed by pressing the ends of a reed stylus into the clay either vertically (to make larger or smaller circles) or at a slant.

Later, when the script became stylized and took on the appearance of cuneiform, the numbers took on a more angular form.

Cryptography was occasionally used so that only a select few could understand the "secrets" of this knowledge, for example, for specialized work, such as the manufacture of glass. Sometimes numbers were used for cryptography. The names of some of the major gods were eventually written as numbers, with Anu, the head of the pantheon, being assigned the number 60.

Techniques and Means of Writing   A stylus was made from a cut reed, trimmed to form a round, pointed, or sloping end; the stylus was then used to draw signs and to mark horizontal lines and vertical columns on lumps of clay that fit into the palm of the hand.

The materials for writing were easily found in the river valleys of the Near East and were simple to use. We do not know how the scribes actually chose, prepared, and stored the clay and kept it sufficiently moist for writing. Clay could be worked into a flat shape, which could be written on while moist and then dried in the sun to last. Many tablets in the libraries of Assyrian kings were actually baked to the same hardness as pottery that had been fired. In other words, once dried, tablets could not be altered; this made them an excellent medium for final records in legal and administrative transactions. Also, many tablets we have today in museum collections were burnt in antiquity when a city was conquered and sacked. Unwanted tablets were reused, thrown away, or sometimes used as floor packing. The first side of the clay tablet to be inscribed is flat, and it is called the "obverse" by Assyriologists; the back of the tablet, or the "reverse," is convex.

Most tablets are either rectangles or squares, but some are round. Some tablets used for magic were made with a perforated handle at one end so that they could be mounted or threaded and worn around the neck or hung on a wall; clay beads were also inscribed for magical purposes. The contents of the tablets (for example, a legal document, a letter, or an administrative text) influenced the shape chosen, such as cones, cylinders, and prisms.

Though the use of clay tablets remained central to the tradition of cuneiform writing, other materials could be used. They were sometimes more expensive, such as hinged tablets with a beeswax overlay. Sometimes tablets were imitated in stone or metal. Monuments and dedications could be incised on stone, ivory, metal, and glass. Large tablets were unwieldy; some have been found as wide as thirty-seven cm. on each side and weighing as much as almost seven kg. Clearly such tablets could not be held in one hand for very long. A scene from a stele ca. 2100 BCE may explain how large administrative and literary tablets were handled: a scribe is shown writing on a tablet that is held for him by his assistant. Otherwise, long texts had to be written on many tablets.

Old Babylonian letter with sealed envelope (ca. early second millennium BCE). ©
BRITISH MUSEUM, LONDON.

When an impression, whether writing or a seal, was made on clay, it
could not be altered once the clay hardened. The practice began in the
fifth millennium BCE with the use of stamp seals on lumps of clay and
continued with cylinder seals throughout Mesopotamian history. In the
second and first millennia BCE, even the illiterate could authenticate a
legal document by using a seal. Seals could even be rolled on lumps of
clay to seal doors, pottery jars, and goods. Some seals belonged to a city
official or, in the case of legal proceedings, a judicial authority. Seals
could be carved on stone, bone, metal, or shell. Different designs and
inscriptions were used to indicate their owners. Later, the practice
changed and the party (or parties) to a legal action impressed a seal or
a substitute such as a finger-nail or garment hem.

Around the time of Sargon (2334–2279 BCE) envelopes were invented;
they were slips of clay formed around the tablet. Envelopes protected
the contents from damage and even fraud; that is, the envelopes safe-
guarded against someone moistening the clay and changing the numbers. Sometimes the text was repeated on the envelope and also sealed.
In the case of a dispute, the envelope could be opened and the contents
examined and compared. Some envelopes opened in modern times have
been found with information written on them different from that of the
tablets inside.

The cuneiform script evolved through time, becoming more standard-ized during times of strong centralized government. Eventually, the form of the signs became unrecognizable from the pictographs of the past. The end of the reed used for writing was cut at an oblique angle, forming a triangular cross-section. As a result, the signs came out wedge-shaped, hence the term "cuneiform," a Latin word meaning "wedge-shaped." By the second millennium BCE, the signs became less complex—only three or four kinds of wedges were used to form signs. Even the number of signs was reduced: similar signs merged, and rarely used signs were deleted. As a result, the number of cuneiform signs known from the Uruk writing was cut in half to about six hundred signs. Nonetheless, many signs still had multiple word and phonetic values. From the be-ginning of the second millennium BCE a scribe could have done his job by using less than two hundred signs.

In the beginning, signs were read according to the normal orientation of the pictures so that pots stood upright and animals' heads were not lying on their sides. The signs were grouped together randomly within the boxes because the signs made sense as a unit. The boxes were ar-ranged in rows read from right to left. When one row was completed, the next row was begun beneath it. When the obverse of the tablet was finished, the tablet was turned from left to right and the reverse was written in a similar manner but starting from the bottom and moving up. When the line instead of the box was used, the direction of writing was like Chinese: in vertical columns beginning in the upper right-hand corner. In the middle of the third millennium BCE, signs were rotated ninety degrees counter-clockwise and read from left to right.

The stylus was also used for other markings; for example, ornamental rulings might be incised around the outer edge of tablets. Check marks might be placed next to every tenth person in account texts and against every tenth line in literary texts. From the second millennium on, nu-merous literary tablets have "firing holes," made by pressing the stylus (or a similar object) straight through the tablet from front to back or side to side, often in an ornamental arrangement. A tablet could be canceled by using a stylus or a similar instrument to draw a mark across it.

EDUCATION AND PROFESSIONAL ACTIVITY OF SCRIBES

Sumer's great achievement was the invention of writing, and an or-ganized system of education was its natural outgrowth. Most people were not literate. With approximately six hundred signs with multiple values, education was confined to the few. Even priests, kings, gover-nors, and judges were illiterate, with few exceptions. Correspondence from Assyrian merchants at Kanesh (Turkey) opens with the standard formula: "Tell Mr A, Mr B sends the following message."[2] That is, the letter was dictated to one professional scribe and would be read to the addressee by another professional scribe. Literacy was highly prized, and only a few rulers, among them Shulgi, Naram-Sin, Lipit-Ishtar, Assur-banipal, and Darius, boasted of their scribal accomplishments.

The oldest documents, the Uruk tablets, consist primarily of economic and administrative records. But we also find lexical lists used by scribes to learn signs to study elementary vocabulary for use in administrative texts, and to categorize the world in which they lived so that an archaic society could better understand itself. The same lists are found about five hundred years later at Shuruppak, the home of the Sumerian Noah, thereby showing the continuity of a tradition.

The archaic texts offer little information about the education or professional activity of scribes. However, the unity in both the appearance of tablets and the writing conventions from different regions of Babylonia suggests the existence of some kind of regulated system of education ca. 3000 BCE. The first detailed information concerning the scribal profession and its social status comes from the Ur III period (2112–2004 BCE). Most probably the purpose of the official Ur III schools was to provide necessary specialized personnel at a time when the demand for scribes was great. From this period come tens of thousands of clay tablets that are administrative in nature, encompassing all aspects of economic life in Sumer. From these texts we learn that there were thousands of scribes, specializing in all branches of the temple and royal administrations. From this we infer that scribal schools must have thrived.

The organization and operation of schools in Mesopotamia are known from the numerous student/teacher exercises, lexical lists, essays on school life, examination texts, and royal hymns where kings refer to their education. This information comes from the first half of the second millennium BCE. After this, small groups of tablets appear at different periods, often retaining the intent of the old tradition but revamping the format.

The student attended school, called a "tablet-house," whose headmaster was called "expert" or "father of the tablet-house." There was a dean who enforced the rules and regulations of the tablet-house, called "supervisor of the tablet-house," and there was even a "man in charge of the whip." Teaching assistants were referred to as "older brothers"; their jobs included writing new tablets for the students to copy, checking the students' work, and listening to memorized lessons. Other faculty members included "the man in charge of Sumerian," "the man in charge of drawing," as well as proctors in charge of attendance and discipline. Mathematics was a separate part of the curriculum, taught by the "scribe of accounting," "the scribe of measurement," and the "scribe of the field." We know neither the hierarchy of the school nor how salaries were paid. When finished, the student became a scribe, literally, a "tablet-writer."

Education was undertaken only by wealthier families; the poor could not afford the time and cost for learning. Administrative documents from about 2000 BCE list about five hundred scribes who are further identified by the names and occupations of their fathers. Their fathers were governors, "city fathers," ambassadors, temple administrators, military officers, sea captains, important tax officials, priests, managers, accountants, foremen, and scribes, in other words, the wealthier citizens of the city. There are references to poor orphan boys adopted and sent to school by generous patrons. There is only one reference to a female scribe at this time. However, cloistered women, celibate devotees of the sun god Shamash and his consort Aya, served as scribes for their own cloister administration. Celibate priestesses may also have devoted themselves to scholarly pursuits.

The Sumerian school may have begun as a temple annex during the third millennium BCE; it was attached to some palaces in the second millennium and later privatized. The first Mesopotamian schools we know of were founded or subsidized by King Shulgi at Nippur and Ur at the end of the third millennium. When in royal service, the scribal school may have composed hymns ordered by the royal court for the king. Three royal hymns actually indicate that they were composed in the school! Sumerian literary texts have been found principally in private houses (some in the scribal quarter of Nippur referred to as Tablet Hill) rather than in the temple complex. In fact, school texts have been excavated at most private homes in the first half of the second millennium, thereby implying that all boys in wealthy families were sent to school.

The actual learning process involved memorization, dictation, writing new lessons and reviewing old ones, reading aloud from a written document, and spelling. The students learned signs, language, and vocabulary through syllabaries (syllabic lists) and lexical lists. The lexical lists provided compilations of botanical, zoological, geographical, and mineralogical information; they also provided important linguistic tools for the study of grammar, bilingual and trilingual dictionaries, and legal and administrative vocabulary. The methods of teaching have given us thousands of "school tablets," often round in shape, with the teacher's copy on one side and the pupil's work on the other. We have the tablets students wrote themselves, from the beginner's first copies to those of the advanced student, whose work could hardly be differentiated from the teacher's. Not every scribe completed the "full course." In fact, the student was probably not required to complete the entire series before attempting the next text of the curriculum. The student copied tablets not only as exercises but at times to build a private library for himself or his teacher.

Despite its professional orientation, the Sumerian school was also a center for literature and creative writing; the Mesopotamian literary "classics" were studied and copied, and new compositions were written. Later, the Akkadians not only used the Sumerian script but also studied the literature of the Sumerians, even imitating their works. The "dictionaries" became a useful tool for learning the Sumerian language, which was no longer spoken by the beginning of the second millennium BCE but enjoyed enormous prestige, much like Latin in Western culture.

The student attended classes daily from sunrise to sunset. We have no information about vacations, but one pupil explained his monthly schedule:

> The reckoning of my monthly stay in the tablet house is (as
>   follows):
> My days of freedom are three per month,
> Its festivals are three days per month.
> Within it, twenty-four days per month
> (Is the time of) my living in the tablet house. They are long days.[3]

The student began school between the ages of five and seven years and continued until he became a young man. We do not know if scribes were expected to have a varied background or to what degree they were expected to specialize as preparation for assuming their posts.

The most complete list of the subjects studied is best represented by "A Failed Examination." The examination involved a comprehensive test by a scribe of his son; it took place in the courtyard of the tablet-house before an assembly of masters.

> *A*: Come, my son, sit at my feet. I will talk to you, and you will give me information! From your childhood to your adult age you have been staying in the tablet-house. Do you know the scribal art that you have learned?
>
> *B*: What would I not know? Ask me, and I will give you the answer.

A series of questions follows:

1. "The element of the scribal craft is the simple wedge; it has six teeth (directions in which it could be written) . . . Do you know its name?"
2. Secret meanings of Sumerian words (cryptography).
3. Translation from Sumerian to Akkadian and the reverse.
4. Three Sumerian synonyms for each Akkadian word.

5. Sumerian grammatical terminology.

6. Sumerian conjugation of verbs.

7. Various types of calligraphy and technical writing.

8. Writing Sumerian phonetically.

9. To understand the technical language of all classes of priests and other professions, such as silversmiths, jewelers, herdsmen and scribes.

10. How to write, make an envelope, and seal a document.

11. All kinds of songs and how to conduct a choir.

12. Mathematics, division of fields, and allotting of rations.

13. Various musical instruments.

The candidate failed, and blamed both the master and the big brother for not teaching him these subjects; he was duly reprimanded:

> What have you done, what good came of your sitting here? You are already a ripe man and close to being aged! Like an old ass you are not teachable any more. Like withered grain you have passed the season. How long will you play around? But, it is still not too late! If you study night and day and work all the time modestly and without arrogance, if you listen to your colleagues and teachers, you still can become a scribe! The scribal craft, receiving a handsome fee, is a bright-eyed guardian, and it is what the palace needs.[4]

We have several essays on school life, which have been named in modern times (1) "Schooldays," (2) "School Rowdies" (or "The Disputation Between Enkimansi and Girnishag"), (3) "A Scribe and His Perverse Son," and (4) "Colloquy Between an Estate Superintendent and a Scribe." "Schooldays" dealt with the daily life of the schoolboy as recounted by an alumnus. It was composed by an anonymous schoolteacher around 2000 BCE, and told a story of school life, not unlike today. It began with the question, "Old Grad, where did you go (when you were young)?" The alumnus answered, "I went to school." The schoolteacher-author asked, "What did you do in school?" The old grad replied:

> I recited my tablet, ate my lunch, prepared my (new) tablet, wrote it, finished it; then my model tablets were brought to me; and in the afternoon my exercise tablets were brought to me. When school was dismissed, I went home, entered the house, and found my

father sitting there. I explained my exercise-tablets to my father, recited my tablet to him, and he was delighted.... When I arose early in the morning, I faced my mother and said to her: "Give me my lunch, I want to go to school!" My mother gave me two rolls, and I set out; my mother gave me two rolls, and I went to school. In school the fellow in charge of punctuality said: "Why are you late?" Afraid and with pounding heart, I entered before my teacher and made a respectful curtsy.

In school the student misbehaved and was caned by different staff members for a variety of offenses such as poor class work, sloppy dress, speaking without permission, rising without permission, going to the school gate, not speaking Sumerian with his Sumerian instructor, and poor penmanship. The teachers gave up on him. Finally, the old grad asked his father's help by feting his teacher and giving him "a bit of extra salary," a new garment, and a ring. The teacher duly praised the student:

Young fellow, because you did not neglect my word, did not forsake it, may you complete the scribal art from beginning to end. Because you gave me everything without stint, paid me a salary larger than my efforts deserve, and have honored me, may Nisaba, the queen of guardian angels, be your guardian angel; may your pointed stylus write well for you; may your exercises contain no faults. Of your brothers, may you be their leader; of your friends may you be their leader, may you rank the highest among the school graduates ... You have carried out well the school's activities, you are a man of learning. You have exalted Nisaba, the queen of learning; O Nisaba, praise![5]

"School Rowdies" was a bitter verbal debate between two classmates, Enkimansi and Girnishag. Each boasted about his scribal talents while insulting the other. In fact, in this composition we have found the first use of "sophomore" (Greek, "clever fool"), but in Sumerian, of course. A sample of this vituperative interchange gives us an idea of the subjects studied:

You dolt, numskull, school pest, you illiterate, you Sumerian ignoramus, your hand is terrible; it cannot even hold the stylus properly; it is unfit for writing and cannot take dictation. (And yet you say) you are a scribe like me.

To which the other replied:

What do you mean I am not a scribe like you? When you write a document it makes no sense. When you write a letter it is illegible. You go to divide up an estate, but are unable to divide up the estate. For when you go to survey the field, you can't hold the measuring line. You can't hold a nail in your hand; you have no sense. You don't know how to arbitrate between the contesting parties; you aggravate the struggle between the brothers. You are one of the most incompetent tablet writers. What are you fit for, can any one say? . . . Me, I was raised on Sumerian, I am the son of a scribe. But you are a bungler, a windbag. When you try to shape a tablet, you can't even smooth the clay. When you try to write a line, your hand can't manage the tablet . . . You "sophomore," cover your ears! cover your ears! (Yet) you (claim to know) Sumerian like me![6]

Finally, the monitor became so enraged with Enkimansi that he threatened to beat him, lock him up for two months, and put him in copper chains. With such strict discipline, pupils sometimes were truant, as in "A Scribe and His Perverse Son." This composition about school life is one of the first documents to use the word for "humanity." The essay began with an amicable exchange between father and son. The father began by asking, "Where did you go?," to which the son replied, "I did not go anywhere." The father rejoined:

If you did not go anywhere, why do you idle about? Go to school, stand before your headmaster, recite your assignment, open your schoolbag, write your tablet, let your "big brother" write your new tablet for you. After you have finished your assignment and reported to your monitor, come to me, and do not wander about in the street. Come now, do you know what I said?

The father had his son repeat what he had said word for word to make sure the boy had paid close attention. The essay then turned into a monologue of fatherly advice and concern:

Come now, be a man. Don't stand about in the public square or wander about the boulevard. When walking in the street, don't look all around. Be humble and show fear before your monitor. When you show terror, the monitor will like you . . . You who wander about in the public square, would you achieve success? Then seek out the first generations. Go to school, it will be of benefit to you. My son, seek out the first generations, inquire of them. Perverse one over whom I stand watch—I would not be a man did I not stand watch over my son.

The father continued, expressing his disappointment at his son's ungrateful and "inhuman" behavior. He was particularly frustrated that
his son refused to follow in his footsteps and become a scribe. Rather,
his son was more interested in being wealthy.

> Yes, I was angry with you. Because you do not look to your hu-
> manity, my heart was carried off as if by an evil wind. Your grum-
> blings have put an end to me, you have brought me to the point
> of death . . . I, never in all my life, did I make you carry reeds to
> the canebrake. The reed rushes which the young and the little carry,
> you, never in your life did you carry them. I never said to you
> "Follow my caravans." I never sent you to work, to plow my field.
> I never sent you to work, to dig up my field. I never sent you to
> work as a laborer. "Go, work and support me," I never in my life
> said to you. Others like you support their parents by working . . .
> But you, you're a man when it comes to perverseness, but com-
> pared to them you're not a man at all. You certainly don't labor
> like them . . . It is in accordance with the fate decreed by Enlil for
> man that a son follows the work of his father . . . I, night and day
> am I tortured because of you. Night and day you waste in pleas-
> ures. You have accumulated much wealth, have expanded far and
> wide, have become fat, big, broad, powerful, and puffed. But your
> kin waits expectantly for your misfortune and will rejoice at it be-
> cause you looked not to your humanity.[7]

Despite his disappointment, the father still blessed his son and called on
the gods to protect him and help him succeed.

In spite of the less than innovative curriculum, the discipline, and the
rivalry between classmates, the students who persevered graduated from
the school. They found jobs, often in the service of the palace or temple,
since the goal of the school was to train scribes for various administrative
positions in these institutions, as well as other positions, such as royal
scribe, district scribe, military scribe, land-registrar, scribe for laborer
groups, administrator, public secretary to a high administrative official,
accountant, copyist ("deaf writer"), inscriber of stone and seals, ordinary
clerk, astrologer, mathematician, or professor of Sumerian. In "Colloquy
between an Estate Superintendent and a Scribe," the graduate has at-
tained a job on an estate. He and his boss, also a school alumnus, discussed their education and work. The estate superintendent offered a
long description about his diligence and obedience as a student, ending
with the admonition, "So you must be courteous to man, supervisor,
and owner, and must make their heart content." The scribe responded
as follows: "The learned scribe humbly answers his estate superintendent." However, the answer was anything but humble:

Now I will let you have the answer to it; as for your ox-like bellow, you will not turn me into an ignoramus with its lack of understanding—I will answer it fully . . . Why do you lay down rules for me as if I am an idler? Anyone who heard you would drop his hands in despair. Let me explain to you carefully the art of being a scribe since you have mentioned it. You have put me in charge over your house (and) never have I let you find me idling about. I held the slave girls, slaves, and (the rest of) your household to their task; saw to it that they enjoyed their bread, clothing, and fat (and) that they work properly. You did not (have to) follow your slave in the house of your master; I did the unpleasant task (and) followed him like a sheep . . . You assigned me the breast (that is, perhaps, the high, unirrigated part) of the field (and) I made the men work there—a challenging task which permits no sleep either by night or in the heat of day.[8]

The estate superintendent then changed his attitude, praising and blessing the scribe's work. The composition ended with the typical, "O Nisaba, praised."

ARCHIVES AND LIBRARIES

The term "archive" is used to designate all records amassed at the time a particular task was carried out by an institution or person; these records may still be kept by those who wrote them or used them. Many tablet rooms were conveniently located for recordkeeping and reference—near the entrance of a palace for registering goods entering or leaving, near a royal audience room, or close to a workshop, kitchen, or warehouse. The palace at Ugarit in Syria had archives located at each of the two entrances to the palace. Ebla's archival rooms were situated both next to the royal audience room and in the administrative quarter. Mari's kitchen archive was conveniently located near the kitchen.

Scribes usually accumulated private libraries through both their own work and their students' copies. Scribes and scribal schools associated with temples and palaces, benefiting from the economic security of their patrons, were able to do scholarly research, thereby accumulating collections of tablets that Assyriologists call libraries.

Small personal libraries can be found in every period, though an unusually large personal library of more than three thousand tablets was found in a priest's house at Tell-ed Der (dated to the seventeenth century BCE). Texts belonging to archives and libraries may be found in the same place. For example, scholars often kept their private archives (for example, legal and administrative records) and professional libraries (such as school, literary, and scientific texts) together, as did the scribe at Ur who ran a school from his home in "Quiet Street no. 7." The majority of information for all periods comes from economic, administrative, and literary texts from temple and palace archives. These large institutions often had separate rooms for filing and storing records.

The first systematic library, and the most famous, was created by King Assurbanipal (seventh century BCE), who boasted of his ability to read and write. Assurbanipal built a library at his palace in Nineveh and sent agents far and wide to stock it with tablets from every field of education, as shown in the following letter: "Hunt for the valuable tablets which are in your archives and which do not exist in Assyria and send them to me. I have written to the officials and overseers . . . and no one shall withhold a tablet from you; and when you see any tablet or ritual about which I have not written to you, but which you perceive may be profitable for my palace, seek it out, pick it up, and send it to me."[9] When brought to Assyria, the tablets were either placed in Assurbanipal's library or recopied. Some tablets were copied exactly, with the scribe leaving blank spaces as in the original but adding, "I do not understand" or "old break." Other tablets were partly or completely rewritten and even adapted to the style of that time. Assurbanipal's library probably consisted of fifteen hundred different tablets with eighty to two hundred lines on each. In general, literary libraries consisted of "classics," standard texts which were recopied for generations. Sometimes new compositions were added, but they were few and far between.

Tablets were stored in a variety of ways. Private individuals stored tablets by wrapping them in either a piece of cloth or a reed mat or by putting them in a jar, basket, bag, or chest. Private archives were sometimes stored in palaces for safekeeping. In Ebla, in northern Syria, the palace archives were stored on shelves; when excavated, the tablets were found where they had fallen when the tablet room was burnt. Tablets could be stacked either on wooden shelves along the wall or on mud-brick benches. The mud-brick benches, found in all periods, were approximately twenty inches wide and placed either in the center of the room or along the walls. Benches were used for storing tablets, for laying out records for reference or filing, and for seating scribes reading or writing tablets. Smaller groups of tablets might be kept in either wood chests or reed baskets, which were sealed; then the door to the room where they were stored was sealed. In a letter to Zimri-Lim (ca. eighteenth century BCE) from his wife, the queen noted that "they opened the door of the room which he indicated, which was sealed with the seal of Igmilum of the secretariat, and took out two baskets of tablets, the baskets sealed with the seal of Etel-pi-sharrim. With their sealings those baskets are deposited with me until my lord's arrival, and I have sealed the door of the room which they opened with my seal."[10] The accounts and correspondence of the Assyrian merchants in Anatolia have been found in sealed jars. Assyrian tablets explain that opening a dead or absent merchant's "safe" was done by a committee of three disinterested parties, who then described the results. Later, in the first millennium BCE temples, large pigeonholes of brick and plaster were built along the walls of an archival room or library.

The systems for storage described indicate that tablets were meticulously filed in order to be readily available for reference. Tablets could be placed on shelves or benches, or in jars, baskets, or other receptacles, according to contents, date, place, and so on. The tablets were placed on shelves or in clay banks tied with strings, with tags attached noting the contents. Some large tablets from the Ur III period as well as the Old Babylonian period contained memos on the edge of the tablet, similar to the spine of a book today. In the first millennium BCE notations were added in Aramaic, Greek, and Egyptian to business documents with a stylus or pen using ink or paint.

LITERATURE: POETRY AND PROSE

Authors and Editors
We do not know the real origins of Sumerian literature. Our only knowledge comes from Berossus, a third century BCE priest of Marduk who lived in Babylon. At the request of the Seleucid king Antiochus I, Berossus wrote *Babyloniaca*, a book about ancient Mesopotamian cultural traditions and history. Berossus recorded that after the Flood, the Babylonian Noah was instructed as follows: "The voice (from the sky) also told them that they were to return to Babylon and that it was decreed that they were to dig up the writings from (the city) of the Sipparians and distribute them to mankind."[11]

The earliest literary texts found so far date to approximately 2400 BCE and are from Ebla, Abu Salabikh, and Fara. We do not know the role of oral tradition in the formation of these compositions. It is possible that generations of storytellers and scribes were involved in creating the final product.

Some scribes signed their names to tablets as early as 2600 BCE. Generally, the authors of literary texts remained anonymous; however, a catalogue from Nineveh listed authors and editors of some well-known compositions such as the *Epic of Gilgamesh*. Later scribes listed their lineage, giving the names of their fathers and even earlier ancestors. Scribes usually described themselves by the simple term "scribe," but sometimes they qualified this with further titles, such as "junior scribe," "exorcist," "astrologer," and so on. A few compositions appear to have been composed by a single author; these works show uniqueness in language, subject matter, and artistic development. In some cases, the texts actually identify the author in the narrative or in an acrostic.

The colophon functions much as the title and imprint pages of a modern book and usually contains the name of the scribe, the date the tablet was written, and the town. The colophon may also include the title of the composition (indicated by a shortened first line of the work), the number of tablets in the series, the catch line of the next tablet, the name of the owner, comments on the original which the scribe had copied, and an invocation of curses against any unauthorized person removing the tablet. The colophon in the *Epic of Creation* at the end of Tablet IV illustrates this process:

(*Catch line*)

He fashioned stands for the great gods.

(*Colophon*)

146 lines. Fourth tablet "When Above." Not complete.

Written according to a wax (covered) tablet whose lines were canceled (that is, crossed out), for Nabu, his lord, Na'id-Marduk, descendant of the Smith family, wrote it for the life of himself and the life of his house, and deposited it in Ezida.[12]

Divine inspiration is acknowledged either directly or indirectly. A god has heard the work and sometimes approved it. The author may even assure us that he has not changed the text from its original version.

Sumerian literature is about equal to Biblical literature in size, but much of Sumerian literature still remains to be discovered. Most is written in the main Sumerian dialect. However, the speeches of women and goddesses in myths and erotic poetry as well as lamentations recited by male singers were written in "the language of women." Most Sumerian literature we have today is from later copies. The Babylonians and Assyrians imitated, revised, and translated Sumerian literature. There are also numerous Sumerian texts with interlinear translations into Akkadian. Sumerian literature influenced Akkadian literature in style, viewpoint, and choice of subject.

During the second half of the second millennium BCE, Kassite scribes, the last great authors and editors of Babylonia, standardized many literary works. New texts entered the canonical corpus at a later date; some were very popular and became widely distributed. As texts were copied and recopied, the scribes sometimes edited the compositions by adding or deleting.

In regard to content, texts were often recopied because they dealt with the human condition, the remote past, heroes, and especially gods. If historical documents were recopied, they reflected universal concerns in regard to events and personalities.

Poetry was generally favored over prose. The language of the texts tended to be simplified over time. Texts that could be either shortened or expanded usually survived over time.

Because few people could read and write, the creation of Mesopotamian literature arose in response to the interests and needs of those who were literate. That is, the texts addressed universal concerns, human dilemmas, or professional interests (for example, for diviners and exorcists). They could be either entertaining or informative. Texts sometimes alluded to or even quoted from other familiar literature.

Categories of Literature
In Mesopotamian tradition, literary compositions are generally named according to the first few words of the text, so that *When Above* is the native title for *The Epic of Creation*, and *He Who Saw Everything* for *The Epic of Gilgamesh*. The ancient Mesopotamians did not divide literature into specific categories, although modern scholars prefer to classify texts as myths and epics, prayers and hymns, essays, wisdom literature, and historiography.

Incantations, the first category of literature to be discovered at Fara and Ebla (ca. 2400 BCE), were written throughout the third millennium BCE. By the beginning of the second millennium, incantations were compiled, organized by subject (such as those against evil spirits), and later provided with interlinear translations into Akkadian. Here is an incantation against an attack by rabid dogs:

> It is fleet of foot, powerful on the run,
> Strong-legged, broad-chested.
> The shadow of a wall is where it stands,
> The threshold is its lurking place.
> It carries its semen [that is, foam] in its mouth,
> Where it bit, it left its offspring.
> (Incantation to survive a dog's bite, incantation of Ea [the god of
>   wisdom and benefactor of mankind]).[13]

Hymns to the gods and their temples are also found at about the same time. Some of the best were composed by the first known author, Enkheduanna, high priestess of the moon god Nanna and daughter of King Sargon of Akkad. She wrote a cycle of forty-two short hymns. In a hymn entitled "The Indictment of Nanna," Enkheduanna used her considerable literary skill as a poet to describe being forced from office and escaping to Ur.

> As for me, my Nanna takes no heed of me.
> He has verily given me over to destruction in murderous straits.
> Ashimbabbar has not pronounced my judgment.
> Had he pronounced it: what is it to me? Had he not pronounced
>   it: what is it to me?

> (Me) who once sat triumphant he has driven out of the
> sanctuary.
> Like a swallow he made me fly from the window, my life is
> consumed.
> He made me walk in the bramble of the mountain.
> He stripped me of the crown appropriate for the high priesthood.
> He gave me dagger and sword—"it becomes you," he said to
> me.[14]

Myths and epics (see Chapters 8 and 9) narrate events about major and even minor deities as well as semi-legendary rulers such as Gilgamesh. Wisdom literature has been given this name because of its affinity to Proverbs, Job, and Ecclesiastes in the Bible. The focus of this literature is man and a concern with moral and ethical problems. Instructions, proverbs, and riddles are the earliest known subcategories of wisdom literature. Instructions offer practical advice; the following paragraph is particularly timely in today's litigious society:

> Don't go stand where there's a crowd,
> Do not linger where there is a dispute.
> They will bring evil upon you in the dispute,
> Then you will be made their witness,
> They will bring you to bolster a case not your own.
> When confronted with a dispute, avoid it, pay no heed.
> If it is a dispute with you, put out the flame,
> A dispute is a wide-open ambush, a wall of sticks that smothers
> its opponents.
> It brings to mind what a man forgot and charges him.[15]

Proverbs continue, sometimes in bilingual form, into the first millennium BCE; the ancient Mesopotamians even organized them into separate collections. Here are a few examples:

> It's not the heart which leads to enmity; it's the tongue which
> leads to enmity.
> Tell a lie; then if you tell the truth it will be deemed a lie.
> Into an open mouth, a fly enters.[16]

Riddles are as old as proverbs, and sometimes their puns and allusions elude the modern reader; for example:

(What is it?)
A house with a foundation like heaven,
A house which like a copper kettle has been covered with linen,
A house which like a goose stands on a (firm) base,
He whose eyes are not open has entered it,
He whose eyes are (wide) open comes out of it?

Its solution is: It's the school.[17]

While the last three lines are clear—the purpose of school is to educate—
the beginning of the riddle is completely obscure to us. Perhaps, unlike
other wisdom categories, riddles do not always bear the test of time. If
we project one hundred or so years into the future, the famous riddle
"What's black and white and re(a)d all over? (Answer: A newspaper)"
may come to be meaningless in the age of computers and CD-ROM.

Next we find royal hymns, celebrating the events and accomplishments of the king. Many hymns to the gods also ended with a prayer
for the ruling king, much like the invocation "God save the Queen!" The
king was regarded as being of both human and divine parentage, with
the human partners representing Ishtar, the goddess of love, and her
lover, Tammuz, the shepherd god. From poetry celebrating this sacred
marriage grew secular love poetry, sometimes addressed to the king or
to be read by him and his bride. In the following poem, Rim-Sin, king
of Larsa (ca. 1822–1763 BCE), takes part in the sacred marriage rite with
a priestess to secure fertility for his kingdom:

> (She)
> Come here, I want to be embraced, as my heart has dictated to
>   me,
> Let us perform lovers' task, never sleep all night,
> Let both of us on the bed be in the joyful mood for love-making!
>
> (She to Him)
> Come together with attractiveness and love-making! Sustain
>   yourself with life!
> Burn out your desire on top of me!
>
> (He to Her)
> My love is poured out for you,
> Take as much as you desire in generous measure.[18]

Because of their unique status, kings acted as both authors and recip-
ients of letter prayers containing individual petitions. Letter prayers were
also written to the gods themselves. For example, in this letter prayer
Apil-Adad addresses his patron god, Marduk, the god of Babylon, and

complains of his god's neglect: "Say to God, my father, thus says Apil-Adad your servant. Why have you been so neglectful of me? Who might there be to give you a substitute for me? Write to Marduk who loves you . . . Let me see your face, let me kiss your feet! Consider my family, old and young! For their sakes take pity on me, let your assistance reach me!"[19] Hymns included lyrical expressions of praise as well as petitions for general well-being. Prayers were pleas for individual well-being. Some literary hymns and prayers were two hundred lines or more in length. Hymns were metrical; prayers could be written in everyday prose, often placed in front of the divine statue or read to the god by a statue of the petitioner. People's names could be miniature prayers, such as "May-the-god-save-me" or "May-I-see-Babylon." Hymns could be songs praising the temple, and in one case a piece of over four hundred lines included brief hymns to the important temples of Mesopotamia.

Hymn writing became such an important creative effort in Sumer that the scribes themselves actually categorized the hymns, adding a special note to the end of each composition, such as "harmony hymn," "musical hymn," "hymn of heroism." Some hymns were classified according to the accompanying musical instruments as lyre, drum, and unidentified string instruments. There are choral refrains and instructions to bow.

At the beginning of the second millennium BCE (the Old Babylonian period) new genres were invented, such as the "congregational lament" to express grief over the destruction of cities and temples. The citizens often regarded this misfortune as the work of a god no longer pleased with them. The laments recalled the historical events leading to the destruction and included an appeal to the god to protect the people from future disasters. In *Lamentation over the Destruction of Ur*, the moon god, Nanna, was beseeched to restore his city. The lament began with Ningal, the city goddess of Ur, sitting down with her harp among the ruins of the city:

> Having placed the harp of mourning
> > on the ground
> > the woman
> is softly, in the silent house
> > herself intoning the dirge:
> "The day that came to be for me,
> > was laid upon me heavy with tears,
> because of which I moan and moan—
> . . . the bitterest of days
> > that came to be for me—"

The hymn continued with reference to the storm of Enlil, a metaphor for the destruction of Ur by barbarian hordes from the mountains:

In those days the storm
        was called off from the country
        —the people mourn—
and its people—not potsherds—
        littered its sides.
In its walls saps had been made
        —the people mourn—
In its high gates and gangways
        corpses were piled,
in all the wide festival streets
        they lay placed head to shoulder
in all the lanes and alleys
        corpses were piled,
and in the (open) spaces
        where (once) were held the country's dances
        people were stacked in heaps.
The nation's blood filled all holes
        like copper or tin (in molds) their bodies
        —like sheep fat left in the sun—
        dissolved of themselves.

Those who have survived appeal to Nanna:

From days of old
        when (first) the land was founded,
O Nanna, have worshipful men,
        laying hold of your feet . . .
so with the dark headed people
        cast away from you,
        let them (yet) make obeisance to you,
with the city laid in ruins,
        let it yet tearfully implore you,
O Nanna!
        with your restoring the city,
        let it rise into view again before you,
and not set as the bright stars set,
        but let it walk in your sight![20]

Related to the lament was the funeral song or elegy, which existed for
both historical figures and everyday people. In the "Elegy for a Woman
Dead in Childbirth," the woman was the narrator. Both husband and
wife pleaded with Belet-ili, the goddess of childbirth, but the goddess
remained unmoved:

How could I not be cast adrift,
    how could my mooring rope not be cut?
The day I carried the fruit, how happy I was,
Happy was I, happy my husband.
The day I went into labor, my face grew overcast,
The day I gave birth, my eyes grew cloudy.

I prayed to Belet-ili with my hands opened out,
"You are mother of those who give birth, save my life!" . . .

[All . . .] those days I was with my husband,
While I lived with him who was my lover,
Death was creeping stealthily into my bedroom,
It forced me from my house,
It cut me off from my lover,
It set my foot toward the land from which I shall not return.[21]

During the Old Babylonian period, Sumerian was taught to Akkadian-speaking students. The students, accustomed to debate, created contest literature, a verbal contest between two characters, for example, Summer and Winter, Pickaxe and Plow, Bird and Fish, Shepherd and Farmer. Some of the essays on school life were similar to the contest literature. The scribes had a special ideogram to describe these dialogues; it was written Man-Man with the second "man" written upside down, that is, "man against man speaking." The contest was judged by a king or god and was followed by a reconciliation between the two contestants. Contest literature was designed for recitation for royal entertainment and religious festivals.

Later philosophical works should be included in the category of wisdom literature. The concept of justice and just rewards evolved slowly in Mesopotamia. Mesopotamians assumed that the gods ruled the universe and that humans were punished for neglecting the gods and rewarded for serving them. Thus, the Babylonian Job did not understand why he was being punished in *The Poem of the Righteous Sufferer*; after all:

I, for my part, was mindful of supplication and prayer.
Prayer to me was the natural recourse, sacrifice my rule.
The day for reverencing the gods was a source of satisfaction to
    me,
The goddess's procession day was my profit and return . . .
I wish I knew that these things were pleasing to a god!
What seems good to one's self could be an offense to a god,

What in one's own heart seems abominable could be good to
   one's god!
Who could learn the reasoning of the gods in heaven?
Who could grasp the intentions of the gods of the depths?
Where might human beings have learned the way of a god?[22]

That is, the sufferer followed the precepts of his religion, yet he was still
unable to figure out what would please the gods. Such sentiments were
already expressed in Sumerian literature.

After the fall of Ur (ca. 2000 BCE), Sumerian became a dead language,
learned only by the educated scribes, who catalogued, copied, and translated Sumerian texts into Akkadian; the scribes even continued to compose texts in Sumerian. The prestige of Babylonian learning went beyond
Mesopotamia's borders. Some compositions continued in bilingual and
even trilingual versions, while others disappeared. An Akkadian literature developed, sometimes revising Sumerian works. New works appeared, such as "The Poor Man of Nippur" in Assyria, a humorous piece
about a poor man cheated by the mayor, whom he later outwits in order
to exact revenge.

We do not know if the general public was familiar with written literature, since only scribes could read and write. Perhaps literature was
written by the scribes as part of their curriculum and even for their own
amusement. We know that there was court poetry. Dialogues may have
actually been performed (see Chapter 8). Some hymns and epics were
recited at religious celebrations. In general, literature was passed down
by the scribes to subsequent generations of scribes.

Literary Devices   Lines of poetry are often paired; meaning is developed by par-
allelism. The same message can be repeated, expanded, or con-
trasted. For example, in *The Poem of the Righteous Sufferer*, the
Babylonian Job laments:

One whole year to the next! The appointed time passed.
As I turned around, it was more and more terrible.
My ill luck was on the increase, I could find no good fortune.
I called to my god, he did not show his face.
I prayed to the goddess, she did not raise her head.[23]

Sumerian literary works do not use meter and rhyme. The meter of
Akkadian poetry is difficult to understand. We do not know whether it
is based on syllables, units of ideas, stress pattern, or some combination
of these.

Sumerian myths and epics lack an intensification of feeling and excitement as the story progresses, so the story does not build to a climax.
The characters appear to be flat. In the case of epic tales about heroes,

the Sumerians did not always integrate individual episodes into a larger whole. However, Akkadian myths and epics have an awareness of storytelling techniques. For example, the hero hesitates before the big battle, thereby intensifying our experience once he ventures forth to fight his opponent. Also, unlike the Sumerians, the Akkadians were able to integrate various stories about Gilgamesh (some with Sumerian antecedents) as well as the beloved Flood story into an epic tale of twelve tablets. In *The Epic of Gilgamesh* there are adventures and encounters with strange creatures, both men and gods. But also central to the story are human relationships and feelings, such as loneliness, friendship, love, loss, revenge, regret, and fear of death. Some myths from first millennium BCE Assyria have a political slant in order to combat the pro-Babylonian factions at the royal court.

NONLITERARY TEXTS

Sumerian historiography included dynastic lists, royal inscriptions, royal correspondence, and royal hymns. The Sumerian King List traced the successive kingships of Sumer and Akkad from before the Flood to the reign of Hammurabi (ca. 1792 BCE). Even Gilgamesh was mentioned. Later king lists outlined the history of Babylonian dynasties, some in bilingual editions. The historical records and dynastic lists from early periods were more unreliable the further back in time they went. There were often discrepancies between the Babylonian and Assyrian accounts, which sometimes placed contemporaneous dynasties in chronological sequence. From the very beginning kings recorded their deeds in a variety of forms which became standardized through time.

We cannot rely on the historical accuracy of these documents—victories were exaggerated, and defeats were never mentioned. In fact, in the battle of Qadesh between the Egyptians and the Hittites, the written records of each nation recorded victory.

The Mesopotamians loved to write letters, many of which have survived. Most were related to business matters, but occasionally we find a personal letter. The letters had a standard beginning, "To A from your servant, B," "Letter (or message) from B: Tell A . . . ," or simply "Tell A," followed by wishes for the recipient's good health. The wishes could be very long-winded, but at the very least stated, "May (a specific) god grant you life." The purpose of the letter followed, and often a variety of topics were addressed. Criticisms, complaints, and commands were strewn with placating words such as "Are you no longer my brother?" or "Are you no longer my father?" The letter ended when the speaker ran out of things to say, or with a standardized ending.

Royal correspondence is some of the most interesting, giving information on many facets of court life and the daily business of running the government, such as repair of flood damage, transportation, and neglect of duties. There were references to war, reports on enemies by the king's spies, and reports on missing persons. In a letter from Shamshi-Adad, the king of Assyria, to his son Yasmakh-Adad, the governor of Mari, various administrative problems were discussed:

> Tell Yasmakh-Adad: Your father, Shamshi-Adad, sends the following message:
>
> I have listened to the tablets you have sent me. You have asked me about the waiving of all legal and financial claims of the northern tribes. (I answer:) It is not appropriate to waive these claims. Should you waive the claims against them, their relatives, the Rabbaya tribes, who are (now) staying on the other side of the river (Euphrates) in the country of Yamkhad, will hear (about this preferential treatment) and be so angry with them that they will not come back here to their home grounds. Therefore, do not waive the claims (of the northern tribes) under any circumstances. (On the contrary), reprimand them severely in the following terms: "If the king goes on an expedition, everybody down to the youngsters should immediately assemble. Any sheikh whose men are not all assembled commits a sacrilege against the king even if he leaves only one man behind!" Reprimand them in exactly this way. Under no circumstances should you cancel the claims against them.
>
> Now to another matter: When I sent you orders concerning the allotting of the fields along the Euphrates as well as the taking over of these fields by the soldiers, you asked me the following: "Should the auxiliaries from Khana who live in the open country take over fields from among those (who live) along the Euphrates, or not?" This is what you wrote me. I have asked Ishar-Lim and other experts for advice, and it is not advisable to reallot the fields along the Euphrates, or even to check on (the rights of the present holders) . . . Every man should keep his holding exactly as in the past. The fields must not become mixed up. Check only the fields of those who died or ran away, and give them to those who have no fields at all . . .
>
> Furthermore, as to what you have written me about having many large boats built together with the small ones, one should construct (only) large boats . . . Moreover, wherever these boats go, they will always be available to you to carry your own barley.[24]

The more personal side of this high-powered relationship between the same father and son is shown in the following letter:

Say to father, Thus says Yasmakh-Adad, your son: I read the tablet that father sent to me saying, "As for you, how long will we continue to guide you? Are you a child? Are you not a grown man? Don't you have hair on your cheeks? How long will you be unable to manage your own affairs? Won't you look at your brother (the heir apparent and the governor of Ekallatum) who leads vast armies? Govern your palace and household!" So Father wrote to me. Now, am I a child?[25]

Observing omens was an important part of Mesopotamian culture. In the first millennium BCE Assyria developed an astrological series. The omens were arranged in fixed form and became canonized. Here is an example from the Assyrian dream omens that explains the symbolic meaning of dreams:

If (in his dream) one gives him a (cylinder) seal with his own name on it: he will have a name (fame) and offspring.

If one gives him a seal with the name of . . . on it: for an important person: poverty; for a person of low status: riches.

If he wears a seal with his name and one takes it away: his son will die.[26]

The king received reports from experts in magic and divination who could interpret the omens, for example,

To the king, my lord (Esarhaddon), from your servant Balasi:

Good health to Your Majesty! May the gods Nabu and Marduk bless Your Majesty.

As to Your Majesty's request addressed to me concerning (the incident with) the ravens, here are the relevant omens: "If a raven brings something into a person's house, this man will obtain something that does not belong to him. If a falcon or a raven drops something he is carrying upon a person's house or in front of a man, this house will have much traffic—traffic means profit. If a bird carries meat, another bird, or anything else, and drops it upon a person's house, this man will obtain a large inheritance.[27]

Economic and administrative documents are known from the beginning of writing in Mesopotamia. Economic documents concern a variety of topics such as sales contracts, warranty deeds, marriage settlements, adoption contracts, inheritance documents, loan agreements, receipts, court decisions, wage memos, and so on. Administrative documents are a bureaucratic tool for recording the movement of goods and the responsibility of personnel; taxes, tribute, yields of temple lands, accounts of animals and animal products, distribution of goods and rations are among the records kept by officials.

Legal documents include law codes and legal decisions. Law codes replaced oral traditions and practices; they showed the king's and god's interest in the well-being of their subjects. They could be used in formulating legal decisions, though laws are seldom cited in these rulings (see Chapter 9).

Writing was created by economic necessity. Developed for administrative purposes, it was soon used in the creation of myths and other categories of literature. Scribes even produced scholastic material for educational purposes. Finally, writing was an important tool for recording historical events.

5

The Sciences

MEDICINE

The reputation of Mesopotamian medicine may have suffered from Herodotus' writing in the fifth century BCE: "They bring out all their sick into the streets, for they have no regular doctors. People that come along offer the sick

Medical Practitioners

man advice, either from what they personally have found to cure such a complaint, or what they have known someone else to be cured by. No one is allowed to pass by a sick person without asking him what ails him."[1] Quite the contrary! Medical practitioners were known as early as the third millennium BCE. Babylonians who were sick could use two types of medical practitioners: the *āšipu*, whose cures were magical, and the *asû*, whose cures were basically medical. A Babylonian proverb suggests the availability of these doctors: "infection without a doctor is like hunger without food."[2] The line between the two practitioners was not hard and fast. Thus, the *āšipu* or exorcist sometimes used drugs, and the *asû* or doctor sometimes used incantations and other magical practices. In fact, the two professionals might even work together on a case, as an Assyrian letter reports: "Let him appoint one *āšipu* and one *asû*, and let them perform their treatment together on my behalf."[3]

Āšipus were also appointed to the temple staff to perform their special functions, such as incantations or expulsion of evil demons from the king. Some *āšipus* served the king and became part of the permanent palace staff. Other members of the royal family and some senior state officials had *āšipus* as part of their permanent staff. But most *āšipus* probably worked outside the temple and earned their income by fees from ordinary people suffering from illness or bad luck.

The profession of *āšipu* normally passed from father to son. We have little information on how the *asû* (doctors) were trained. All we know about their hierarchy comes from their use of titles: physician, chief physician's deputy, and chief physician. There is little information about surgeons (see below). Midwives were women. An early second millennium tablet mentions a woman doctor. Also, the "physician of an ox or donkey," a veterinarian, is noted. A first millennium tablet refers to an eye doctor.

Doctors conducted a clinical examination, taking the temperature and pulse of the patient. Also, any discolorations of the skin, inflammations, and even the color of the urine were noted. Tablets also mention contagious diseases, as in this letter written by Zimri-Lim, king of Mari, to his wife Shibtu (ca. 1780 BCE):

> I have heard that the lady Nanname has been taken ill. She has many contacts with the people of the palace. She meets many ladies in her house. Now then, give severe orders that no one should drink in the cup where she drinks, no one should sit on the seat where she sits, no one should sleep in the bed where she sleeps. She should no longer meet many ladies in her house. This disease is contagious.[4]

The Code of Hammurabi described fees that were paid according to the social status of the patient. Private physicians were rarely mentioned at the turn of the second millennium BCE. Most physicians were attached to the palace. Letters from Mari and Amarna mention court physicians being sent abroad to impress foreign rulers. A military officer, writing from battle, asked that an *asû* be sent in case one of his men were hit by a slingshot. A humorous story called the "The Poor Man of Nippur" notes the physician as having a special hairstyle and carrying a fire-scorched pot (perhaps to mix his herbs). Other texts described the physician bringing a wooden box or leather bag of herbs.

People in ancient Mesopotamia were able to identify the natural origin of some illnesses that resulted from overexposure to heat or cold, overeating, eating spoiled food, or drinking too much of an alcoholic beverage. In the initial stages of the development of medical practices, the *āšipu* would read over the list of sins the patient might have committed. The ancient Mesopotamians believed that sin lay at the cause of the patient's illness. Once the sin was identified, the *āšipu* would be able to exorcize the demon causing the illness. For the ancient Mesopotamians, "sin" included crimes, moral offenses, errors and omissions in ritual performance, and unintentional breaking of taboos. The offended gods or demons could strike directly; that is, "the hand" of various gods or demons was thought to cause illness. Therefore, illness indicated a kind of black mark against the patient. Incantations were recited to exorcize the demon, and foul substances were used to purify the body by using enemas, induced vomiting, fumigation, and inhalation. Sometimes sympathetic magic was used. The *āšipu* might substitute an animal to offer the disease another place to inhabit. Or the demon might be bribed with gifts that he or she might find useful on the journey away from the patient. At the same time certain symptoms were also identified. Thus, disease was believed to be caused by both a demon and recognizable symptoms; remedies were prescribed to expel that particular demon; for example, in the case of epilepsy, the doctor ordered the patient to place "the little finger of a dead man, rancid oil, and copper into the skin of a virgin goat; you shall string it on a tendon of a gerbil and put it round his neck, and he will recover."[5]

As a number of symptoms and prognoses of diseases were identified, omen series were developed. In time, medicine began to use materials of therapeutic significance. Some of the remedies were related in shape or color to the disease. For example, jaundice was treated with yellow medicine. Also, the exact time for collecting herbs was noted—indispensable knowledge even for today's herbalists.

There was a god called Ninazu, meaning "Lord Doctor," whose son used a rod intertwined with serpents as the insignia of the medical professional. Mesopotamian medicine was transmitted to the Greeks along with Egyptian medicine, laying the ground for Hippocratic reform of the fifth century BCE. However, in its two thousand or so years of existence, Mesopotamian medicine made little progress. The doctors still resorted to superstition and magical explanations. Though they could offer rational explanations for many symptoms and diseases, they never tried to collect data and theorize.

Medical texts are found from the third millennium BCE on, but most come from Assurbanipal's library at Nineveh. Texts come from Sumer, Babylon, Assyria, and even the Hittite area. Medical texts are basically of two kinds: descriptions of symptoms and lists of remedies.

Symptomology and Diagnoses in the Medical Texts

The greatest number of medical texts are part of an omen series which deals with the activities of the *āšipu* and begins with the words, "If the exorcist is going to the house of the patient," followed by what the *āšipu* might see on his way to the patient's house or at the door. This introductory series includes such chance encounters as, for example, the following:

If (the exorcist) sees either a black dog or a black pig, that sick
   man will die.
If (the exorcist) sees a white pig, that sick man will live [. . .]
If (the exorcist) sees pigs which keep lifting up their tails, (as to)
   that sick man, anxiety will not come near him.[6]

This section is followed by a description of the disease and frequently
the prognosis, "he will get well" or "he will die." Treatment is rarely
mentioned. In one section the symptoms are organized according to the
parts of the body, starting with the skull and ending with the toes. Usually the diseases are attributed to the god or demon who caused them.
For example:

If the patient keeps crying out "My skull ! My skull!" it is the
   hand of a god.
If he grinds his teeth, and his hands and feet shake, it is the hand
   of the god Sin; he will die.[7]

In one section the prognoses are arranged according to the daily progress
of the illness. Each section identifies the disease, which in one case is
jaundice:

If a man's body is yellow, his face is yellow, and his eyes are
   yellow, and the flesh is flabby, it is the yellow disease.[8]

The last part of this omen series was assigned to medical problems of
women and children, including pregnancy, childbirth, and malnutrition.
Some omens tried to predict the sex of the child from the pregnant
woman's complexion, body shape, and so on. This section even included
favorable and unfavorable days for a pregnant woman to have intercourse.
The medical texts concerning the *asû* or doctor are organized in a manner similar to the omen texts; however, here specific symptoms are listed
with directions on administering medication. The texts reveal an extensive list of herbal remedies, some of medicinal value; also, the texts describe the identification and treatment of many kinds of illnesses, among
them intestinal obstructions, headaches, tonsillitis, tuberculosis, typhus,
lice, bubonic plague, smallpox, rheumatism, eye and ear infections, di-
arrhea, colic, gout, and venereal diseases such as gonorrhea. The Babylonians also recorded abnormal and monstrous births in their omen
literature. They even recorded the hallucinations of a patient and their
meaning. For example:

If, when he was suffering from a long illness, he saw a dog, his
illness will return to him; he will die.

If DITTO he saw a gazelle, that patient will recover.

If DITTO he saw a wild pig, when you have recited an
incantation for him, he will recover.[9]

Mental illness was certainly known. The royal family of Elam seemed
to suffer particularly from what the texts describe as "his mind
changed," meaning "he went off his rocker," not a change of policy.
Sexual impotence was also recognized as having a psychological basis.

Particularly interesting is the omen literature describing dreams of falling, flying, and walking around naked and the ancient interpretations,
such as: "If a man flies repeatedly, whatever he won will be lost" or "If
in his dream a man walks about naked . . . troubles will not touch this
man."[10]

The oldest medical text known to us, a list of prescrip-
tions, was written at the end of the third millennium BCE.   **Prescriptions**
Saltpeter (potassium nitrate) and salt (sodium chloride)
are the minerals most often mentioned. However, the prescriptions also
make use of milk, snake skin, turtle shell, cassia, thyme, fir, fig, and date.
The samples were stored as either solids or powders to be used in preparing remedies—salves and filtrates (extracts) to be applied externally;
or powders, often dissolved in beer, to be taken internally. Unfortunately, these Sumerian prescriptions failed to indicate the quantities to
be used, the amount to be administered, and how often this medicine
should be taken. Perhaps whoever wrote this tablet wanted his professional secrets protected. Or perhaps these details were not considered
important.

A tablet written in the first millennium BCE was divided into three
columns of more than 150 items; the tablet lists (1) what part of the plant
to use, (2) the disease it was meant to cure, and (3) how to administer
the medicine, that is, frequency, time of day, necessity of fasting, and so
on. Methods of administering the drugs included baths with hot infu-
sions, enemas, vapor inhalations, and blowing liquids through a reed or
tube into the mouth, nose, ear, penis, or vagina.

An Assyrian handbook found in the libraries of Asshur and Nineveh
lists more than four hundred Sumerian words for plants, fruits, and other
substances, with about eight hundred Semitic synonyms. Approximately
half of these plants have medicinal value.

We have little information about surgery. Probably medical
expertise was acquired by training and observation—experi-   **Surgery**
ences not described in handbooks. As early as 5000 BCE skeletal
remains attest to trepanation, an operation involving removal of part of

the scalp and a piece of the skull bone. Trepanations were performed when the skull was fractured or to relieve headaches and epilepsy. We also know that court physicians were called to affirm that any officials having access to the harem were castrated; though we assume that castration was performed by physicians, we do not know this for a fact. One surgical instrument, the lancet, was called a "barber's knife."

In general, the Mesopotamians knew little about anatomy and physiology; they were restricted by the religious taboo against dissecting a corpse. Animal anatomy may have helped, but the Mesopotamians dissected only the liver and lungs of perfectly healthy animals for divinatory purposes.

The liver was regarded as the seat of various emotions and the heart of intelligence. The ancient Mesopotamians recognized variations in pulse rate but never went a step further in understanding how blood circulated.

The Code of Hammurabi indicated that surgery was performed, and surgeons were able to set broken bones. The laws also tell us that the punishment for surgical mistakes was mutilation and even death.

MATHEMATICS

The Number System   Numbers were written on cuneiform texts from the earliest, ca. 3100 BCE, to the last text found in 75 CE. The method for writing numbers developed as did the rest of the cuneiform script—becoming more stylized and angular through time.

The number system was always a combination of the decimal system (counting by tens) and the sexagesimal system (counting by sixties). Babylonian mathematics used the sexagesimal system; the decimal number system was rarely used in mathematical calculations. Base 60 is preserved in the way we tell time, that is, 60 seconds to a minute and 60 minutes to an hour, and in measuring a circle as 360°. From 2000 BCE to 75 CE, Babylonian numbers used place-value notation or a positional number system, which was developed in the fourth millennium BCE. Place-value notation uses a very limited number of symbols whose magnitude is determined by position (the higher values on the left and the lower values on the right). That is, for every place a number moved to the left, its value was multiplied by 60, and for every place it moved to the right, it was divided by 60. The numbers were written as follows:

1   2   3   4   5   6   7   8   9

| 10 | 20 | 30 | 40 | 50 | 60 | 600 | 60² | 60²×10 |

The same symbols were even used for writing fractions. Therefore, in place-value notation the number indicates:

$$60 + 40 + 5 = 105$$
$$60^2 + 40 + 5 = 3645$$
$$\text{or } 1 + 45/60 = 1.75$$

Thus, in the sexagesimal system every number remained an integer because the system was intended to serve only as an instrument of calculation. Fractions were also eliminated. Knowledge of reciprocals is essential to our understanding the solution of mathematical problems. Division is not performed. Instead, numbers are multiplied by reciprocals. For example, in the sexagesimal system the reciprocal of 5 is 12. In other words, the reciprocal of a given number is another number which when multiplied with it yields 60.

The system of place-value notation allowed a great deal of flexibility in calculation and stimulated the growth of higher mathematics and astronomy. Among ancient peoples, only the Mesopotamians developed place-value notation; it is similar to our own Hindu-Arabic system. That is, our own decimal system is a place-value or number position system; for example, the symbol 5 means "fifty" in the number 53 and "five" in the number 35—the value of "five" is determined by its position in a number.

The Babylonian system had two inherent disadvantages: (1) it was confusing and, therefore, not used in many daily economic activities, and (2) there was no special sign for zero, to separate the different units. To understand the difficulties that arise from not having zero, a number like 353 could be read as 3053 or 3503 or even 3530. Some Old Babylonian mathematicians sometimes compensated by leaving blank spaces for zero or by using a special sign that indicated a space between words. A sign for zero was eventually invented sometime in the first millennium BCE, though it was never used at the end of a number. The lack of the zero sign was probably tolerated because of the amplitude of base 60, which included a large number of factors (1, 2, 3, 4, 5, 6, 10, 12, 15, 20, 30).

Numbers could be used for cryptography. The Mesopotamians assigned a numerical value to each sign. Thus, every name had a corresponding numerical value. So, during construction of his palace at Khorsabad, Sargon stated, "I built the circumference of the city wall 16,283 cubits, the number of my name." Also, the major gods were assigned numbers according to their position in the divine hierarchy. Thus, Anu, the head of the pantheon, was assigned 60 in the numerical hierarchy, Enlil 50, Ea 40, Sin 30, Shamash 20, Ishtar 15, and Adad 10.

Mathematical tablet with problems concerning the areas of complicated geometric shapes. 90 cm × 75 cm. © BRITISH MUSEUM, LONDON.

Algebra
Babylonian mathematicians developed a mastery of algebraic skills, even though there was no graphic symbol for the unknown. Instead, the Babylonians used a method called false value. Here the unknown is provisionally designated by 1 in order to find the coefficients and thus solve first degree (linear) and second degree (quadratic) equations. Examples of first or second degree equations in Babylonian mathematics show that the scribes had all the necessary algebraic tools, such as reduction of similar terms, elimination of the unknown by substitution, completing the square, and, in second degree

equations containing two unknowns, using $\pm$ in a single algebraic statement.

The Babylonians never took additional steps to prove statements and formulate theorems. Rather, the scribes merely performed the operations leading to the solution without explaining them. Algebraic problems in school exercises were constructed with an eye to their solution, so that ancient mathematicians rarely encountered an irregular number, that is, a prime number which is not a factor of base 60.

The Babylonians displayed a considerable knowledge of geometric shapes and geometric formulas. They even used **Geometry** the Pythagorean theorem more than a thousand years before Pythagoras and applied principles of similarity. However, whenever a geometrical problem was posed, its purpose was to find length, width, volume, and so on. That is, the method of solution was algebraic. Triangles were usually right-angled or isosceles. Areas of quadrilaterals, regardless of shape, were generally solved by an approximate formula which averaged the opposite sides and multiplied them by each other. This formula was also used in calculating the size of fields. The Babylonians generally used a gross approximation of $\pi = 3$ (see also 1 Kings 7:23, $\pi = 3$), though a coefficient list from Susa (Iran) suggested a more precise value of $\pi = 3\frac{1}{8}$.

Babylonian mathematics lacked basic geometric terms and concepts; there were no words for angle, slope, perpendicular, or parallel. The invention of the geometry of angles must be credited to the Greeks.

The conversion of units of measurement required the mastery of ratios between units. For these computations, **Metrology—** the scribe memorized or consulted tables. The system of **Weights and** weights and measures was essentially sexagesimal, that is, **Measures** a "load" (which could be carried by either a man or an animal) was equal to sixty minas, and a mina was equal to sixty shekels.

Part of the scribal education involved mathematics. Instruction was both oral and written. Colophons referred **Mathematical** to "questioning by the teacher." But our primary source **Texts** of information is the large number of school tablets excavated, in particular mathematical tables.

The phrasing of the problem texts is highly condensed. The problem texts are translated as follows: the teacher, referred to as "I," is used in the description of the problem, and the student, referred to as "you," is used for operations performed in solving the problem. For example,

> A cistern was 10 "rods" square, 10 "rods" deep.
> I emptied out its water; (using) its water, how much of the field
>   did I irrigate to a depth of 1 "finger"?
> Put aside 10 and 10 which formed the square.
> Put aside 10, the depth of the cistern.[11]

In problems that give details of the method of solution, intermediate results are sometimes signaled by the phrases "keep in your head" or "that your head keeps."

The mathematical texts, for the most part, belong to two distinct periods, separated by more than a thousand years: approximately eighteenth century BCE and the last three centuries BCE. The cuneiform mathematical texts can be divided into three main categories: (1) the table texts, (2) the coefficient lists, and (3) the problem texts.

The mathematical tables dealt with the following: multiplication, reciprocals (for division), squares and cubes, square roots and cube roots, exponential tables, logarithms, and metrological tables of length, area, monetary conversion, and weight units. The table texts are probably older than the problem texts. The table texts were meant for students at the elementary level of scribal education and were probably used extensively outside the schools as well. The problem texts were exercises for more advanced students and dealt with matters of practical value.

The coefficient lists contained fixed values for a series of items, organized more or less by categories (for example, geometric shapes, bricks, and metals) to be used in solving various types of mathematical problems. The coefficient lists were concerned with both nonmathematical operations and mathematical ones as, for example, the appearance of a list of string names and numbers in a musical instrument, comprising a catalogue of musical intervals in a coefficient list.

The problem texts can be broadly divided into two categories: (1) algebraic/geometric problems, and (2) practical problems, that is, problems concerned with the realities of Mesopotamian life. The tablets contained as few as one problem or as many as several hundred. The majority of tablets were one-problem texts. The tablets varied, giving all, some, or none of the details for solving the problem. Sometimes the problems were accompanied by drawings (not to scale). Also, some collections of mathematical problems were coordinated with the same data, and some even had the same answer. The algebraic/geometric texts generally dealt with plane geometric figures, that is, with problems of areas, not volumes. The problems were solved by a series of equations with up to six unknowns and even to the eighth degree. For the most part, solid geometric figures were dealt with in the practical problems where they referred to bricks and brickworks, excavations of canals, and earthwork constructions such as walls, dams, and ramps. The practical problems also dealt with other matters such as prices, commerce, inheritance or division of property, the water clock, field plans, herd growth, reed bundles, and standard measuring containers.

ASTRONOMY

The Babylonians surpassed their neighbors in the ancient Near East in their knowledge of astronomy and mathe- **Purposes of** matics. The Babylonians and Assyrians kept detailed rec- **Astronomy** ords of their observations of the position and movement of heavenly bodies. They combined these observations with their mathematical proficiency to give birth to mathematical astronomy.

By the seventh century BCE precise astronomical observations influenced the development of a more accurate calendar. The Mesopotamian calendar was lunar, based on observation of the moon throughout its history, that is, "Nanna (the mood god), fixing the month and the new moon, setting the year in its place." Each lunar month consisted of 29 or 30 days, and a year was approximately 354 days. The month names usually referred to an important ritual observance or agricultural event. An extra month (called an intercalated month) was added approximately every three years to align the lunar and the solar calendars.

The ancient Mesopotamians were aware of both the lunar and solar calendar, but the lunar calendar took precedence. In fact, in their mythology the Sumerians depicted the moon as the father of the sun. An intercalary month was added to guarantee that the religious festivals, which were connected to the lunar calendar, were observed at the proper time. By the eighth century BCE a regular intercalation of seven months every nineteen years was established; its accuracy in reconciling the lunar and solar calendars is still admired. By the fourth century BCE, mathematical astronomy was used for this intercalation. The calendar produced was called the Metonic Cycle, which was the basis of the later Jewish and Christian religious calendars.

Besides the seasonal and lunar cycle, the Mesopotamians were influenced by the cycle between the equinoxes, the period during which the sun and moon competed for time in the sky. The two six-month equinox cycles were important in instituting a cultic calendar and were reinforced by the seasons—the summer, which began around March, and the winter, which began around September. The equinox refers to the two times during the year when the sun and moon cross the celestial equators and both the night and day are approximately the same in length.

As we know, the division of the hour into sixty minutes is a Babylonian legacy. However, the division of the day into hours was influenced by both the Babylonians and the Egyptians. The Babylonian day, which began at sunset, comprised twelve "double hours," each consisting of sixty "double minutes." Each day was also divided into six equal parts for calculation and observation. At the same time, the Egyptians divided the day, that is, from sunrise to sunset, into twelve

unequal parts, depending on the season of the year. Hellenistic astronomers took the next step—they divided the twelve double hours into
twenty-four units of equal length. Thus, the twenty-four-hour day was
created.

Astronomical Texts

The first records we have of astronomical observations are
the "Venus" tablets, which were composed to preserve
omens for King Ammi-saduqa of the seventeenth century
BCE, the fourth king after Hammurabi. Though not com-
pletely reliable, the Venus tablets are still useful in determining ancient
chronology (see Chapter 1). Over the centuries the astrological omen
series grew; it was preserved up to the fall of the Assyrian and Babylonian empires. The omens cited the heliacal rising of planets, eclipses,
the appearance of the new moon, the length of the day, and the paths
of the planets among the stars. These observations were recorded in order to catalogue predictions concerning the king and his country; for
example: "In the night Saturn came near to the moon. Saturn is the 'star'
of the sun. This is the solution: it is favorable to the king (for) the sun
is the king's star." Unfortunately, the rising and setting of planets close
to the horizon were obscured by a haze of dust. Thus, the Babylonian
observations were not completely accurate. Earlier astrological omens
referring to King Sargon were collected as part of a series toward the
end of the second millennium BCE.

At the end of the second millennium BCE the Assyrians developed
astrolabes, which combined mythology with observational astronomy.
According to the mythology, there were three main stations of the sky
under the aegis of three great gods: Anu (the head of the pantheon), Ea
(the god of wisdom), and Enlil (the god of wind). This concept provided
the framework for organizing the positions of major constellations, stars,
and planets according to different months. The information was arranged either in three columns or in three concentric circles which were
divided into twelve sectors. The three columns or concentric circles represented the three stations. A column for the twelve sectors symbolized
the twelve months of the year and the heliacal rising of each star in its
respective month. The Mesopotamians compared the wandering planets
to wild goats and the fixed stars to tame goats. Two astrolabes have been
found, and they depict the length of a day.

In everyday life water clocks were used to measure units of time. Water clocks were either cylindrical or prismatic. Time was calculated by
filling a vessel of specified height to a marked line with water and then
letting the liquid escape through a hole in the bottom. A set of these
bowls could be used in conjunction with the water clock to measure short
and long portions of time.

Late Babylonian astronomical tablet with constellations incised. From left to right, Corvus (raven) pecking at the tail of Hydra (serpent), Mercury (star), and Virgo (holding a spike). © LOUVRE MUSEUM, PARIS.

Through observation and calculation, the Mesopotamians were able to compile tables of fixed stars and the distances between them. The results were amazing considering the available equipment: tubes used as view finders, the water clock, a rudimentary sundial, and the *polos*, a kind of shadow clock. The distance between the stars found on the Tropic of Cancer was even measured using three systems: (1) time between the passages of two stars at the meridian according to the weight of water escaping from a water clock, (2) the arc, and (3) length according to either linear measurement or according to degrees.

Basic knowledge of astronomy was collected and organized into a three-tablet series called mul.apin ("plow-star" = Andromeda), named after the first entry. This series was found in Assurbanipal's library; it included a list of stars arranged in three parallel "roads," with the middle one following the equator, along with references to the planets, to complexities of the calendar, and to observations of Venus' disappearance and reappearance behind the sun. From the seventh to the second century BCE astronomical "diaries" were kept; they were primarily based on monthly or yearly observations but contained a number of predictions, in particular relating to the moon, the planets, solstices, equinoxes, Sirius phenomena, meteors, comets, and so on. In addition, the diaries noted the weather (rain, thunder, lightning, fog, haze, cold, cloudburst, hail, overcast, etc.), prices of various goods, the river level, and historical events. The astronomical diaries of previous years were collected in goal year texts in order to predict astronomical phenomena in the coming year, that is, the goal year. Included in the diaries for 164 and 87 BCE were references to Halley's Comet. The Assyrians kept records of lunar eclipses, which they were able to predict.

The most important texts deal with mathematical astronomy and can be dated from 300 BCE to the beginning of the Christian era. Texts known as ephemerides recorded the daily and monthly positions of the moon and the planets (Jupiter, Venus, Saturn, Mercury, and Mars). Procedure texts augment this information with rules for calculating the ephemerides. The ephemerides record full and new moons for as much as two years and eclipses for more than fifty years. Almanacs predicted the length of each month, the rising and setting of each planet, the zodiacal positions of the planets, eclipses, equinoxes, and the movements of Sirius for the coming year. Other tables listed information such as lunar velocity and daily solar and lunar motions. The mathematical astronomy of Mesopotamia was highly sophisticated. The tables of new and full moons were accurate. In fact, it was a Babylonian astronomer, Kidenas, who calculated the length of the solar year with a margin of error of 4 minutes and 32.65 seconds. Mathematical astronomy developed at the same time as the Greek mathematics of Euclid and the Greek astronomy of Hipparchus. However, unlike the Greek astronomers, the Babylonians never synthesized their data into a cosmic theory.

Astronomical computations were also essential to the invention of the zodiac and horoscopic astrology. The Mesopotamians believed that what happened in the heavens was mirrored on earth. Thus, Mesopotamians believed that the movements of heavenly bodies could be connected with gods, kings, and countries in order to make predictions. At first, astrological omens were used to explain only the future of the country and its ruler. However, the shift to horoscopic astrology required a method for relating celestial phenomena to individuals. Here the zodiac came into play and, along with it, a year of twelve thirty-day months was created. By the fifth century BCE, the zodiacal belt was partitioned into twelve zodiacal signs of 30 degrees each. The first known Babylonian horoscope was cast for a child born April 29, 410 BCE. Astrology and mathematical astronomy were associated with separate social and intellectual circles. Astrology was the basis for the reputation of "Chaldean" science, which extended through the whole of Europe.

TECHNOLOGY

We know about Babylonian science and technology from cuneiform tablets. The technical vocabulary is extensive, but, unfortunately, many of the words cannot be translated. We also have archaeological evidence confirming both advanced knowledge and technology in many fields. However, often technological equipment is not recognized by archaeologists because they do not know exactly what they are looking for (see Chapter 11 for a discussion of crafts).

NATURAL SCIENCES

The ancient Mesopotamians tried to understand and organize the world around them. To this end, they made inventory lists of animals, plants, minerals, and so on. They even made lists of the gods! Lists of objects were recorded as early as the third millennium BCE, but a definite sequence within categories was not established until much later.

During the second millennium BCE, some lists became canonized. A series of about forty tablets was organized and named after the first line, "interest obligations." The work is an exhaustive survey of the world the Mesopotamians knew, including real and mythical animals, foods, manufactured objects, and so on. The organization was not always clear. For example, trees were listed in Tablet 3, but the rest of the plants in Tablet 17. Later, during the first millennium BCE, explanations or commentaries were added to bridge the gap between Sumerian and Akkadian.

Early attempts to deal with the natural sciences produced the Sumerian lists, which were expanded by the Babylonians. **Zoology** The Babylonians were aware of a variety of species, though their categories differ from ours. For example, a comprehensive list of land animals was extended to include insects and worms. Body parts of both humans and animals were grouped together. During the first millennium BCE there were lists of drugs made from animals, flowers, and minerals, along with the illnesses they were meant to cure. As we can see, the lexical lists did not clearly define the boundaries between animal, vegetable, and mineral. Less information was given about birds and fish in these lists. Nevertheless, animals, birds, and fish were accurately depicted in the reliefs.

The lexical lists are not our only source of information about the nat-

ural sciences. Lists of terrestrial omens described animals and their behavior. Real and fantastic omens were included, such as a lamb with ten
feet. Other texts tell us of animals living in the wild at the time (for
example, the small horse of the steppes, with a head resembling that of
a camel and a short, thick, stiff mane) or animals that have now become
extinct (for example, a long-bearded ram with widely separated curving
horns). Certain literary texts give useful information about identifying
birds and even spell out bird calls. Also, we have a list of eighteen varieties of edible fish sold at a market in Larsa (near the Persian Gulf) ca.
2000 BCE.

In a ninth century inscription, King Assurnasirpal II stated, "I captured
alive with my hand, herds of wild oxen, elephants, lions, ostriches, male
and female monkeys, wild asses, gazelles, deer, bears, panthers . . . all
the beasts of plain and mountain, I collected in my city of Nimrud, letting the people of the land behold them."[12] We do not know whether
these animals were kept in cages or allowed to roam in a safari park. In
the eighth century BCE King Sennacherib set up a safari park around
Nineveh, where "the cane-brakes developed rapidly; the birds of heaven
. . . built their nests, and the wild swine and beasts of the forests brought
forth young in abundance."[13] That is, Assyrian kings created the first
zoos and safari parks in their capital cities.

Botany   Lists of terrestrial omens described plants and their location.
Some drugs came from foreign countries, thus emphasizing the
importance placed on medicinal herbs even at an early date.
Medicinal commentaries also listed plants according to their appearance,
for example, a plant called "hound's tongue." Also, the parts of each
plant were listed from the flower to the root.

The curiosity of the Assyrians and Babylonians also led them to collect and bring home rare species of plants to create the first royal botanical garden. The Assyrian king Tiglath-pileser I (1114–1046 BCE) spoke of
taking rare fruits from abroad and planting them in his orchards in Assyria. King Sennacherib (704–681 BCE) brought the cotton plant to Assyria. Applying the principles of "scientific" organization, the
Babylonian king Merodach Baladan II (721–710 and 703 BCE) arranged
his garden in plots, with each plot organized to contain plants according to their uses.

Mineralogy   The Mesopotamians also knew a large variety of stones;
some rare and beautiful ones—such as lapis lazuli, jasper,
carnelian, agate, rock crystal—semiprecious stones, and
others were made into cylinder seals and jewelry. In fact, there were
many lists of magical stones from Babylonia and Assyria, and they usually begin with lapis lazuli, which was imported from the east and was
especially in demand. Precious stones such as emeralds were rarely used,
and then only in the later periods.

CARTOGRAPHY AND GEOGRAPHY

There is little evidence of the mechanics of surveying. We know that the land registrar, whose primary concern was   **Land** assessing real estate taxes, was involved in surveying. He   **Surveying** used a triangle, rods of different lengths, a measuring rope, and a peg, which was driven into the ground to hold the measuring line. Later the clay peg was used ceremonially; the peg was inscribed with the recorded sale and embedded in a house wall.

Fields were surveyed by pegs and ropes from the Early Dynastic period (ca. 2800 BCE) on. By this method, a relatively regular polygon could be marked and measured in order to approximate the area of an irregular shape.

The fields measured were triangles, trapezoids, rectangles, squares, and circles. The shapes of fields were the same (squares and circles excepted) in both the drawings and descriptions found in economic and administrative documents. In field plans dated to approximately the eighteenth century BCE and the last three centuries BCE, the measurements of all sides are given in order to compute the actual area. Earlier field plans gave only enough measurements to calculate the approximate area. Therefore, more comprehensive measurements reflected historical changes in land ownership, because private owners needed to determine a more accurate measurement of their properties.

The Babylonians drew maps of local areas such as field plans, estate plans, and ground plans of temples and   **Map-making** houses as well as maps of more distant regions such as larger areas, districts, and towns. They also gave us the famous *mappa mundi* or world map, which portrays the Babylonians' vision of the world with Babylon as its center. The maps were of practical value in daily life. They could be used for surveying, building, conducting business transactions, taxation, traveling, and waging campaigns. Sometimes maps were cited in litigation.

Babylonian maps are limited in number. Nevertheless, they exhibit common characteristics through the millennia. Most important, they were drawn as if seen from above, that is, what we today call a "bird's-eye view." The maps were drawn with little attention to angles, scale, and orientation. They used mostly straight lines, since curved lines were difficult to draw on clay. Even rivers and canals were depicted as angular forms rather than winding curves. But sometimes canals were portrayed by parallel lines filled by wavy ones (a convention still used by cartographers and called "water lining"). The name of the canal was inserted with the designation "canal" to remove any ambiguity. Cities, camps, fields, and so on were designated by rectangles or circles. Streets or highways were indicated by double or single lines with the name of the street written inside or along the lines. Only one map from Nuzi had a rather pictorial drawing of mountains as a series of semicircles drawn closely together and in two rows.

Maps of immediate localities included building plans and field plans. Ground plans were usually of private houses, but there were also plans of public buildings and temples. Field plans were the most common type of survey and occurred throughout Mesopotamian history. The field plans ranged from simple areas of land to complex ones which, in turn, were subdivided for calculation. The drawings were usually rough sketches, and the fields were depicted as rectangles, triangles, or trapezoids. The amount of information given on the field plans varied considerably and could include compass directions, notations in the field plan or along the border (to show adjacent fields, canals, or buildings), the name of the field, the year in which the survey was made, the commissioner of the survey, a summary of calculations, and the name of the surveyor. However, frequently the only information given included measurements of the sides and the area.

Maps of large areas of the country consisted of both district maps and city maps. For example, a map found at Nippur and dated to the second millennium BCE showed nine towns, three canals, and a road. City maps presented either cities or sections of cities as, for example, in maps of Babylon, Nippur, and Asshur. Temples, palaces, rivers, canals, walls, and fortifications were indicated. Sometimes distances and areas were given. No private houses were noted. A city map of Nippur, dated to the second millennium BCE, is particularly interesting because it was drawn to scale with such remarkable accuracy that it proved similar to plans drawn by an American expedition during their excavation of the city. The careful portrayal of this well-fortified city may indicate a military use for this map.

The *mappa mundi* reveals the Mesopotamian, indeed the ancient Near Eastern, view of ancient cosmography. The earth was seen as a round disc encircled by the ocean (depicted by a double ring) with Babylon at its center and the Euphrates flowing through the middle of the earth. Other cities and districts were marked on the map, but they were not placed in geographical order. The text on the tablet explained the map as a chart of the "Seven Islands," regions lying between the "Earthly Ocean" (also called the "Bitter River") and the "Heavenly Ocean." The signs of the zodiac, belonging to the "Heavenly Ocean," were also described in the text. These seven islands beyond the "Bitter River" were drawn as triangles around the edge of the circle. The cartographer noted the exact distance between them and added a descriptive note about the fifth region, "country where the sun is not seen." We may conclude that the Babylonians knew of the polar night, at least by hearsay. The concept of the cosmos as portrayed by this map was accepted for a long time, but each nation saw its own capital as the center of the universe.

Some tablets contained itineraries, with the distances between one town and another and the amount of time needed **Itineraries,** for the trip. In a second millennium BCE itinerary called **Etc.** "The Road to Emar," a route was described from Iràq, through northern Syria and southern Turkey. All stations listed were approximately one day's travel from each other. If more than one night was spent at a particular caravanserai, it was duly noted, for example, "where the chariot broke down" or "when the troops rested for two days." Each day's journey was approximately 25–30 kilometers, corresponding to the speed of travel by foot or upstream by boat at this time. There were also survey lists of empires, provinces, and minor localities. These surveys included the distances and/or identifications of boundaries which could be converted into maps. Both the itineraries and survey lists offered further proof of commerce, communication, and trips made throughout the Mesopotamian empire and its adjacent territories.

Geographical lists are another source of information. They included the names of lands, cities, bodies of water, and sometimes mountains. These lists were recopied, with omissions and additions, from the middle of the third millennium BCE on. The lists were arranged by subject matter (countries, rivers, cities, and so on), and even alphabetically; unfortunately, they tell nothing about geographical location.

Finally, we learn of various geographical names through myths, epics, and economic and historical texts. For example, Aratta, a city-state most probably in northwestern Iran near the Caspian Sea, is described in Sumerian myths and epics as the rival of Uruk. Aratta was known for its stone, metals, craftsmen, and artisans. Magan and Melukkha were written about in texts from the time of Sargon the Great (2374–2239 BCE) to the middle of the first millennium BCE. Sargon recorded that boats from Magan (Oman), Melukkha (Indus valley), and Dilmun (Bahrain) dropped anchor in his capital, Agade (not yet located). Melukkha was described as the place of "black men" and its people as "men of the black land" or "black Melukkhaites." "The black land" was described in myths, epics, and economic documents as a prosperous, populous country, full of trees, reeds, bulls, birds, various metals, and carnelian. Magan was known for copper and stone. In Sumerian mythology, Dilmun was a spiritual paradise. However, economic documents recorded that "the ships of Dilmun brought ... wood as a tribute from foreign lands." Merchants brought back information of foreign lands from their travels. Also, there were always foreigners in Mesopotamian cities. The Sumerians and later the Babylonians and Assyrians knew about the geography, economy, political organization, religious beliefs, and customs

This map of the world is a Late Babylonian tablet, which claims to be a copy of an older original. The Babylonians represented the earth as a round disc encircled by the ocean (depicted as a double ring) with Babylon (a rectangle placed just above the middle of the map) placed at the center of the earth and the Euphrates flowing through the middle. Other cities and districts are designated by circles and rectangles; the names were written on most of these shapes, but not in geographical order. The accompanying text explains the map as a chart of the "Seven Islands" regions between the Earthly and Heavenly Oceans. The islands beyond the Earthly Ocean are represented by a series of triangles with their bases on the circle. The fifth region is described "where the sun is not seen." Ht. 12.2 cm. © BRITISH MUSEUM, LONDON.

of foreign countries and their peoples. From archaeological and literary evidence, the world the Mesopotamians knew extended to the north to Anatolia, the Caucasus, and westerly parts of central Asia; to the south to Egypt; to the east to India; and to the west to the Mediterranean Sea, Cyprus, and Crete.

6

Society, Part I: City Life, Country Life, Nomadic and Semi-Nomadic Life

CITY LIFE

The cities of Mesopotamia were sizable (100 acres or more) and well populated. They functioned as political, even imperial, capitals, trade centers, and principal shrines of a region.

Definition of a City

Cities were not the same as city-states. A city was characterized socially by a complex economic structure and by allegiances based on the urban community rather than on the tribe; the city was distinguished physically by public buildings and a strong city wall. Because the city protected the people from invasion, its citizens were very loyal. A city-state was an administrative unit that could contain several cities.

The average Sumerian city, and, most probably, later cities, included three parts. First, the city itself referred to the walled area, which included the temple or temples, the palace with residences for royal officials, and the houses of the citizens. Second, the "suburb," called the "outer city" in Sumerian, consisted of houses, farms, cattle folds, fields, and gardens, all furnishing the city with food and raw materials. We do not know how the "outer city" extended or whether it was protected by secondary walls or by fortified outposts, the latter known from the Neo-Babylonian period. Third, the wharf section, functioned not only as a wharf, but also as the center of commercial activity. The wharf had administrative independence and separate legal status for the citizens transacting business there. Foreign traders had stores here, and their needs were met by the tavern keeper of the wharf. Of course, not every city followed this three-part scheme. A few Mesopotamian cities were characterized by specific topographical features, as the following: Asshur was on a cliff, reached by a monumental stairway, and Borsippa straddled both sides of a lake.

During the fourth millennium BCE larger settlements, or "cities," can be distinguished from the smaller sites, or "villages." In their own languages neither the Sumerians nor the Akkadians distinguished between city and village; both languages used the same word to refer to permanent settlements. Manors and certain rural settlements were given specific names, distinct from "cities."[1]

The cuneiform documents confirmed that a small number of old and important cities enjoyed privileges and exemptions; that is, their legal status differed in essential points from that of any other community. In Babylonia, these cities were Nippur, Babylon, and Sippar; in Assyria, the old capital Asshur and subsequently Haran in Upper Mesopotamia. The inhabitants of these "free cities" were exempt from conscripted labor, military service, and taxes. The privileges accorded the inhabitants of these cities were under divine protection. Their status, called *kidinnu*, had both legal and religious implications (see Chapter 11).

The standard of living for a typical city was only slightly above subsistence level. The city enjoyed real prosperity only when its king was victorious and brought back from his campaigns booty, tribute from subject cities, and gifts of intimidated neighbors. The spoils of war were added to the wealth of the ruler and redistributed among the military hierarchy and the bureaucracy, thereby raising the standard of living of the city. The temples grew rich and were elaborately decorated; temple personnel were allotted grants in land. Decorating the palace and temple drew traders, who brought typical imports (metals, timber, precious stones) as well as luxury items (certain spices, perfumes, wines, finery, rare animals). Only a few of the Babylonian cities prospered for more than one or two short periods, and most not at all. Affluence was soon replaced by a wretched existence, with people living among ruins, the sanctuaries dilapidated, and the city walls disintegrating. The citizens were debt-ridden under the authority of greedy administrators. The inhabitants soon fell prey to invading enemies and raids of people living in the open country. Once a city was destroyed, the remaining inhabitants continued to live in the ruins, preserving the city's name through the millennia.

In Babylonia, kings built either fortified seats of government or small fortresses against possible invasions. Fortresses were also constructed in outlying or rebellious areas. In Assyria, new cities were established by the king for political or military purposes. Occasionally an extensive wall was built to seal off a threatening frontier, such as the wall erected against the invading Amorite tribes, and, much later, the Median wall built between the Tigris and Euphrates (see Chapter 3).

The policy of both Babylonian and Assyrian kings was to urbanize outlying sections of the country. In this way, the kings ensured the safe passage of caravans involved in overland trade and solidified nomadic or unsettled populations so that they could be controlled. Further colonization provided increased agricultural production, income from taxes, conscripted workers, and soldiers. Assyrian kings often founded cities on virgin soil as new capitals to be populated by their administrators, workers, and craftsmen captured in wars. They even claimed conquered cities, which they renamed and repopulated with prisoners of war or deported peoples to ensure Assyria's control.

The shapes of cities varied. Usually the wall of a Mesopotamian city was constructed in either wide curves or **City Planning** in rectangular, often symmetrical designs. Other shapes were found, such as ovals (Ur and Uruk), triangles (Der), diamonds (late Babylon), rectangles (Sippar), trapezoids (Nineveh), and squares (Dur-Sharrukin and Nimrud). In Zinjirli in northern Syria (second millennium BCE), the outer wall was almost a perfect circle, with one hundred wall towers; it enclosed a circular inner city, with a palace, a temple, barracks, and other structures. Often round cities were built after the collapse of the Babylonian and Seleucid empires. We even have a map of Nippur, drawn on clay; it is the only Mesopotamian city map found to date and is true to scale.

Both rectangular and round city plans have been traced to similar military encampments depicted on Assyrian reliefs. Such simple geometric figures were the conventional way for either migrating tribes or armies to arrange their camps. Assyrian military camps, whether rectangular or round, included the royal tent, with the sacred standards, consistently placed off center, near the stockade which surrounded the rows of tents.

Southern cities were similar to northern cities along the Euphrates in their dependence on agriculture. But as northern settlements were transformed from villages to cities in the third and second millennia BCE, the small mounds of the early settlements were used as raised platforms upon which to build their temples and palaces on a high citadel, sometimes separated from the rest of the city by their own fortifications. Whether the Assyrians occupied an old settlement or founded a new one, they separated parts of the city by elevation, whereas the southern cities used the maze of waterways for this purpose.

In the south the city was the primary settlement pattern, situated along canals; the rural population inhabited more temporary sites that shifted as the waterways changed course. In the north permanent villages, some dating back to the Neolithic period, were distributed regularly across the fertile land.

In the south, land was divided by numerous canals into areas of intensive cultivation; southern marshes supplied reeds, fish, and birds; the wasteland could be used "as is" for seasonal grazing. In the north, land was ready for either tell-size agriculture or grazing. Northern cities were divided by elevation into upper and lower towns, that is, citadels and residential areas. In the south, land was more valuable in irrigated zones. But in the north, city and country property were of equal value. Such geographic differences suggest that no one concept of city planning could completely satisfy different needs.

The sites in the south were bare, showing the results of millennia of sandblasting by summer winds. But the sites located in the north were partially vegetated and bore signs of intense water erosion. Because of these regional variations, the southern sites preserved kilns, canals, and even entire buildings on the surface, thereby furnishing clues to the overall urban layout.

Urban centers often grew because of their temples, which served the religious needs of the people, and also because of their administrative and economic functions. By the beginning of the fourth millennium BCE, the cities operated as hubs for negotiating among different groups inhabiting Mesopotamia, such as the herders of the desert, the fishermen of the marshes, and the farmers of the plains. Later the cities became centers of communication and trade between Mesopotamians and the people of far-off mountain areas, which provided materials Mesopotamia lacked, such as stone, metal, and wood. A network of trade routes ran through the open country among commercial centers. However, there was little traffic on these routes. Traveling was dangerous due to marauders from the deserts, migrants, runaway slaves, and wild animals. Only army contingents, foreign ambassadors traveling under military protection, royal messengers, and donkey caravans, carrying loads from city to city, dared to travel these routes. In fact, there were few periods in the history of Mesopotamia when private persons could travel freely and private letters could be sent from city to city. The Assyrian kings, recognizing the need for safe travel and communication, built roads and maintained them by conscripting workers from nearby villages.

By 3500 BCE, in cities like Uruk, the temple organized Mesopotamian society. The temple was built on a raised platform and could be seen for miles around. The temple generated writing, government, a judicial system, fine art, architecture, and so on. For the first five hundred years of Mesopotamian history, the temples alone controlled most facets of society and the economy.

By approximately 2800 BCE, territorial disputes erupted in the south.

Monumental fortifications were built to maintain security and define boundaries between rural and urban areas. But these wars required leadership, and so another major urban institution emerged—the palace. Mesopotamian cities now had two centers of power: the palace, which controlled the political and military arena, and the temple, which regulated the economy and religious life. Monumental fortifications were built to maintain security and to define boundaries between rural and urban areas.

In the third and early second millennia BCE, some Assyrian villages became centers of political power and expanded, often abruptly, into cities. Temples were built on the mound of the old settlement, and new fortifications were constructed to enclose a larger, lower town. At some northern sites, the citadel mound was located at the edge of the new city, next to the city wall.

Residential areas were crowded with houses, workshops, shrines, and other structures. The cuneiform tablets provide **Residential** a limited description of residential areas. Both textual and **Areas** archaeological data confirm that neighborhoods were not based on wealth; the house of a prominent official could stand next to the house of a poor fisherman. Workshops have even been found in residential areas. We know that cities were divided into several residential neighborhoods, but we lack information on the exact size and organization of these neighborhoods. Some texts have acknowledged local leadership within these areas.

In the third millennium BCE in the Diyala region, there were spacious houses with recognizable lavatories, consisting of a brick platform with a wide slit. However, the houses of ordinary peasants were very simple one-story buildings containing one or two rooms with little equipment. The building material depended upon what was available in the vicinity; in Mesopotamia mud brick was used to build a peasant hut, which survived as the *serifah,* common in Iraq until the 1950s.

Excavations at the city of Mashkan-shapir have provided the best picture of the layout of a southern Mesopotamian city to date. In the nineteenth and eighteenth centuries BCE, Mashkan-shapir was the second capital of the kingdom of Larsa as well as an important trade center. The city was suddenly abandoned ca. 1720 BCE and was never reoccupied in any significant way. The main roads of Mashkan-shapir ran either parallel to canals or at right angles to them, with bridges or ferries to link neighborhoods. The residential areas were connected by a network of streets, and most homes were entered through narrow alleyways and culs-de-sac. The layout of the narrow streets was like a maze. The street surfaces were uneven, in part due to the constant rebuilding of homes on previous foundations that were never leveled, and in part because garbage was dumped into the streets. Dogs and other scavenging ani-

Modern village of *serifahs* (reed huts) in the swamps of southern Iraq. COURTESY OF W. J. HEIMPEL.

mals ate some rubbish, but the rest was dried by the sun and walked on. At Mashkan-shapir all residential areas included artisans; some areas even provided evidence of craft specialization, such as the production of pottery, copper-bronze smelting, and lapidary work.

Archaeology and texts have provided no evidence of either a central marketplace or a commercial quarter in Mesopotamian cities. Textual references to wine shops around squares have still not explained the role of these stores in the distribution of goods. Some small buildings in residential areas have been identified as shops, but the archaeological evidence is shaky; furthermore, the texts rarely mention shops. Perhaps the agriculture products and crafts were traded near the centers of production or importation, such as workshops, city gates, and wharves. The establishment of markets was a late development, stimulated by the extraordinary size of the cities, which led to the creation of supply markets. Thus, the markets served to link those who lived inside the city to those who lived outside.

Most archaeologists have calculated populations based on 200 persons per hectare (1 hectare ≈ 2.5 acres) in southern irrigated areas. The resulting figure correlates with textual information. That is, the populations of major cities in southern Mesopotamia ranged from 10,000 to nearly 100,000 people. Such estimates should be regarded as maximum populations of cities in their heyday. The archaeological evidence, however, has suggested that the population density in the south was approximately 100 persons per hectare, similar to rural villages of today in southwestern Asia. The population of the cities changed as their political fortunes changed. Unfortunately, calculating the population of northern cities has been more difficult, because large residential areas have rarely been excavated.

The Population

With the advent of the Neo-Assyrian empire, the temple and palace became one complex built on high citadel mounds, which were walled off from the rest of the city. Stone replaced brick as the primary construction material. In this way, a city within a city was created from which ordinary citizens were excluded. This inner city has endured as a distinctive pattern of urbanism even today in Eurasia, namely, the Kremlin of Moscow and the "Forbidden City" of Beijing. The term *kirhu*, used to describe this characteristic of Mesopotamian urbanism, is neither Akkadian nor Semitic, thus implying that the citadel city was foreign to Mesopotamia.

Excursus: Capital Cities of the Neo-Assyrian Empire

Unlike older cities in which the citadel was in the center, new capital cities, particularly those built by Assyrian kings, were often raised above the plain on a terrace the same height as the city wall. The entrance to the citadel was located in the lower city, so the king had to pass through the city whenever he left the palace.

Cities used their watercourses to reinforce their fortifications. Archaeologists have excavated a number of bridges both within and outside the main walls. A fortified building was constructed near the city walls to house weapons and booty. The workshops of armorers, who made weapons, horse fittings, chariots, and other equipment, were located next to this complex. Large stone horse troughs also found near Nineveh (Nebi Yunus) were probably meant to provide water for the imperial cavalry. The citadels of both Nineveh and Nimrud (Calhu) used wharves for trade and river communication.

Sennacherib's own building inscriptions furnished a detailed description of Nineveh which coincides with the archaeological data. Nineveh had two settlement mounds: (1) Sennacherib's palace, covering one hectare, and (2) the "back palace" or imperial armory. The two mounds were about a kilometer apart and separated by the Khosr River. The two mounds united at the city wall, which enclosed an area of more than seven hundred hectares, making Nineveh the largest city in Middle Eastern history. Sennacherib described his city as filled with plazas, fields, gardens, and a large botanical and zoological park next to his palace. The park was irrigated, and the excess water from the canal system was fed into an area that created a man-made swamp for canebrakes, water birds, and wild pigs. Sennacherib also gave the citizens of Nineveh plots of two acres on which to plant orchards.

Sennacherib initiated his massive building program at the border of the earlier lower town. Here were the houses of the rich and powerful citizens of the seventh century BCE. On the east was Sennacherib's great Royal Road; traces remain of its stone pavement. Sennacherib, in describing the Royal Road, connected its construction with widening the roads through the artisan-market areas.

Nebuchadnezzar's Babylon, an Architectural Marvel in the Ancient World According to Herodotus, Nebuchadnezzar enhanced the ancient capital of Babylon with his building and renovation projects. The topography of the ancient capital, described by Herodotus in detail, matched well with archaeological excavations of the city. The remarkable sights included the ziggurat, the famous Hanging Gardens (one of the Seven Wonders of the Ancient World), and the museum next to Nebuchadnezzar's new palace. Babylon was more or less square, covering approximately 1,000 hectares, and bisected by the Euphrates. The Euphrates itself could be crossed by a bridge that rested on five piers.

The city walls of Babylon can be traced. According to Herodotus, the outer wall extended more than eight kilometers and had enough space on top for a four-horse chariot to turn around. The most detailed and best preserved gate was dedicated to Ishtar; its thirty-six-foot-high walls are still standing. The walls were constructed of deep-blue–glazed bricks with molded figures of bulls and dragons in yellow and white.

Nebuchadnezzar's Southern Palace had five courtyards surrounded by offices, royal apartments, and reception rooms. In a corner of the palace, archaeologists found an underground crypt. There, a three-shafted well in one of the cellars appeared to have been some kind of hydraulic lifting system, perhaps the water source of the Hanging Gardens of Babylon. Farther south, the Processional Way came to the main temple complex, the dwelling place of Marduk. Here stood the ziggurat, the famous Tower of Babel. Today only 300 square feet of its foundations remain. Nearby was Esagila, Marduk's main temple, with a golden statue of Marduk, restored by Nebuchadnezzar II.

Before Desert Shield and Desert Storm, Saddam Hussein had plans to restore the city of Babylon. In the tradition of Mesopotamian kings, he planned to put his name in one of the bricks. From September 22 through October 6, 1994, Hussein hosted a celebration billed as "From Nebuchadnezzar to Saddam Hussein: Babylon Invokes Its Glories on the Path of Jihad and Glorious Development." A poster featured his profile superimposed on that of Nebuchadnezzar II at the top and the famous glazed bricks with lion friezes and a turreted gate at the bottom.

City Institutions

The main institutions of each city were the temple and the palace (see above). The main temple was always located in the highest part of the city but not necessarily in the center. Ziggurats were often built near the temple. The other urban institution, the palace, was not as easy for archaeologists to find because it was not built on a platform like the temple. During times of political centralization, capitals were governed by kings, and cities were ruled by governors. Power lay with three groups: the temple, the king, and senior members of ancient or wealthy families.

No matter how powerful the central royal administration, there were still problems to deal with on a local level. For example, city authorities were held responsible for the security of goods and strangers and also for apprehending robbers or murderers. If city authorities were unable to find the criminals, the city was obligated to compensate the victim(s). Other cases handled locally included inheritance, family disputes, and conflicts between citizens that did not involve the prerogatives of the king or the temples. Local government also chose citizens for labor or military service for the state.

Thorkild Jacobsen compiled information from disparate sources to make a case for "primitive democracy" in the Early Dynastic period. The city assembly acted as a forum for public discussion and decision. Jacobsen used the models in later myths and epics in which the gods acted in their assembly to reach political and military decisions by consensus.

In the Sumerian myth of Gilgamesh and Akka, decisions in Early Dy-nastic Uruk were based on the advice of both the elders and the young men of the city. The cycle of Uruk myths suggested that there was a bicameral assembly including an "upper house" or "executive council" of city elders. One or more officials were designated to govern the pro-ceedings in the assembly. Eventually, the assembly became little more than a local council, its powers appropriated by the ruler.

The assembly members, we assume, were citizens, the "sons" of the city, but we have no direct evidence on how assembly members qualified for their positions. We presume that originally the assembly included the heads of each household, with "the elders" playing a major role. These assemblies exchanged letters with the kings, arguing with the king for confirmation of their exemptions and privileges. "The city and the el-ders" survived into the Old Babylonian period, but only as a law court; the real seat of power moved to the palace. We are not sure where the assembly met.

During the Old Babylonian period, cities were further divided into administrative districts called "wards," which were governed by the heads of households and the mayor. The Akkadian word for "ward" is closely related to the word for (city) "gate." That is, the assembly of the ward may have met at the city gate, and the mayor performed his duties there. A tablet from Eshnunna lists Amorites "living in the city" accord-ing to their wards, each named after the first man of each group.

Canals, Streets, and Walls   Unlike all other sites in the ancient Near East, southern Mesopotamian cities were comprised of many mounds. The depressions between these mounds were once canals, which separated the cities into component parts. For ex-ample, at Larsa the canals divided the administrative-religious areas from residential (or artisan) neighborhoods. The canals divided the city internally and yet connected it with distant territories for communication and trade. The canals also provided water for the residents of the city. At Ur, for example, canals were associated with harbors. Cuneiform tablets indicated that trade activity was carried out near the harbors of all southern Mesopotamian cities. Because the canal system was also the primary means of communication between different villages or cities, offices were constructed on the riverbanks to control trade and regulate the rates of exchange. The Mesopotamians referred to these business administrative offices collectively as "the wharf."

Mesopotamian cities, both large and small, were divided as well as united by streets and canals. City streets were not paved until the As-syrian period of the first millennium BCE. Sennacherib enlarged Nine-veh's squares, pulled down buildings to let light into alleys and narrow streets, and straightened and widened various streets to create a main ceremonial avenue. He had his Processional Way paved with limestone blocks. Sennacherib, proud of his Processional Way, wanted to preserve it:

> At that time I enlarged the site of Nineveh, my royal city, I made its "market streets" wide (enough to) run a royal road. . . . In days to come, that there might be no narrowing of the royal road, I had steles made which stand facing each other. Fifty-two great cubits I measured the width of the royal road. . . . If ever (anyone of) the people who dwell in that city tears down his old house and builds a new one, and the foundation of his house encroaches upon the royal road, they shall hang him upon a stake over his (own) house.[2]

The final sentence is Sennacherib's only reference to citizens' housing, but it demonstrates that citizens could build their homes where they wanted and according to whatever plan, as long as they kept away from the king's highway. Both inside and outside the city, major roads probably ran parallel to the canals and rivers, much like today. Other main streets were laid at right angles, demarcating blocks of approximately one hectare. Coincidentally, both the average size of a small Mesopotamian village and the size of a residential area were one hectare.

All major Mesopotamian cities were enclosed by fortifications, which separated the city itself from its surroundings. Walls were usually built at the edge of the settlement mound so that later they could be extended to include nonsettled areas. In Mashkan-shapir, a southern Mesopotamian city dated to the second millennium BCE, a fortification system surrounded the entire city. The city wall was pierced by gates for boat traffic and gates for land travel. Because the roads usually ran parallel to the canals, the two gates were close together.

Walls served both symbolic and practical purposes. Rulers celebrated building a new wall, and when a city was conquered, standard military practice was to demolish its fortifications. Sometimes city walls proved to be either too big or too small. For example, at Ur, the ancient Early Dynastic walls inhibited the growth of its population later in the Old Babylonian period. Suburbs could be built outside the city walls, but security would be sacrificed. Or, more practically, a wall could be built to enclose a larger space. Expansion usually reflected an increased population. Also, new political rulers needed new palaces and administrative buildings, which could not fit in already densely populated areas. The capital cities needed housing for visiting officials from other centers and accommodation for increased commercial activity.

The area of Sennacherib's capital city, Nimrud, increased from 72 hectares to 400 hectares. Sennacherib built a great inner wall which was forty bricks thick and 180 courses high, that is, 12 meters thick and 13.5 meters high. There were fifteen gates piercing the wall. North and south of the city were more parks, and the cultivated land of the city probably extended eight to sixteen kilometers beyond a great outer wall.

A New Year's Chapel belonging to the city was located outside the city walls. Once each year, the statue of the main city god was carried in a procession and accompanied by its worshipers to this sanctuary. Sometimes a sacred road passed through a special gate to the outlying sanctuary to the temple.

Water Supply and Sewage Disposal
The sources of drinking water in Mesopotamia were the Twin Rivers and their canals; for many cities these remained the main sources of water down through the first millennium BCE. But some palaces, especially in Assyria, got their water supply from deep wells, safe from pollution. For the most part, large cities were built near water supplies. Smaller cities survived if they had many springs, wells, aqueducts, or cisterns.

In Nimrud many wells were dug to a depth of ninety feet to protect the city's water supply in times of siege. In 1952 excavators cleared one well and found it still able to provide five thousand gallons a day. In that well archaeologists found a wooden pulley wheel bearing the wear of rope marks, and many pots, some with rope still around their necks, which formed a chain of vessels operated by a windlass to draw water from the well. Sennacherib described a similar device when he rebuilt his capital, Nineveh: "In order to draw water daily, I had ropes, bronze cables and bronze chains made, and I had beams and cross-bars fixed over the wells instead of poles."[3]

King Sennacherib had an aqueduct constructed from Jerwan, a village 9.6 kilometers away, to supply Nineveh, his capital, with water for drinking and irrigation. This aqueduct, over 270 meters long, anticipated later architectural plans in every detail. The entire structure used about two million stones, each weighing a quarter of a ton. The water flowed over the aqueduct floor, which was hardened earth waterproofed with bitumen and lined with stone. The aqueduct extended over the valleys on arches and was fed by many small streams, thereby guaranteeing an adequate supply of water to the city.

Pure water was especially important in the ancient Near East. At the Hittite court, water for the king had to be strained; records noted that one time the king found a hair in his water jug and ordered the guilty water carrier put to death. Mesopotamian texts also referred to the risk of death from drinking contaminated water. For the Assyrians, cleanliness was essential, particularly for ritual purposes.

The health of a community was directly connected to its ability to eliminate human waste without contaminating its water supply. As early as the third millennium BCE, royal palaces and even the homes of the rich had indoor lavatories. Usually the lavatories were placed against outside walls, with a seat over a terra-cotta drainage pipe. Human waste was often carried to a distant river through a complex system of drains and sewers beneath the streets. Manholes were used to keep the sewers clear. Of course, bathrooms were a luxury most could not afford. Archaeological excavation has demonstrated that the homes of ordinary workers and peasants had no lavatories, not even communal bathrooms. Instead, the poor would defecate outside in orchards, in fields within city walls, and in surrounding fields. In Mesopotamia having human waste outdoors was not necessarily a health hazard, since the hot sun dried and sterilized fecal matter within hours. But if human waste was too close to a water supply, the water could become contaminated. In King Sennacherib's palace, the throne room had a bathroom adjacent to it, a feature common in palaces.

A typical bathroom had a floor of burnt brick waterproofed with bitumen, which was plastered on the lower parts of the walls. A depressed part of the floor had one or two drainage holes with stone plugs. A seat could have been built over the drainage holes. At Nuzi, a provincial Mesopotamian town, a luxury toilet was unearthed in the residential section of the Government House. The "seat" was made of two marble slabs. Low platforms beside the toilet were probably stands for water jars, used for "flushing."

Garbage was usually thrown into the streets and empty lots with layers of ash, perhaps indicating incineration. There was no municipal rubbish collection. Animal teeth and bones at Mesopotamian sites show that both pigs and dogs were found in all parts of the city; they probably played a role in the disposal of garbage. Scavenging pigs and dogs roamed around Babylonian cities, and among the Hittites these scavengers even wandered inside the palace of the king. These animals were only prohibited from crossing the threshold of the place where the food for the king or the god was prepared. In time the scavenging pigs were eaten (except by people such as the Israelites, for whom the pig was taboo). However, if this meat was not thoroughly cooked, the flesh transmitted dangerous Trichinella worms. Rodents also thrived in the constant presence of garbage, with rats carrying fleas, an agent of the bubonic plague.

THE COUNTRYSIDE

The city served as a political center and military refuge to its surrounding villages. Cuneiform sources do not record any conflict between people living in the open countryside and city-dwellers. In fact, the residents of the city owned farms and estates in the countryside.

In the Old Babylonian period these villages governed their own territory, regardless of whether they were politically dependent or independent. The Laws of Hammurabi (CH §23) stipulated that the village or city was responsible for crimes committed within its domain: "If the robber should not be seized, the man who has been robbed shall establish the extent of his lost property before the god; and the city and the governor in whose territory and district the robbery was committed shall replace his lost property to him."[4]

The elders and the mayor acted on behalf of the village, thus setting the pattern later adopted in the city wards. Consensus was required for the organization of water rights, fallow land, and other agricultural affairs. Old Babylonian correspondence documented the role of the village in local government. A letter states, "The village has given me 10 iku (= 3.6 hectares) of land, the holding of a soldier who campaigned with me and who has no heir (literally, whose "hearth is extinguished)."[5]

NOMADIC AND SEMI-NOMADIC LIFE

Nomads were shepherds who migrated with their herds through areas not suited for cultivation. Early nomads in the Near East were never more than one day's travel from a water hole. Nomadic groups also had bases to which they returned periodically. For example, both the Amorites and Aramaeans used Jebel Bishri as their headquarters, between the Euphrates and the main oasis of Tadmor (Palmyra).

Nomads belonged to social groups larger than the family, such as the tribe or clan. The political organization of nomads varied from small, decentralized "egalitarian" groups to large, hierarchical "chiefdoms." Many nomadic tribes or clans farmed and raised animals on the outskirts of settlements. These tribes have been termed semi-nomads or transhumants. Today we use the term "bedouin," borrowed from Arabic, to refer only to camel-nomads, who cross the desert by dromedary, an animal whose capabilities are superior to those of the ass.

Nomads did not leave written records; even archaeological remains are meager relative to those of the sedentary or settled people. Despite the progress of archaeologists in their field methods and scientific techniques, we have only a bare outline of nomadic life in ancient times. Because of this lack of information, archaeologists are forced to consider traditional peoples of the modern Near East for insights into the ancient nomadic way of life, a study called ethnoarchaeology. The tribal organization of modern nomads, as well as their techniques of farming and herding, is believed to simulate a way of life that began in prehistoric times.

Frank Hole, an archaeologist known for his use of the ethnographic study of nomads and archaeological fieldwork, joined a group of Luri nomads (in Iran), even migrating with them in the spring. En route in southwestern Iran, he discovered a Neolithic site, which was part of a larger area that would soon be leveled to improve irrigation. After completing his ethnographic study of the Luri nomads, Hole returned. But the site had already been leveled, and remains of a nomadic tent site were exposed. He also learned that the Luri nomads with whom he traveled used to camp near this site before the Shah's government resettled them.

Sayid Ali, one of the older nomads in the group, asked Hole why they were digging at this site, which he called "just a nomad camp."[6] Sayid Ali examined each of the uncovered tent sites and their orientation to the prevailing wind. From his observations, Sayid Ali was able to determine the season of occupation, the size and layout of the campsite, and whether the tent belonged to a leader or to an average person. While cleaning out one of the tent sites, Ali was even able to show Hole where the fireplace was by using the back wall as a point of orientation. Then from the fireplace, Ali took several steps to the front of the tent and turned a number of steps to the left. Here he found the ash dump where the ash was deposited each day after the fireplace was cleaned. To Hole, the connections were apparent: the spatial layout of a tent and of its surroundings had remained the same over time. Unfortunately, today little remains for us to study, as the traditional ways of life throughout the region have almost disappeared.

The traditional view of scholars on nomadic-sedentary relations in the Near East stressed their mutual antagonism. This opinion was influenced by ancient Near Eastern textual sources, written by scribes who lived in the city: the authors stressed the uncivilized behavior of nomadic groups and their potential danger to sedentary society. For example, the Gutians were described in a derogatory manner:

> not classed among people, not reckoned as part of the land,
> . . . people who know no inhibitions,
> With human instinct but canine intelligence and monkeys'
> features. (*The Curse of Agade: The Ekur Avenged*)[7]

In another text, the "Weidner Chronicle," the Gutians are described as people "who were never shown how to worship god, who did not know how to properly perform the rites and observances."[8]

Desert nomads were ever present, and their campsites were regarded as a threat to the city-dwellers, as found in descriptions of the Amorites:

> a tent dweller . . . wind and rain . . . who digs up truffles from the hills, but does not know how to kneel; who eats raw meat; who has no house during the days of his life, and is not buried on the day of his death. (*Myth of the Wedding of Amurru*)[9]

Since that time the Amorites, a ravaging people, with the instincts
of a beast . . . the sheepfolds like wolves; a people which does not
know grain. (Inscription of Shu-Sin)[10]

The Amorites were well documented in early Mesopotamian sources.
In Sumerian, the Amorites were called MAR.TU and in Akkadian Amurru,
meaning "west," that is, Semitic-speakers who originated in regions west
of Sumer and Akkad. Mesopotamian sources regarded the Amorites as
a threat. In fact, the kings of Ur built a defensive wall called "the wall
that keeps Tidnum (an Amorite group) away" (see Chapter 3). However,
many Amorite individuals were assimilated into Mesopotamian settlements and assumed various positions in society. When the Third Dynasty of Ur fell, Amorites became the rulers of many Mesopotamian
cities. Most prominent among these rulers was Shamshi-Adad I (ca.
1830–1776 BCE), who created a state encompassing nearly all of upper
Mesopotamia and whose ancestors were described as those "who lived
in tents"—that is, nomads. His famous Amorite contemporary in the
south, Hammurabi (1792–1750 BCE) of Babylon, also derived his lineage
from the same tent-dwelling ancestors. The Amorites sometimes split
into "Sons of the North" and "Sons of the South," but the two groups
were basically the same. In a letter, Zimri-Lim (1782–1759 BCE) was portrayed as governing both the sedentary Akkadian population of Mari
and the Khanaeans of his own Amorite origins: "If indeed they come to
the banks of the Euphrates, is it not like beads in a necklace, distinguished because one is white and one black? Thus, they say: This village
is Bin-Simal ('Sons of the left = North'), this village is Bin-Yamina ('Sons
of the Right = South'). Is it not like the flood-waters of a river in which
the upper confronts the lower?"[11] The royal archives of Mari (ca. 1810–
1760 BCE) documented the relationship between sedentist central authority, also Amorite, and the migratory routes of the nomadic Amorites.
The kingdom of Mari kept careful watch on the movements of these
Amorites and even tried to control their migratory patterns. The Mari
state frequently employed tribal members in corvée labor and military
service.

Though nomadic invaders and uncivilized peoples from the Zagros
Mountains were sometimes despised for lacking the basic qualities of
civilized people, contact with Mesopotamians could "civilize" the "uncivilized." A Sumerian poem composed in honor of Ur declared that
even a native of Markhashi, a mountain region of Elam, became civilized
once he resided in Ur.

Recent studies have shown that nomads were economically dependent
on the sedentary population, particularly for grain. But nomads were
difficult to govern because they lacked ties to the community. Most nomads were shepherds, which meant that they wandered far away to find

grazing land. When their relations with the villagers were friendly, the nomads were employed as shepherds in exchange for grazing rights. Sometimes nomads grazed their herds on sedentists' fallow fields, and their animals provided dung as fertilizer. Nomads were employed as agricultural workers, as laborers on public projects, and as soldiers. The state allotted plots of land to soldiers, so nomads could become sedentary in this way. The Amorites bred donkeys, used by farmers and soldiers as draft animals; also, donkeys were probably sold to merchants for their caravans. Nomads were involved in trade and at times controlled the trade routes between Mesopotamia and the west. The nomads also furnished animals and their local know-how for commercial ventures. By the end of the second millennium BCE, camels gave nomads the ability to move to desert areas far away from the sedentist zones of the Levant and Mesopotamia, while still retaining ties to these sedentary communities.

Near Eastern agriculture was always a risky business, at the mercy of severe environmental or climatic difficulties, greedy governmental authorities, and crop damage in times of war. Within this framework, domestic animals were "capital on the hoof."[12] As an economic strategy, herding predominated in pastoralism, but other activities were also performed, such as hunting, gathering, trading, and agriculture. The nomadic way of life may have served as an alternative when farming was no longer feasible.

The desert population renewed itself by absorbing other Semitic tribes; for example, the Amorites (ca. 2200–2000 BCE) preceded the Aramaeans (ca. 1200–1000 BCE) who, in turn, preceded the Arabs (800 BCE). Because they had no permanent territorial claims, these groups were identified by tribes. Descent from a common ancestor was of great importance to tribal affiliation. The genealogy of tribes was, perhaps, more theoretical than literal. Tribal affiliations changed, tribes constantly absorbed other tribes, and individuals even changed their tribal status.

Political upheavals brought the Amorites and later the Aramaeans on the scene due to widespread abandonment of rural settlements. According to the texts, the mobility of nomads was aided by domesticated horses (third millennium BCE), which gave them a distinct military advantage in raids against settlements. That is, nomadic raids succeeded during times of weakness in settled communities.

In time each nomadic group was absorbed into other populations or became sedentary. Traditionally, this process was viewed in terms of successive stages in which the tribes were transformed from nomadic barbarism to settled life. Passing through social strata, some nomads eventually became princes or kings and, as "town-dwellers," founded dynasties.

The nomads living closer to urban civilization gradually assimilated into sedentary society. Part of the tribe established a winter home near the village, cultivating fields around the settlement; another part moved the flocks further north each summer in search of grazing. That is, nomads followed migratory routes which were carefully planned every year. The annual migration may have followed particular routes to known encampments, where the grazing rights were drawn between other nomads and the settled population.

The Aramaeans were first mentioned in twelfth century BCE texts of the Assyrian king Tiglath-pileser I, who conducted a sequence of campaigns against Aramaean nomads. Ensuing Aramaean attacks on Assyria during Tiglath-Pileser I's reign corresponded with famines and crop failures. When Assyrian kings conducted a series of campaigns to the west in the late tenth century BCE, the Aramaeans had formed a nexus of petty states, many named after tribal ancestors, such as Bit-Adini ("House of Adini"), on the great bend of the Euphrates, and Bit-Bakhiani ("House of Bakhiani"), in the upper Khabur plains. Beginning in the ninth century, Aramaean rulers kept their own records, written in their own language, Aramaic.

Camels were first domesticated in the third millennium BCE in Arabia. By the end of the second millennium BCE, camel nomads from Arabia began a thriving trade in incense and spices from southern Arabia to the markets of the Levant and Mesopotamia. Since camels can survive on less water than sheep or goats, camel pastoralists were able to roam vast expanses of arid desert, while sheep-goat nomads could not.

CLASS AND SOCIETY

Hammurabi's law code furnished much information about class and society as corroborated by contemporary documents from the ancient Near East. Mesopotamia's social structure was based on economics; that is, Mesopotamian society was divided into two groups, those who owned property, especially land, and those who were dependent upon the wealthy—the "haves" and "have-nots." Mesopotamia did not have warrior or priestly classes. Hammurabi's law code named three basic social strata, the *awīlum*, the *muškēnum* and the *wardum*; the latter means "slave," the only term which can easily be translated. Any legal distinction between *awīlum* and *muškēnum* disappeared after the Old Babylonian period.

Awīlum, "man," usually translated "freeman," that is, free from debt, also implied a "gentleman." Possibly the *awīlum* was a landowner or head of a household. The *awīlum* had obligations to the state to pay taxes and perform military service. Upon his death, his property was divided among his sons.

Muškēnum is an Amorite term, literally meaning "the one prostrating himself." Whenever the *muškēnum* appeared in relation to the *awīlum*, the "freeman" or "citizen," the status of the *muškēnum* was inferior. The *muškēnum* often served at the palace in exchange for rations or land allotments. Numerous legal provisions may have been necessary in order to identify the *muškēnum* with the palace because he was not protected by customary law.

After 1500 BCE the word *muškēnum* appeared in texts with the connotation of "the poor." With this meaning, the *muškēnum* made its way into Hebrew, Aramaic, and Arabic, and much later, into the Romance languages, namely, French (as *mesquin*) and Italian (as *meschino*).

The first slaves captured by Mesopotamia were men or women seized in raids on the mountains, so that the ideograms for "slave" and "slave-girl" were composed of the signs for "man" or "woman" plus the sign for "mountain." Initially the economy could not accommodate captives, so they were killed. Later the kings saved captives and organized them into gangs serving as laborers or soldiers; the king could still kill them since he "owned" them. The slaves worked with conscripted laborers and some hired workers to construct roads, dig canals, build military fortifications, erect temples, till the crown lands, and work in palace factories. State slaves lived in special barracks; their names, ages, and lands of origin were recorded. Temple slaves were drafted from both prisoners of war and the offerings of private citizens. Preclassical societies, however, were never economically dependent upon slave labor. These societies began increasingly to use slaves as domestics, as military conquests brought in more prisoners of war.

In the third millennium BCE, citizens went into debt slavery because they could not repay loans to the aristocracy. Penniless men and women sold themselves or their children into slavery or were seized by creditors. By the eighteenth century BCE, debt slavery was well established, with five of Hammurabi's laws regulating aspects of it.[13] In fact, in the Old Babylonian period, Mesopotamian kings would issue, at the beginning of their reigns, a reform edict of "righteousness" or "justice," which included economic measures such as freeing citizens from debt slavery. In later times, children were often given to temples to save their lives in times of famine. In first millennium BCE Babylonia, these temple slaves represented an important economic class which was able to rise to important positions within the temple administration.

Babylonian merchants sold foreign slaves: Subarians from the north were much in demand. The cuneiform texts showed that slaves were frequently bought and sold, sometimes with an implied warranty; that is, if a slave suffered an epileptic attack within one hundred days of purchase, the seller was obligated to take back the slave.

During the Old Babylonian period the average price for a slave was approximately twenty shekels of silver, but sometimes as much as ninety. The average wage paid to hired laborers was ten shekels a year. Therefore, landowners preferred to hire seasonal laborers, because it was cheaper than owning slaves for agricultural work.

The slave became the property of his owner. If he tried to escape, he was severely punished. Runaway slaves were rare, but according to one text, on their foreheads was marked "A runaway—seize him!" A slave was often distinguished by a characteristic lock of hair, though others wore tags or fetters. The authorities were responsible for capturing runaway slaves and returning them to their masters. The theft of slaves was punished severely, with special laws applied to palace slaves.

Private slaves were relatively uncommon and were employed largely in domestic service. Slaves born in the house had special status. In the Old Babylonian period, they were often adopted to care for their adoptive parents in their old age. Upon the death of their "parents," the slaves gained their freedom. Slaves had certain legal rights: they could take part in business, borrow money, and buy their freedom. If a slave, either male or female, married a free person, the children they had together would be free.

Social distinctions were not fixed. The slave could be freed, and the free man could be enslaved by debt. A man without land could become a landowner. There were several ways to become a landowner. Kings rewarded administrators with grants of land. A wealthy merchant could buy land. In fact, in regions where law customarily forbade the sale of ancestral land, the wealthy merchant could circumvent this prohibition by legal fiction; that is, he would be adopted by the seller and thus inherit his land. There was social mobility at the very top. For example, a man who was not of royal birth could become king (see Chapter 3). According to tradition, Sargon's father was unknown, which meant he was of humble birth. Since the king was the chief representative of the god on earth, the priests and scribes created the necessary divine link in *The Legend of Sargon*. The legend told that Sargon was the son of a high priestess who bore him secretly because she was prohibited from having sexual relations with a man. A high priestess was often of royal lineage and often the consort of a god. Therefore, the son of a high priestess was certainly worthy of being king. Hammurabi, an Amorite, explained his rise to kingship in the prologue to his laws: "At that time, the gods Anu and Enlil, for the enhancement of the well-being of the people, named me by name: Hammurabi, the pious prince, who venerates the gods, to make justice prevail in the land, to abolish the wicked and the evil, to prevent the strong from oppressing the weak, to rise like the sun-god Shamash, over all humankind, to illuminate the land."[14]

Ethnic divisions, with few exceptions, played no role in ancient Mesopotamia. Many ethnic groups entered Mesopotamia, and all eventually assimilated. Even former Assyrian enemies who resided in cities ruled by their conquerors were treated as "equals"; they were never called barbarians, "Asiatics," or other derogatory names, as corroborated by Neo-Assyrian royal inscriptions.

Fringe groups existed, particularly those whom the Assyrians deported as early as the thirteenth century BCE. Assyrian reliefs often depicted women and children in wagons, while the men were on foot. Only some of the deportees became slaves; many more worked on public projects, and others, if qualified, were incorporated into the army. Craftsmen were able to ply their trades, particularly when their skills were in great demand. In most cases, the assimilation of resettled peoples was encouraged. Of those deported and resettled, the Aramaeans were the largest group. However, because many Aramaeans had already invaded Babylonia and Assyria through the plains, these newly arrived Aramaeans were easily assimilated.

7

Society, Part II:
Private Life

PRIVATE HOUSES

Houses in ancient Mesopotamia were built of the same materials as those in Iraq today: mud brick, mud plaster for the walls, mud and poplar for the roofs, and wood for doors and doorframes; all materials available around the city. The purpose of a house in southern Iraq was to provide shelter from the twelve hours of unrelenting heat—the climate from May to September. Bricks were made from a mixture of clay and chopped straw, packed into molds, and then left to dry in the sun, often in the first summer month (May–June), also called "the month of bricks."[1] Baked bricks lasted longer but were expensive to manufacture; consequently, they were used only to construct luxurious buildings. In the Old Babylonian period (ca. 1900–1595 BCE) baked bricks, bitumen and lime plaster, were used to waterproof the lower parts of the wall, which were subject to deterioration from rising dampness.

Ancient houses, particularly those made of sun-dried brick, often collapsed. The Laws of Hammurabi devoted five sections to this problem (§§229–233), noting in particular the builder's responsibility:

> If a builder constructs a house for a man, but does not make his work sound, and the house that he constructs collapses and causes the death of the householder, that builder shall be killed.
>
> If it should cause the death of a son of the householder, they shall kill a son of that builder.[2]

The roof was usually constructed from planks of palm tree wood, then a cover of reeds and palm leaves, and finally a layer of earth. Stairs of wood or brick led to the roof, where vegetables could be dried in the sun, a cool breeze enjoyed, and sometimes rituals performed.

In the third millennium BCE the average house was a thick-walled mud hut, usually without windows. When windows were present, they were made from clay or wooden grilles set in the wall. Artificial lighting was supplied by lamps, which were often shaped like small shoes filled with sesame seed oil and a wick made from wool, a reed, or some other plant. The rooms of these houses showed little evidence of architectural planning. Doors between rooms were so low that people had to stoop as they went through. Frequently, two adjacent houses shared a common wall. Under such circumstances, both neighbors were responsible for the wall.

Usually doors were made of wood; they were set in a wooden frame, which was painted red, the color that frightened evil spirits and kept them from entering. Occasionally, doors were made from ox hides—sometimes as many as ten ox hides. Small, crude statues meant to ward off evil were buried beneath the outer door or inside, along the walls, in lavatories, and, especially, in the bedroom.

Houses of the wealthy were often large, their rooms designed around a square courtyard. However, in cities, where space was limited, there might be rooms on only two or three sides of the courtyard. Poorer areas might not even have a courtyard. When present, second stories replicated the plan of the ground floor and were constructed on an extra thick foundation wall for support. In larger homes, the rooms and their uses have been easier to identify, such as reception rooms, kitchen and courtyard, fireplaces, and water installations. Some houses had storage rooms for valuables. These rooms could be sealed by a metal hook attached to a doorknob; clay covered the hook and knob, over which a cylinder seal was rolled to secure the premises (see Chapter 4). Sometimes, a room might be set aside as a sanctuary.

Lavatories were found from the third millennium BCE; they were designed as a platform above a pit or drain, sometimes with a seat of bitumen for comfort. The palace at Eshnunna (ca. 2300 BCE) had six lavatories with raised seats of baked brick. There were even five rooms for bathing. Bathing rooms were a feature of houses of the rich. Inventories of bathing room furnishings have supplied us with a list of their contents, namely, tubs, stools, jars, and mirrors. All lavatories and bathing rooms were connected with drains leading to a main sewer approximately one meter high and covered with baked bricks. Each lavatory had a large water pitcher, some found with a pottery dipper to help flush the waste. Assyrian palaces dated to the first millennium BCE had an elaborate drainage system, which emptied its waste into the river (see Chapter 6).

Based on available data, city houses changed in size over time. No single house should be regarded as typical. For example, in the third millennium BCE the houses at Uruk and Fara covered approximately four hundred square meters in surface area. However, during the second millennium the size of the average Old Babylonian house at Ur was less than one hundred square meters. We also have house models from various cities in ancient Mesopotamia.

The residences of ancient Mesopotamia housed creeping things such as scorpions; a group of omens referred to scorpions that fell from the ceiling onto a man or his bed. There were even magical and herbal treatments to treat scorpion stings. Snakes also crawled through the house in search of rodents in the branches and mud that formed the roof and ceiling. Here again omen texts referred to snakes falling out of the roof onto a man or his bed—sometimes this was considered a lucky omen. Even the walls of houses were decorated with different colored species of ants and cockroaches. A number of omen texts indicated the significance to be attached to animals that might be met both inside the house and on its walls—reptiles, lizards, scorpions, cockroaches, beetles, and others.

Household furnishings varied according to the time period, the location, and the wealth of the owners. The furniture of a typical private house was different from that found in palaces. Ancient furniture, like modern furniture, **Household Furnishings** was most often made from wood and other organic materials which decayed over time. Consequently, archaeological finds of ancient furniture are rare, except for places such as Egypt, where the hot, dry climate inhibited decay.

The furniture designs from the third millennium BCE continued to be used in the second millennium BCE. Mari texts have provided a detailed description of how royal furniture was constructed and what it looked like. The texts recorded the use of cords, sinews, and glue in constructing furniture; leather was used for upholstery.[3]

The greatest variety of sources for furniture comes from the first millennium BCE, namely, texts, illustrations, and numerous archaeological finds from Assyria. The furniture was either made in Assyria, imported, or brought back as booty or tribute from neighboring countries. In fact, records of booty and tribute often listed furniture among the most valuable objects.

Stools were used for menial work at the beginning of the third millennium. They were usually made of reeds on a wooden frame. There were even folding stools with crossed legs as well as stools with carved legs and sides.

Chairs had legs, backs, and even arms. Their frames were made from various hardwoods; seventeen kinds of wood were listed. Sometimes chair frames were inlaid with copper, bronze, silver, gold, or carved ivory. Chairs were often painted. Their seats were covered with leather, palm fiber, or rushes, or padded with felt. Loose linen slipcovers were even designed for the chairs.

Chairs came in many shapes and sizes: thrones, sedan chairs for transportation, and armchairs (from which Sennacherib is shown watching the siege of Lachish). Reliefs from Khorsabad showed Sargon II presented with two kinds of tables, a chair or throne, and a footstool with lion's paw feet set on conical bases. Assyrian furniture has been found with bronze panels of griffins and winged deities in addition to calf or bull head finials decorating the arms. Ivory fittings, the work of Phoenician and Syrian craftsmen to decorate furniture, were found at Nimrud (Calhu) and Fort Shalmaneser. The series included plaques depicting animals, sphinxes, griffins in floral settings, seated or standing figures holding branches beneath winged discs, and "women at the window" (perhaps prostitutes making themselves visible to potential clients).

Babylonian thrones were similar in style to Assyrian thrones. Literary evidence supports a connection between the furniture of the two kingdoms. Babylonian furniture was greatly prized by Assyrian monarchs. Assyrian kings were also portrayed relaxing on couches. The legs of the couches were decorated with small panels showing carved ivory moldings, women in a windowlike setting, and recumbent lions supported by tapered, conelike feet. These couches may have been imported from Phoenicia or Syria.

Meals were eaten at tables. Tables, tray tables, and offering stands were used throughout the third millennium, as confirmed by texts and art. Assyria has provided us with actual tables, models of tables, and illustrations of tables on reliefs. Like stools and chairs, tables were made of wood and sometimes decorated with metal. In first millennium BCE Assyria, the table was usually a small square on four ornamented legs, terminating at the bottom in either an ox hoof or a lion's foot. Tablecloths were mentioned in Babylonia, that is, "a linen cloth on the gold table of the god Shamash,"[4] and illustrated in cylinder seals. Table napkins were held by a servant who offered them to those dining so that they could dry their hands after washing them at the end of the meal.

Beds were usually made of a frame and supporting base of wood, though sometimes rope, interwoven reeds, or crisscrosses of metal strips were used. The bed provided support for mattresses stuffed with wool, goat's hair, or palm fiber. Bedding included linen sheets, mattresses, cushions, and blankets. Medical texts often mentioned patients who "took to their bed." Of course, not everyone owned a bed; the poor slept on straw or reed mats.

We have few illustrations of beds from the third millennium; in fact, beds were often omitted from furniture inventory lists of this period. An

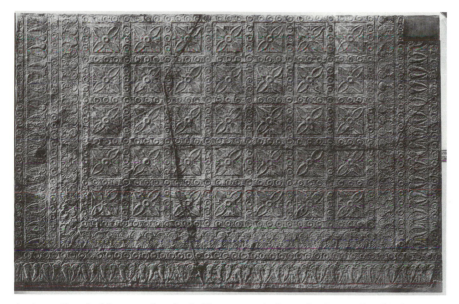

A stone threshold, carved to look like a rug, is from the Sennacherib's (704–681 BCE) South-West Palace at Nineveh. 50.8 cm × 96.5 cm. © BRITISH MUSEUM, LONDON.

Old Akkadian source alluded to a wooden bed with fruit decoration and slender feet. However, by the end of the third millennium, a number of beds were described in texts as constructed from reed and wood and overlaid with gold, silver, or copper. Beds had legs that often terminated with an ox hoof or claw. But some beds looked like shallow wooden boxes.

Tablets refer to bedside mats, thereby raising the issue of floor coverings. The palace may have used carpets. Some floors at doorways were decorated by limestone slabs carved to imitate carpeting. Carpets were luxury goods that served two functions: they affirmed the wealth of their owners and decorated the wall or floor.

Household goods included containers for storing utensils and provisions. Baskets, skins, clay bins, and large wooden chests were used for storage. Crates were used for storing vegetables. Containers were waterproofed to hold liquids. Wine was stored in special jars of several gallons' capacity, which were sometimes marked with the volume.

The design of both eating and drinking vessels varied greatly through time. Platters, bowls, and cups were made of pottery, wood, stone, or metal in different sizes. Ladles were used for scooping up liquids. Ostrich eggs were used for fine vessels. As for cutlery, a large number of single-pronged bone forks have been found. Knives, their blades made from either bronze or iron, were common. Knives were sharpened on small flat whetstones about the size of a finger. Spoons were manufactured from bitumen, metal, wood, terra-cotta, and occasionally ivory.

Food was prepared in an oven, found within the house or in the courtyard. Pots were made with small handles through which a rope could be passed to hang them out of the reach of rats and mice. Other cooking utensils included a copper frying pan, a sieve pot, and kettles for water. Neo-Babylonian dowries recorded that women received equipment for brewing date beer. Smaller jars were used for oil, clarified butter, or beer. A mortar and pestle, made of baked clay or stone, were used to pound some cereal foods and legumes, and hand mills, made from imported volcanic rock, were used for grinding barley, sesame seeds, and spices.

Household Slaves   Household slaves were usually female, but male slaves could also reside with the family. Sometimes as many as ten male and ten female slaves resided in a single household.

The children of slaves belonged to their owners. When large estates were divided, the slaves were included in the division of property and could be sold.

Slave owners encouraged slaves to marry in order to increase their wealth. The children of such marriages belonged to the master, who was free to sell them individually. But separating members of a family was rather uncommon.

A slave could, upon the master's consent, marry a free woman. Even if she brought no dowry with her, both she and her children remained free. If she brought a dowry and invested it with her enslaved husband, who later died or abandoned her, the widow's dowry was returned to her, but only half the profits—the other half belonged to her husband's master.

Slave-girls could be considered concubines, whether supplied by a barren wife as a surrogate or owned by the husband (see CH §§170–74 and below). If, as a concubine, the slave bore her owner children, she still remained a slave and could be sold. After her owner's death, both she and her children were given their freedom.

If a female slave was purchased by a married woman to act both as her servant and as her husband's concubine, the slave was still the sole property of the wife. The law codes provided, but did not require, that the children of this union could inherit from the paternal estate.

FAMILY LIFE

The term "nuclear family" refers to a married couple and their children. In ancient Mesopotamia the nuclear family was called a "house," and a man was expected "to build a house."[5] To achieve this goal, he married one woman. If she was unable to bear children, he could take a second wife or a concubine, or the couple could decide to adopt children (see below, "Adoption"). On average, from two to four children survived early childhood; the initial number of children born remains unknown. An extended or expanded household refers to a group of people who resided together with one or more relatives besides children. In ancient Mesopotamia, the extended household might include unmarried sisters, widowed mothers, and underage brothers; it was called "the house of the father." These family members referred to each other as "brother" or "my [own] flesh and blood."[6]

In the ancient Near East the family was patriarchal. The father was head of the family and wielded authority over his wife and children. The Laws of Hammurabi (§195) reflected the cultural attitudes of the time, stating, "If a son strikes his father, they shall cut off his hand."[7] The father was head of the family until he died. His rule was law. In case of debt, the father could offer slaves as well as any member of his family to his creditor to satisfy his obligation. The father had the right but not the obligation to redeem them. If he died and left unmarried children, the eldest son became head of the family and administrator of the estate. If the children were young, their mother might be given the authority of "fatherhood."[8]

Men were identified by their father's name. Therefore, having a son and heir was of great significance for the family; a son could support his parents in their old age and perform the proper rites after their death. In the first millennium BCE, free citizens were identified by their given name, followed by their father's name and that of an ancestor who lived centuries ago; that is, X, the son of Y, the descendant of Z. Slaves were not given a family name. Sons and daughters lived in their father's home until they left to establish their own household or to marry into another. An excerpt from a distribution list (rations as payment for services) portrayed family life in Kish, a northern Babylonian city:

30 liters—Ishtar-gamelat, his wife

20 liters—Ahassunu, his daughter

20 liters—Ikuppi-Adad, his son

15 liters—Shamash-andulli, his son

House of Ishme-Adad

30 liters—Humusi, his wife

20 liters—Ibbi-Adad, his son

20 liters—Tabni-Ishtar, his daughter

15 liters—Rabi-sillashu, his son

20 liters—Munawwirtum, his slave-woman

10 liters—Ad-mat-ili, her son

House of Sin-ishmeni[9]

An Assyrian census list from the first millennium BCE recorded the farmers and their holdings in the district of Haran. The census also listed the names of the family members, for example:

Adad-duri, farmer,

Nashukh-dilini, his adolescent son,

1 woman; total 3.

30 units of land, 15 cultivated thereof;

1 orchard,

1 cow.

Total of the estate Arrizu

in the administrative district of Haran.[10]

This census list in its entirety showed that the Assyrian villager was usually monogamous. Some of the sons at home were reported to be adolescents, and some of the daughters "of marriageable age." According to this census list, there were 1.43 children per family; however, this statistic indicated families too small even to maintain the population and may have excluded some circumstances. For example, daughters may have left to set up their own households. Adult sons could have departed for military duty or other state service.

Childbirth, Infancy, and Infant Mortality
Prenatal care involved the use of amulets, herbal potions, rituals, and incantations. Amulets were objects believed to have magical and protective power, bringing luck or averting evil. In order to produce the necessary magical effect, amulets were worn by a person or placed at a specific location.[11] A woman in labor wore an image of the demon Pazuzu or his head to counteract the evil of Lamashtu for herself, her unborn children, and her newborn child. Lamashtu also caused miscarriage and crib death. This female demon was known to slip into the house of a pregnant woman and touch the woman's stomach seven times to kill the baby. Lamashtu also kidnapped the child from the wet nurse.[12] Pazuzu was depicted with a canine face, extraordinarily bulging eyes, a scaly body, a snake-headed penis, talons, and sometimes wings.[13] Metal or stone plaques against Lamashtu were engraved with an image of Lamashtu on one side and an incantation against the female demon on the other. Rows of demons and divine symbols were also engraved on these plaques.[14] Lamashtu was depicted as having a lion's head, donkey's teeth, naked breasts, a hairy body, stained hands, long fingers and fingernails, and bird talons.[15] She clutched snakes in her hands, while a piglet and puppy suckled at her breasts.

Texts described prescriptions for making a barren woman conceive and for giving birth easily: "Total: 21 stones to help a barren woman to become pregnant; you string them on a linen thread and put them around her neck.''[16] If a woman became sick during pregnancy, the prescribed treatment involved plants mixed over a fire to which oil and beer were added. Woolen material was saturated with this mixture and then placed in the woman's vagina twice daily. The treatment was supplemented by anointing and bandaging.

To help a woman in labor, she was given the bark of a tree to chew. Her stomach was massaged with ointment and/or a rolling-pin of magic wood was rolled over her. Midwives or female relatives could be present at the birth. A myth called *The Cow of Sin* was recited; the story was about the Maid-of-the-Moon-god (the moon god's consort in the shape of a cow), who also had a difficult delivery until Anu, the head of the pantheon, anointed her with oil and ''waters of labor pangs'' (that is, amniotic fluid). The myth ended with the following incantation: ''Just as Maid-of-the-Moon-god gave birth easily, so may the maid having a difficult delivery give birth.''[17]

If these remedies proved unsuccessful, magic was invoked. The woman visited a mortuary and the following incantation was recited:

> The woman [is] having a difficult delivery . . . The baby is held fast . . . She who is creating a child is shrouded in the dust of death. Her eyes fail, she cannot see; her lips are sealed, she cannot open them . . . [The woman is now represented as speaking:] ''stand by me . . . O merciful Marduk! Now am I surrounded with trouble. Reach out to me! Bring forth that sealed-up one (that is, the unborn child), a creature of the gods, as a human creature; let him come forth! Let him see the light!''[18]

Some incantations portrayed the unborn child as a ship with unidentified cargo—boy or girl?—on a dark sea.

''Female problems'' related to pregnancy and childbirth were often described in the medical texts. There were numerous prescriptions for a physician to treat a woman with complications after childbirth. One text provided a prescription to abort a fetus.

Death in childbirth and infant mortality were imminent dangers. Many texts referred to Lamashtu (alias Daughter of Anu), the female demon who threatened the life of both mother and child. A poignant elegy described the perils of childbirth in a series of dialogues between a husband and wife and prayers to the mother goddess:

> ''Why are you adrift, like a boat, in the midst of the river,
> your rungs in pieces, your mooring rope cut?''
> ''. . . The day I bore the fruit, how happy I was,
> happy was I, happy my husband.
> The day of my going into labor, my face became darkened,

the day of my giving birth, my eyes became clouded.
With open hands I prayed to the Lady of the gods (the mother
    goddess)
You are the mother of those who have borne a child, save my
    life!"
Hearing this, the Lady of the gods veiled her face (saying),
". . . why do you keep praying to me?"
[My husband, who loved me], uttered a cry,
"Why do you take from me the wife in whom I rejoice?"
". . . [All] those [many] days I was with my husband,
I lived with him who was my lover.
Death came creeping into my bedroom:
it drove me from my house,
it tore me from my husband."[19]

Lullabies, originating from incantations, were sung to stop babies from crying so that the gods would remain undisturbed. The ancient Mesopotamians believed that human "noise" enraged the gods and provoked them to do evil.

Soon after birth the baby was given a name. Akkadian proper names were unique in the Semitic world because many of them reflected the family's feelings about the newborn, such as "My god has had mercy on me" or "Sin has heard my prayer." The name of King Sennacherib means "the god Sin has replaced a brother," thus indicating that even the royal family was affected by infant mortality. Children were also named for their grandfathers. Names could be changed when adults assumed administrative positions; at that time they took a name praising their king's divine status.

Birth abnormalities were listed in the omen texts because of their significance in daily life. The texts reported a child born with only one foot, Siamese twins, and a hermaphrodite. Quadruplets were noted as a normal but unusual birth. Malformed babies were considered evil omens; a ritual was performed, and then the babies' bodies were tossed into the river. Also, the illnesses of infants and children were described in great detail in an omen collection and in magical texts. But infant and child ailments were not even mentioned in therapeutic medical texts.

A newborn baby was at risk if the mother failed to produce milk. The rich could hire a wet nurse, but the poor faced certain death of the child. Children were nursed for two or three years. Nursing also served as a means of birth control because women are relatively infertile while nursing. The infant slept in a basket. As the baby grew, his mother or nurse wore a sling to carry him around. The birth of boys was considered a blessing. Infant exposure was probably more common for daughters than sons.

We know little about how children were raised. The emotional bonds

Woman feeding child with a goatskin bottle. This detail can be seen in the top right of a relief from the Southwest Palace at Nineveh. The women are being deported after a campaign in Babylonia. © BRITISH MUSEUM, LONDON.

between children and their parents were very strong. Many of the gods were referred to as either father or mother. Numerous terra-cotta figurines, mostly miniatures, portrayed a naked woman carrying a child on her arm. Parents sold their children only in times of dire circumstances (see Chapter 6). Babylonian and Assyrian lists described the life cycle as follows: a child at the breast, a weaned child, a child, an adolescent, an adult, and an elderly person. The height of the child was given in cubits.

Children were usually adopted when there was no male heir. The simplest form of adoption was that of a newborn, **Adoption** abandoned right after birth "to the dog" while still "in (its) water and blood."[20] Older children were adopted by reimbursing their parents for the expenses of feeding and raising them. These transactions were recorded as if they were sales. Adults could become part of another family by their own will, called "arrogation." Even slaves could be freed and adopted as sons. The reason for adoption and arrogation was to have a son to care for his parents in their old age. The adoptive parents agreed that the child would be their heir, regardless of how many natural children were born to them after the adoption. Breaking the agreement had severe consequences; if the parents did this, they were either fined or lost their entire estate; if the son left them, he lost his freedom.[21] One adoption contract has what one may call "boilerplate" to insure the immutability of the adopted heir's status:

> Yahatti-Il is the son of Hillalum and of Alittum. He shall enjoy their good times and suffer their bad times. If Hillalum, his (adoptive) father, and Alittum, his (adoptive) mother, say to Yahatti-Il their son, "You are not our son," they shall forfeit house and property. If Yahatti-Il says to Hillalum, his father, and Alittum, his mother, "You are not my father. You are not my mother," they shall shave him and sell him for silver. Even if Hillalum and Alittum have many sons, Yahatti-Il is the heir, and he shall take two shares from the estate of Hillalum his father; his younger brothers shall divide the (remaining estate) in equal parts. A claimant who raises a claim against him infringes on the taboo of Shamash, Itur-Mer (god of Mari), Shamshi-Adad and Yasmah-Adad, and shall pay 31 minas of silver, (as reparation) in a capital case. 18 witnesses. Date.[22]

In a letter between a son and his biological mother, the young man complained, "Though you bore me, and his mother adopted him, you do not love me as (much) as his mother loves him."[23] From this letter, we can conclude that the parties to an adoption could have emotional bonds as well as economic ones.

Adopted children were responsible for providing financial and physical security for adoptive parents in their old age. When the parents died, the adopted heirs were obligated to bury and mourn their parents (see "Death and Burial" below).

The laws concerning adoption differed from place to place. For example, in Nuzi, land could only be transferred to a family member. Therefore, in order to sell land to a nonfamily member, the buyer was "adopted" so that he could receive his share of the inheritance. In Elam, where the king and queen were brother and sister, adoption was into "brotherhood" or "sisterhood," the latter allowing a concubine to become a family member.[24]

An unmarried woman could adopt a daughter. She had the right to permit her daughter to marry or to work as a prostitute. The adopted daughter was not a slave. Like an adopted son, she would take care of her mother in her old age.

Marriage and Sexual Relations
Reconstructing marital relationships in the ancient Near East has proved a difficult task. Generally, marriage was monogamous, even among the gods. Happy marriages flourished in ancient times; a Sumerian proverb mentioned a husband boasting that his wife had borne eight sons and was still ready to make love. Like people the world over and throughout time, ancient Mesopotamians fell deeply in love. Texts re-

ferred to ensuing depression in the case of rejection. To remedy this situation, the man or woman prayed to a god or used a magic spell. Some magic rituals came with a guarantee, promising, if the man performed it: "this woman will speak to you whenever you meet her, she will be powerless to resist and you can make love to her." In the case of lovers' quarrels, the man might also resort to charms or spells with similar claims: "with this charm she will not sleep alone; she will be loved."[25]

The law codes addressed various aspects of marriage. Legal documents were drawn to define property rights—a kind of ancient prenuptial agreement. A unique document from Ur recorded the expenses, gifts, and payments incurred by the father of the bride over a four-month period during the negotiations over the marriage of his daughter.

Customs varied over time and place, but the process of marriage included at least four stages: (1) the engagement, (2) payments by the families of both the bride (dowry) and the groom (bride-price), (3) the bride's move to her father-in-law's house, and (4) sexual intercourse.

The legal definition of marriage is found in the Laws of Eshnunna §§27–28, in which marriage included a contract as well as a feast:

> If a man marries the daughter of another man without the consent of her father and mother, and moreover does not conclude the wedding feast and contract for her father and her mother, even if she lives in his house for a full year, she is not a wife.
> If he concludes a wedding feast and a contract for her father and her mother, and he marries her, she is indeed his wife; the day she is caught lying with another man (literally, "in the lap of another man"), she shall die, she will not live.[26]

The contract described in the Laws of Eshnunna was between the two families, commonly represented by the fathers. For the groom's family, the contract concerned payment of the bride-price, which was a considerable sum of silver in the Old Babylonian period. The bride-price was an act of good faith, insuring the groom's right to the bride.

Both the bride-price and the dowry could be paid in installments until the first child was born, at which time the balance of both payments was due. The marriage was legally finalized, and the mother assumed the legal rights of a "wife."

The bride-price was equal in value to the dowry provided by the bride's family. The dowry consisted of household utensils, silver rings (a form of ancient coinage), slaves, and even fields. In addition to these items, the dowry in later periods included other household goods such as furniture, textiles, and jewelry. The bride brought her dowry with her. A husband could use his wife's property and manage it with his own assets.

Terra cotta plaque of a loving couple from Diqdiqqeh (ca. first half of the second millennium BCE). Ht. 10.5 cm. © BRITISH MUSEUM, LONDON.

In Old Babylonian times the dowry was often itemized. A document was drawn to specify that the bride's father "sent it and her into the house of A, her father-in-law, for B, his son."[27] The document concluded with the payment to be made by the groom's family in the event of divorce. If the groom died or had a change of heart, his father could insist that the bride be given to one of the groom's brothers if one were available and of age. That is, the bride married into her husband's family—she did not marry an individual.

The marriage contract was also an oral agreement, probably accompanied by formal or symbolic actions and marriage vows. The words recited at marriage can be reconstructed from the spoken formula of divorce, namely, "You are not my husband" and "You are not my wife"—that is, an annulment of words cited in a wedding described in a magical text: "I will fill your lap with silver and gold: You are my wife, I am your husband."[28]

Not much is known about the wedding ceremonies. Among wealthy families, the wedding party lasted several days or even weeks. The groom and his family customarily gave gifts to the bride and her family at the wedding celebration. These gifts included food for the wedding feast and prenuptial celebrations leading up to it. Also, gifts of clothing, jewelry, and other valuables could be added. During the wedding celebration, the bride was covered with a veil that the groom removed. Once married, women were not veiled in Babylonia. Legal texts imply that married women were veiled in Assyria.

The next step in the marriage process varied. Since girls often married young, as teenagers, the young bride might either continue to live in her father's house or move to her father-in-law's house. Assyrian texts spoke of brides who were "four half cubits high (about three feet)." Under these circumstances, consummation occurred later. The groom was usually ten years older than his bride.

Even if the bride continued to reside in her parental home, the groom could visit his father-in-law's home in order to consummate the marriage. This event was accompanied by traditional ceremonies. The bridegroom might be accompanied by a male companion, and both would reside in the father-in-law's house for a period of time. Marriage was euphemistically alluded to as "calling at the house of the in-law." In the trial record a man from Ur was described as follows: "He called at the [father-]in-law's house, he got a son and a daughter."[29] A bed, included in dowry lists, was used to consummate the marriage. There are extant terra-cotta models (some of which include a couple in the throes of passion), and royal hymns spoke of beds used for making love.

The virginity of the bride was a matter of concern. The "best men" of the bride were a group of "friends" who protected her against dangers and were responsible for her chastity.[30] After the wedding night, they displayed "the bloody sheet."

When virginity was disputed, the courts called on expert female witnesses to offer testimony. A letter from Mari described the situation of a betrothed girl: "The 'wife' of Sin-iddinam declared as follows: Before Sin-iddinam took me, I had agreed with [the wish of] father and son. When Sin-iddinam had departed from his house, the son of Asqudum sent me the message 'I want to take you.' He kissed my lips, he touched my vagina—his penis did not enter my vagina. Thus I said, 'I will not sin against Sin-iddinam.' "[31] In an earlier trial in Nippur, a man denied physical penetration using the same words. Obviously, penetration was the criterion to establish whether a woman—virgin, betrothed, married or slave—was raped or seduced, in order to determine culpability.

Incest was also addressed in the law codes. In the Laws of Hammurabi §§155–56, if a father-in-law had sex with his son's bride-to-be, the law demanded a fine of half a mina of silver, and the girl could return to her family home with her dowry and marry someone else. However, if his son had consummated the marriage and incest was committed, the father was sentenced to drowning. Other forms of incest were treated in the law codes, namely, cases of a man with his sister, his niece, his daughter, his mother-in-law, or his mother after his father's death. The last offense was considered particularly loathsome, and the punishment was to burn the mother and son.[32]

With rare exceptions, a man could not have more than one formally recognized wife at a time. Both Babylonian law codes and court proceedings indicated that only under exceptional circumstances was a man permitted to have more than one wife at the same time. For example, the Laws of Hammurabi (CH §148) allowed the husband to take a second wife when his first wife was incapacitated by illness; however, he could not divorce his first wife, whom he was obliged to support until her death. The case of the married but celibate priestess was also addressed; in this case, the second wife was often her sister. Uru-inimgina included polyandry (a woman with more than one husband) among the social abuses he chose to reform.

In Assyria a man could raise a concubine to the status of wife. The Middle Assyrian laws explained the procedure: "If a man intends to veil his concubine, he shall have five or six of his comrades, and he shall veil her in their presence, he shall declare 'She is my wife.' She is (then) his wife."[33]

The concubine was permitted to wear the veil only when she accompanied the legal wife outdoors. Her status remained secondary, and, in the event that the legal wife bore sons, the children of the concubine could not inherit. The concubine was chosen from among the slaves and was still expected to perform her duties for the legal wife, such as carrying her chair when she went to the temple and assisting her in her toiletries.

Assyrian laws detailed which classes of women must and must not be veiled. A married woman had to be veiled in public, but prostitutes were strictly forbidden from this practice. Should a prostitute be veiled, she would be severely punished by being caned fifty times and having pitch poured over her head.

Both Mesopotamia and Syria demonstrated interest in erotic art. There were handmade or molded clay figurines of naked women, as well as cylinder seals and terra-cotta or pierced metal plaques depicting various positions for sexual inter- **Sexual Practices** course. Erotic art was found in temples, tombs, and houses and may have reflected a genre somewhere between official and popular art. The art from the Amarna period (fourteenth century BCE) was rather graphic in depicting sexual intimacy and sensual pleasure. Cylinder seals with erotic scenes were not very common. Plaques illustrated a variety of subjects: squatting women spreading their legs apart with their hands; couples standing facing each other, with the woman guiding the man by holding his member with her hand; and couples having intercourse from behind. The omens also spoke of anal intercourse between a man and his wife, that is, a man "keeps saying to his wife: 'Bring your backside.' "[34] However, the most common position for sexual intercourse was the "missionary position." Another position described was the woman on top of the man, perhaps alluded to in the Amorite saying, "You be the man, let me be the woman."[35]

Anal intercourse may have been used as a means of contraception. The priestesses were said to have had anal intercourse to avoid pregnancy. Contraception was used, particularly by certain priestesses, "who by skillful ways keep their wombs intact,"[36] possibly by herbs or charms. Nevertheless, "accidents happened," and unwanted babies were left in the street to die or to be eaten by a dog. Occasionally, we learn of a passerby grabbing the child from a dog's mouth.

Some plaques depicted a woman leaning against a mud-brick tower, perhaps the town walls, where prostitutes usually lived and worked. In some tavern scenes one or more persons were shown drinking from vases or cups. The taverns, run by alewives, were houses of pleasure where men drank, listened to music, and had intercourse with prostitutes. The walls of the taproom were decorated with clay plaques of naked women or other erotic scenes. Ishtar, the goddess of love, was the patron of taverns.

There were also love lyrics and love charms, which are abundant for some periods and nonexistent for others. Love lyrics between human beings were formulated as a dialogue, often accompanied by a musical instrument. The poems were narrative, with a beginning, a middle, and an end. The songs were characterized by passionate love and sexual desire for the beloved. Themes related to marriage pervaded the poetry, such as the bridal sheets laid out on a marriage bed. The beauty of the bride was described by her natural attributes as well as her jewelry. The

Terra cotta plaque of a nude woman holding her breasts which was made from a mold. Such clay figurines were cheap replicas and part of popular art. They may have had cultic value, perhaps as household gods; some were found buried under the house. © YALE BABYLONIAN COLLECTION, YALE UNIVERSITY, NEW HAVEN.

love stories occurred at sunset or later, in the streets, squares, and homes. The poems incorporated all the senses: touch, smell, sight, taste, and hearing. The metaphors used, the apple tree and the pillar of alabaster, which may rise in a garden or stone, referred to the male and female sexual organs, respectively. Incantations praised the qualities of the genitals but demonstrated little interest in breasts.

Texts spoke of women menstruating for six days as "hit by the weapon."[37] During this time, women were considered unclean and released from work. A man who touched a menstruating woman was also regarded as unclean for six days.

Men sometimes suffered from sexual dysfunctions such as impotence and premature ejaculation. To help reverse impotence, a group of rituals was performed and various medicinal preparations, including ointments and aphrodisiacs, were used. Though alluded to, no treatment for premature ejaculation was mentioned; perhaps the ancients believed that time and practice would eventually provide a cure.

Male homosexuality was described from the third millennium BCE onward in Mesopotamia. Texts referred to sodomy between men as well as between men and boys. The Babylonians did not condemn this practice. But male prostitutes were either despised or considered laughable. Homosexual acts were never clearly depicted in visual art, with the possible exception of cylinder seals in which the gender of the protagonists is questionable. However, the Assyrians did not follow the Babylonian policy of "live-and-let-live" in regard to homosexual practices. During the Middle Assyrian period (ca. 1300–1100 BCE), homosexuality was severely punished. According to the Middle Assyrian laws: "If a man sodomizes his comrade and they prove the charges against him and find him guilty, they shall sodomize him and they shall turn him into a eunuch [that is, castrate him]."[38]

Lesbianism was seldom mentioned. The women of ancient Mesopotamia seemed much more interested in taking male lovers. The Code of Hammurabi described a wife who took a lover, whom she encouraged to murder her husband so that the lovers would be free to marry. In this case, the wife was punished by impaling her.[39] If the cuckolded husband caught the lovers, he could bring them up on charges before either the king or judges. If the couple was found guilty, Middle Assyrian law provided for several courses of punishment: "If the woman's husband kills his wife, then he shall also kill the man; if he cuts off his wife's nose, he shall turn the man into a eunuch and they shall lacerate his entire face; but if [the husband wishes to release] his wife, he shall [release] the man."[40]

Eunuchs ("those not having a beard") were quite common, but a man who became a eunuch as a punishment was exceptional. Eunuchs served at court, and many of them became high officials—an administrative practice that continued up to the nineteenth century CE in the Turkish and Persian empires. However, not all Assyrian courtiers were eunuchs, a point emphasized by a list of courtiers that included both eunuchs and non-eunuchs. In Assyria, as elsewhere, a small proportion of males failed to develop normally and became natural eunuchs; many of them were possibly male prostitutes.

The Mesopotamians recognized that sex had a religious component. There were religious prostitutes—male, female, and neuter—associated with some temples. Reference to temple sexual activity was more common for Babylonia than for Assyria. Although male prostitutes were often eunuchs, this was not always the case. Certain priests in the cult of Ishtar were homosexuals; they were also accomplished in dancing and cross dressing. The ancient Mesopotamians' problem with homosexuals and prostitutes stemmed from the fact that they did not have children (prostitutes appear to have had an understanding of birth control).

Divorce   Divorce usually was initiated by the husband. He could divorce his wife, but he had to return her property and sometimes pay a fine. The divorce was accompanied by the symbolic act of cutting the hem of the wife's robe—the reverse of knotting the original bride-payment in her robe.

Social stigma was attached to divorce, therefore, it was not undertaken without grave cause, such as adultery by the wife or a childless marriage. Many Old Babylonian marriage contracts forbade the wife to divorce her husband, often by threatening her with penalties customary for adultery: drowning in the river, being pushed from a tower, or impalement. The wife could even be sold into slavery. Also, at various times in ancient Mesopotamia, if a woman expressed the desire to divorce, she could be thrown out of her husband's home penniless and naked. The conditions of the divorce were influenced by whether or not the wife had sons. If the woman had no sons, the husband's family did not care if she returned to her father's house or went elsewhere. However, some agreements and Assyrian and Babylonian marriage contracts permitted either the husband or the wife to divorce; each was fined the same amount in silver. This arrangement contrasted markedly with the inferior position of women under Middle Assyrian law. It seems that the status and independence of specific women gave them equal rights in the marriage; possibly these women were independent widows or the daughters of rich families.

Since marriage was treated as a bond between families, its purpose was to secure sons to perpetuate the male line, but an infertile marriage did not result in an automatic divorce. Both law and custom allowed a barren wife to supply a slave-girl as her surrogate to bear children, who were legally considered the wife's children. Another arrangement permitted the childless wife to adopt a second woman as her sister and permit that woman to marry her husband. The exact same principles of law were applied to a priestess, who was permitted to marry but not to have sexual relations with her husband; she, too, could provide a surrogate to bear sons.

In Assyria, if a woman's husband abandoned her, did not support her, or left no sons who could support her, she could take another husband after five years. Her first husband could not reclaim her. If a woman did not wait for the five-year period to elapse, but went to live with a man and bore him children, her husband could return and take her children on his return. However, if the first husband was absent for reasons beyond his control, such as being captured, he could reclaim his wife after the five-year period. He then had to provide the second husband with a replacement.

We know a great deal about beliefs concerning death and the afterlife in ancient Mesopotamia. Numerous sources described their funeral and mourning practices, the cult of the dead, burial practices, funerary offerings, visits from ghosts, the organization of the netherworld, and causes of death.

Death and Burial

Many literary texts struggled with the meaning of death and dealt with the fortunes of the dead in the netherworld. Surprisingly, creation myths generally excluded the institution of death. In a later version of *Gilgamesh*, Uta-napishtim (the Babylonian Noah) advised Gilgamesh about death:

> No one can see death.
> No one can see the face of death.
> No one [can hear] the voice of death.
> But savage death snaps off mankind . . .
> Suddenly there is nothing.
>
> They (the gods) established life and death.
> Death they fixed to have no ending.[41]

In both *Gilgamesh* (the epic of a hero-king) and *Atra-khasis* (the Babylonian Flood Story) the gods created death. The gods solved the problem of overpopulation through sterility, miscarriage, and religious celibacy.

Death was not the end. Man had a soul or ghost, which he inherited from the slain god whose body was used in creating man. When man was accorded traditional burial rites, he could descend to the kingdom of the dead below the earth, the lowest realm of the universe.

The ancient Mesopotamians did not speak of death for fear of summoning it. Instead, they referred to death by using a host of euphemisms: "to cross the Khubur"; "to go up to/toward heaven" (meant only for kings of the Third Dynasty of Ur); "to go to one's fate"; "to be invited by one's gods"; "to come to land on/reach/take refuge in one's mountain"; "to go on the road of one's forefathers."[42] The Mesopotamians' practice was not so different from our own; we refer to death by terms such as "passed away," "no longer with us," "may he/she rest in peace," and so on. All things said and done, the ancient Mesopotamians accepted death as a fact of life.

In ancient times (as today), a person preferred to die in his own bed, surrounded by his loved ones. The dying person was moved to a special funerary bed with a chair placed at the left. A specific formula was recited to release the soul from its body, and the chair served as a seat for the soul. The soul received its first funerary offerings on the chair.

In order to prepare it for burial, the body was washed and the mouth tied shut. The corpse was anointed with oil or perfume, clothed in clean garments, and accompanied by as many personal items as the family could afford—weapons, toiletries, jewelry, and other objects. Most bodies were simply buried without being preserved for eternity. The body and grave goods were laid out for public viewing (the Mesopotamian version of a wake) shortly before the funeral. Of course, members of the royal family were expected to provide lavish funeral displays.

The dead were buried in a coffin, sarcophagus, or tomb. The poor were wrapped in a cloth or reed mat and provided with a few simple pottery vessels, stone beads, a copper pin, or the like. Kings and wealthy commoners buried their dead in individual or communal vaulted chambers built below the floors of the palace or house. The sarcophagi of kings were often impressive. Family members and servants who died at home were interred in the family crypt, older bodies being pushed aside to make room for new bodies. Other families buried their dead in public cemeteries. Those who carried the body to its final resting place were paid. Burial officials were also compensated with first rights to the funerary bed and chair and the clothing in which the person died (which was removed when the body was washed). The edicts of reforming kings such as Uru-inimgina (ca. 2350 BCE) tried to ensure that the amounts charged for such services were not excessive.

After burial, mourning rites could last as long as seven days for a prominent person. Both relatives and close friends were supposed to display their grief openly. For the death of the king, queen, or queen mother, the subjects mourned publicly. Professional mourners, both male and female, were hired to increase the number of mourners and to lead the laments. Sometimes prostitutes were recruited for this service. Laments could be sung a cappella or accompanied by a musical instrument, or even the rhythmic beating of the breast. A few funeral laments have been found expressing grief and eulogizing the dead, as in *The Epic of Gilgamesh*:

> Hear me, O Elders of Uruk, hear me, O men!
> I mourn for Enkidu, my friend,

> I cry out bitterly like a mourner . . .
> an evil demon appeared and took him away from me!
> My friend, the swift mule, fleet wild ass of the mountain, panther
>   of the wilderness . . .
> Now what is this sleep which has seized you?
> You have turned dark and do not hear me.[43]

Mourning rites were not meant to end prematurely. The so-called Babylonian Job complained, "The grave is open, my jewelry is ready (to be placed in the grave); before I had died, the wailing (for me) was finished."[44]

Mourners also expressed their grief in the way they dressed. They were expected to remove their finery, tear their garments or clothe themselves in sackcloth, take off their turbans or cover their heads with their clothes, and move about unbathed and ungroomed. Fasting was another expression of grief. The ancient Mesopotamians accepted men openly displaying their sorrow, but only women tore out their hair or scratched their cheeks and breasts. Once the dead were interred, the official mourning period drew to a close, marked by purification ceremonies and a return to normal dress and grooming habits.

The ceremonial rites for mourning for Ishtar's spouse, Tammuz/Dumuzi (as for other dying and returning fertility gods), were described in detail in myths and cult songs meant to accompany rituals. During the ceremonial mourning for Dumuzi some vessels used for offerings to the deceased were broken, torches were carried around the funeral bed three times, and incense was burned.[45] These rites were performed in order to protect the living from contamination by the dead. Niches for funeral lamps were found in graves at various sites. The tombs of high-status individuals also contained a niche where an engraved funerary inscription was placed.

The dead depended on living relatives to provide them with funerary offerings. The eldest son of the deceased was primarily responsible for providing a continuous series of funerary offerings, perhaps an explanation of why he received an additional share of the inheritance. Offerings to kings corresponded to the deluxe menus they enjoyed on earth; these offerings were made at the new and full moon, and at an extended celebration during the month of Abu (July/August). War heroes received special offerings associated with the royal cult; they were portrayed as relaxing on couches while served by their family. Stillborn children were described as playing "on a table of gold and silver with honey and flowing beer."[46] Shrines were dedicated to their collective spirit.

In the royal cult, all ancestors of the reigning king received individual offerings regularly. But ordinary people provided individual offerings to those relatives they knew personally, such as their fathers, mothers, brothers, sisters, grandfathers, and grandmothers. More distant relatives were lumped together as a common ancestor. A few legal texts, from Susa of the Old Babylonian period (1900–1595 BCE) and from Nippur of the Middle Babylonian period (1595–1000 BCE), specifically required a woman to perform rites of the ancestors' cult. The family ghosts of ordinary people received cold water, bread, hot broth, beer flavored with roasted grain, flour, oil, wine, honey, and occasionally the rib section of a sacrificed animal. The food was set at the place of burial, and liquids were poured through a pipe in the earth. To ensure that the intended ghosts received the offerings, the names of the dead were called. Sometimes a statue of the deceased housed his spirit for offerings. Ghosts were usually helpful, often intervening on behalf of family members. But if the deceased were neither buried nor accorded the proper funerary rites, their ghosts were considered dangerous.

Several times a year ghosts were permitted to leave their homes in the netherworld and return to earth for brief visits. At the end of *Ishtar's Descent to the Netherworld*, Dumuzi was said to return during his festivities in Du'zu (June/July), and there was also a general return of the dead in Abu (July/August). During these celebrations, the ghosts were wined and dined. Then they returned by a special river road to the netherworld on boats, which floated down the river.

During life in the upper world, the gods were able to control population growth, but in the realm of the dead, the population always increased. The netherworld was called "earth," "great earth," and "extensive earth." It was also the "land of no return."[47] There were two traditions explaining how humans entered the netherworld. According to one tradition, the road to the netherworld passed through the demon-infested steppe land, across the Khubur River, and then through seven gates with seven gatekeepers. Another version described a road to the netherworld crossed by boat down one of the rivers of the upper earth and across the *apsû* (the sweet waters under the earth) to the lower earth, where Ereshkigal, queen of the dead, ruled. The latter road was taken by the dead returning home from their annual visits with their families, by babies about to be born, and by the occasional demon. Situated in the bowels of the earth, the netherworld was described as a dreary place:

> To the gloomy house, seat of the netherworld,
> To the house which none leaves who enters,
> To the road whose journey has no return,
> To the house whose entrants are bereft of light,
> Where dust is their sustenance and clay their food.
> They see no light but dwell in darkness,
> They are clothed like birds in wings for garments,
> And dust has gathered on the door and bolt.[48]

Despite this paradigm, the dead were not always gloomy, because Shamash (the sun god) visited daily on his travels through the sky. Also, the inhabitants were not reduced to eating mud; rather, they imitated life above: eating bread and drinking clear water. A complex bureaucracy similar to that of the upper world governed below. There was a royal court, presided over by King Nergal and Queen Ereshkigal, who were outfitted in royal regalia and lived in a lapis lazuli palace.

The bureaucracy of the netherworld was described in great detail, particularly in the dream of Kumma, in which he visited the netherworld, where he met many members of the bureaucracy, some described as half-man and half-animal. The Anunnaki, the court of the netherworld, welcomed each ghost, taught him the rules of the netherworld, and assigned him a place there. The female scribe of the netherworld checked the names of the newcomers against a master list so that no unexpected visitors from the upper world arrived.

Besides the court of the Anunnaki, there were two other courts of the netherworld. Gilgamesh, the legendary king of Uruk, presided over one court; however, we know little about it. The sun god Shamash presided over the other court in his daily rounds. In effect, the circuit of the sun god allowed him jurisdiction in both the upper and lower worlds. Shamash decided problems between the living and dead, such as punishing ghosts who harassed the living and ensuring that lonely and forgotten ghosts got their fair share of funerary offerings.

The netherworld courts did not render a Last Judgment as in the Christian tradition. In fact, neither the dead man's virtues nor sins on earth were considered when assigning him a place. The worst punishment dispensed to a sinner was denial of entry by the gods of the netherworld. In this way, the sinner was sentenced to sleeplessness and denied access to funerary offerings. Foreigners were permitted to enter the Mesopotamian netherworld. Lepers were allowed entrance, but they were kept safely apart from the rest of the dead.

The rate of death resulting from childbirth remains unknown. Infants were buried in jars beneath the living-room floor. At Nuzi a jar containing the remains of an infant burial was found under a private home; the jar was in the shape of a breast—a poignant memorial. Abnormal pregnancies, maldevelopment of the infant, and gross physical abnormalities of the fetus resulted in the death of mother and child. The live birth rate must have exceeded the death rate since enough children survived to maintain the population, and, in fact, from the fourth millennium BCE onward, the populations grew. In the third millennium BCE, Mesopotamia and Egypt each had a population of approximately one million; the life expectancy (with rare exceptions) was approximately forty years. Since death usually occurred at an early age in antiquity, diseases associated with old age were rare.

Those who survived the physical dangers of early childhood could expect to enjoy a relatively long life. A late text reflected that for man the age of forty years was "prime"; of fifty, as "a short time" (in case he dies that young); sixty, as "manhood"; seventy, as "a long time"; eighty, as "old age"; and ninety, as "extreme old age." In a wisdom text from the Syrian city of Emar, the gods allotted man a maximum lifetime of 120 years.[49] To see one's family in the fourth generation was considered the ultimate blessing of extreme old age. Surprisingly, a number of people actually reached extreme old age. Several kings had long reigns, such as Shulgi of Ur (48 years), Hammurabi of Babylon (43 years), and Assurbanipal of Assyria (42 years). We know that the mother of King Nabonidus lived for 104 years—she told us so in her autobiography. Archives have shown that some individuals lived at least seventy years.

Battle casualties were the major cause of death among adult males. Those captured on military campaigns most probably died of exhaustion and maltreatment. Those who managed to escape from their victors died of exposure, hunger, and thirst. The people besieged within their cities suffered from disease and starvation, sometimes resorting to cannibalism.

"Acts of God," such as flood, drought, famine, or plagues of locusts, affected entire communities. Floods were generally local but extremely destructive, causing a high death rate. Locusts involved wider areas of land, starving both men and animals.

Several infectious diseases were so severe that clinical patterns were observed by the ancients. Diseases that caused a high mortality rate were (1) tuberculosis (ca. second millennium BCE); (2) pneumonic and bubonic plague, the most lethal diseases to infect man; (3) typhus, particularly the human louse-borne type of disease, often associated with famine, filth, and other disabling conditions in war; (4) smallpox, probably a mutant of cowpox virus affecting domestic cattle; and (5) leprosy, which was rarer and less infective but more chronic.

Southern Mesopotamia was the most heavily populated area of Mesopotamia, and therefore more conducive to the outbreak of epidemics, such as bubonic plague. The word for epidemic disease in Akkadian literally meant "certain death" and could be applied equally to animal as well as human epidemics. An omen reported plague gods marching with the troops, most likely a reference to typhus, which often afflicted armies. Tablets reported cities and even whole countries which were struck by some fatal epidemic, sometimes lasting years. An Akkadian myth, *Erra*, was written as a result of a plague at Babylon; the myth was believed to ward off further attacks when hung on the wall of the house. Old Babylonian letters described performing rituals, avoiding crowds, and purifying cities once the god had "calmed down."

The diseases caused by viruses were first reported in the second millennium BCE. These viruses may have infected their animal hosts earlier; however, in the second millennium, the increasing density of urban populations and the close contact between domestic animals and man gave rise to two strains of diseases, one in man and one in animals.

PROPERTY AND SUCCESSION

Each city followed different customs concerning inheritance. Generally, the eldest son was favored in the following ways: (1) he might receive two shares instead of one; (2) he might be allocated an extra agreed-upon proportion of the total estate, at least 10 percent; and (3) he might be allowed to choose his share, while the others drew lots.[50] The estate was physically divided after the father's death so that the married brothers would be able to set up independent households.

The eldest son may also have inherited the family home because of his duties, since in some places and periods the building housed ancestral tombs beneath it. From Early Dynastic times through the Old Babylonian period, the dead were commonly buried within the house. Separate cemeteries existed both inside and outside the city. An Old Babylonian document described the division of household property, the eldest son receiving "a share, together with the shrine." Some inheritance documents have informed us that the eldest son regularly received the "offering-table of the shrine." At Ur houses had separate rooms designed as shrines, identified with the baked brick family vault.

Though the eldest son often received a larger share of the inheritance, often real estate was not divided in order to conserve the revenue. In ancient Sumer, the custom was to leave the estate undivided; all became the property of the eldest son, who was the designated heir and leader of the family. The eldest son was obligated to support all of his siblings.

Usually the eldest son inherited certain entitlements. For example, at Nippur, the heir received temple offices, and he usually had first claim on the family residence. In later periods all of the brothers divided the estate equally, but the eldest son received an additional share. In Old Babylonian times, documents described in detail how property rights remained within the nuclear family. When the head of the household died, the brothers divided the estate. Family members could remain in the house after the father's death, but the actual division of the rooms might be postponed until much later, sometimes until the grandchildren divided the house among their families.

If the house was large enough to accommodate the brothers separately, it was divided. Mesopotamian inheritance laws often resulted in subdividing a single home into many smaller units. Mud brick was used to block old doorways, and new doorways were cut where necessary. When a house was inherited (or sold), the rooms were counted and their area measured ("roofed floor space").[51] Beams and doors were considered a valuable part of the house; specific doors have been listed in sale or inheritance texts.

The custom of giving a preferred share to the eldest son was prevalent in southern Babylonia; elsewhere, the brothers divided equally. Many house-sale documents of Old Babylonian times were merely "paper transactions" in order to provide compensation for the transfer of ownership of very small parts of the family home which could not in practice be occupied. Elizabeth Stone, a historical archaeologist, working with textual, architectural, and ethnographic data, established residential patterns in Old Babylonian Nippur.[52] She correlated information in the cuneiform texts with actual houses and rooms that had been excavated.

The division of the paternal estates among the heirs was recorded in inheritance documents. Land, houses, furniture, slaves, animals, and also religious and military duties were divided. An Old Babylonian document from Nippur itemized the division of goods and duties, ending with the following clause: "The heirs of Imgua of their free will divided by lot and swore by the name of the king not to raise claims against one another in future."[53] In some cases, daughters could inherit, and then daughters were treated legally as sons. However, this practice has been attested in fringe areas, such as Nuzi and Emar, not in Babylonia and Assyria.

According to the patrilinear system, property was divided among sons or the surviving male line. The children of a dead brother also inherited. Nasty uncles were sometimes libelous in casting slurs on the paternity of a baby born posthumously. In the following case, the boy's uncles questioned his paternity once he was old enough to lay claim to his inheritance:

Ninurta-ra'im-zerim, the son of Enlil-bani, approached the (court) and faced the court officials and judges of Nippur, (and testified): "When I was still in the womb of Sin-na'id, my mother, Enlil-bani my father, the son of Ahi-shagish, died. Before (my mother) gave birth Khabannatum, my paternal grandmother, informed Luga, the herdsman, and Sin-gamil, the judge, (and) she sent a midwife and (the midwife) delivered me. When I grew up, in 20th year of Samsu-iluna . . . (his uncles attempt to question his paternity) . . ." The court officials and the judges investigated the case. They read the earlier tablet with the oath. They questioned their witnesses, and discussed their testimony . . . The witnesses who knew the paternity of Ninurta-ra'im-zerim, affirmed (it) by oath and they (the judges) ordered the case brought back to the assembly.

(Witnesses testified:) "Until she (Sin-nada) gave birth, they (the mother-in-law, the herdsman, the midwife and the judge) looked after her. We know that Ninurta-ra'im-zerim is the offspring of Enlil-bani."[54]

Such procedures suggested that the birth of important people was witnessed. There were also tablets with baby footprints, indicating their paternity, and the seal of the witness.

Wills were written prior to the father's death, a practice found in Old Assyrian documents and outlying areas. These wills preserved the rights of the eldest son but also made allowances for separate bequests. A father could disinherit either an adopted or a natural son; the mother could have the same paternal authority upon the death of her husband. Disinheritance was a unilateral act, but the court had to ratify this action for legal purposes. The court could moderate or rescind a father's action if the father acted either in haste or unfairly. If a child said to his parents, "You are not my father" or "not my mother," he could be thrown out of his family home and disinherited.

The head of the household could also present gifts during his lifetime which were not included in the division of the estate. This provision was important for daughters who needed an appropriate dowry. If the father died before the dowry was arranged, the sons were obligated to allocate part of the estate for their sisters. A widow did not inherit from her husband's estate if there were sons. However, her husband could separate some of his property to provide for his wife when he died.

The widow gained access to her dowry once her husband died. If she had no children, her dowry would become the property of her brothers and their descendants. A widow could continue her husband's business by herself. But if she remarried, she lost this right. Contracts from Emar described a woman leaving to remarry, by performing a symbolic act, "to place her clothes on a stool"; then she left without her possessions. When a woman died, her dowry was inherited by her biological children, both male and female. If she had no children, her dowry was returned to the estate of her brothers and their descendants.

The dowry a woman brought increased the estate of her husband, particularly in land or slaves. However, her marriage reduced the estate of her own family. This situation could be remedied by marrying within the family or by other manipulations, as in the case of Lurindu. She married a much older man, a childless widower. Because she could potentially bear children, her family was able to give a smaller dowry. Sometimes a man married his brother's widow in order to keep her dowry in the family.

When a girl became a priestess, the brothers had to support her. Her brothers managed her property, and, upon her death, her brothers or descendants would inherit it. In this way, estates could be conserved. However, sometimes priestesses adopted another priestess or slave and chose to leave their property to their adopted daughters—a situation that led to much litigation.

The extended family was more involved in joint ventures the further back we go in time. The family cultivated the land jointly rather than dividing and fragmenting their property—a practice still maintained today in rural communities throughout the world, so that successive generations do not inherit impractically small plots of land.

The hereditary system functioned in another way. Usually a son learned his father's trade or profession by observing and helping at an early age. He was able to take over his father's position in due time, as a scribe, an artisan, and so on. Current research has shown that the Old Babylonian buildings where the school texts were discovered were actually private houses. The schoolmaster lived there with his family and taught his sons his art at home. Some scribal families can be traced through several generations. Children were also apprenticed to craftsmen; apprenticeship contracts stipulate the responsibilities of both parties. An artisan would take a boy (often a slave) into his house and teach him his profession: cook, carpenter, singer, or seal cutter, for example.

WOMEN'S ROLES

Women's social status was similar to men's. But women were never the legal equal to men. The position of women was generally higher in the early Sumerian city-state because of the importance of goddesses in the Sumerian religion. Later, in Mesopotamia, when Sargon (2334–2279 BCE), the Akkadian king, rose to power, the Akkadians took part in Sumerian religious observances. To ensure religious legitimacy, Sargon was the first king in a long line of monarchs to appoint his daughter, Enkheduanna, as high priestess of the moon god, Nanna, at Ur. Enkheduanna was a highly accomplished poet.

The kings of the Ur III Dynasty (2112–2004 BCE) were praised by the songs of their royal women. Female scribes have been identified as the authors of lullabies for the crown prince, long songs to the king, and even laments. Though scribes were usually men, there were women scribes in Old Babylonian Sippar and Mari. Some were even the daughters of scribes. At Sippar, female scribes worked at the cloister, which also functioned as an economic institution of that city. These women scribes recorded the transactions of the members of the cloister. From Mari, we know the names of at least ten female scribes. Nine of them were slaves; they received small rations, indicating the low regard in which they were held. Slaves with scribal skills were sometimes given to princesses as part of their dowries.

Only one fragment of an Old Babylonian vocabulary text lists female scribes as scholars. There were female counterparts to diviners, physicians, performers, and artists. But, once again, their activities were eclipsed by males in the same jobs.

In the second millennium BCE free women at Nuzi, a Mesopotamian provincial town, played an active role in the economy and in the courts. Though women were not always allowed to participate in the economic spheres, once they participated, they took part in the same range of business transactions as men, ensuring their legal equality with men. Women could acquire land by purchase, inheritance, and royal grant. The real estate ranged in size from simple rural structures to complex urban structures to extensive agricultural estates. In one instance, a free woman owned land in at least six towns. Women sued and were sued regarding the title and ownership of land. The inclusion of free women at Nuzi in real estate transactions was particularly important because ownership of property at Nuzi was the path to power and wealth.

Women had less control of commercial life despite their legal parity with men. A woman could take part in business with her husband's permission. Women also became involved in economic activities when men were not available. That is, widows, particularly those responsible for minor children, could inherit, become head of the surviving family, and administer the family estate. Though loans could be given interest-free, women usually charged interest when they lent silver.

Women had little control over the management of either real estate or slaves. A woman's dowry became part of the estate of her in-laws and was managed by the head of the house, that is, the father or the eldest son. Therefore women used loans as an opportunity for financial gain. Women from wealthy families received additional sums of silver or precious metal as part of their dowry; they then made a profit for themselves on this capital by separate investments. The property a woman accumulated on her own was referred to as in her "hand," "tied in the corner of her garment," or "in her basket"—different expressions used through time.[55] The surviving wife was called "wife of So-and-so." The term "widow" in Mesopotamia was reserved for destitute women and their children, called "orphans."[56]

Women could serve in various temple jobs, such as priestesses. These were mostly very wealthy young women, including even a princess! They lived in cloisters and were forbidden to marry. Only priestesses of Shamash (the sun god) were permitted to marry, but they did not have children. Some women became temple prostitutes. Orphans and illegitimate children, both boys and girls, wound up in the temples, possibly exploited by the practice of temple prostitution, described in graphic terms by Herodotus. The cloister was also staffed by managers, officials, scribes, laborers, and personal female slaves. The most famous cloister was in Sippar.

Cloisters were an Old Babylonian institution. When the priestess entered the cloister, she received her dowry, which consisted of real estate and movable property, notably "ring money," which included a coil of silver and other jewelry. Wealthy families sent one daughter with a sizable dowry (typically including houses, fields, orchards, and household slaves) to a cloister to pray on behalf of her family, as a young priestess explained in a letter to her family: "At morning and evening offering I always pray before my Lord and my Mistress for your health. I have heard of your illness, and I am worried. May my Lord and my Mistress not fail to protect you on the right hand and on the left! Every day, at the light, I pray for you before the Queen of Sippar."[57]

The priestesses were supported in part by contributions from their brothers. The brothers managed the property, and, upon the priestess' death, her property reverted to the brothers or their descendants. In this way, estates were conserved. Only the priestesses of Marduk (the patron god of Babylon) were permitted to keep their dowries, and their brothers could not lay claim to their estates. Priestesses took part in a variety of business activities, such as buying, selling, and leasing fields. These business ventures were funded by their "ring money." The profits might be willed either to the brothers of the priestess or to a faithful slave, who might be emancipated with the proviso that the slave take care of the priestess in her old age and perform the proper burial rites. Many tablets recorded the business activities of the priestesses, who proved to be excellent businesswomen.

In a hymn, the goddess Gula (the patron goddess of doctors and healing) described the stages of a woman's life: "I am a daughter, I am a bride, I am a spouse, I am a housekeeper."[58] In other words, women were never completely independent from men in the roles they played in their lifetime.

In ancient Mesopotamia the most important role of a woman in marriage was to bear children, particularly sons, who were preferred as heirs. Women who bore no children were in a difficult position. When the husband predeceased his wife and left no will, the widow was permitted to continue to live in his house and to be supported by his children. However, if she had children with a previous husband, the children of her second marriage could return the widow to the children of her first marriage. The lack of regard for the widow's situation was stated in the Middle Assyrian law: "She shall go wherever she pleases."[59] The Middle Assyrian law code allowed widows the freedom to cohabit with a man without a marriage contract; however, after two years, the

widow would legally become a wife despite the lack of a marriage contract. At Asshur a long tablet of Middle Assyrian laws has fifty-nine
clauses concerned with matters related to women.

Few references have been found to women outside the patrilinear
household. Widows and orphans were protected by the charity of a
righteous ruler. Prostitution was an option, and prostitutes were found
in public places in the city—the tavern, the harbor, or under the city
wall. Prostitutes dressed to attract business, wearing a special type of
leather jacket. They were forbidden by law to wear a veil outdoors, as
respectable married women did. An Assyrian text described a prostitute
having to untie her undergarment to prepare herself for clients. As in
the classical world, the whore was often pictured as leaning out of a
window. Alewives were also a part of city life, but whether these women
were considered "respectable" remains unclear.

FASHIONS

Clothing was worn throughout western Asia for modesty
and for protection against the elements. The main sources of   **Clothing**
information have been sculptures, bas-reliefs, and cylinder
seals. Unfortunately, their colors are no longer visible. The first information about clothing and grooming appeared at the end of the fourth
millennium BCE with the advent of sculpture and writing, where rich
and powerful men were usually depicted more often than women and
children.

We do not know much about clothing before the development of
sculpture and writing ca. 3300 BCE. Before the invention of textiles, sheepskins, goatskins, and fleeces were worn, as depicted in Sumerian cultic
art. Sheep were sheared or plucked for their wool. Goat's hair was also
used. Men wore a belted sheepskin which hung down above the ankles.
Women wore a toga-like garment, sometimes secured by a pin from
which hung a string of beads or a seal.

The materials used to make clothing were the same throughout the
ancient world. Though leather was used in early times, the most common
material for clothing was wool. Linen was used for better garments or
for clothing for priests and statues of the gods. Felt made of low-quality
wool or goat hair was used for shoes, linings, and cushions. Cotton for
clothing did not become available until Sennacherib introduced it into
Assyria ca. 700 BCE. Silk was introduced later. There is evidence that the
warp-weighted vertical loom, which was able to produce a tapestry
weave, was in use by the third millennium BCE.

The manufacture of textiles became a major industry. Letters from numerous sites of the eighteenth century BCE, particularly from Mari, have
provided information about the use of dyes, reversible fabrics, and

clothes stitched with appliqués, tiny beads, or embroidery. The famous dye produced from Maoris shells, called Tyrian purple, was produced before 1200 BCE at Ugarit, where piles of shells were found. At the royal tombs at Nimrud (eighth century BCE) gold appliqués have been discovered. Textiles were traded and given as royal gifts.

In the Old Akkadian period (ca. 2330–2193 BCE) male fashions changed; instead of being bare from the waist up, men began to wear robes draped over one shoulder. Pleated and draped material was used for robes and men's kilts. Waterproof sheepskins were replaced by wool textiles in soft folds, with intricately knotted fringes at the hems and edges. In mountainous regions they wore shoes with upturned toes. Women's fashions also began to change. Though they continued to wear a toga-like garment wrapped around the body, the material was sometimes draped over both shoulders to form a V-shaped neckline. Short-sleeved dresses, some with rounded necklines, were introduced.

During the Neo-Sumerian and Old Babylonian periods (1900–1595 BCE), styles for men and women remained the same, with minor variations. Men continued to wear robes, but the ends and hems of their garments became more elaborate. The fringes of robes were sometimes impressed on contracts instead of a seal. From about 1400 BCE on, both Assyrian men and women wore fringed bolts of cloth wrapped around the body and held in place by a belt, with the long, tasseled ends hanging down between the wearer's legs. Kilts were also worn, sometimes under robes.

But by the first millennium BCE, fashions had changed. Assyria has provided two sources of information about clothing. The main source comes from art objects, such as sculptures, bas-reliefs, plaques, carved ivories, and cylinder seals. Lexical texts also catalogued many words relating to clothing. The texts listed many different qualities of textiles, from cheap materials for servants to those worn by royalty.

Men wore a tunic or several fitted tunics; these garments were short-sleeved and belted at the waist and covered men from their necks to their knees. Sometimes the upper part of the tunic had straps running diagonally from each shoulder and crossing the chest. People of higher status, such as officials and military officers, added a cloak to this outfit. In fact, the royal harem edicts stated that if a courtier were negligent, he would be stripped of his cloak—clearly a status symbol.[60] The cloak was usually made of wool, or sometimes linen, in blue, red, purple, and white. There was an over-garment apart from the cloak, which had no armholes and was put on over the neck.

The Assyrians were usually barefoot, even when they went to war. When they wore footwear, they usually wore sandals with a wedge heel and straps over the top of the foot and around the big toe. Sometimes more elaborate footwear was depicted, such as calf-length boots (worn by hunters or warriors) or shoes covering the whole foot. We know less about women's footwear, although Assurbanipal's queen was shown wearing a kind of slipper, covering the front half of the foot.

Prisoners of war were often naked. The Assyrians stripped whole groups of the population during campaigns. One text described a conquered population as so impoverished that they wore garments made of papyrus, the ancient equivalent of paper.

With the fall of Babylon to the Persian king Cyrus (539 BCE), the people of western Asia wore the fashion of the conquerors—a clothing tradition based on pants.

Men were usually shaved bald, but some wore their hair longer. During the Early Dynastic period (2900–2350 BCE) women's hairstyles and headdresses showed great variety. The hair was worn long, but elaborately plaited **Hairstyles and Headgear** and piled on top of the head, held in place either by a net or a scarf, or covered with a pleated headdress. The women also wore jewelry in their hair.

Excavations at the Royal Cemetery at Ur, ca. 2600 BCE, have shown women wearing strands of gold willow leaves with beads of lapis lazuli, carnelian, and gold in their hair. Their hair nets were of gold ribbon and their hairpins silver, with large blue (lapis lazuli) and red (limestone) flowers. Also, the women wore gold and silver hair ribbons, but one woman had her hair ribbon rolled up—obviously, she did not have time to put on a ribbon for her own funeral. These elaborate hairstyles may have affected the men's hairdos. A gold helmet from the Royal Cemetery was decorated with a thick metal braid wrapped around the head and coiled in a chignon at the nape of the neck. This was the hairstyle of royalty and was later worn by King Sargon.

In the Old Akkadian period, men were either shaved bald or wore their hair and beards meticulously waved. Women's hair was styled into a large chignon from the top of the head to the beginning of the neck. Women also used hair bands, hair nets, and hairpins made of bone, copper, silver, or gold. During the Neo-Sumerian and Old Babylonian periods both men and women continued to style their hair as before.

In Assyrian reliefs, men were depicted with a full beard and mustache, waved and curled at the ends. Priests, doctors, and slaves wore distinctive hairstyles. Greying hair was treated by a lotion and an incantation. Gods, royalty, soldiers, and religious personnel wore headdresses associated with their status or ceremonial functions.

Objects made of gems and precious metals were used as decoration in life and at death. Jewelry was worn by men, women, **Jewelry** and children and even decorated the garments of divine images and statues. Artistic representations show us how jewelry was worn at different times, the styles, and who wore them. Also, Sumerian and

Akkadian texts have provided abundant information on jewelry and jewelers' workshops. Literary texts, as, for instance, the Sumerian myth of Inanna and Dumuzi, described the goddess of love preparing for her bridegroom by bathing, perfuming herself, combing her hair, and putting on clothes and jewelry:

> Rings of gold
>   I put on my hands,
> little stone beads
>   I hung around my neck,
> straightened their counterbalance.[61]

Jewelry was exchanged as gifts between rulers, provided as wedding gifts and inheritances, and included in dowries. The tablets also recorded precious metals (but rarely jewelry) taken as booty during military campaigns.

Perhaps the most important source of information on Mesopotamian jewelry is the Royal Cemetery of Ur. Here, hundreds of burials, mostly dating to the Early Dynastic period (2900–2350 BCE), were unearthed by Sir Leonard Woolley. A group of sixteen tombs contained a lavish display of jewelry, weapons, and vessels made of precious metals, musical instruments, and other decorative art objects. Some of the most impressive objects were the contents of the undisturbed tomb of "Queen" Puabi. Next to Puabi's body was a lapis lazuli beaded crown with gold figures of animals, fruits, and flowers. Necklaces made from beads of gold, silver, lapis lazuli, carnelian, and agate were strung in close-fitting collar necklaces. Gold, silver, and copper pins with heads of lapis or carnelian were used to fasten clothing. All of the women at the Royal Cemetery of Ur wore crescent-shaped earrings.

The representational arts showed an increase in the amount of jewelry worn by both men and women from the Akkadian period on, particularly strings of beads and bangles worn at the wrists. By the end of the third millennium BCE, women wore multistrand heavy necklaces with long counterweights hanging down their backs to counterbalance the necklace.

The archaeological record for the second millennium BCE has provided few examples of jewelry. Three royal tombs were found in the Northwest Palace, built by Assurnasirpal II (883–859 BCE), at his new capital of Nimrud. One tomb held hundreds of pieces of gold jewelry, including a gold crown with medallions inlaid with agate "eye beads" (against the "evil eye") and cloisonné scenes executed with precious and semiprecious stones.

In Assyria, both men and women wore jewelry, such as earrings, amulets, cylinder seals, and bracelets. The ancients, like people today,

passed jewelry down through the generations. Women wore ankle bracelets, a practice still surviving among peasant women in Iraq.

We know little about Neo-Babylonian jewelry, although texts refer to
jewelers and goldsmiths associated with the Eanna temple in Uruk, and
the house of a bead maker was discovered in Babylon.

Jewelry, including earrings, beads, pendants, bracelets, and anklets, was found in private homes together with toiletries, such as pots of unguents for the body and hair, mussel shells containing kohl (blue eyeshadow), combs **Cosmetics and Perfumes**
made from wood or ivory, and tweezers and mirrors of copper, silver,
and even gold. The mirrors were usually made of highly polished
bronze, which provided a reflecting surface.

The evidence for cosmetics is meager. Women used cosmetics, both
for their eyes and complexion. White, red, yellow, blue, green, and black
pigments were found in cockle shells in tombs in the Royal Cemetery at
Ur. Some texts referred to cosmetics, but these texts are very difficult to
interpret. A second millennium BCE myth about the Sumerian goddess
Inanna (later called Ishtar, the goddess of love), described her preparations for descent to the underworld. "She daubed her eyes with ointment
called "Let him come, let him come."[62] Clearly, eye makeup was considered sexy, and a good marketing name was important even in ancient
times. The base of eye cosmetics was antimony paste, which was applied
with a carved ivory pin. Rouge was mentioned in a synonym list; in
Sumerian it translates as "gold paste" and in Akkadian as "red pigment
of the face."

Aromatic substances became a major industry in Mesopotamia; they
were used for medicine, magic, ritual, and cosmetics. Women played a
major role in the manufacture of perfumes. In fact, a woman was listed
as the author of a series of recipes for making perfumes. Aromatic plants
were steeped and simmered in water for several days, put in oil, and
then skimmed.

FOOD AND DRINK

The diet of the people of Mesopotamia was based on barley, which
was used to make unleavened bread and beer. Barley and other cereals
were ground with portable millstones to produce various grades of
flours. The flour was then mixed with water (usually without any leav-
ening agent) to produce assorted breads. Other grains such as millet,
emmer wheat, rye, and, in the first millennium BCE, rice, were also used
to make bread or cereal. The breads were described as first quality, ordinary, black, or white. In the Royal Cemetery at Ur in the tomb of
Queen Puabi, there were pieces of unleavened bread made from finely
ground flour.

Specialty breads were made by "beating in" various fats, such as sesame oil, lard, mutton "butter," and fish oil. The oil was sometimes seasoned or flavored to disguise the rancid taste that the fat would have quickly acquired in the heat of ancient Mesopotamia. Honey, ghee, sesame, milk, fruit juices, cheese, and fruits could be added to the dough. High-quality breads and cakes were meant for the royal table. One text lists the ingredients to make cakes that "have gone to the palace": 1 *sila* of butter; ⅓ *sila* of white cheese; 3 *sila* of first quality dates; ⅓ *sila* of Smyrna raisins, to which "excellent" flour was added.[63]

There were many varieties of beer, an important part of the Mesopotamian diet; the literal translation was "barley-beer" because there were no hops. The Sumerians at Ur enjoyed dark beer, clear beer, freshly brewed beer, and well-aged beer as well as sweet and bitter beers. Until Hammurabi's time, women brewed beer, and the craft was protected by female gods.

In taverns beer was drunk from a common vat and had to be strained. The ends of drinking tubes were perforated by small holes to act as a filter. Ration lists for palace employees recorded the distribution of one quart to one gallon a day of beer, depending on the rank of the recipient.

Unlike beer, wine could be made only once a year, when the grapes ripened, but wine had a longer shelf life when stored in a sealed jar. Sumerian texts never described how wine was manufactured. It was referred to as a very expensive and rare commodity, found in areas of natural rainfall in the highlands. Even in Nebuchadnezzar's time, wine was called "mountain beer" or "bright wine like the uncountable waters of the river."[64] Many wines were named after their places of origin. Though wine consumption increased over time, it was still a luxury item, served only to the gods and the wealthy. Women ran wine shops (ca. 1800 BCE) which certain priestesses were prohibited from entering upon penalty of death.

Wine was readily available in ancient Assyria. About two thousand liters of wine were stored in special vessels at the Nimrud palace. Between 791 and 779 BCE, many tablets from Nimrud described the wine ration to the royal household as less than a half-pint per person. Other products of the vine included grape juice, wine vinegar, and raisins.

The Sumerians also drank milk: cow's milk, goat's milk, and ewe's milk. Milk soured quickly in the hot climate of southern Iraq. Ghee (clarified butter) was less perishable than milk, as was the round, chalky cheese, which could be transformed back to sour milk by grating it and adding water. The texts do not mention the processing of sheep's milk before the Persian period, at which time it was made into a kind of cottage cheese. Other dairy products included yoghurt and butter. Many kinds of cheeses were produced: a white cheese (for the king's table), "fresh" cheese, and flavored, sweetened, and sharp cheeses.

Soups were prepared with a starch or flour base of chickpeas, lentils, barley flour, or emmer flour. Other ingredients were onions, lentils, beans, mutton fat or oil, honey, or meat juice. The soups were thick and nourishing—a meal in a bowl.

Onions were basic to the ancient diet; the onion family included leeks, shallots, and garlic ("white onion"). The onions were described as sharp, sweet, or those "which have a strong odor." Lentils and chickpeas were staples in the ancient diet. Other vegetables included a variety of lettuces, cabbage, summer and winter cucumbers (described as either sweet or bitter), radishes, beets, and a kind of turnip. Fresh vegetables were eaten raw or boiled in water (al dente).

Dates were a source of sugar, and the date palm was used to make date wine. Other fruits commonly grown were apples, pears, grapes, figs, quince, plums, apricots, cherries, mulberries, melons, pomegranates, as well as pistachios.

Meat was also a part of the ancient Mesopotamian diet. At Drehem in southern Mesopotamia massive barns housed numerous flocks and herds, which were then redistributed for sustenance and cultic needs. The animals were delivered alive and then slaughtered by a butcher. But some animals were dead on arrival. Both types of meat were considered fit for human consumption. The meat from already dead animals was fed to soldiers, messengers, and cult personnel. Among the many deliveries recorded, workers at the textile workshop at Lagash received six sheep with bread and salt.[65]

Meat was expensive. Mutton, beef, and goats were part of the ancient Mesopotamian diet. The gods and the king received large rations of meat. Cattle allocated for food or sacrifice were fattened. A letter from Mari mentioned an ox intended as a palace offering that was so fat it could not stand.[66] There was no prohibition against the consumption of pigs, still found in great numbers in southern Iraq's marshes. In Sumerian times pigs were tended in large herds, their scavenging supplemented by barley feed. Fat meat was prized because it was in short supply; for this reason, pork was valued. A Sumerian proverb stated that slave-girls were to be given lean ham—pork was too good for them![67] Because of the shortage of pasture land, there were few cattle. Horseflesh was eaten. A lawsuit in Nuzi (ca. fourteenth century BCE) recorded a case in which the defendants were accused of stealing and eating a horse. Dead asses were fed to the dogs. Poultry, geese, and ducks were raised for meat and eggs; the hen was introduced in the first millennium BCE.

The rivers were filled with fish, turtles, and eggs. A Sumerian text (ca. 2000 BCE) described the habits and appearance of many species of fish. Fish was an important source of protein in the diet, and many kinds were listed from the third and second millennia. Fish was served to the king. But ordinary citizens also ate salt and fresh water fish, although they preferred fish bred in "fish ponds" or reservoirs. After the Kassite period (1595–1158 BCE), fish became less popular.

Many herbs and spices were available, such as salt, coriander, black and white cumin, mustard, fennel, marjoram, thyme, mint, rosemary, fenugreek, watercress, and rue (an acrid, green leafy plant). A Sumerian proverb explained:

> When a poor man dies, do not revive him.
> When he has bread, he has no salt; when he has salt he has no bread.
> When he has meat, he has no condiment; when he has a condiment, he has no meat.[68]

The Sumerians did not use sugar; instead, they substituted fruit juices, particularly grape and date juice. Only the very rich could afford honey, which may have been imported. "Mountain honey" as well as "dark," "red," and "white" honey were mentioned in texts. "Date honey" actually referred to a syrup made from the dates, not a real honey.

Many foods were preserved for times of need. Cereals were easy to keep. Legumes could be dried in the sun. A variety of fruits were pressed into cakes. Fish and meat were preserved by salting, drying, and smoking. Ice was brought from the highlands and stored in icehouses for cooling beverages.

Some fruits and vegetables could be eaten raw, but breads, cakes, and meats all required cooking. Meat could be cured, dried, roasted, boiled, and "touched with fire." Fish was described as "touched by fire" and "placed upon the fire," possibly referring to glowing coals. Even some breads were cooked in the coals. A grill could be used for cooking over the flames. The vocabulary for cooking pots, whether clay or metal, was extensive. The Sumerians used several types of ovens such as a clay oven and a kind of barbeque. Some pottery molds unearthed from the kitchen area of the Mari palace (ca. eighteenth century BCE) were circular, with designs of animals; others were shaped like fish. These molds were probably used to prepare dishes for the king.

The Sumerians ate two meals a day. They bragged about their highly developed cuisine and compared it to that of desert nomads, whom they believed had no idea of the ways of civilized life. They described the nomads as eating raw food and having no idea how to make a cake with flour, eggs, and honey. Despite their boasts, we have no way to evaluate the Sumerians' culinary ability—to date we have not a single recipe from them.

We are fortunate to have a series of recipes on three tablets from Babylon ca. 1700 BCE, dubbed the Yale Culinary Tablets because they are part of the Yale Babylonian Collection. These tablets contained thirty-five recipes.[69] Many dishes were cooked in water to which fat was added, but the consistency of the liquid after cooking—broth, soup, vegetable porridge, or sauce—was never described. Meat broths were often named after the kind of meat used, that is, "venison broth," "gazelle broth," "goat kid broth," "lamb broth," "ram broth," and even "spleen broth." The list also included both pigeons and francolins (wild hens). There were even vegetable broths. All broths were seasoned with a variety of mineral, plant, and animal products. Some recipes indicated their geographical or cultural origin such as Elamite or Assyrian. A recipe for preparing francolins in broth provides us with the following information:

> Split the birds open, clean well with cold water and assemble in a cauldron to "sear" them. Remove from the fire and clean well again with cold water. Sprinkle with vinegar and rub all over with crushed mint and salt.
> Put beer in a clean cauldron and add fat. Clean the birds well with cold water and assemble all the ingredients in the cauldron. When the cauldron is hot, remove from the fire, sprinkle with vinegar and pat with mint and salt. Variant: clean a cauldron, put in clear water as well as the birds, and put it on the stove. Remove from the fire, clean well in clear water, and rub all over with garlic from which you have squeezed out the juice . . .
> Assemble the ingredients in a pot with water; a piece of fat from which the gristle has been removed, a carefully measured amount of vinegar, and, as desired, pieces of "aromatic wood" soaked in beer, and stripped rue leaves. When it comes to a boil, add *samidu* (a spicy plant), leek and garlic mashed with onion. Put the birds in this broth and cook.[70]

In this recipe, as in others, hygiene was a matter of great concern. After each step in preparing the dish, the cooked piece was washed well and wiped. The recipe included "side dishes" and garnishes.[71] Since presentation was important, prepared meat was accompanied by fresh greens, garlic, and vinegar or salt, and garnished with a porridge of grains and legumes. Another recipe included five or six garnishes and a pastry crust.

The Yale Culinary Tablets comprise the first cookbooks. Since only scribes were able to read and write, these "recipes" may have been read to the cook. Texts refer to professional cooks, "the great cook" and "the chief cook." One chef even left the mark of his seal, which he claimed King Ibbi-Sin gave to him personally. Women played almost no role in royal kitchens. Female servants were employed only to mold barley.

The Yale Culinary Tablets did not include the amounts of ingredients and the necessary cooking times, information that may have been learned by observation and oral instruction. Also, instructions for preparation of many foodstuffs we know to have been eaten in large quantities, such as fish, eggs, crustaceans, turtles, locusts, and so on, were omitted. Traditional methods of cooking were rarely mentioned, for example, radiant heat in a closed chamber (the "domed oven"), indirect heat in hot ashes or roasting, by direct exposure to flame (broiling or grilling), and spit-roasting. Possibly these tablets belonged to a library of similar texts dealing with the "science" of cooking, which a teacher used to instruct a student.

8

Recreation

Everybody loves a good time, and the Mesopotamians were no exception. Sports, games, and entertainment were part of their everyday life. Some games had religious or magical significance, and others were just for fun. The lunar month of the Mesopotamian calendar had twenty-nine or thirty days. Six days were designated holidays, three days lunar festivals, and three more for relaxation. Both the monthly and annual holidays were times for games and entertainment.

HUNTING

The Assyrian kings were famous hunters of lions, elephants, ostriches, wild bulls, and other beasts. Though the king preferred to hunt the larger, more aggressive animals, other beasts would do. The sport had both religious and political implications: as a successful hunter, the king proved that the gods favored him and that his power was therefore legitimate. Good triumphed over evil.

The Syrian plain was often the scene of the Assyrian royal hunt, but lions were also caught in Africa and brought to Assyria, where they were kept in game reserves until the hunt. The hunts were carefully orchestrated. From a booth above the wooden cage, a servant raised the door and released the lions, who were attacked by dogs and beaters. The beaters' job was to beat the lions with sticks and drive them toward the king. The king killed the lions from his chariot with a bow or spear. Sometimes the king was shown on foot, killing the lion by holding his

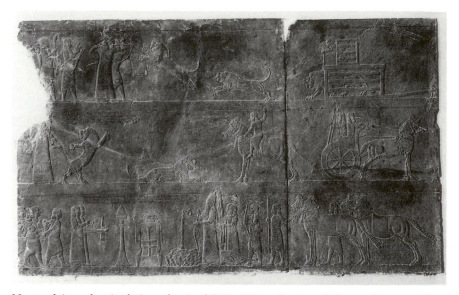

Hunt of Assurbanipal. Assurbanipal (669–627 BCE) enjoyed the royal sport of lion hunting, which often took place once the lion had been captured. These panels probably decorated the king's private apartments. Each register is to be read from right to left. In the top register a lion is released from its cage by a small boy or eunuch, who is protected from the lion by a smaller cage. The lion advances left and the king shoots him with arrows. The kill is unsuccessful and the lion leaps at the king, who is guarded by a shieldbearer and eunuchs holding extra arrows. In the central register an Assyrian chariot team distracts the lion, while the king approaches from behind, grabbing the lion by the tail. The king's right hand holds a mace (damaged here) to hit the lion over the head, as described by the accompanying inscription. In the lower register the dead lions are brought in from the left. A musician plays a harp, while the king pours a libation of wine over the bodies of four lions and makes an offering to the god with a tall stand for burning incense, and the elaborate altar set with a cloth for holding an offering which includes a leg of meat. Ht. ca. 1.69 m. From Nineveh, North Palace. © BRITISH MUSEUM, LONDON.

mane and thrusting a sword into his prey. The hunt became a public event. After the hunt, as part of a religious ceremony, the king poured a libation over the dead lions to atone for the harm he had done them and to appease their angry spirits. He also recited a devotional speech attributing the success of the hunt to his patron goddess. At the end of the hunt the servants picked up the dead animals. The formal hunt was continued by the Persian kings. The popularity of this sport is attested to by both information in the tablets and lifelike hunting scenes carved ad nauseam on Assyrian palace walls.

SPORTS

Both boxing and wrestling were depicted in art. Terra-cotta plaques showing boxers imply that boxing was a popular sport. In one plaque the boxers are beside two men beating an enormous drum, perhaps in time with their motions. In the *Epic of Gilgamesh* there is a reference to a wrestling match between Gilgamesh and Enkidu.

A form of polo may also have been played, but with men astride the shoulders of other men rather than on horses, as in Mesoamerica. Again, in the *Epic of Gilgamesh* there is a reference to Gilgamesh oppressing his subjects by tiring the young men with endless contests of this polo and then taking sexual advantage of the young women.

BOARD GAMES

Board games have actually been recovered through archaeological excavation. The boards were usually stone or clay (in Egypt and ancient Israel they were wood or ivory). Some were from Esarhaddon's palace and displayed the royal legend. Board games were played with various kinds of pieces and even dice. Two of these games were similar to those of ancient Egypt. The first, the game of twenty-squares, involved a race using pieces that moved according to rolls of the dice. The game of twenty-squares was played not only by the rich, since large clay bricks have been found with the board crudely drawn. Palace guards even passed their time playing the game of twenty-squares; in fact, a game board was scratched into the pedestal of one of the pair of bull-colossi guarding King Sargon's palace gates at Khorsabad. The second type of board game, the game of fifty-eight holes, is an early model for cribbage.

Two lot-boards, one connected with the twelve signs of the zodiac, contained instructions on the back about how the game was played. We learn how to draw the eighty-four sections on the ground and the names of the pieces (eagle, raven, rooster, swallow, and an unidentified bird). In fact, the lot-boards used a word for game piece, "doll, figurine," like "man" in chessman. The pieces were moved when dice made from astragals (the joint bones of oxen or sheep) were thrown. This game, called "asha," is still played today by women in the Jewish community of Cochin in southern India.

In general, games were accompanied by objects that were thrown and objects that were moved. Thrown objects included dice, probably of Indian origin, which have been dated to all periods and found at sites throughout Mesopotamia. The dice are cubes of bone, clay, stone, and even glass. They have the numbers 1 through 6 incised on them. However, unlike modern dice, on which the sum of the opposite sides is always 7, ancient dice have opposite sides which are usually numbered

Game board from the Royal Cemetery of Ur (ca. 26th century BCE). The game board of twenty-squares is made of a mosaic of shell, bone, lapis lazuli, red paste and red limestone. The board is hollowed to contain the placing pieces, seven black shale counters inlaid with five white spots and seven of shell inlaid with five lapis lazuli spots. Length of board, 27cm, width 12 cm. Diameter of playing pieces: 2.2 cm. © BRITISH MUSEUM, LONDON.

consecutively. Other objects thrown included joint bones, throw sticks, and stones. Stones, described as desirable or undesirable, were put as lots into a container, drawn, and played once certain prayers were made to the gods to oversee the game. Moved objects included the game piece referred to as "doll, figurine," as well as birds, dogs, circular pieces, and other shapes such as small clay cones and pyramids.

TOYS

Both action and nonaction toys have been found. Some, like today's toy guns, were miniaturized weapons of the time; these included slingshots, bows and arrows, and boomerangs or throw sticks. Other action toys and games included the spinning top, rattles, jump ropes (sometimes called "the game of Ishtar"), puck and mallet, hoop, balls (seals are shown with jugglers and balls), and the buzz or button (a disc or piece of pottery with holes for strings). Nonaction toys were used by children to play "house" or "grown-up." For their role-playing children used miniature furniture such as tables, beds, stools, dolls, and a variety of small-sized animals. Model vehicles clearly mirrored the time with miniature carts, wagons, chariots, and ships for children.

The front of a terra cotta model of a chariot (ca. 2000 BCE). The figure of a king (left) with his feet on the mountain facing the god (right). Divine symbols are in the registers above their heads. This may have been a toy or a gift to the god. Ht. 16.3 cm, W. 11.1 cm. © YALE BABYLONIAN COLLECTION, YALE UNIVERSITY, NEW HAVEN.

MUSIC

From the Early Dynastic period, if not before, music was a part of royal and religious festivals. Singers and musicians were featured at festivals, as were snake-charmers, bear trainers, and jesters. Singers were both male and female; they sang in the royal courts and in the temple,

Restored lyre from the grave of Puabi at the Royal Cemetery of Ur (ca. 26th century BCE). The lyre was made of inlaid wood. The cow's head was made of gold and lapis lazuli attached to the sounding box of the lyre. Ht. 1.125 m. © BRITISH MUSEUM, LONDON.

where they sometimes functioned as priests. Their repertoire consisted of celebratory music, laments, and literary works (see below). Singers were often accompanied by musical instruments.

Musical instruments belonged to the string, wind, and percussion families. Stringed instruments, pipes, and a clay whistle were even recovered from excavations. Eight lyres and two harps, including an elaborate example of a lyre inlaid with shell and trimmed in gold, were found at the

Four musicians, a detail from the second register of a four register scene dealing with the military, perhaps suggesting this group is a military band. Of the pair of musicians on the left, one man plays the hand drum, the one behind him, a lyre, and of the pair of musicians on the right, one plays a harp and the one behind him cymbals. Ht. 37 cm. © LOUVRE MUSEUM, PARIS.

Royal Cemetery of Ur. There are also many examples of both the harp and the lyre throughout the Near East, but there are fewer examples of the lute. The pipe, a wind instrument, existed as either a single or double pipe. Trumpets were used for communication (as in battle) rather than for music. Three kinds of drums are known: a hand drum or tambourine, a drum in the shape of a sand-glass which was used by the temple priest to appease the god, and a kettledrum, which was beaten in the temple courtyard during eclipses of the moon. Also, cymbals and bells were used. Second millennium tablets from Babylonia, Assyria, and Ugarit in Syria described music theory, naming nine strings of the harp, and using a heptatonic scale. A whole psalm praising the moon goddess Nikkal was found complete with libretto and score at thirteenth century Ugarit. Complete scores were also kept on file.

Musicians were sometimes shown playing solo, but often several musicians were pictured together, carrying harps, lyres, and various other instruments, suggesting an ensemble. The musicians might also accompany dancers or singers in royal and religious festivals. Sometimes musicians were even shown dancing. Musicians were also depicted in military scenes, accompanying the army as they marched.

DANCING

Reliefs show dancing done in time to music, singing, and clapping. Dancing was mentioned in the tablets but usually in reference to the cult and not as an independent activity. At the annual feast for the goddess Ishtar and other goddesses, whirling dances were done in her honor by both men and women. Circle dances were usually performed by women. Acrobatic dancers took part in cultic activities.

BANQUETS

Bas-reliefs show kings and queens banqueting in lush gardens, attended by servants, and entertained by musicians. In a relief from Khorsabad, the nobles sat at tables of four. In front of them was placed a dish of food as they toasted the king, raising a rhyton (cornucopia-shaped drinking cup) with a base in the shape of a lion's head.

When King Assurnasirpal II built his new capital at Nimrud, he hosted a huge banquet to celebrate opening ceremonies. A historical summary of the event provides us with a detailed menu, the number of guests, and their country of origin:

> When Assurnasirpal, king of Assyria, inaugurated the palace in Calah, a palace of joy, built with great ingenuity, he invited into it Assur (the Assyrian national god), the great lord and the gods of his entire country. He prepared a banquet of 1,000 fattened head of cattle, 1,000 calves, 10,000 stable sheep, 15,000 lambs—for my lady Ishtar (alone) 200 head of cattle (and) ... 1,000 spring lambs, 500 stags, 500 gazelles, 1,000 ducks, 500 geese ... 10,000 doves ... 10,000 assorted small birds, 10,000 assorted fish, 10,000 jerboa, 10,000 assorted eggs; 10,000 loaves of bread, 10,000 jars of beer, 10,000 skins with wine ... 1,000 wooden crates with vegetables, 300 containers with oil, 300 containers with salted seeds ... 100 containers of parched barley ... 100 containers of fine mixed beer, 100 pomegranates, 100 bunches of grapes ... 100 pistachio cones ... 100 with garlic, 100 with onions ... 100 with honey, 100 with rendered butter, 100 with roasted ... barley, ten homer of shelled pistachio nuts ... ten homer of dates ... ten homer of cumin ... ten homer of

thyme, ten homer of perfumed oil, ten homer of sweet smelling matters, . . . ten homer of *zinzimmu*-onions, ten homer of olives.

When I inaugurated the palace at Calah I hosted for ten days with food and drink 47,074 persons, men and women, who were bid to come from across my entire country, also 5,000 important persons, delegates from the country Sukhu, from Khindana, Khattina, Hatti, Tyre, Sidon, Gurguma, Malida, Khubushka, Gilzana, Kuma and Musasir (capital of Urartu), also 16,000 inhabitants of Calah from all ways of life, 1,500 officials of all my palaces, altogether 69,574 invited guests . . . furthermore I provided them with the means to clean and anoint themselves. I did them due honors and sent them back, healthy and happy, to their own countries.[1]

The menu, despite difficulties in translation, has furnished us with an outline of the banquet: (1) meat dishes such as sheep, cattle, and some game; fowl, mostly small and aquatic birds; fish and jerboa, and a large variety of eggs; (2) bread; (3) beer and wine in identical amounts; (4) side dishes (mostly pickled and spiced fruit, and a large variety of seeds and onion); (5) dessert (sweet fruits, nuts, honey, cheese) and savories; most are still not identifiable. Finally, perfumed oil and sweet-smelling substances were listed.

PERFORMANCE OF LITERARY WORKS

Literary works were sometimes sung. The compositions display a poetic structure syntactically and rhythmically. Stanzas are usually composed of four to twelve verses, sometimes more.

Kings were the subject of hymns (which sometimes named the musical instrument for accompaniment) and historical romances. The king and his court were often the audience for these literary works, as well as for new compositions. The royal house may even have commissioned the scribes to compose hymns and other works. King Shulgi claimed he wrote his own.

Some literary works became part of the cult, such as the *Epic of Creation*; this myth was recited and its battle scene reenacted at the Babylonian New Year's festival. Other texts were clearly cultic, and their instructions indicated that they be recited for particular rituals.

Some literary works showed awareness of an audience. At the beginning of the *Epic of Gilgamesh*, the narrator praised the accomplishments of King Gilgamesh and asked his listeners to examine his monuments— the temple, the city wall, and even the lapis lazuli tablet buried in the wall's foundation as part of an ancient "time capsule" of information.

Dialogues such as *The Babylonian Theodicy* and the *Dialogue of Pessimism*

Relief of Assurbanipal's garden party. The king and queen are shown relaxing in their garden. Attendants fan them while food is brought for their banquet. A musician plays a harp. In the second tree from the left hangs the head of King Te'umman. © BRITISH MUSEUM, LONDON.

might be performance pieces, with the two speakers clearly delineated like actors in a script. *The Babylonian Theodicy* is a dialogue between a sufferer and his friend discussing age-old questions such as why the gods allow man to suffer and why good things happen to bad people. The sufferer says:

> Your reasoning is a cool breeze, a breath of fresh air for mankind,
> Most particular friend, your advice is excellent.
> Let me put but one matter before you:
> Those who seek not after a god can go the road of favor,
> Those who pray to a goddess have grown poor and destitute.
> Indeed, in my youth I tried to find out the will of (my) god,
> With prayer and supplication I besought my goddess.
> I bore a yoke of profitless servitude:
> (My) god decreed (for me) poverty instead of wealth.
> A cripple rises above me, a fool is ahead of me,
> Rogues are in the ascendant, I am demoted.[2]

Among the friend's standard pious replies, we find:

> Adept scholar, master of erudition,
> You blaspheme in the anguish of your thoughts.
> Divine purpose is as remote as innermost heaven,
> It is too difficult to understand, people cannot understand it.[3]

The conclusion is that men are unjust because the gods made them that way, and the sufferer challenges the gods to take care of him. The *Dialogue of Pessimism* is a more humorous treatment about the purpose of life. The scene is a series of exchanges between a master and servant. Each time the master suggests a plan of action, the servant obsequiously puts a positive spin on it; the master then suggests doing the exact opposite, and the slave once again finds other "words of wisdom" to support his master, as in the following exchange:

> "Servant, listen to me." "Yes, master, yes." "I will do a good deed for my country." "So do it, master, do it. The man who does a good deed for his country, his good deed rests in Marduk's basket." "No, servant, I will certainly not do a good deed for my country." "Do not do it, master, do not do it. Go up on the ancient ruin heaps and walk around, look at the skulls of the lowly and great. Which was the doer of evil, and which was the doer of good deeds?"[4]

Only at the conclusion does the servant finally offer an independent opinion about life and his master:

"Servant, listen to me." "Yes, master, yes." "What, then, is good?"
"To break my neck and your neck and throw (us) in the river is
good. Who is so tall as to reach to heaven? Who is so broad as to
encompass the netherworld?" "No, servant, I will kill you and let
you go first." "Then my master will certainly not outlive me even
three days!"[5]

Other dialogues featuring a verbal contest between two characters—
such as Summer and Winter, the Pickaxe and the Plow, the Date Palm
and the Tamarisk—are followed by a judgment and reconciliation in
which the contestants leave as good friends. Possibly these compositions
were performed, but we cannot be sure.

In some cases, we can only speculate as to how broad the audience
was—whether these works were performed only before the royal court
or before the general public. Certainly, the literature reflects an awareness of taste and standards of the time.

9

Religion

RELIGIOUS VIEWS OF EARLY MAN

The past 150 years of excavations have yielded remains of temples, statues, and religious artifacts. Unfortunately, most excavated temples were found empty, their contents stolen or brought to a safe place. Written sources include myths, "manuals" explaining the religious ideology, rituals, hymns, and prayers. Common religious beliefs were also expressed in letters and administrative documents. Even personal names could communicate religious beliefs, for example, "I-Was-Spared-on-Account-of-Ishtar," "May- I-Not-Come-to-Shame, O Marduk," and "Assur-Knew-My-Loyalty."[1]

Texts often described the transcendence of the gods, their superiority and rule over man, because of their power and intelligence:

> Who could learn the reasoning of the gods in heaven?
> Who understands the intelligence of the gods of the underworld?
> Where have human beings learned the way of a god?[2] (*Poem of the Righteous Sufferer*)

Myths, in particular, answered questions for ancient peoples about origins and existence by helping ancient civilizations make sense of the world around them. The myths were often about the gods and their activities and about our world and how it was created.

Creation was an important theme in mythology and was explained by

Votive statues from Tell Asmar from the Square Temple. The statues represent worshipers and were set in the temples to pray perpetually for the health and well-being of the donor. Their hands are clasped in prayer. Ht. of largest figure, 72 cm. COURTESY OF THE ORIENTAL INSTITUTE OF THE UNIVERSITY OF CHICAGO.

separation of the primeval matter, which was watery, solid, or a mixture of the two. According to *Enuma elish* (the Akkadian *Epic of Creation*) there was nothing in the beginning except primordial Apsu (male), the sweet waters, and Tiamat (female), the waters of ocean. The origin of the universe was traced to their union. For the Sumerians, creation began when Enlil, their chief god, separated a single body of matter into a two-level universe in order to prepare the world for mankind, as in the following excerpt:

> Enlil, to bring forth the seed of the land from the ground,
> Hastened to separate heaven from earth,
> Hastened to separate earth from heaven.[3]

The phrase "the seed of the land" referred to the Sumerians. In general, the people of ancient Mesopotamia rarely questioned how the primordial elements came into being. A bilingual Sumero-Babylonian incantation explained it as a concept of spontaneous generation from water:

Clay figurines (ca. mid-third millennium BCE). These clay figurines are probably from northern Syria. The left and center figures appear to be men. The right figure has one hand under her breast. The figures are made from molds and clay pellets were added for eyes, beard and necklace. Ht. ca. 85 mm. © YALE BABY-LONIAN COLLECTION, YALE UNIVERSITY, NEW HAVEN.

> Heaven was created of its own accord.
> Earth was created of its own accord.
> Heaven was an abyss, earth was an abyss.[4]

In all the Mesopotamian creation stories, creation always resulted in heaven and earth, since the ancients clearly saw that both existed. Any creation story also included one of two basic versions of the creation of the human race. In one version the human race sprouted from the ground like plants; in the other, mankind was created from clay, mixed with divine blood, and molded into figurines. In ancient Mesopotamia, divine blood, sometimes combined with divine spittle, was necessary to infuse the clay with life. Man was created to take over the gods' work, so the gods could rest. In time, the world became overpopulated, and the gods brought a flood.

Trespasses against the gods were often the main topic in Sumerian sources about religion. There were numerous words for sins. The native terms distinguished their gravity. At the end of the second millennium BCE, the text *Šurpu* (literally, ''burning'') listed two hundred acts and omissions as sins, including not speaking one's mind, causing discord in the family, neglecting a naked person, and killing animals without reason. The confessional lists of trespasses contained unintentional sins as well as ancestral sins. The gods punished the sinners they forgave, but if the gods refused to forgive the sinner, that person could not be helped. In reality, the wicked often fared better than the righteous.

Ancient Mesopotamians regarded personal well-being as being tied to correct worship of the gods. If an individual sinned or a community neglected the proper rites, disorder, plague, earthquake, fire, or other evils could befall the entire community. There was little hope for a better life after death—life in the underworld was, for the most part, miserable for all (see Chapter 7).

The religion of the priest was focused on the image of the god and on the temple. The priest was concerned with the religious service—sacrifices and hymns of praise. Royal religion differed from that of the priest and the ordinary citizen. The king alone undertook prayers, fasts, mortification, and taboos. But the religion of the common man still remains largely a mystery. For the average person, religion was ceremonial and formal rather than intense and personal. Each Babylonian had a personal god to whom he gave regular offerings and from whom he made specific requests, such as a cure from illness. The personal god also mediated with higher gods on the worshiper's behalf. The Babylonian relationship between the worshiper and the personal gods can best be described as benefits for the worshiper in return for his offerings. If the process did not succeed, the supplicant threatened to abandon his god and seek another; nonetheless, as one proverb noted, "You cannot teach your god to run like a dog after you."[5]

DEVELOPMENT OF THE PANTHEON

Early Mesopotamians regarded the supernatural forces that controlled their world as mysterious and impersonal. Such forces are called *numina* (plural of Latin *numen*). Early man believed that storms, rivers, lakes, marshes, mountains, sun, wind, and fire were all living beings. The religious beliefs of the Sumerians took form in Eridu, one of the oldest Sumerian settlements. For them, water was a numinous power, a supernatural life force.

During the fourth millennium BCE, ancient Mesopotamians worshiped forces in nature, that is, the powers of fertility. Spring was brief, and its fertile powers declined as the dry, hot summer came. Myths explained the alternation of fertility and sterility. The progressive humanization of the supernatural forces emerged from the human need for a meaningful relationship with them. Eventually, this led to a growing preference for the human form over older, nonhuman forms (*numina*) and a preference for organizing the gods according to human patterns of family and profession.

The third millennium BCE ushered in a period of war. Kingship began as a temporary office during times of danger. When the emergency passed, the king no longer held power. Once war became chronic, the office of the king became a permanent position. He had both an army for defense and labor to maintain the city wall. A new literary form developed, the epic tale, which took its place beside the myth. In the epic, man was represented by the hero-king, who represented society's will in peace and in war.

Once in office, kings tried to find ways to maintain their position. Before acting, the king had to know the gods' will and properly carry out their orders to protect the community from divine wrath or neglect. There were "standing" orders such as cultic activities and maintenance of the temple. Sometimes the ruler received specific instructions from the gods in dreams or in omens. Occasionally, the king impiously defied divine authority revealed through the omens. The ruler metaphor was extended to the gods. Nature gods were transformed into city gods or heads of state. In their roles as rulers, the gods were expected to protect their realms against outsiders.

In addition to their cosmic roles, the gods were assigned powers conferred on them by such high-ranking gods as An, Enlil, or the whole divine assembly. For example, Enki, god of the fresh waters (rivers and marshes), was charged by An with such duties as the following:

> To clear the pure mouths of the Tigris and Euphrates, to make verdure plentiful,
> make dense the clouds, grant water in abundance to all plough lands,
> to make grain lift its head in furrows and to make pasture abundant in the desert, to make young saplings in plantations and in orchards sprout where planted like a forest.[6]

During the first half of the second millennium BCE, the Semites came to power and Sumerian culture came to an end. When the Sumerians disappeared from the scene, the Semites continued to develop Mesopotamia and its religion. They still maintained the ancient religious structures they had inherited from the Sumerians, but the religion took on a Semitic coloration, gods gradually becoming detached from their embodiment in nature. The majority of Semitic gods were male.

In the national cults the great gods of the Sumerian pantheon were equated with parallel Semitic gods. The polytheistic view of the ancients allowed them to accept the gods of other nations. The rank of the gods reflected the political relationships between nations. In their political role, the gods and goddesses constituted a "Primitive Democracy," which met at Nippur in an assembly presided over by An and Enlil.

Here political decisions such as war were discussed and humanity's crimes were judged.

Once the gods were no longer associated with natural phenomena, they became anthropomorphized. Their cities regarded them as rulers and sought political aid and protection against external enemies and internal lawlessness. For example, Ningirsu entered into an agreement with King Uru-inimgina to protect widows and orphans.

The gods were regarded as an aristocracy of great landowners, the country's powerful upper class. The gods created man to serve them; this concept was expressed in numerous Sumerian and Akkadian myths, hymns, prayers, historical texts and royal inscriptions, and in art. The pantheon included various administrators and divine artisans. In this way, man's world was reflected in the heavenly world of the gods. In time the gods and their world were modeled on the world of humans. The gods had wives (usually secondary figures), children, courtiers, and servants, similar to a human ruler, but without human boundaries. The relations between different city gods were defined through family ties.

Descriptions of the heavens refer to seven or three heavens, each made of a different precious stone.[7] The gods were assigned various functions, which varied in importance according to their rank in heaven. The city prince assumed a special status as the earthly representative of the city's god.

The increasing intermingling of Akkadians, immigrating Amorites, and Sumerians throughout Mesopotamia changed the theology of the time. The tendency was to merge with the Sumerian religion. The gods of neighboring peoples were often integrated within their own pantheon. However, the Babylonians rejected Assur, the god of the hated Assyrians.

From the second millennium BCE to the first millennium BCE the gods were identified with the political ambitions of their nations. Marduk (Akkadian, "son of the storm"), patron god of Babylon, and Assur, patron god of Assyria, became head of their respective pantheons when their cities became the capitals of their nations and empires.

On a personal level, there was a growing closeness between man and god, resulting in a relationship with a personal or family god. The ancient Mesopotamian felt that his good luck and fortune were attached to his personal god, and this fortune was described in the phrase "to acquire a god." The omen literature indicated that a favorable portent could designate, "that house will acquire a god, that house will endure," and a bad portent could indicate that "that house will grow poor, will not acquire a god."[8] The ancient Mesopotamian addressed his personal god (or goddess) by name, asking him to intervene with more powerful gods in his role as protector. Mesopotamian man lived in the "(protective) shadow" of his personal god.[9] On a personal level, the pious worshiper believed that his god(s) cared deeply about him and his welfare.

The personal god had requirements similar to those of a human parent:

> Daily, worship your god
> with offerings, prayers and appropriate incense.
> Bend your heart to your god;
> That befits the office of a personal god,
> prayers, supplication,
>   pressing (the hand to) the nose (as greeting)
> shall you offer up every morning,
> then your power will be great,
> and you will, through the god
>   have enormous success.[10]

In the second millennium BCE the problem of the righteous sufferer became part of the Mesopotamian religious consciousness. Two main works, *The Poem of the Righteous Sufferer* (also referred to as the Babylonian Job) and *The Babylonian Theodicy*, considered the workings of divine justice. Both works arrived at the same conclusion: in reality, the wicked often fared better than the righteous.

Various mythological themes became popular, namely, death, the demons in the netherworld, and divine wars. Death was graphically described. An was flayed and his head cut off; Enlil's eyes were plucked out.[11] The growing cruelty paralleled the increased political roles of the gods. The gods of political enemies became the embodiment of the enemies themselves and were treated with cruelty. The gods were drawn into political conflict, with their statues and temples at the mercy of their conquerors. Politico-religious pamphlets were equally brutal. For example, one text was written to discredit the New Year Festival of Babylon in the eyes of the Assyrians; ritual instructions were even included in order to stage a trial of the god Marduk for his sins against Assur.[12]

For the most part, the Assyrians worshiped the same gods as the Babylonians, but the Assyrians' gods did not always play the same roles as their Babylonian counterparts. Assur, the patron god of the city of Asshur, became the chief god of an ever-expanding empire. Oaths were taken in Assur's name, and prayers were offered to him in personal matters.

By the Neo-Assyrian period the temple buildings and their staffs had become enormous; income from temple lands and traditional offerings were insufficient to support the temple personnel. The major cults depended on the king for extra income and upkeep of the building. The Assyrian king came to represent the god Assur. "Temple" and "palace" were no longer separate. The king was the chief priest of the state, and his presence was required at various rituals (although sometimes he could send a piece of his clothing as his replacement). Even though he was head of the official religion, he was still subject to various taboos and fasts.

THE COMPOSITION OF THE PANTHEON

The gods were named in a canonical list (ca. third millennium BCE), which contained almost two thousand entries. Most of the listed gods had Sumerian names. But as a result of political events, the gods gained Semitic characteristics (see "Development of the Pantheon," above). The number of gods increased in the Neo-Sumerian period; the Sumerians themselves estimated that there were 3,600 (60 × 60) gods.

The gods' list outlined the basic structure of the pantheon. Anu, the sky god, originally was chief god of the pantheon. Later, some of his attributes were assigned to Enlil and later to Marduk in Babylonia and Asshur in Assyria.

The strongest divine personalities appealed most to worshipers, and these gods absorbed the powers of the minor gods. For example, Inanna, whom the Semites equated with Ishtar, was the goddess of love. Later she absorbed the powers of a number of goddesses, such as the divinity of the planet Venus and the goddess of war. By the time the Mesopotamian empire came to an end, there were about thirty major gods.

Just as a human leader administered power through members of his own family and other subordinates, so the chief god in a local pantheon was envisioned as surrounded by members of his family, ministers, and servants. There was a patron deity for every profession and activity, such as a god of brick making and a god of brewing. Many local pantheons developed.

The Older Generation of Gods From the third millennium BCE onward, **An** (Akkadian, Anum) was the head of the pantheon. His name meant "sky," and he was the god of the sky. All things on heaven and earth conformed to his will, because his command was "the foundation of heaven and earth."[13] As the ultimate source of all authority, An was associated with the highest authority on earth, the king, whom he designated as ruler.

According to the official pantheon, the great god list called An-Anum, An's female consort was **Antum**, a female derivative of An. From her breasts, the clouds brought forth her milk, the rain. **Ki**, "earth," was sometimes designated as his consort as well. He impregnated her with his sperm, the rain, and she gave birth to trees, reeds, and all other vegetation.

Enlil, "lord wind," played an active role in human affairs, initially as the national god of Sumer. Enlil originally held the Tablets of Destiny, on which the fates of men and gods were decreed. Later his role was

assumed by Marduk. Enlil was the moist wind of spring and the creator
of the hoe, the farmer's most versatile tool. Enlil displayed a two-sided
nature, as the benign wind of spring and also as the destructive storm.
His consort was the grain goddess **Ninlil**, "lady wind," whom, according to one myth, he raped. A tribunal of gods found him guilty, and
Enlil went to the netherworld, where Ninlil followed him and bore a
number of underworld deities.

Ninkhursaga was ranked number three, after An and Enlil. Her name
means "Lady of the stony ground" or "Lady of the foothills"; originally
she was the numinous power in the alluvial stony ground, in the east at
the foothills near the Iranian mountains and in the west at the stony
Arabian desert. She was the goddess of birth for pregnant animals, providing shelter for them in the hut, fold, or pen. She also acted as midwife
to the gods.

Enki (Akkadian, Ea) was the god of the fresh waters and a benefactor
to mankind. He was the source of all secret magical knowledge. At the
beginning of the second millennium BCE, he replaced Ninkhursaga in
the ruling trio—reflecting the increasingly male-dominated society of
the times. Enki was known for his cleverness—he usually prevailed in
conflicts with other gods by using his brains. His name means "Productive Manager of the Soil," and in this capacity he provided the irrigation waters for much of southern Mesopotamia. When water moistened
clay, the material produced would be molded into a variety of shapes.
Enki was also named "Image Fashioner," and in this role was the patron god of artists and craftsmen such as potters, bronze casters, stone
cutters, jewelers, seal cutters, and so on. Enki also had the power to purify and cleanse mortals. In an omen series called "The Bathhouse,"
Enki supervised the purification of the king from the evils of a lunar
eclipse.

A rather ribald myth about Enki, the god of wisdom, and Ninkhursaga
was probably told at the king's court to entertain coarse seafarers visiting
from Dilmun (Bahrain). The story recounted Enki's seduction of Ninkhursaga, who then turned down his marriage proposal. Later Enki
seduced Ninkhursaga's daughter and finally her granddaughter. Ninkhursaga warned her granddaughter, who was a spider; but she was suc-
cessfully wooed by Enki, who brought whatever wedding gifts she
demanded. When Enki left, Ninkhursaga extracted his seed from the
spider's womb and then threw it on the ground. Various plants grew
from Enki's seed. Enki saw the plants, named them, and then ate them.
Enki found himself pregnant from the plants, but being male, he could
not give birth. He was in agony. Finally, Ninkhursaga was persuaded in
her role as birth goddess to help him deliver many gods, including the
goddess of Dilmun.

The older generation of gods represented the major elements of the universe: the sky, winds, foothills, and underground water. The younger generations of gods, the grandchildren and great-grandchildren of An, represented the moon, the sun, the morning and evening star, the thunder cloud, and the rainstorm.

The Younger Generation of Gods

Nanna (Akkadian, Sin) was the full moon, the crescents, and the new moon. He was described as follows:

> Nanna, great lord,
> light shining in the clear skies,
> wearing on (his) head a prince's headdress,
> right god bringing forth day and night,
> establishing the month,
> bringing the year to completion.[14]

Ninurta, "Lord Plow," represented the humid thunderstorm of spring, which made the soil easy to plough. He was depicted as a hybrid creature, a huge lion-headed eagle, gliding with its wings extended and thunder roaring from its mouth. A series of myths about Ninurta described the hydraulic cycle of the waters.

Utu (Akkadian, Shamash), whose Sumerian and Akkadian names mean "sun," was entrusted with the responsibility of dispensing justice to both gods and men. Utu was placed to guard the boundaries "for heaven and earth." Thus, the universe became subject to one law and one judge—everybody and everything in existence could be brought to justice. This concept gave rise to the "just war," that is, doing battle with wrongdoers.

Inanna (Akkadian, Ishtar) was the sister of Utu. She embodied the roles of different goddesses and was called "Lady of a myriad offices."[15] By the second millennium BCE, Ishtar became the best-known and most widely worshiped Babylonian deity, and the name Ishtar came to be the generic word for "goddess."

According to various myths, Inanna was the goddess of the date storehouse, the goddess of shepherds, and the power behind the thundershowers of spring. Inanna was the Morning Star and Evening Star. As the Morning Star, Inanna marked the awakening of man and beast. As the Evening Star, she designated the end of the day's work for men and animals. She was also the goddess of love and sexuality as well as patron goddess of the harlot and alehouse.

Netherworld Deities

The netherworld was governed by a king, **Nergal**, and a queen, **Ereshkigal**. Their administrative staffs included, among others, minister to the queen, **Namtar** (literally, "fate"), the judges, **Utu** and **Gilgamesh**, and the gatekeeper **Neti**.

In Mesopotamian theology the gods never aged or died of natural causes. They could, however, die a violent death, such as younger gods killing older gods in a struggle for succession, defeated rebel gods being punished by death, or in monster-slaying.

REPRESENTATIONS OF THE GODS

The image of the god was central to the official religion of ancient Mesopotamia. The god was believed to be present in his or her statue. When the image of the deity was carried off in war, that god remained absent until his statue was returned. The importance of these statues has been shown by the wide distribution of cheap, clay replicas as well as statues of minor gods. In fact, a son could inherit his father's "gods."

Creating a divine image was a solemn ceremonial task for the temple workshops. Mesopotamian gods were usually fashioned to look like men, and they participated in most human activities such as eating, drinking, making love, losing their tempers, sulking, weeping, and sleeping.[16]

The statues were made and repaired in special workshops. Most temple images were fashioned from precious wood. Small decorative ornaments of gold or silver were sewn onto the clothing of the gods. Pectorals and a horned crown were added to complete the god's outfit. The clothing was changed according to ritual and ceremonial requirements. Some images were seated since their thrones were mentioned.

As early as the third millennium BCE, the images also underwent various rituals to sanctify them in special ways. The most elaborate ritual, the "washing of the mouth," was performed at night and accompanied by an appeal to the stars. The animation of the divine statue required several stages: mouth-washing conducted in the workshop; carrying the statue in a procession to the river bank, where a second mouth-washing took place; placing the statue facing west, then facing east, and making offerings to numerous gods, planets, certain fixed stars and constellations, and finally all the stars. The role of the astral deities in the ritual was to irradiate the wooden statue, which was adorned with precious metals and stones. Also, a secret ritual of consecration was performed to endow the gods with "life" by opening their eyes and mouths to see and eat.

The divine statues were then placed on a pedestal in the inner sanctuary. Here the gods "lived" with their families and were served by a staff of minor gods who, in turn, supervised human workers such as divine musicians, handmaidens, a counselor, and a secretary who screened cases submitted to him for decision.

The gods of Mesopotamia were identified by their symbols or standards, horned crowns, and by garments of gold (see above). The symbols sometimes replaced or accompanied the traditional statues. If the statue was carried off or destroyed by the enemy, the symbols could substitute for the statue in all its ritual functions.

The divine statues accumulated wealth through dedications of clothing, jewelry, and paraphernalia. For example, King Ibbi-Suen of the Third Dynasty of Ur brought a valuable gold jar, which he dedicated to Nanna. The jar was part of the booty from a campaign in Elam and stood in Nanna's bedroom at the top of the ziggurat of his temple at Ur. This bath pitcher was considered too sacred to be seen by the ordinary citizen.

Inventory lists kept account of the accumulated wealth of the gods, as in the following example: "Inventory of the treasure of Ishtar of Lagaba: 2 gold rings; 1 gold vulva; 19 gold flowers; 2 gold rods; 2 gold dress-pins; 2 silver earrings; 1 [. . .] of carnelian; 4 cones; 6 cylinder seals; 2 stamp seals; 1 chain of electrum; 6 ivory pins; 1 large ring of carnelian; 2 fleeced skirts; 3 linen robes; 6 woven headbands; 4 [. . .] headbands; 5 headdresses; 1 cover; 3 bronze cups; [x] lamps."[17]

Specific animals were associated with certain gods and often became their symbols, such as the dog for the goddess of healing, Gula, the lion-snake-eagle for Marduk, and the goat-fish for Ea. These emblems were called "gods," "standards," "weapons," "drawings," and even "seats," because the symbols were often placed on the pedestals used for the gods themselves.[18] The symbols retained their associations for more than three millennia.

SERVICE TO THE GODS

Ancient Mesopotamians believed that man was created to serve the gods. This principle was interpreted literally, so the image of the god was cared for, fed, and clothed. The temple administration included the chief priest, various kinds of exorcists, singers, musicians, scribes, and the staff who supervised the temple businesses. The temple staff purified the temple.

According to a detailed text from the Seleucid period, the divine statues in the temple of Uruk were served two meals daily. The first meal was served in the morning when the temple opened, and the other was served at night, immediately before the doors of the sanctuary were closed. Each meal included two courses, called "main" and "second."[19] From descriptions of divine meals, the following sequence can be reconstructed. First, a table was placed before the image. Water for washing was offered in a bowl (even the gods had to wash up before eating!). Then a variety of beverages, special cuts of meat, and fruits were brought to the table.

When the gods ate, they were hidden from both priests and human beings by linen curtains drawn around the statue and table. Music was played during the meal, and ritual fumigation was performed. At the end of the meal, the table was cleared. The curtains were opened and then drawn shut so the gods could wash their fingers. Clearly, the statues of the gods did not and could not eat. In reality, the meal of the god was scaled to feed the temple staff and their families. Also, the food from the divine meal was sent to the king for consumption, perhaps daily or only on special occasions.

In order to serve the god, the temple was designed like a royal palace, with well-equipped kitchens, a reception suite to receive visitors, bedrooms, additional suites for the god's family and servants, a courtyard, and stables. Many temples featured a wharf where the god's boat was moored so that he could visit other deities or his country home in spring and summer.

Enormous amounts of food were provided to temple administrators and craftsmen. For example, one text listed a daily total of more than 500 kilograms of bread, forty sheep, two bulls, one bullock, eight lambs, seventy birds and ducks, four wild boars, three ostrich eggs, dates, figs, raisins, and fifty-four containers of beer and wine, in addition to other offerings.[20]

The best agricultural products and the best animals (cattle, sheep, and goats) were sent to the temple, to be used in three different ways: (1) as daily food served to the divine image, (2) as income or rations for the temple staff who supervised and prepared the divine meals, and (3) to be accumulated for future use or trade. The temple also relied on funds supplied by the royals, wealthy citizens, and, occasionally, booty.

PLACES OF WORSHIP AND THEIR FUNCTIONS

The temple represented the communal identity of each city. The temple was usually located in the center of the city. It was both the largest and tallest building in the city. At each temple worshipers could meet one or more gods to make requests of them. Most gods had a dual function; they both served as the god of a particular place and were the patrons of some particular aspect of life.

The temple was built mostly of mud bricks, but the facades and walls were elaborately decorated. Mud brick columns and half-columns graced the temple, sometimes imitating palm trunks. The most important temples had several courtyards and principal entrances, which led to the temple cella. There was even an ante-cella in front of the cella. The architecture of the temple was carefully planned. Miniature bricks were found at one ancient temple—they were probably used to construct a scale model! Throughout the history of ancient Mesopotamia there was continuity in religious architecture. In the third millennium BCE, temples became the symbolic focus of the city and its surrounding countryside as well as of the state and its rulers.

Stone statues were commonly placed inside temples to act as substitutes for the worshiper, standing before the gods in a state of continuous prayer. Ritual texts described parts of the temple forbidden to outsiders and ritual actions "at a place which is not public." The immense enclosure surrounding the ziggurat at Babylon allowed the people to observe ceremonies, but only from a distance.

Architects designed stepped towers called ziggurats. The ziggurat had a rectangular base and three staircases, which met at right angles and led up to the high temple. The first proper ziggurat was built by Ur-Nammu (2112–2095 BCE), the first king of the Third Dynasty of Ur. Ur-Nammu's piety and attention to building and restoring shrines led to his posthumous deification.

Sanctuaries were considered public places of worship, though, in reality, only the "clergy" visited them. According to texts from the Old Babylonian period, individuals sometimes donated small chapels to the temple. There were also wayside shrines containing numerous votive objects.

The temple was regarded as the god's "house" or "estate," and managed like a secular institution. The temple could own property in more than one place and take part in various productive and commercial activities. The range of the temple's economic activities included cultivation of cereals, vegetables, and fruit trees; management of sheep, goats, and cows; manufacture of textiles, leather, and wooden items; and promotion of trading links with foreign lands. These enterprises necessitated storerooms, granaries, and workshops within the temple enclosure. Some temples lacked sufficient space for expansion in the crowded quarters of the old shrine. In these cases, additional buildings were spread throughout the city and countryside.

Though the temple accumulated capital, rural estates, and craft industries, it was not only a capitalist institution. Evidence of the social conscience of the temples could be found in loans of barley made interest-free to individuals in time of famine. A few sale documents recorded the purchase of children for an unspecified price by the high priest of the temple—transactions which implied the temple's practice of taking in poor children, illegitimate children, and orphans.

The temple also served as a forum for various judicial proceedings, particularly the taking of solemn oaths (possibly for a fee). The gods or their symbols even left the temple to go on location in order to settle human affairs such as boundary disputes or the distribution of shares in a harvest.

Regular offerings were distinguished from those for special occasions such as the great feasts, emergencies, or celebration of joyous events. Enormous offerings were presented at annual festivals. Sacrifices included animals, incense, oil, and butter.

Human sacrifice was occasionally practiced in ancient Mesopotamia. The most striking case was found at the sixteen Royal Tombs of Ur. The principal body was interred in a large pit more than thirty feet deep, lined with stone or brick. In a ritual ceremony, the king's staff was killed or drank poison; in one case as many as seventy-four people, mainly women.

Another form of human sacrifice was practiced in Assyria through the first millennium BCE. When omens foretold grave danger to the king, a substitute king was appointed to rule during this perilous time. Thus, any evil fated for the king befell his substitute. At the end of the substitute king's reign of one hundred days, he and his spouse were ritually killed. An Old Babylonian chronicle reported that Erra-imitti of Isin had Enlil-bani installed as the substitute king; however, Erra-imitti was scalded with hot broth and died, so that Enlil-bani now was his successor.

WORSHIPERS

Hymns and prayers have provided us with a window into the religious beliefs of the ancient Mesopotamians. Individual prayers followed a fixed pattern: (1) at the beginning there was an invocation praising the deity; (2) the middle section, which varied in length, was devoted to the complaints or petitions of the worshiper; and (3) the end included anticipatory expressions of appreciation and praised the god again.[21] The style of these prayers was not very interesting. They used stock phrases, epithets, and hymnal quotations. Many examples of liturgical poems have been found; they expressed feelings of respect, fear, and spirituality. These liturgical poems were addressed to a particular god, before whom the worshiper bowed and appealed for mercy, sometimes through flattery. Only poems composed outside the cult showed more sincere feelings and poetic style—personal requests referring to a specific and very personal experience. Prayer was used for a variety of purposes, such as imparting magical effectiveness to sacred paraphernalia and warding off the evil effects of eclipses and bad dreams. Special prayers expressed laments or complaints; others conveyed blessings. Thus, when man enjoyed economic prosperity and spiritual peace, he attributed his situation to the presence of supernatural powers that either filled his body or guarded him. Conversely, a man blamed his misfortunes, illnesses, and failures on the absence of such protection.

Obedience to the gods was a cornerstone of religious behavior; these obligations included a large number of positive and especially negative prescriptions (taboos). A few examples taken from a list contained the following: one could not invoke the god's name while brandishing an axe, nor drink from a cup of unbaked clay, nor tear out twigs from the steppe or break reeds in the canebrake, nor urinate or vomit in a waterway, nor take away a clod of earth from a field, and so on.[22] The gods inevitably punished humans for their transgressions through accidents, sudden disgraces or illnesses, or unexpected catastrophes.

Prayers were mostly linked with rituals. The rituals were carefully described in a section at the end of the prayer to regulate the actions of the worshiper or priest. The ritual section included the details of sacrifice and the precise time of the offering. The links between the acts and offerings of the prayer were fixed. For example, the merchants who sailed down the Gulf to trade in Bahrain brought "thank offerings" upon their safe return home. They paid a proportion of their cargo to the Temple of Nanna at Ur, which capitalized their venture. Sometimes they added a silver boat, which the scribes recorded as a gift coming "from the prompting of his heart."[23]

RELIGIOUS PERSONNEL AND SERVANTS

Lists of temple personnel have given us a clearer picture of how the temple operated. The staff included cultic, administrative, and domestic staff (such as craftsmen). For instance, the staff at Ninurta's temple at Lagash consisted of the following:

The High-Priest

The lamentation-priest

The purification-priest

The high priestess

The *nadītum*-priestess

The chief *qadištum*-priestess

The diviner

The snake-charmer

The miller

The guard

The fuller

The fuel-carrier

The water-carrier

The oil-presser

The cow herder

The (copper-)smith

The steward

The boatman

The boat-tower

The weaver

The courtyard-sweeper

The barber

The water-pourer

The mat-maker

The runner

The stone carver

The king's butler

The palace guard

The house supervisor

The accountant

The treasurer

The cupbearer

The overseer of the oil-pressers

The scribe[24]

Cultic personnel took care of the gods' needs, placing offerings before them, keeping them clothed and sheltered, and performing rituals. According to Sumerian religious practices, priestesses served as the chief attendants to gods, and priests similarly served goddesses. However, most of the temple staff performed routine tasks such as sweeping the courtyard, guarding the doors, and managing the temple staff and property. From the Akkadian period on the priest's head was shaved, so the barber was part of the temple staff. Another Ur III text provided a list of 180 "musicians" (both vocal and instrumental) and 62 "lamentation-priests" (who chanted) in the temples of Lagash. Music played an important part in both temple and state rituals. Musicians and lamentation-priests were often mentioned together in temple rituals.

The responsibility for arranging the songs of the rituals belonged to the lamentation-priests. The lamentation-priests had to be able to read and sing difficult rituals. They were literate and sometimes acted as scribes. A well-connected lamentation-priest could collect a variety of appointments at different temples.

The duties of the musicians were to sing the songs properly and accompany them with musical instruments. Musicians, both male and female, were often mentioned in large numbers in connection with palaces, escorting the Assyrian kings on their campaigns. The Assyrian kings also captured musicians in their campaigns and brought them back as part of their booty. They included among their ranks snake-charmers and bear wardens as part of a ritual circus performance.

Religious personnel received bread "returned from the sanctuary."[25] That is, the temple staff received regular allotments from the temple income, namely, food, drinks, textiles, wool, and silver goods. Temple personnel always included "live-in" staff. In the Old Babylonian period the regular staff was reduced, perhaps reflecting the separation of temple and palace. Both priestly and domestic offices were treated as prebends (temple offices). Though many prebends became unnecessary, they continued to be inherited, sold, or even rented. The practice of prebends began in the Ur III period and became an elaborate institution during the Old Babylonian period, when temple offices were gradually converted into commercial shares. Certain offices changed hands every few days, but others required specialists, such as craftsmen, scribes, and permanent administrators. Temple offices were usually inherited by the eldest son upon division of the estate. But in time the prebend was subdivided so that individuals might execute their duties only one day a year. During the Seleucid period the prebends were calculated by scribes, who divided the offices into a long and complex total of fractions to convince the purchaser that he was buying a large fraction of the day. Prebends were lucrative, so that their holders wanted the sanctuary to function according to the old rites, which gave them a guaranteed income.

Female religious personnel consisted of various types of priestesses. The high priestesses (Akkadian, *entum*) were cloistered to offer prayers on behalf of their male (and female) relatives (see Chapter 7). They also took part in the Sacred Marriage as attested by cloisters containing a bedroom within the shrine at various excavated sites.

The cloister at Sippar, a large walled enclosure, served as the residence of a whole community of *nadītum*-priestesses. Their cultic role was unclear. The word *nadītum*, "fallow," referred to the women's unmarried or virginal status. At Sippar the *nadītum*-priestesses did not marry. In other communities, such as Babylon, *nadītum*-priestesses could marry but remained celibate.[26] The priestess did not enter the household of her husband but was able to leave an inheritance to her adopted sons or daughters (see Chapter 7). She was given a dowry to set her up in her new home. The Laws of Hammurabi (§§178–180) allowed the *nadītum* a life interest in any property given to her by her father, or, if bequeathed in writing to her, an absolute right to it.[27] The *nadītum* was not reclusive—she was active in business and family life. The priestesses were from wealthy families, and some were even royalty. The cloister staff also included managers, officials, scribes, laborers, and personal female slaves.

Other female religious personnel, mostly in temples of Ishtar, took part in cultic prostitution as part of fertility ceremonies. Greek authors reported that every woman had to offer her body to a stranger in the temple of the goddess of love. Herodotus described temple prostitution as follows:

> The most shameful of the customs of the Babylonians is this: every woman must sit in the shrine of Aphrodite once in her life to have intercourse with a strange man. Many women who scorn to mix with the others, because they are rich and proud, drive to the temple in covered carriages drawn by teams of horses and stand there with their retinue. But most sit in the precinct of Aphrodite, wearing a wreath of string round their heads. . . . And through all the women are passages marked off running in all directions, along which the strangers walk to make their choice. Once a woman has taken her seat, she does not go home until one of the strangers has thrown money into her lap and had intercourse with her outside the shrine; and when he throws the money, he has to say, "I call you by Mylitta," because the Assyrians call Aphrodite Mylitta. The amount of the money does not matter; for the woman will never refuse, because that is against the law, as this money has thus become sacred. She follows the first man who throws money and refuses no one. After the intercourse, she has discharged her duty to the goddess and goes home, and it is then impossible to seduce her, however large the offer. So handsome, tall women can leave soon, but the ugly ones have to wait a long time because they cannot fulfill the law; and some of them stay there for three or four years. There is a similar custom in Cyprus.[28] (Herodotus 1.195–200)

Another group, the "sacred women," were dedicated to the god Adad; they were expected to bear or nurse children, and were probably not prostitutes.

Orphans, children of the poor, and children of insolvent debtors were dedicated as temple slaves. In times of famine, widows gave children to be temple slaves to save them from starvation, but the children stayed with their mothers until they were able to work. Marriage of temple slaves replenished the slave personnel. Privately owned slaves were sent to the temples by their devout masters. During the Neo-Babylonian period, prisoners of war were offered as slaves to the temple.

Most slaves dedicated to the temple were branded, but sometimes the slave mark was a wooden or metal tag on the slave's wrist. The status of a branded slave was passed down at least to the third generation.

Temple slaves were marked on the wrist or the back of the hand with symbols of the gods to whom they were dedicated; for example, a star tattoo was Ishtar's symbol; a spade, Marduk's; and a stylus, Nabu's. Temple slaves were further identified by their own name plus their father's.

When slaves or workers ran away, they were branded or marked, placed in shackles, and returned to work. Also, when slaves refused to work, they were placed in shackles. The demand for shackles was so great that the temples regularly placed orders for their manufacture. Rebellious slaves were sometimes confined to temple prisons.

Temple slaves worked under strict supervision and lived in city districts specially set aside for them, though some owned their own houses or lived in rented lodgings. Numerous texts involving judgments about temple slaves note their harsh treatment. Temple slaves often attacked their overseers and even high temple officials.

Slaves who worked for the temple year round were placed on a permanent allowance, receiving barley in the form of grain or flour, dates, and vegetable oil. Some slaves even received beer, salt, and occasionally meat. The temples also supplied clothing and footwear to their slaves, though slaves often received wool to weave their own garments instead of clothing.

Some slaves, who led an independent economic existence or did not work under the direct, regular supervision of temple officials, were obliged either to pay monetary remuneration or to provide the temple with finished products such as bricks and garments.

RELIGIOUS FESTIVALS

The cultic relationship between the city and its god was formalized at cyclical festivals, such as the New Year's Festival and the festival of each temple and its god. The festivals were usually centered around a cult drama which was reenacted to institute the necessary function. A ritual text specified that "the people of the land will light fires in their homes and will offer banquets to all the gods. They will speak the recitations."[29]

The common man was only able to communicate with the deity through communal religious events such as cyclical festivals and mourning ceremonies. The role the general public played in these elaborate ceremonies remains uncertain. But at the very least the public could observe the great processions as the divine image was carried in a procession through the spacious yards of the temple compound or through certain streets of the city.

When deities left the temple, they showed themselves to the public, took stock of their city, visited their country home, and met with the gods of other cities to determine the fate of the nation or to receive the blessings of major gods. Outdoor rituals involving the god-statues of more than one city helped to maintain theological unity on a national level. With the collapse of the Ur III dynasty, these visits were seldom mentioned, although the gods continued to leave their temples to go on local journeys to settle legal disputes.

Myths spoke of gods and goddesses leaving their homes to visit their friends and relatives. These visits reflected actual ceremonies in which the divine statue was transported for both regular calendar festivals and for special occasions. There were many regular festivals in Babylonia, including festivals of thanksgiving and sheep-shearing. Various cities had their own calendar of seasonal feasts. For example, there were special calendar days for the delivery of first fruits and the offering of the first dairy products of the year. This ritual act was recognized both as a religious celebration and as an exchange of products between the cattlemen in the south and the farmers in the north of Mesopotamia.

The most common festivals were connected with certain days of the month which corresponded to the phases of the moon. The concept of self-generation was usually associated with the moon, which waxed, waned, and finally vanished during each (lunar) month. The ancients believed that the moon actually died at the end of each month, went down to the netherworld, and then came to life again by its own efforts. Special offerings were made on the day the moon was invisible and believed to be dead, "the day of lying down." On this day Nanna descended to the netherworld to render judgment and make administrative decisions there with other deities.[30] When Nanna had completed his duties in the netherworld, he reappeared in the skies as the new moon. A partial or total eclipse of the moon was considered an ominous event. The great gods asked Sin (the moon god) how to avoid the evil omen portended by the eclipse. Purification rites were a general feature of the Mesopotamian cult in order to keep the moon free of defilement during eclipses.

The greatest festival of all was celebrated at the New Year. In Neo-Babylonian times the New Year's Festival took place during the first eleven days of Nisan, the month of the spring equinox. For the first few days, ceremonial ablutions and prayers were performed, but on the evening of the fourth day the whole of the *Epic of Creation* was recited in public, or perhaps reenacted like a medieval mystery play. The *Epic of Creation* told how the universe was created through Marduk's victory, thereby providing assurance to the Babylonians that the world as they knew it would continue unchanged. The fifth day included more ritual purification. The god Nabu arrived from Borsippa to participate in the festival, and so did the king. The king was permitted to enter the inner sanctuary but only after the high priest had removed the royal insignia. The king was humiliated by having his cheek slapped and his ears pulled. Then he knelt before Marduk and assured the god that during the year he had not committed any sins or neglected Esagila and Babylon. After a speech by the priest, the king's insignia were returned to him, and once again he was slapped on the cheek. The more painful his slap, the better, because the tears in the king's eyes signified that Marduk was well pleased. In the evening the king participated in a ceremony in which a white bull was sacrificed. The rest of the ritual text is lost, but from other sources we know that later ceremonies included the famous procession to the New Year's house outside the city. During the parade, the king "took the hand of Marduk," leading him from his shrine along the Processional Way and through the Ishtar Gate. Then the king took part in the so-called Sacred Marriage.

The Sacred Marriage was a fertility drama celebrated in select cities. The date-growers in Uruk celebrated the Sacred Marriage as the power in the date palm to grow and bear fruit, and the herders, dependent on pasture and breeding, believed that consummation resulted in fertility in nature. In this rite the ruler, the priest-king (EN), or king (LUGAL) represented the god. His sexual union with the goddess, Inanna, played by a high priestess or perhaps even the queen, resulted in all of nature being fertilized. The Sacred Marriage was based on the myth "The Courtship of Inanna and Dumuzi" (see Chapter 7). The Sacred Marriage was celebrated at the New Year's Festival when offerings associated with "setting up the bed" were recorded.[31]

SORCERERS, EXORCISTS, AND DIVINERS

Human existence depended on pleasing the gods, but the gods also relied on their human servants to do their work. The gods were easily provoked and ready to destroy man for the most minor offenses, particularly for disturbing their sleep. But since the gods did not want to labor, they also rescued human beings in several myths.

Unjust punishment was expected by the citizens of a totalitarian state. Throughout Mesopotamian history, men complained about the capricious and unfair treatment of the gods in their prayers. "Fate" and "Evil Day," demons of death, brought men and women to the netherworld. Numerous "Evil Days" represented the god's decision to end an empire—that is, collective death.

Magic and Sorcery Magic and sorcery were widespread; they were part of experience and faith in ancient Mesopotamia. There were spells and counter-spells ("releases") for every facet of life. There were no boundaries separating "magic" from "cult" and "religion."

"Magic" included religious behavior that tried to influence man's success, well-being, health, and wealth. There were two major forms of magic: black magic, which brought harm to people, and white magic, which tried to turn away evil caused by demons, malevolent powers, and humans. Since black magic was dreaded, sorcerers were summoned to cancel spells that brought trouble or misfortune to an individual. Most tablets described white magical activities.

The ancient Mesopotamians lived in a world of supernatural forces that constantly threatened their lives and well-being. So, the ancient peoples had a philosophy of life controlled by permanent fear of something negative prowling in the dark—an unknown power lying in wait to harm them. Both evil demons and human sorcerers could strike a person at any time.

Sometimes a specific demon or sorcerer could not be held responsible for the decline of the victim's well-being. Rather, the afflicted person had committed a sin unknowingly, resulting in a "ban" or "curse," which alienated him from the favor of the god(s). Once the individual became aware of his "sin," the situation could be remedied. However, if the reason for divine anger remained unclear, magic was used.

Two compendia, called *Šurpu* and *Maqlû* (both meaning "burning"), were consulted; they contained spells addressed either to deities known for their exorcistic powers or to fire, which was used to destroy figures representing the enemies of the sufferer. The prayers varied greatly in style, content, and literary merit. They contained mythological allusions, folkloric imagery, hackneyed phrases, and abracadabra-like sequences of words.

Šurpu and *Maqlû* were used for different purposes. *Šurpu* contained a collection of spells and rituals that described all possible types of misbehavior, such as cultic negligence, domestic trouble, uncharitable conduct, cruelty to animals, and unintentional contact with ritually unclean people or places. *Šurpu* was concerned with the purification rites for the offender-victim. Objects carrying the sufferer's misdeeds were burned or discarded. As a result the patient was released from the evil effects of his previous actions. *Maqlû* was concerned with burning the image of the witch by fire.

The texts noted the importance of identifying the perpetrator, who, in all surviving witchcraft texts, was unknown to the victim. Several law codes referred to procedures to be followed in cases of sorcery. Because an accusation of sorcery was hard to prove, the accuser himself could face death. For this reason, "witchcraft trials" were avoided whenever possible. Only a fragment of a single letter reported that certain women were accused of witchcraft, but again, we hear nothing of witch trials.[32] In cases in which evidence and testimony were not easily refutable, the standard procedure was to bring the case before the divine judges of the river. Immersion in the "Divine River" brought a verdict of guilt (drowning) or innocence (survival). For example:

If a man charges another man with practicing witchcraft but cannot bring proof against him, he who is charged with witchcraft shall go to the divine River Ordeal, he shall indeed submit to the divine River Ordeal; if the divine River Ordeal should overwhelm him (that is, he drowns), his accuser shall take full legal possession of his estate; if the divine River Ordeal should clear that man and should he survive, he who made the charge of witchcraft against him shall be killed; he who submitted to the divine River Ordeal shall take full legal possession of his accuser's estate.[33] (Laws of Hammurabi §2)

Omens   A large group of omens revealed a predetermined situation, which was avoided by magical means. Omens involved two types of divine revelation given to individuals: (1) a warning about a specific danger predicted by an observable fact, or (2) a notification of a propitious development in the future. Omens were the main way in which Mesopotamian gods communicated their intentions and decisions. That is, the Babylonians believed that the gods disclosed their intentions to humans by signs in natural phenomena and world events. These signs could be interpreted through prolonged observation and deep study. The most common forms of divination were examination of the entrails of sacrificial animals (extispicy) and observation of the stars and planets (astrology). Other forms of communication, though rarely used, were oracles, prophecy, necromancy, or incubation (that is, spending the night in a sanctuary in order to receive a dream message).

Omens were either solicited or unsolicited. In the case of a solicited omen a specialist examined or observed a situation he deliberately induced. The gods could then be asked for advice in a specific situation. Omens predicting disaster for an individual called for the speedy performance of a specific rite to prevent the threat from becoming reality. Rituals were as diverse as the divine signs prompting their use—such rituals were often recorded on individual tablets, each designed for a specific situation.

Unsolicited omens, such as a solar eclipse, the birth of a baby with two heads, or the appearance of a wild animal in the city, could be seen by anybody, and even the casual observer could be affected. If the sign foretold evil, the observer could ward off its evil effect by preventive rites. Signs observed at an individual's house related primarily to that particular person; events that happened in the community (for instance, a wolf seen in town or an untimely regional thunderstorm) affected a city or district. Events in the capital could have consequences for the state administration. Terrestrial or celestial omens, such as earthquakes or eclipses, affected the whole country and its representatives, the king, the court, and their politics or warfare. Preventive rituals were recorded in various ways. Sometimes they were written on individual tablets, each designed for a specific occurrence. At other times, the ritual instructions and incantations were part of an omen series, so the specialist had easy access to all information necessary.

The common man, upon seeing an omen, probably contacted the nearest literate person, a priest, a scribe, a diviner, an exorcist, or even the local authorities. There was no one specialist to deal with unsolicited omens. If none of these people had access to the necessary manuals, they could contact a more erudite specialist or a higher authority, as in the following case:

> To my lord, from your servant Sumkhurabi: In Great Zarrum, among the flocks of sheikh Zazum, a malformed lamb was born, but while I was staying with my lord in Mari, nobody informed me. As soon as I arrived in my district, they brought it to me, telling me the following: "It had one head, (and) its face looked like a ram's face; it (also) had just one breast, heart and (set of) entrails. From its umbilical cord (down) to its loin there were two bodies, but during birth one of its shoulders was ripped off, and (later on?) somebody crushed its head." Now I had it sent immediately to my lord. My lord should inspect it! (Letter from a governor to the king of Mari, Old Babylonian period)[34]

Diviners were specialists who solicited omens from the gods and interpreted the signs. A diviner (literally, "examiner") communicated with divine forces through extispicy, hepatoscopy, lecanomancy, and libanomancy. Diviners also used a variety of procedures to avoid evil events, such as oral formulas, manual rituals, and prayers. The Mesopotamian diviner's most important tool was a copper kettledrum covered with the hide of a black bull. There were rituals describing the ceremonies to provide a new drumhead. The process involved the ritual preparation of a bull chosen to be slaughtered, tanning its skin, and then installing its hide on the drum. After the bull had been slaughtered and its heart burned, they prepared the animal's skin and mourned its death. The bull was given a ritual burial, but its meat supplied food for the priests—as was done with any other sacrificial animal. Unlike exorcists, diviners did not belong to the priesthood of a particular temple. Most diviners known to us by name worked directly for the crown; they were either palace scholars or were attached to local governments or the army. The diviner could have no physical defects and had to be of free descent.[35]

Both private individuals and state officials consulted diviners on all important matters. Diviners usually received communications from the gods through extispicy; the diviner requested the gods to "write" their messages on the entrails, especially the liver, which the diviner "read"

Liver model inscribed with omens. This model records how the liver of a sacrificial lamb looked when the stairs collapsed as Sin-iddinam (1849–1843 BCE) entered the temple of Shamash. Ht. 74 mm, W. 69 mm. © YALE BABYLONIAN
COLLECTION, YALE UNIVERSITY, NEW HAVEN. See A. Goetze, *Old Babylonian Omen
Texts*, Yale Oriental Series 10 (London and New Haven, Yale University Press,
1947), no 1.

by examining the organs. Sometimes the diviners used liver models, interpreting the signs in order to locate or record unusual features. The
diviners had extensive handbooks that listed every conceivable defor-
mation, mark, or discoloration, often further defined by location and
significance.

Hepatoscopy, the type of divination in which the liver of a sacrificed
animal was examined, continued to be the main way of consulting the
will of the gods, even when astral divination gained in importance. In
fact, portents from celestial omens were verified by the questions sub-

mitted to the liver diviner or haruspex. A "letter of recommendation" addressed to the king named twenty-three well-trained scholars and described the haruspex in glowing terms—"he is expert in divination."[36]

Extispicy, the form of divination based on examination of the intestines of slaughtered animals, was used to foretell future events. Extispicy involved at least one animal for each inquiry, so private citizens probably resorted to this technique only in extraordinary circumstances. The diviner was also able to perform cheaper, though less precise, methods for soliciting a divine message, such as lecanomancy (observing the pattern of oil poured onto water, or vice versa) and libanomancy (observing smoke generated by a censer). Also, prayers to the stars, particularly to Ursa Major, the Wagon of the Babylonian sky, were employed by the fortune teller to obtain a reliable omen through a dream. There is a compendium of such information in the Assyrian Dream-book.[37] During first millennium BCE Assyria, there were professional "observers of birds" in the king's service. They furnished reports on omens derived from the movement of birds. The observers of birds were also interpreters of dreams.

The methods of divination described above sought answers on a binary level. The client, king or citizen, through the medium of the diviner, asked for a "yes" or "no" from the gods for a specific problem or situation.

In the case of an ambiguous reading, the signs were counted, and a mathematical majority of positive or negative aspects were totaled to determine the final verdict. If the totals were the same for positive and negative answers, the process was repeated. There was no immediate danger in a negative sign, as long as the situation under investigation was properly postponed or even canceled in due time. Because of this, no follow-up rituals were required. The handbooks used for interpreting the divine signs were organized by topic and followed a format: the omen was listed in the conditional clause (the protasis), "If such-and-such is seen (or happens)," followed by an apodosis that described the portended event in a declarative clause. The list could be expanded indefinitely by variations on the protasis. For example, multiple births were enumerated from two up to eight or nine. Some omens were traced back to historical events of the past, when the occurrences were observed for the first time. Thousands of different signs were collected, and the resulting texts were expanded into purely theoretical "science" by adding scores of conceivable or inconceivable possibilities.

Astral magic is the art of harnessing the power of the stars through prayers and rituals. Professional diviners **Astral Magic** and exorcists practiced astral magic to foretell the future, avoid evil portents (apotropaic rituals), and find the most auspicious moment to undertake a task. An extensive collection of celestial omens described the influence of astral deities on man. Eventually the art of celestial divination became a scholarly discipline.

Prayers to stars were just a few lines or a few words that briefly stated the petitioner's appeal. The reason for turning to the particular god or celestial body was not usually stated. In dire circumstances, divine favor was requested by enumerating the names of stars, the names of gods, natural forces, various rivers such as the Tigris and Euphrates, and so on.

In the *Prayer to the Gods of the Night* the stars and constellations of the night sky were present during the diviner's lonely vigil before dawn when he examined the liver. The night was calm and dark, and the moon and Venus were not visible. The fire on the roof and the constellations provided the only sources of light.

> They have retired, the great ones.
> The bolts are drawn, the locks in place.
> The noisy crowds are still and quiet,
> the open doors have now been closed.
>
> The gods and goddesses of the land—the Sun, the Moon, the
>   Storm, the Morning-Star—
> have gone to where they sleep in heaven,
> leaving aside judgement and decree.[38]

The diviner stood on the roof of the temple and regarded the world below. He concluded his prayer to the celestial bodies for a successful reading:

> May the great gods of the night:
> shining Fire-star,
> heroic Erra,
> Bow-star, Yoke-star,
> Orion, Dragon-star,
> Wagon, Goat-star,
> Bison-star, Serpent-star
> stand by and
> put a propitious sign
> in the lamb I am blessing now
> for the haruspicy I will perform (at dawn).[39]

"Lifting-of-the-hand," a type of prayer named for the accompanying gesture, was offered collectively to "stars" or to "all stars," often called "gods of the night."[40] These prayers were also addressed to constellations, such as the Wagon (Ursa Major), the True Shepherd of Anu (Orion), the Pleiades, the Scorpion (Scorpius), and the Arrow Star (Sirius).

During the first millennium BCE gods were identified with stars. Divine powers became consolidated in a single god. The three highest gods, Anu, Enlil, and Ea, were not equated with individual stars, constellations, or planets. Instead, they represented the entire sky. The major planetary gods were the sun, the moon, and Venus. The sun was the god of justice, and the Scales (the constellation Libra) were called "Shamash's star of justice."[41] The moon was the most important to the ancient Mesopotamians, because it was used to fix their calendar, which was based on lunar months. Sin, the moon god, was the father of both Shamash (the sun god) and Ishtar (Venus). Sin was partial to sorceresses, who could "draw down the Moon." The two celestial appearances of Venus and Mercury were known from early times.

The descriptive names the ancient Mesopotamians ascribed to their planets confirmed their astronomical knowledge. For example, Mercury was called the Leaping One; Saturn (the slowest), the Steady One; and Mars, the Red Planet or the Enemy. Observational astronomy and recognition of the periodicities of heavenly phenomena began in the Old Babylonian period, but mathematical astronomy did not emerge until the fifth century BCE. Babylonian constellations were named after the shapes of their configurations, specifically, human figures, animals, or common objects. These names were either similar or identical to the names of constellations in Classical Greek antiquity.

Hemerologies from Mesopotamia enumerated auspicious days for undertaking a particular kind of business or activity, such as building a house, marrying, or offering prayers and sacrifices to the god or goddess. One of the most common taboos referred to eating fish and leeks on the seventh day of the seventh month.[42] Hemerologies, even in abbreviated form, always included the "evil" days (7, 14, 19, 21, 28). Particular days were named for fasting and sexual abstinence.

There was no clear distinction between the two types of celestial observation, "astronomy" and "astrology." The specialists in these fields either worked together or were experts in both fields. In the case of celestial omens pertaining directly to the king or state, the divinatory science of astrology was generally restricted to specialized scholars associated with the palace or the main temples of the land.

The astronomer was the "expert in celestial matters."[43] The astronomers made regular reports to the king on the monthly sighting of the new moon as well as special reports on various celestial and meteorological phenomena.[44] The meanings of lunar and solar eclipses, other stellar occurrences, and meteorological phenomena were collected and standardized in an omen collection called *When Anu, Enlil*. The astronomer was even called the "scribe of *When Anu, Enlil*," referring to that same celestial omen series. The series included seventy tablets of omens referring to the welfare of the king and the country.

The stars influenced human actions and acted as mediators, like saints, between man and god. In their role of communicating with gods, the stars were the supplicant's messengers, as in the following prayer:

> may the star itself take to you (goddess) my misery;
> let the ecstatic tell you, the dream-interpreter repeat to you,
> let the (three) watches of the night speak to you.[45]

Mesopotamian life harnessed the powers of the stars (1) to cause harm or protect from harm; (2) for amulets and charms; (3) for confirming favorable or unfavorable times; and (4) for medicine, from acquiring the herbs or other medicinal substances, through preparing and administrating the medications. Moonless nights were particularly appropriate for gathering herbs. The stars transformed ordinary substances into potent ones, effective in magic, medicine, or ritual. Stars also provided reliable answers to the queries of the diviner.

The most influential area of Mesopotamian divination was astrology. The ancient Mesopotamians combined here their belief in omens with observational astronomy, mathematical calculation, and eventually the prediction of the movements of heavenly bodies. Western astronomy was later founded on these early records.

The Healing Arts
There was no clear distinction between medicine based on "rational science" and medicine based on magico-religious techniques. Two professions provided health care to the population, the "magical expert" (*āšipu*) and the "physician" (*asû*; see Chapter 5).

Ghosts
Mesopotamians used the native term for a "dead person" interchangeably with the word for a "ghost." A corpse was fully human in appearance (though sometimes skeletal), but a ghost was not. Old souls were recycled as new human beings; otherwise, the dead would have dangerously outnumbered the living.

Unfriendly ghosts pursued, seized, bound, and even physically abused their victims; they even entered their victims through their ears. Ghosts bothered people by appearing uninvited at their homes, assaulting them in city streets, or haunting their dreams. Persons who traveled through uninhabited areas were particularly susceptible to attack by ghosts, sometimes conjured up by sorcerers. The gods sent ghosts to haunt sinners, in particular, murderers. Also, the sorcerers and sorceresses used black magic "to seize a ghost and tie him to a man" and "to hand over an image of the man to death."

Even the most unhappy ghosts could be rendered harmless by performing the correct magical procedure. Methods of dealing with annoying ghosts included tying of magic knots, manufacturing amulets, smearing on magical salves, drinking magic potions, pouring out libations while reciting incantations, and burying a surrogate figurine representing the ghost. Other ghost rituals were similar to those used against demons, demonstrating that the souls of the human dead were immortal and possessed demonic powers.

As long as offerings were made without interruption, a ghost would remain more or less peaceful. Ghosts of the dead returned to haunt the living because they had not received the proper burial rites or their share of the funerary offerings. In order to put a stop to their roaming the earth and perpetrating acts of vengeance, the ghosts were appeased with offerings, the same as those regularly given to the dead. Offerings usually consisted of various types of water, vinegar, watered beer, ashes, and breads or flour made from roasted grain.

The preferred method for consulting ghosts involved the preparation of an ointment. Incantations included instructions for preparing the salve, which was composed of a variety of ingredients, some unusual, as centipede dust, frog intestines, lion fat, and goose-bone marrow. The preparation was smeared on the practitioner's face in order to enable him to see and speak with the ghost. Alternatively, the salve could be rubbed on a figurine or skull that housed the ghost. If the application of ointments failed, the practitioner tried another ritual, an apotropaic ritual of "undoing," called *namburbû*, for which professional ghost raisers could be hired.

Demons were shapeless forms of evil. The names of many Mesopotamian demons are known to us, but few have been **Demons** individually described. Often they appeared in groups of seven, for which a generic incantation such as the following could be used:

> They are seven, they are seven,
> They are seven in the depth of the primeval water,
> They are seven adorned in heaven.
> They are not male, they are not female,
> They are drifting phantoms.
> They have no spouse, never bore a child,
> They do not know the result of their actions,
> They do not pay attention to prayers and offerings.
> They roam about the streets to cause trouble on the highway.
> They are seven, they are seven.[46] (From a Sumerian spell against
>   the *utukku*-demons)

A few demonic figures were described in detail, such as Lamashtu and Pazuzu. Lamashtu, Anu's daughter, brought evil on her own initiative, attacking pregnant women, young mothers, and babies. Many incantations against her recount her ugliness and evildoings:

Face of Khumbaba. Khumbaba, the demon who guards the Cedar Forest in *The Epic of Gilgamesh*. In this example, probably from Sippar, Khumbaba is depicted as the entrails of a sacrificial animal. Ht. 8 cm. © BRITISH MUSEUM, LONDON.

She comes up from the swamp,
is fierce, terrible, forceful, destructive, powerful:
(and still) she is a goddess, is awe-inspiring.
Her feet are those of an eagle, her hands mean decay.
Her fingernails are long, her armpits unshaven . . .
The daughter of Anu counts the pregnant women daily,
follows on the heels of those about to give birth.
She counts their months, marks their days on the wall.
Against those just giving birth she casts a spell:
''Bring me your sons, let me nurse them.

In the mouth of your daughters I want to place my breast!"
She loves to drink bubbling human blood,
(eats) flesh not to be eaten, (picks) bones not to
be picked.[47] (From *Lamaštu* series, tablet 1)

Lamashtu was depicted on many amulets, which were meant to discourage her by having the demon view her own image. The ritual texts accompanying the incantations used various magical techniques, most commonly effigies of Lamashtu being killed, destroyed, buried, dispatched downstream, or sent to the desert.

Another well-known demon was Pazuzu, who was often called upon to neutralize Lamashtu. *Ardat-lilî*, the "Maid of the Storm"(or "*lilû's* girl"), was the prototype of the Biblical Lilith, a frustrated bride, incapable of normal sexual activity, love, and childbearing. Her frustration was transformed into vengeance against young adults—causing impotence in men and sterility in women.

Those who died unmarried joined a special class of demons called *lilû* (female *lilîtu*). *Lilû* and *lilîtu* entered people's homes by slipping through the windows. They looked for victims to fulfill the role of the husbands and wives they had never had. If proper precautions were not taken, the victim was carried off to an early death to become part of the next generation of *lilû* and *lilîtu* demons.

Demons had no cult, received no offerings, and exploited humans mercilessly. The demons who preyed upon people were called the "Seven Evil Spirits," each one given a name such as "Evil Fate," "Evil Constable," or "Disorder." The evil spirits brought diseases on their own initiative. The counterparts to the "Evil Spirits" were the "Evil Ghosts," that is, the souls of the dead that returned to earth for food and drink. Many evil spirits were believed to be the children of two senior gods, Anu and Enlil, who were not always friendly to mankind.

Not all demons and spirits were ill disposed; some were protective spirits, such as the human-headed winged lions and bulls that guarded the gates of Assyrian palaces. The Assyrian king Esarhaddon explained how the guardians fulfilled their duty: they were made of stone "repelling the evil one according to their form."[48] In an inscription Sennacherib boasted that the protective spirits were made from "the *pindû* stone which at the time of my forefathers was (considered) too precious to be (worn) around the neck."[49]

Rituals of "Undoing of Such-and-Such an Evil" (Akkadian, *namburbû*) were inserted immediately after the evil omen. Usually *namburbû* rituals included an incantation accompanied by actions to transfer the evil portent to a disposable object. At the first sighting of the new moon, a male or female figurine, called a "doll," was fashioned. The

Other Rituals and Incantations

Bronze head of Pazuzu. This amulet is suspended near a woman in labor to protect her and her baby from Lamashtu, the child-snatching demon. Ht. 10.5 cm, D. 6 cm, Wt. 1113.6 gm (ca. 8th–7th century BCE). © BRITISH MUSEUM, LONDON.

Winged bull colossus. One of a pair of colossi guarding an entrance to palace of
Sargon II (721–705 BCE) at Khorsabad. On the base, roughly scratched is the grid
for twenty squares, possibly incised by guards or those waiting for entrance.
Behind the bull is a winged protective deity with a bucket and cone. Gypsum.
Ht. 4.42 m. © BRITISH MUSEUM, LONDON.

exorcist was instructed to "throw the doll behind you into the river, and the evil will be loosed."[50] Offerings and purification rites were added "for safety's sake"—to ensure the benevolence of the god who sent the ominous warning. Incantation-prayers, similar to *šu-ila* ("Lifting-of-the-Hand"), appeared next to, and sometimes in place of, magical spells. An incantation was actually addressed to the respective god or goddess directly, as in the following example:

> Shamash, king of heaven and earth, judge above and below,
> Light of the gods, guide of mankind,
> Who judges the cases of the great gods!
> I turn to you, seek you out.
> Command among the gods life (for me),
> May the gods who are with you speak favorably of me.
> On account of this dog that has urinated on me,
> I am afraid, anxious, frightened.
> Deliver me from the evils of this dog,
> Let me sound your praises![51] (*namburbû* prayer from the Neo-Assyrian period)

Some *namburbû* rituals were used in contexts unrelated to ominous portents, to seek help and protection from a specific god. The main characteristic of all *namburbû* texts was personal divine involvement, which was reflected in the ritual.

Rituals for building temples were extremely important; they accompanied the construction through all its major stages, from selecting the site to the final consecration. The rites of "Opening/Washing of the Mouth" were used to purify and introduce the divine images of worship into the temple. These rituals were repeated whenever the cult statue came into contact with something impure, for example, through repair work or illegitimate intrusions by noncultic personnel (see "Representations of the Gods," above).

In nocturnal rituals the moon and sun could combine their influences for healing. Thus, two dates, two regularly occurring planetary events (a lunar and solar eclipse), were specifically designated for dispensing potions and for performing rituals (see "Religious Festivals," above).

Some rituals required that both the sun and the moon be present on the fifteenth day of the month, against a spirit of the dead, a "persecuting ghost," who haunted a man. This ceremony was performed at dawn, when the full moon set and the sun rose. The exorcist was instructed to clothe the patient and draw blood by making cuts on his forehead with an obsidian (knife). The patient then sat in a reed hut, facing north. The exorcist made an incense offering of juniper and libated cow's milk to

Sin at sunset in addition to an offering of cypress and libated fine beer to Shamash at sunrise. Then the patient recited the following incantation seven times: "To my left is Sin, the crescent of the great heavens, to my right the father of mankind, Shamash the judge, the two gods, ancestors of the great gods, who determine the lots for the far-flung people. An evil wind has blown at me, the persecuting ghost persecutes me, so that I am worried, I am troubled, disturbed as I face your verdict. Save me so that I not come to grief." Then the patient left the reed hut to change his clothes, put on a pure garment, and uttered another incantation three times, asking Sin to remove his illness.[52]

Many situations in everyday life required, or at least benefited from, the use of magico-religious techniques. "Potency" rituals provide the clearest example for manipulative magic. These spells and instructions were used to seduce, to rekindle passion, and particularly to enable the male partner to sustain an erection. A little magic could go a long way by inducing sexual desire that may have not existed previously. Lovers addressed prayers to Venus, the planet of Ishtar, the goddess of love. The accompanying ritual instructed the supplicant as follows: "you set up a reed altar before Ishtar-of-the-Stars, you make offerings" and, having prepared six times two figurines, "you burn (them) before Ishtar-of-the-Stars." A "woman whose husband is angry with her" prayed to Ishtar, calling to her "in the midst of the sky";[53] this was one of the few love charms women recited to seduce their lovers to return. The ritual activities prescribed in these texts employed certain objects which were magically "enriched" with the power of love, often derived from the sexual organs of certain animals. These objects were brought into physical contact with the desired partner. The spells usually referred to the strong sexual potency of animals, accompanied by vivid descriptions of sexual techniques, desires, and fantasies—all directed at stimulation and arousal before intercourse:

> Let the wind blow, let the orchard sway,
> Let the clouds gather together, and raindrops fall!
> Let my potency flow like running river water!
> Let my penis be (as taut as) a harp string,
> Let it not slip out of her![54] (Potency incantation, Neo-Assyrian
>   period)

Many other genres and uses of magico-religious rituals were available to the ancient Mesopotamians, such as the generic incantation for "reconciling a man's god or goddess with him" or incantations for calming a baby—"Let Mother Get Her Chores Done." The baby incantations revealed the themes and style of earlier lullabies.

Magical
Paraphernalia
Magical protection was necessary for both palaces and private residences. Protective spirits were placed near windows, drainpipes, and doorways—that is, places through which demons might enter. The manufacture and use of prophylactic figurines, many of which have been found throughout Mesopotamia, were described in great detail. The statues were buried beside the threshold. Some of these were dogs with names such as "Don't stop to think, bite!" and "Loud of bark."[55]

A compendium called "the nature of the stone is" listed numerous stones used for appeasing divine anger, preventing migraine, and being received favorably by the king. The power of the stone was defined by its material and its nature. For example, magnetite was of special interest, and its epithet described its magnetic attraction. The epithet "capturing" may refer to magnetite's being captured with other rebellious stones by Ninurta in the Sumerian myth "Lugal-e." The popular etymology of hematite was explained as "the stone of truthfulness, he who wears it will speak the truth, only a pious man may wear it."[56]

Besides handbooks, there were shorter lists of herbs, stones, or a combination of herbs, stones, shells, and various other magical paraphernalia. The list of enumerated "stones" included beads of metal (namely, silver, gold, copper, iron, or tin) and beads of various minerals such as antimony. The stones were rarely qualified except as being "male" or "female" (the same as herbs). Male and female stones were listed in magical texts, stone lists, and "glass texts," which explained how to make glass.[57] There were even references to natural markings, such as "which shows a (moon?) crescent," and some shells were specified as having seven spots.[58]

Amulets were widely used; they were found in every possible location from royal palaces to poor neighborhoods. That is, magico-religious thinking crossed social and economic classes. Various stones were strung on a cord of wool and worn as charms around the neck, on the right or left wrist, or the right or left ankle. A small tablet listed "eleven stones for blurred vision, to string on red wool . . . while you recite a charm, and tie it on his left hand."[59] Other amulet stones were placed on the chest or the abdomen. Prescriptions for various illnesses included long lists of beads, enumerated in groups for each string. The string or the individual drew its power by being exposed to the stars.

PROPHETS

Male and female prophets, literally "ecstatics" or "frenzied persons," were believed to be selected by the gods for a specific occasion or time period to convey information to an individual or group. The deity usu-

Clay dog. Models of mastiffs are deposited in groups of ten, with their names inscribed on them, and each pair is painted in the following five colors: red spots, red, yellow-white, green-blue, black, as prescribed ritually in texts. The clay figurines protect against disease and, as such, were associated with Gula, the goddess of healing. This dog (ca. 645 BCE) is painted red and bears the inscription "Catcher of the enemy!" Ht. 4.5 cm, L. 7 cm, D. 1.9 cm. © BRITISH MUSEUM, LONDON.

ally initiated the communication, but the recipient could also induce communication. The prophet received his information from visions, dreams, auditions, and more mechanical media such as divinatory techniques. Once the prophet received the message, he would repeat or rephrase it in oral or written form—often poetically—to provide inspired insight into the situation. Prophetic activity was widespread throughout the ancient Near East, although only a small number of prophetic texts has survived. After the eighth century, prophecy became a cultic activity in Assyria—the sayings of both male and female prophets were recorded in tablet series.

Akkadian prophecies usually contained "predictions" of events that had already happened, although some were genuine forecasts.[60] The language of these prophecies drew heavily on predictive statements (or apodoses) of omens. The accounts used formulaic expressions that re-

Amulet of lion-headed god. Crudely manufactured, the figure on the front of the amulet and the inscription on the reverse are crudely scratched. At the top is a hole so that the amulet could be suspended. The human-bodied figure has the head of a lion and the claws of a bird. He protects against evil demons and illnesses. Ht. 27 cm, W. 25 cm. © YALE BABYLONIAN COLLECTION, YALE UNIVERSITY, NEW HAVEN.

vealed the identity of the recipient and the place where the revelation occurred. The largest number of Mesopotamian prophetic texts was discovered in excavations at Mari.

Oracles were sometimes similar to prophecies and communicated by priests. An Assyrian oracular message was sent by Ishtar to a priest, which he, in turn, reported to Assurbanipal as follows:

> The goddess Ishtar who lives in Arbela entered. Right and left quivers were suspended from her. In her hand she was holding a bow and (her) sharp sword was drawn ready for battle. You were standing before her and she spoke to you like a real mother. Ishtar, most exalted among the gods, called to you, instructing you as follows: "Wait to the attack; wherever you plan to go, I am also ready to go" ... She repeated her command to you as follows: "You will stay here where you belong. Eat, drink wine, enjoy yourself, praise my divinity, while I go and accomplish that work to help you achieve your heart's desire. Your face will not be pale; your feet will not be shaky; and you will not need to wipe off sweat at the height of battle" ... Then she went out in a fearsome way to defeat your enemies, (namely) against Te'umman, king of Elam, with whom she was angry.[61]

This Assyrian oracular text referred to a historical event. According to Elamite records, Te'umman and Assurbanipal were constantly at war. When Assurbanipal was at Arbela, he was told of the mobilization of Te'umman's army against him. Ishtar of Arbela, the goddess of war, provided Assurbanipal with a favorable oracle. Assurbanipal's army entered Elam, and Te'umman was caught and beheaded. The oracle clearly combined politics with religion. That is, the gods of political enemies became enemies of each other; the gods were credited with brutality toward their human enemies.

Kings did not always believe the predictions of diviners, as shown in a letter addressed to King Esarhaddon, who was known for being superstitious: "This is what it (the text) says about that eclipse that occurred in the month of Nisan: 'If the planet Jupiter is present during an eclipse, it is good for the king because in his stead an important person at court will die,' but the king closed his ears—and see, a full month has not yet elapsed and the chief justice is dead!"[62] At times the professional honesty of the diviners was doubted. In diviners' reports to Assyrian kings, the diviners go to great lengths to interpret bad omens to have a favorable meaning. In order to obtain a true report, King Sennacherib of Assyria separated his diviners into two groups—much as today's scientists use a control group.

10

Government

THE KING

The Mesopotamian king was considered the gods' representative on earth. An Akkadian proverb provided the metaphor: "Man is the shadow of a god, and a slave is the shadow of a man; but, the king is the mirror of a god."[1] Both political and religious events on earth were believed to be mirrored and explained by events in heaven.

Secular government was universally in the hands of a single ruler, who was almost invariably male. The name of the ruler's position varied from city to city. For example, some rulers held the title *sanga*, "chief accountant (of the temple)," perhaps reflecting the economic basis of their authority. At other times the king was called *en*, originating from high priestly office. In several cities the ruler was referred to as *ensi*, "city governor." Finally, *lugal*, "king" (literally "great man"), was a title accorded to the most powerful *ensi*. Hammurabi put an end to the institution of the *ensi* once and for all by using its Akkadian equivalent, meaning "farmer."

The kings also held various titles, such as "the strong king" (meaning the legitimate king); "the legitimate king" (in reality, a usurper); and "the king of the four corners (of heaven and earth)" (emphasizing the king's expansionist policies).

Unlike the Egyptian pharaohs, who were regarded as gods, the kings in Babylonia and Assyria were usually considered mortals. In exceptional cases, certain kings had themselves divinized. Cultic structures similar to those of the traditional gods were built for some kings.

Mesopotamian kingship had a religious dimension. Me-
Legitimization   sopotamian theology incorporated the concept that king-
of the King   ship was one of the basic institutions of human life,
designed by the gods for mankind. The gods were de-
scribed as choosing the king, that is, "taking his hand." The gods were
even credited with some role in his creation, birth, and upbringing. Divine approval was necessary because there were no unequivocal secular
criteria.

Rulers often cited the fact that their father or other ancestors preceded
them as ruler. Ancestry constituted some form of legitimacy, but inheritance of office by the eldest son was not strictly followed. Rulers could
be succeeded by their brothers. Members of the royal family who had
no claim to the throne defended the legitimacy of their usurpation
through divine calling.

Safeguarding the king was of great importance. A large number of
omens referred to safety or danger to the king, and divination was used
to protect the monarch. The king was subject to various religious stric-
tures in order to safeguard him against an evil day or an evil omen. On
some occasions the Assyrian king had to fast for several days until the
new moon appeared. The kings wore the clothes of a nanny, remained
indoors, donned a white robe for several days, and stayed for a week in
a reed hut like a sick person.

The ruler was chosen from among the population of the city, and his
acceptance by the people was important. The king's rule could come to
an end if his people revolted. The inscriptions of Uru-inimgina, a usurper
(from Lagash, ca. 2350), described his reform of social injustices and his
concern for the welfare of the citizens, particularly the orphan and the
widow, as part of his claim to legitimacy.

Installation ceremonies were held at Ur, Nippur, and Uruk and involved three symbolic acts similar to those used by today's monarchies:
"coronation," "enthronement," and taking a mace or "scepter."[2] A Sumerian epic explained that when kingship was brought to earth after the
Flood, it was represented by three symbols: the crown, the throne, and
the scepter—images that recurred numerous times in hymns addressed
to the king; other royal emblems were added, as in the following hymn
to Rim-Sin, King of Larsa:

> May An fix the holy crown on your head,
> May he install you grandly on the throne of life,
> May he fill your hands with the scepter of justice,
> May he bind to your body the mace which controls the people,
> May he make you grasp the mace which multiplies the people,
> May he open for you the shining udder of heaven, and rain
>   down for you the rains of heaven.[3]

Reconstruction of an Assyrian Throne Room, originally a colored print, published by A.H. Layard in *The Monuments of Nineveh*. Layard described this hall as restored from actual remains found in the ruins. Winged human-headed lions guard the entrance. On the lower parts of the walls are stone bas-reliefs, copied from actual examples found at Nimrud, but arranged here without regard to their original positions. The drawing of the ceiling was purely speculative. © BRITISH MUSEUM, LONDON.

The king's family, including his children, nephews, and cousins, were trusted members of the royal house and paid with nepotism. As far back as Sargon, the king's daughter was appointed the priestess of the moon god, Nanna, at Ur. **The Royal Family**
The dedication of a daughter as a priestess was considered important enough to be mentioned as a major event in the names of the years of a king's reign.

The household quarters of the king were quite separate from the administrative section of the palace. The king had a problem keeping order among the women in his household. In addition to any wives or concubines the king might have taken, a large number of other women arrived at his court, either sent from foreign princes seeking dynastic alliances or brought as part of the booty from conquered cities. Life could become tedious and tense, and a series of edicts from the fourteenth through the eleventh centuries BCE referred to the king's wives and other women cursing and arguing among themselves. If a member of the palace staff listened to women quarreling or singing, he risked a severe beating and having one of his ears cut off. Among the women themselves, discipline was harsh. A palace lady had the right to give her maid thirty strokes of the rod for a first offense, possibly so viciously inflicted that the girl might die; in this case, the lady herself was liable to punishment.

There were stringent rules about courtiers meeting with palace women. When an official had to enter the palace, all the women had to be hurried from sight to an area outside the harem quarters. The chief wife and the royal concubines lived, at least at the Assyrian court, in a harem guarded by eunuchs. Under no circumstances could a courtier approach within seven paces of a woman to speak with her; if they had a rendezvous and were discovered, both were put to death. If a palace woman called to a courtier when she was undressed and he caught a glimpse of her while answering, he was severely beaten.

Reigning or even powerful queens were the exception. Normally the queen was the king's consort and had no royal functions. Short inscriptions by queens were rare but indicated that a few strong women often exercised considerable influence, also documented in letters. In Assyria, King Sennacherib deeply loved his Syrian-born wife, Naqiya-Zakutu, and even ensured that her death was recorded in the Babylonian Chronicle—an extraordinary event. When Sennacherib was murdered by one of his own sons, the crown prince, Esarhaddon, could not be installed for three weeks. So for three weeks control of Assyria fell into the hands of the queen mother, Naqiya-Zakutu. The queen mother continued to wield considerable power during the early years of the reign of Assurbanipal, her grandson. Royal officials feared her.

The Palace Complex

The secular bureaucracy in the palace was probably modeled on the traditions of the temple. The major temples created a bureaucracy to administer and keep detailed records of its employees and of the commodities under its supervision.

As territories expanded, each independent state became a province. The bureaucracies of the former regime were maintained, but usually an outsider was selected to govern. By the middle of the second millennium BCE, the old system of provincial governors evolved into petty kingdoms in which larger states were administered as districts, each with a governor—a policy adopted by Hammurabi, among others. The king retained some form of limited sovereignty by appointing a trusted nominee.

In the Old Babylonian period, the king regulated most of the palace activities both inside and outside the palace, such as craft industries, agricultural estates, and business activities. Reports were made to King Hammurabi himself about the collection of revenues from both the temple and the palace. Tax collectors were forced to collect the full tab or make up the deficit themselves. King Hammurabi paid attention to even the smallest details in his letters, describing time and labor devoted to building and maintaining canals and defense walls. The king also kept a close eye on his officials, who defended themselves against charges of negligence in their letters.

As the palace organization grew, the complexity of palace architecture came to reflect new requirements, such as the installation of a throne room and audience hall. Within the royal court there might be several subcourts, such as that of the queen mother or crown prince, along with their staffs. The crown prince sometimes had his own palace, called the "House of Succession." The provincial governors might even have a palace in the capital, apart from the royal palace.

The palace complex served a variety of functions. It was the residence of the king, his family, and household servants. It housed the government and administrative offices as well as workshops. Household goods and royal treasure were stored there. Ceremonies of state took place at the palace. Provincial officials sent regular provisions for the palace personnel and livestock.

The king was chosen by the gods to provide prosperity and righteousness. As ruler, he was responsible for the welfare of all subjects, especially the poor and the weak. Temple offerings made by the king had both religious and political overtones; that is, the temple personnel accepted the king's offerings because he was the recognized ruler. Divine approval of the king's actions resulted in prosperity. **Duties of the King**

Mesopotamian rulers built and rebuilt temples. Rulers were depicted carrying a basket of earth or builder's tools thrown over their shoulder. Sometimes rulers carried the first basket or molded the first brick of a temple. The king ordered the fashioning of images of the gods. He also provided income to maintain the temple staff and took part in festivals.

The king could delegate responsibilities. He could not participate in every local ritual in person as required, so he sent representatives from his family, much like kings and queens of present-day monarchies. The king also took part in emergency rituals to avoid evil omens.

ADMINISTRATION OF JUSTICE

The king was directly responsible for administering justice on behalf of the gods, who had established law and order in the universe. The king was considered the final judicial authority for all appeals within his realm. Though appeals were made to him, he often referred them back to the lower authorities.

Mesopotamian judicial institutions had clear procedural guidelines for settling disputes. The facts had to be clearly established before a verdict was rendered. Oral testimony was taken from two contestants; witnesses were called from either side; and documents, if available, were presented. In one case the judges accepted a fifty-two-year-old text that was in such bad condition that "the envelope of the tablet was broken, so they extracted the tablet from inside to read it."[4]

If the facts of the case were not clear, judges might write to local authorities to have witnesses sent or request further investigation locally. At the end, the penalty had to suit the crime. Judicial tasks were carried out by local councils, judges and courts, and the king. For example, in a lawsuit Ilusha-khegal, a priestess, claimed that she had not received full payment for land sold to the current owner, Belessunu, a priestess and wife of Addi-liblut. An excerpt from the case illustrates the judicial procedures followed:

> The judges requested from Ilusha-khegal (to provide) witnesses that Belessunu, the *nadītum* (-priestess), had not paid her the silver, or (documentation for) the debt-document which they had made out to her for the remainder of the silver, but they (that is, the documents) did not exist and she did not produce them; whereas Addi-liblut did produce the sealed deed for 1 SAR of house, and the judges read it, and questioned the witnesses who were written in the deed and they gave evidence before the judges in front of Ilusha-khegal that she had received 15 shekels of silver as the price of 1 SAR of developed property (literally, "a built house"), and Ilusha-khegal conceded it. The judges examined their case, and because Ilusha-khegal had disowned her seal they imposed a penalty on her and made out this tablet renouncing her claim.[5]

Judicial Procedures   The court of first resort in early Mesopotamia was the local council, which included the elders and mayor of the village or city quarter. Their decisions, both judicial and administrative, were announced by a public herald. Correspondence showed that though the local council passed judgment, the council (and even the litigant) could refer the case to a higher court.

Judges presided by the Early Dynastic period, sometimes in conjunction with the ruler of the city-state. Attorneys were never mentioned. In the Old Babylonian period the town mayor and elders usually settled minor local disputes, while other cases were brought before the whole town to render a decision. At times one party and his witness(es) were required to testify under oath, usually in the presence of the god's symbol, which was rented from the temple. Lying under oath was hindered by the fear of divine vengeance in cases of perjury. When there was contradictory evidence, the divine judges of the river were summoned to decide the case by the River Ordeal. Immersion in the "Divine River" brought a verdict of guilt (drowning) or innocence (survival). The River Ordeal was reserved for cases in which grave accusations could not be decided by any other means, for example, perjury, sorcery, adultery, and homicide. Evidence for execution of the death penalty is almost wholly lacking.[6] Both the death sentence and mutilation were perhaps oral pronouncements, and only civil cases involving compensatory damages were transcribed.

There was no Akkadian word for "court," and the term used implied that the case was brought before a judge or benches of judges who sat at the gate or in the temple courtyard. We do not know the credentials of these judges and how they were chosen. Some judges seem to have been appointed when necessary, possibly from among the "elders" and prominent secular and temple officials. There is some evidence for the appointment of more permanent judges, known as "judges of the king," who were also responsible for administrative duties. By the beginning of the Old Babylonian period some men were given the professional title of "judge." Judges were expected to display high standards of professional conduct, as noted in the Code of Hammurabi (§5): "If a judge tried a case and made a decision and had a sealed document executed, but later changed his judgment, they will convict that judge of changing his judgment: he will pay twelve times the claim involved in that case, and they will remove him in the Assembly from his judgment seat, and he will not sit in judgment with the judges again."[7]

A good deal is known about the administration of justice. There were court officials who ensured that the court's decision was executed. The Old Babylonian courts had a sheriff (literally, "soldier") whose duties included recovering property and bringing a baby to court to record its birth. Another official attached to the court was a barber, who gave slaves the hairdo characteristic of their status. Later the barber performed unrelated tasks such as destroying tablets nullified by a royal edict.[8] A herald also was an official at the court; his duties involved announcing official information. It was the herald who publicized the loss of a seal and its dates, so any documents sealed after that date would be deemed invalid. He also advertised a runaway slave, announced government conscriptions, and presided over house sales. The king himself could hear cases, and any citizen could appeal directly to the king. The lower courts might refer a case to the king.[9] Murder trials traditionally were the king's domain.

The king might require that the two opposing parties take oaths. Letters described Hammurabi judging and supervising cases. Sometimes penalties affected the entire community; for example, §23 stipulates that if a man was robbed but the robber was not caught, the local authorities had to compensate the victim for his loss. The code included both civil and criminal matters. Preserved also are the texts of some "decrees" considered to be royal decisions. For example, two decrees in the edict of Ammi-saduqa of Babylon (1646–1626 BCE) concern offenses punishable by death:

> The wholesale and retail merchants [who have used] a false seal (in order to certify their "documents"), will be put to death.
>
> The representative of the king or the local governor who has forced upon the family of a worker attached to the king, grain, silver, or wool, in order to make him harvest or perform work for his own profit, will be put to death. His victim will keep everything that was given to him. (Edict of Ammi-saduqa §§18 and 22)[10]

After ca. 1500 BCE, the kings of both Babylonia and Assyria issued decrees of exemption from various kinds of conscripted service such as military obligations and corvée labor as well as a moratorium on debts to certain cities.

Legally Valid Transactions   Contracts could be either written or oral. Legal formulas were recited in certain cases, for example, "You are not my wife" (divorce) or "You are not my father" (resulting in disinheritance of an adopted child). Symbolic acts were described in legal documents such as "crossing of the pestle," in which a slave stepped over a pestle as a symbol of servitude,[11] or striking one's forehead, which indicated agreement to act as a guarantor in a transaction. In time, symbolic acts were phased out.

The law regarded a document as proof that a transaction had occurred in a legally valid manner. There are innumerable extant Sumerian, Babylonian, and Assyrian legal documents. All major business transactions and agreements required a contract.

Legal documents recorded purchases, employment, and exchange of goods and property. In addition, there were partnership deeds, gifts, deposits, and debt certificates. Marriage and adoption contracts as well as inheritance documents were rare. Certain legal documents included established formulas, while others had more flexible language. Usually documents began with a precise description of the matter at hand. Contracts involving money or property often noted that they were not made under duress. Large fines were imposed on anyone breaking the agreement. The body of the text was followed by a list of witnesses, sometimes including their respective seals. Winesses could be called to testify in order to verify the transaction. Neo-Babylonian documents often included curse formulas in case any party broke the agreement. Finally, documents might include the place and date, but not always.

Documents were often enclosed in sealed clay "envelopes," which contained a copy of the contract inside, or at least important excerpts from it. In the case of a dispute, the envelope could be opened and compared with the text inside.

At the beginning of a king's reign, edicts were announced, rather than recorded, in order to provide **Royal Reforms** short-term relief from social and economic injustices. **and** The first known edict was from Uru-inimgina. Royal **Law Codes** edicts have been found through the reign of Hammurabi and after, when they became a regular institution.

The next step taken by the king was recording collections of laws. The law codes began with a prologue written in the style of a royal inscription, followed by a collection of laws, which formed the main body of the text. An epilogue contained curses against those who should try to deface or alter a stele. Each collection was a new, independent legal work, but some laws were quoted verbatim from previous collections. Most of the laws were formulated like omens, including a conditional clause and a statement: for example, "If a man has committed robbery, he will be killed." None of the legal collections was organized systematically; cases of penal, civil, trade, and work laws alternated with each other.

The most complete law code by far was the Code of Hammurabi (ca. 1750 BCE). A relief of King Hammurabi of Babylon (1792–1750 BCE), receiving the insignia of royal power from Shamash (the god of justice) was portrayed at the top on the front of the stele. The last seven of these columns were erased by Shutruk-Nakkhunte, the Elamite king, who took the monument as part of his booty (ca. 1595 BCE). There were 282 cases, taking into account the missing portion in the middle. The penal law was much harsher than older laws. The death penalty was a common punishment. Mutilations (such as cutting off a hand) as well as beatings were frequently prescribed. Hammurabi termed his laws "cases of justice." Many copies of the Code of Hammurabi were made on stelae and clay tablets and have been found from the time of Hammurabi through the Seleucid period. Late texts included commentaries in order to facilitate understanding of the code.

The Code of Hammurabi may have represented a collection of decisions, customary law, legal innovations, and designations of areas in need of amendment. The codes may have standardized traditional practices. We do not know for certain to what extent the codes were actually implemented in judicial practice.

In both the prologue and epilogue, the word used for laws is "decision," perhaps referring to royal decisions. The key to understanding the purpose of the legal code may be found in the epilogue: "Let the wronged man who has a case go before my statue (called) the 'King of

Stele of the Code of Hammurabi (1792–1750 BCE). The stele has a prologue, a law code, and an epilogue, inscribed in 3,500 lines on both sides of this diorite stele. At the top Hammurabi stands before Shamash, the sun god and god of judgment. Ht. 2.25 m, Wt. 4 tons. © LOUVRE MUSEUM, PARIS.

Justice' and have my inscribed stele read and hear my valuable words. Let my stele reveal his case; let him see the law which applies to him, and let his heart be at rest."[12] The stele was placed in Babylon before a statue of Hammurabi, erected in the twenty-second year of his reign.[13]

Alternatively, the code may have been a model for just royal decisions, as also described in the epilogue: "To the end of days, forever, may the king who happens to be in the land observe the words of justice which I have inscribed on my stele . . . let that stele reveal to him the accustomed way, the way to follow, the land's judgements which I have judged and the land's decisions which I have decided."[14]

Hammurabi's laws were not statutes in the modern sense; to date, only one reference has been found to his laws among thousands of court records, in a contract dealing with the cultivation of land (dated in the fifth year of Hammurabi's successor). The penalty clause stated that, in the case of a breach of contract, the cultivator will be treated "according to the wording of the stele."[15]

Some cases in public documents were settled in a completely different way from the Code. In comparing the Code of Hammurabi with contemporaneous administrative and legal documents, we find numerous omissions and contradictions in the law code.

As for Assyrian laws, Old Assyrian documents and letters cited laws which were part of a merchant statute, based on either Assyrian or local laws. Middle Assyrian laws have been found in a fragmentary state. The first tablet, almost completely preserved, concerned women. The second dealt with property rights, and the third dealt with slaves, livestock, and goods. According to the Middle Assyrian laws, the status of women was low. Punishments in all cases were exceedingly harsh, including the death penalty, beatings up to one hundred blows, forced labor, and various mutilations. River ordeals were frequently used by judges to decide guilt or innocence. There was no further codification of law in Assyria after the second millennium BCE.

WARFARE

Warfare often arose as the result of wealth, control of the Tigris and Euphrates for transportation and irrigation, boundary disputes, and the need to acquire luxury goods such as timber, stone, and metals. City walls originally may have been built to protect livestock from wild animals and poachers. Some early walls did not encircle the city fully and were perhaps used as barriers against flooding. Once erected, the walls displayed the wealth and power of the ruler; sometimes they were even richly decorated.

The people of the ancient Near East explained warfare as the will of the gods. In 714 BCE, Sargon II attacked his northern neighbor, Urartu; he issued a report to the national god which was probably read publicly at the New Year's Festival, justifying his invasion and claiming divine approval:

I, Sargon, king of the four regions (of the world), ruler (shepherd) of Assyria, guardian of the . . . of Bel-Marduk . . . the rightful king, whose words are gracious, whose aversion (abomination) is falsehood . . . because I had never yet come near Ursa, the Armenian, and the border of his wide land, nor poured out the blood of his warriors on the (battle)-field, I lifted my hands, praying that I might bring about his defeat in battle, turn his insolent words against himself, and make him bear his sin.

Assur, my lord, heard my words of righteous (indignation), they pleased him and he inclined to hear my just prayer. He granted my request.[16]

Sargon II claimed that he was punishing Urartu on behalf of the gods because of the impiety of its king. Sargon allowed the surviving Urartian army and its allies to flee, realizing the propaganda value of the reports they would spread about the mighty Assyrian army.

Divine support for royal campaigns was also described by oracle texts from Ishtar of Arba'il, as leader of battle. Royal inscriptions often referred to her as the goddess who goes at the king's side into battle, although reliefs portrayed standards of other gods accompanying the king in battle.

Each step of the campaign was checked in advance by extispicy, which was accompanied by very specific questions, such as, "Will Kashtaritu (ruler of Karkashi in Media) and his troops, or the troops of the Cimmerians, or the troops of the Mannaeans, or the troops of the Medes, or of any other enemy capture that city Kishassu?"[17] Diviners probably accompanied the army on all its campaigns. Omens referred to death in military campaigns by phrases such as "the one who goes in front of the army," "a famous soldier," "a hero," and the diviner who might "fall" (in battle).[18] Other dangers described in the omens were approach, ambush, surrounding, assault by the enemy, and so on.

All nations developed practices to curb the savagery of war; unfortunately, the conventions were not uniform, thus giving one army an advantage. For example, the Egyptians had a ban against surprise attacks, even postponing a battle until the enemy was ready to fight. However, the Hittites accepted the element of surprise as a legitimate military tactic, as is known from their attack against the headquarters of the Egyptian king.

Psychological Warfare   The Assyrians publicized their atrocities in reports and illustrations for propaganda purposes. In the tenth and ninth centuries BCE, official inscriptions told of cruelty to those captured. Most were killed or blinded; others were impaled on stakes around city walls as a warning. The bodies were mutilated; heads, hands, and even lower lips were cut off so that counting the dead would be easier. These horrifying illustrations, texts, and reliefs were designed as a warning to frighten the population into submission.

Assyrian strategy for conquering foreign territories included siege warfare, pitched battles, and psychological warfare. The Assyrians did not have a navy and turned to the Phoenicians when they had to go to sea. Because sieges and pitched battles took much energy, time, and manpower, the Assyrians preferred psychological warfare whenever possible. When the Assyrians decided to conquer an area, they first tried rhetoric to persuade or threaten people into submission without a fight. The Bible (2 Kings 18:17–19:8; 2 Chron. 32:9–19; Isa. 36:1–37:8) recorded Sennacherib's invasion of ancient Israel. Sennacherib was occupied, so he sent his chief cupbearer along with other senior officers and an army to Jerusalem. When the Assyrians approached the gates, King Hezekiah of Judah sent senior officials to greet them. The cupbearer delivered a message from the Assyrian king, challenging their reliance on Egyptian support, claiming, "You rely, of all things on Egypt, that splintered reed of a staff, which runs into a man's hand and punctures it if he leans on it!" (2 Kings 18:21). The cupbearer mocked the size of their army compared to Assyria's. He taunted the people on the wall in their own language, urging them to surrender and turn against Hezekiah. The chief cupbearer promised peace and prosperity if they submitted to Assyria. The attempt failed—both Hezekiah and his people refused to answer.

When surrounding the capital city and shouting to the people inside failed, the Assyrians' next tactic was to select one or more small cities to attack, usually ones that could be easily conquered. Then the Assyrians committed extreme acts of cruelty to show how the entire region would be treated if the inhabitants refused to surrender peacefully. Houses were looted and burned to the ground, and the people were murdered, raped, mutilated, or enslaved—acts all vividly portrayed in the Assyrian stone reliefs and royal inscriptions in the palaces. The Assyrian troops regarded looting and rape of a conquered city as partial compensation. The king, of course, appropriated the largest and choicest share of the booty for himself; these items were enumerated in royal inscriptions and shown on reliefs. The king's share consisted of luxury goods such as gold, silver, and ivory used to decorate the palaces and temples. The annals of Assurnasirpal II vividly described such tactics:

> In strife and conflict I besieged (and) conquered the city. I felled 3,000 of their fighting men with the sword. I carried off prisoners, possessions, oxen, (and) cattle from them. I burnt many captives from them. I captured many troops alive: I cut off of some their arms (and) hands; I cut off of others their noses, ears, (and) extremities. I gouged out the eyes of many troops. I made one pile of the living (and) one of the heads. I hung their heads on trees around the city. I burnt their adolescent boys (and) girls. I razed, destroyed, burned, (and) consumed the city.[19]

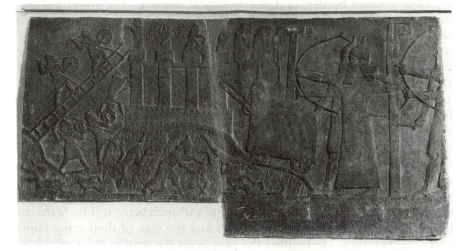

Tiglath-pileser III relief shows the attack on an enemy town. The Assyrians are attacking on both sides. The archers are on the right with a battering ram with large spears in order to break through the walls of the fortifications. Battering rams also served as platforms for the archers. On the left, Assyrian soldiers held spears and shields while attacking across a moat and scaling ladders. The effects of the siege are shown: three enemies are impaled on stakes, two thrown over the walls, some of the bodies have been stripped, and an Assyrian soldier is shown beheading a captive below. Those on the turrets raise their hands in surrender. 90 m. © BRITISH MUSEUM, LONDON.

This type of "psychological" warfare was especially convincing, and the inhabitants, "overwhelmed by the fearful splendor of the god Assur," surrendered.

Controlling conquered areas was often a problem, with vassal states either withholding annual tribute or in open rebellion. If repeated attacks failed to quell the population, the Assyrians transported large numbers of people to another area. Assyrian kings began deportation in the thirteenth century BCE, but the practice became state policy during the ninth century BCE, numbers reaching one-half million deportees.

The Assyrians found mass deportation beneficial; it provided labor colonies to work on the monumental building programs, to cultivate new farmland, and to produce more food for the growing urban population. People were also deported to curb nationalistic longings. Persistent rebellion was treated with harsh retribution. The detested king of Hamath (in Syria) was publicly flayed while still alive, as graphically depicted on one of Sargon II's reliefs. A king's head was considered a prized trophy: Assurbanipal displayed the head of the defeated king of Elam on a tree in a royal garden while he feasted there with his queen.

Tiglath-pileser III relief of women and children prisoners and scribes recording spoil. A double-walled, turreted town, located in a palm-growing region, has already been captured. The battering-rams stand next to the wall. At the top, two scribes record the booty; one scribe records with stylus and table in cuneiform and one with pen or brush writing on skin or papyrus in Aramaic. Cattle are being driven by captors as part of the booty. At the bottom, women and children are being transported in two ox-carts. L. 2.90 m. © BRITISH MUSEUM, LONDON.

Early Dynastic monuments clearly illustrated battles fought and armies conscripted. The texts from the Early Dynastic period described frequent armed confrontations both within The Land (Sumer) and against external invaders; other documents recorded lists of those in the military, chariots, and weapons. The first clear reference to a standing army came from the Akkadian Dynasty. King Sargon (2334–2279 BCE) spoke of 5,400 soldiers eating before him. Later King Shulgi (2094–2047 BCE) described the formation of specific military units, among them a unit of spearmen.[20] At all periods, documents describing the administration of the army were few. Such texts usually involved the conscription of soldiers and efforts to avoid the draft.

Military Service and Conscription

The most successful method of conscription, the *ilkum*, was devised in the Old Babylonian period. This practice involved exchanging land ownership in return for military service. However, in times of peace, state service was substituted. If a citizen was conscripted for the royal campaign and failed to appear, he would be executed. The Code of Hammurabi forbade hiring substitutes to perform military duties. However, a few contracts involved the hiring of a substitute or bartering commercial debts and credits to designate a substitute.[21] Lists distinguished between soldiers, substitutes, and reserves.

The texts described parallel systems of conscription for nomads, vassal states, foreigners, and so on. For example, Khaneans from the middle

Euphrates were drafted for policing activities. Kassites were conscripted for their skills as horsemen. "Reserves" from the sedentary villages (literally, "backup men") were designated for the royal corps, and were not to be called up for any other purpose.

Soldiers were allocated plots of land in return for military service by the military administration throughout Mesopotamian history. Such land could be inherited. The Code of Hammurabi allowed certain classes of society, namely, priestesses and merchants, to sell their *ilkum* plots, but other citizens could not.

> The field, orchard, or house of a soldier, a fisherman, or a state tenant will not be sold.
>
> If a man purchased a field, orchard or house of a soldier, fisherman, or a state tenant, his deed will be invalidated (literally, "his tablet will be broken"), and he will forfeit his silver. The field, orchard or house will return to its owner.[22] (Code of Hammurabi, §§36–37)

Military units consisted of ten, fifty, and one hundred men. Larger units were formed according to the needs of warfare. As the Assyrians conquered foreign territory, part of the male population was incorporated in the Assyrian army. Near the end of the Neo-Assyrian empire, the majority of the troops were not Assyrian. Eventually, these population groups received all the economic and social rights of native Assyrians. Thus, a society evolved within the Assyrian empire that was very mixed in both race and language. The size of military forces increased through the Iron Age as the Neo-Assyrian empire expanded. Shalmaneser III (858–824) BCE mentioned a force of 44,400 men; a century later an inscription of Tiglath-pileser III mentioned a force of 72,950 men. The militia of Sargon II (721–705 BCE) numbered 90,580, and grew to 208,000 under his son Sennacherib.[23] The reliability of these figures remains open to question.

Sennacherib divided the royal corps into two or three contingents, perhaps headed by the queen and by the crown prince. Usually, we expect the queens' roles to have been nominal in military affairs. An unpublished inscription referred to Sammuramat (Greek, Semiramis), wife of Shamshi-Adad V, mother of Adad-nirari III, and daughter-in-law of Shalmaneser III, as being instrumental in a victorious campaign that established the boundaries among three territories.

Once the Assyrians conquered a region, systematic administration took place as an extension of the military. The king himself took on a dual role; he was head of state and commander-in-chief of the army. Three officers served immediately under the king: (1) the field marshal, who executed the king's military orders and led the troops in the king's absence, (2) the vice-chancellor, who advised the king on affairs of state, and (3) the majordomo, who alone had direct access to the king. The chain of command was not fixed; in fact, the king often gave direct orders to officers at any level.

The appointment of officials was a "pork barrel" for patronage and nepotism. A provincial governor considered his province to be his personal property, from which he tried to obtain as much profit as possible. The concept of "integrity of office" did not exist; bribes or gifts were routinely given to influence a decision. Public office was a potential source of personal wealth, and provincial governorships were the most lucrative offices.

The occupants of a chariot were called the "rein holder," "shield-bearer," and "third man." The king's bodyguard was drawn from the chariotry corps. The army included cavalry, chariotry, engineers, infantry, and supply personnel. When the king did not lead the army into battle, his commanding officers spearheaded the campaign. The major cause of death among adult males was death during war in the line of duty.

Terms distinguishing the different types of soldiers have been difficult to understand. Various types of foot soldiers depicted on reliefs also appeared in royal inscriptions. Foot soldiers served in various capacities, for example, as swift messengers on horseback, as laborers cutting new roads before the advancing Assyrian army, and at the front breaking through city walls.

With the growth of the Assyrian army, a new building known as the "review palace" was developed. An inscription of Esarhaddon clearly stated its purpose: "For the ordinance of the camp, the maintenance of the stallions, chariots, weapons, equipment of war, and the spoil of the foe of every kind."[24] The review palace had huge internal courtyards, ideal for mustering the troops, as well as numerous storage rooms and living quarters.

The Neo-Babylonian dynasty did not provide us with as much information as the texts and reliefs from the Neo-Assyrian empire. Possibly Babylonian temples played a larger role in military affairs; for example, temples owned "bow-fiefs," or allotments of land which still carried the specific obligation on the cultivator to serve as an archer or to supply a substitute.

The soldiers' weapons were often used as tools in their daily life. Hunters used slings and nets. Nomads were prob- **Weapons** ably well armed and kept supplies of metal. Sedentary communities brought elaborate military equipment such as chariots, carts, and protective armor. Different contingents were distinguished by their clothing and weapons.

Each troop had its own patron deity and standards of other gods accompanying the king in battle. For example, Old Babylonian texts mention the gods Nergal or Erra on the right and Adad on the left, that is, a right and left wing. Weapons used by kings and gods were deified and given names.

Starting with the Early Dynastic period, foot soldiers or infantrymen used a variety of weapons such as axes, adzes, large shields, spears, maces, and bows and arrows. Daggers, sickle-swords, and homemade-looking blades wrapped around the end of a wooden shaft were followed by swords, invented in the second millennium BCE. Defensive weapons included small round shields, round helmets, and protective armor, even used for the horses, particularly at the neck.

Later texts listed lance-bearers, shield-bearers, and archers. In Mari palaces and administrative centers supplied military equipment. In the first millennium BCE iron became the metal of choice for weapons. Engineers were important for building bridges and roads for the army, primarily during the first millennium in Assyria.

Chariotry became important during the second half of the second millennium when the Hurrians and Hittites first introduced masses of light, spoke-wheeled chariots drawn by teams of horses—usually racehorses, which were well trained. Originally, the chariots carried only a bowman and a driver; later a shield-bearer was added to the group.

There were two main types of chariots: the four-wheeled "battle-car," a heavy vehicle with wheels of solid timber, and the two-wheeled chariot, which may have been made for the hunt. In the first millennium horses from Nubia were used to pull the heavier chariots.

Charioteers wore body armor made from copper or bronze platelets which overlapped and were attached to leather garments, the whole gear weighing as much as fifty-seven pounds and issued by the palace treasury. Scale armor protected the charioteers from arrows. Helmets were sometimes plumed and covered in metal scales or made from hammered sheet-iron; one set of body armor required 400 large copper scales for the corselet, 280 small scales for the sleeves, and 190 scales for the helmet. Such precise information has come to us mostly from texts and reliefs.

Military Operations Historical records described armies in pitched battle, long-term sieges around fortified cities, long-distance campaigns to foreign countries, bedouin razzias, and invasions by barbarian hordes. Since war was a seasonal activity, sedentary communities drew on greater man-power during nonagricultural periods.

In the second millennium BCE the political and military operations spanned more than 1,000 kilometers from the Mediterranean to the Persian Gulf. The correspondence between the Assyrian king Shamshi-Adad I (ca. 1830–1776 BCE) and his sons, the governors of Ekallatum and Mari, showed that routes were carefully planned, including daily itineraries, using knowledge of the local area and of logistical requirements.

Shamshi-Adad's courier service was so fast that some of his dated letters record the time of day. Spies or informers gathered intelligence which messengers passed with due speed to the king. The royal roads were kept in good repair for the king's messengers; otherwise, the roads were generally in poor condition.

The Assyrians had a system of posting stations located along the major routes at regular intervals of a day's march (30 kilometers), so that the king's messengers could rest and get fresh teams of mules to pull their chariots. By this system of posting houses, under ideal conditions a messenger could travel from Nineveh in northern Mesopotamia to the Levant in a matter of several days. The courier's business was dangerous because he might be hijacked for his message. The Mari texts described using beacons in a series of signal fires in order to transmit a message over the entire country.[25]

Shamshi-Adad appointed governors over various districts under his control. Permanent garrisons were situated in each town, and additional troops were called up for each campaign from both the sedentary and nomadic population. Before each campaign lists were drawn up specifying the men taking part and arranging the distribution of provisions. Censuses were also instituted.

Siege warfare developed as a special category of military strategy. Outer and inner walls were often built in front of a fortification wall, which had towers and a complicated design of gates to thwart the enemy. Sometimes these fortifications were built next to a river. There were more elaborate fortifications in mountainous regions. The attacking army might redirect the courses of rivers in order to make both walls and buildings collapse. The battering ram was used to pierce enemy fortifications. Mari correspondence was full of references to siege towers which were preassembled and floated downstream. Wooden scaffolds and ramps were also used to scale the battlements. Roads were made of interlocking short sections of planks to form a portable surface for transporting loaded wagons across muddy or swampy areas. Staging posts at major passes and borders at intervals along the main roads were marked by stelae and rock-cut images of the Assyrian king. Mules were often used for difficult terrain.

Bridges were built in order to cross rivers. Individual soldiers also used inflated sheepskins to reach the riverbank walls by floating. (The verb "to swim" was not known in Mesopotamia.) Sennacherib was the first king known to cross the bays of the Persian Gulf with a naval flotilla, using warships built by the Greeks.

Royal inscriptions described the destruction in conquered lands, namely, demolition of walls, public buildings, orchards, and irrigation systems. Other documents suggested that complete destruction was viewed as a last resort. To spare themselves the expense of destructive campaigns, the Assyrians spent a good deal of effort to persuade foreign people to submit willingly. The letter describing Sargon's eighth campaign related how various detachments made a show of force, marching around to amass tribute and to organize an administration. Only after these measures were taken did the Assyrians confront intransigents. Other military tactics included night marches, surprise attacks, deceptive operations, and the service of spies and infiltrators; they were all devices to save time and keep casualties to a minimum.

CONSEQUENCES OF WAR

At the end of the battle, cities, houses, and individuals were looted. In the local wars in Sumer and Akkad, the city temples were treated with respect, since their gods were members of the same pantheon. However, booty was taken from temples of enemies. The *Lamentation over the Destruction of Ur* described the Elamite desecration of the innermost temple sanctuaries and destruction of decorations. The Hittites boldly carried Marduk's statue into exile upon their capture of Babylon.

Division of Spoils   There were conventions governing the distribution of the spoils of war. The king took the largest and most valuable share of the booty for himself; these items were enumerated in royal inscriptions and depicted on reliefs. From the eighth to the seventh century BCE we have wall paintings of pairs of scribes, one writing with a stylus on a tablet and the other writing with a pen on a leather or papyrus scroll; that is, one writing in Akkadian and one writing in Aramaic in order to record the spoil.

The king's portion consisted of luxury goods such as gold, silver, and ivory, used to decorate the Assyrian palaces and temples. Military leaders often shared in the division of spoils with the king; in addition, they received large estates of agricultural land as a reward for prowess, valor, and victory. Assyrian troops considered loot and rape from a conquered city as part of their pay.

The kings of Akkad presented at least token gifts to the gods from their booty. Stone bowls, inscribed "booty of Elam" or "booty of Magan," have been found at various sites. The tradition of making a dedication to the appropriate temple survived into Assyrian times, in fact, even into the classical world.

Treatment of Prisoners   One of the most valuable spoils of battle was the people. In the Ur III period some tablets recorded long lists of women and children. Males were not included in these lists, perhaps because they were often killed, tortured, or mutilated.[26] Occasionally captured soldiers were sacrificed to the gods. Official propaganda of the third millennium BCE described piling up enemy corpses into heaps and burying them in large mounds, thereby ensuring that they would harass their descendants as restless ghosts.[27] Sometimes women and children were included as part of the general massacre, but usually they became slaves.

Other deaths were also attributed indirectly to warfare. Those who were able to flee from their conquerors often died of exposure, starvation, or thirst. Those besieged within their cities also suffered from starvation and disease. They sometimes ate the women and children, but cannibalism was a rare occurrence.

Prisoners of war were often taken on long marches. Often naked, they were put in neck-stocks, their hands bound behind their backs; or they were enmeshed in a net. Since heavy chains were expensive, the prisoners were often blinded en masse. When brought to their captors' land, they could still perform certain tasks, such as carrying water from a well or canal with a bucket and a rope.

At the end of a war, prisoners were brought to the victors' land. Some prisoners were incarcerated and used as bargaining chips in political negotiations.[28] Other prisoners were held hostage for ransom, some becoming laborers in a "house of bound men" for a limited time. Such practices have been confirmed by ration lists and "death certificates" for prisoners of war.

Diplomatic correspondence described treaty (literally, "touching the throat") and disengagement negotiations. At **Peace and** this time the repatriation of citizens became an issue. At the **Alliance** conclusion of a treaty, the two parties swore an oath and performed rituals. For example, at Mari, the ritual was "to kill asses" as part of the ceremony.

In peace treaties both parties swore by the gods to obey the terms of the treaty. If one side attacked the other, the gods punished the offending party. Prospective agreements included these clauses, thereby promoting future cooperation rather than settling past differences. A letter to a god at Mari traced a broken agreement back to the alliance between earlier kings. The writer emphasized that breaking an oath was considered a religious sin. International treaties also secured succession. Parties to the treaty agreed to support their allies militarily. The treaties also included extradition clauses. In his *Letter to the Gods*, Esarhaddon demanded the extradition of his brothers who had murdered his father.

Before the end of the third millennium BCE, international alliances were formalized by treaties. By the middle of the **Vassals and** second millennium BCE, treaties explicitly outlined the na- **Overlords** ture of the relationship between the parties. But most treaties between vassal(s) and overlord dated to the first millennium BCE.

A minor kingdom usually became a vassal of a major one because vassalage was its only hope of survival or because it offered economic advantages. The king would formally initiate his vassal by anointing his head with oil, and then he would announce the terms of the treaty. Both parties accepted the treaty under oath. Such terms limited the vassal's right to an independent foreign policy and sometimes even economic activities. For example, a Hittite king required one of his vassals, the state of Amurru in Syria, to take part in economic sanctions—a trade embargo—saying that no Syrian merchant could go to Assyria, and no Assyrian merchant could go to Syria.[29] Vassals had to pay annual tribute and serve in the army. In return the overlord defined and defended the boundaries of his vassal states. If a foreign temple was damaged, the Assyrians helped to rebuild and restore it for the sake of the foreign gods. Esarhaddon's vassal-treaties were presented in writing in May 672 BCE. They required affirmation of loyalty by his vassal states and periodic renewal.[30] The vassal-treaties further stipulated that only a successor nominated by the king should receive their allegiance. No vassal was to harm the crown prince designate by giving him poisoned food or drink; no one was to practice witchcraft or enrage the heir's personal god or goddess. Any plot, rumor, or revolt had to be reported. The vassal was obligated to capture and put to death the crown prince's assassin and his whole family, "shedding blood for blood," in order to remove the murderer's descendants and their name from the land. Esarhaddon added a list of curses to any vassal who would violate his treaties, as follows:

> May Assur, father of the gods, strike you down with his terrible weapons . . . May Girra, giver of food to young and old, extermi-nate your name and your progeny . . . Just as the mule has no de-scendant, may your name, your descendants, (and) the descendants of your sons (and) your daughters disappear from the land . . . may your enemy squash you. May they strangle you, your wives, your sons, (and) your daughters with a cord.[31]

Babylonia was a special case. It could not be treated by the Assyrian imperialists as a territory to oppress and exploit. Historical, ethnic, relig-ious, and cultural ties would neither have allowed the Assyrians to treat their southern neighbor in this way nor permitted the Babylonians to accept such a subordinate status. The Assyrian empire needed secure borders in Babylonia for their armies to march through on the way to conquer western Asia. The Assyrians tried to use puppet kings whom they married to their daughters in order to manipulate the Babylonians.

Tribute

During the Neo-Assyrian period, the annual campaign usually began in spring, once the army met at a given point. A show of force was usually sufficient to ensure voluntary pay-

Scenes of tribute on Black Obelisk of Shalmaneser III (858–823 BCE) containing twenty panels on all four sides. Over each panel is an inscription describing the scene below. The top panel shows the Sua, the Gilzanite, bowing before the king. The top panel shows Jehu, the son of Omri, bowing before the Assyrian king. The king is accompanied by attendants, one holding a parasol and the other a club. The tribute includes camels being led away, double-humped camels, a monkey, gazelle, and lion. The bottom panel includes further tribute such as vessels of precious metals. The Ht. 2.02 m, W. 0.60 m. © BRITISH MUSEUM, LONDON.

ment of tribute. Tribute and taxes levied on conquered areas included costly goods, but also more practical items such as horses for the military and grain stored locally as rations for the troops. Vassal territories paid tribute as part of their treaty obligations. Major provinces paid large sums, but peripheral areas, such as the Anatolian states, usually sent token gifts.

INTERNATIONAL RELATIONS

The political map reflected a lively diplomatic scene. Messengers traveled widely both within and beyond the borders. Some messages were conveyed orally, but rulers generally used extensive written documentation to regulate their officials and to communicate with their allies. Because of written correspondence, ambassadors were able to represent their rulers in making agreements. Nevertheless, high-level meetings still took place between rulers. For example, the king of Ugarit (a port city in Syria) visited the palace at Mari, and Zimri-Lim himself went on a diplomatic mission to the Mediterranean.[32] The crossing of frontiers must have required careful advance planning. Kings probably traveled with an entourage, some of whom were armed.

Diplomatic Relations Kings sent ambassadors on special occasions or as residents at other courts in order to establish and maintain diplomatic relations. They usually brought a gift of great rarity or of high-quality craftsmanship. The exchange of gifts was one part of the reciprocal relationship between the king and his guest. Particular gifts were requested, and sometimes the recipient complained about a gift. Dynastic marriages also were a feature of international relations, used to cement relations between ruling families everywhere.

The king fed and housed any visitors from outside the state at royal expense, even if they were not accommodated in the palace itself. The Mari archives recorded the daily royal menu on thousands of tablets. In addition, there were banquets for special events such as religious festivals and visits by foreign ambassadors. Occasionally we find mention of more distinguished guests, such as the Hurrian ruler of Nineveh and his entourage of more than one hundred followers.

Ambassadors enjoyed certain diplomatic immunities: their property was protected, and they were sometimes exempt from customs duties. Sometimes their activities made them unwelcome, and their rulers were requested to remove them. But regardless of the ambassador's popularity, his person was inviolate.

An ambassador at a foreign court might have to conduct negotiations on behalf of his king; knowing that he might come under pressure to compromise, the king sometimes gave him detailed written instructions for his negotiations.

Usually ambassadors returned home soon after completing specific negotiations, but sometimes the foreign ruler might detain them for several years because of problems between the two kings. Diplomatic protocol required an ambassador to return with a substantial gift from the foreign king. Sometimes the ambassador was delayed because the foreign king was unable or unwilling to send a lavish gift. Returning an ambassador without a gift was tantamount to breaking off diplomatic relations.

Gifts were also brought by strangers and subjects alike when permitted an audience with the king, but the king was not easily accessible to all the people because he was subject to many taboos. Usually only the superintendent of the palace had direct access to the king, much like the Chief of Staff to the President of the United States. The crown prince could have an audience with the king when the astrological omens were auspicious. Courtiers often received gifts to speak to the king on behalf of suppliants.

Assimilation was the result of immigration, deportation, and mixed marriages by people such as merchants or longtime residents abroad. Prisoners of war were often re- **Assimilation** settled in the land of the victorious king. There was relatively little prejudice against them, and through time they or their descendants could acquire full rights of citizens and even rise to positions of importance.

The major powers accepted assimilation, even taking active steps to support it. For example, King Sargon II of Assyria (721–705 BCE) built a new capital, Dur-Sharrukin (Fort Sargon), and populated it with vassals, "peoples of the four quarters (of the world), of foreign tongue and divergent speech." In order to ensure their becoming good Assyrians, he explained, "Assyrians, fully competent to teach them how to fear god and the king, I dispatched them as scribes and sheriffs (superintendents)."[33] There were also interpreters. King Assurbanipal described the arrival of an ambassador from a remote country (perhaps Lydia in Asia Minor), saying:

> He reached the border of my land. When the people of my land saw him, they said to him, "Who are you, stranger, from whose country a messenger never came here?" They brought him before me in Nineveh, my capital. But of the languages of east and west, over which (the god) Assur had given me authority, there was no one who spoke his language. His language was strange, and they could not understand his speech.[34]

From the second millennium BCE onward, rulers frequently corresponded by mail. Major archives have **Communications** been discovered at Mari on the middle Euphrates and **Between Rulers** at El-Amarna in Egypt. More than three hundred letters were found at El-Amarna from Hittite, Babylonian, Assyrian, and Mitannian kings and from Egyptian vassals in Syria and Palestine. The language commonly used was Akkadian, the language of diplomacy.

Kings used kinship terms such as "father," "son," or "brother" in addressing each other. For example, calling a ruler "my father" implied his seniority, and "my brother," equality. Some rulers were touchy about their status and took offense at familiarity. For example, at the beginning of Assyria's ascent as an international power early in the thirteenth century, Adad-nirari I (1307–1275 BCE) addressed the great Hittite king in terms of brotherhood, only to be rejected: "Why should I write to you about brotherhood? Were you and I born of the same mother?"[35]

On appropriate occasions, such as accession or illness, vassals were expected to send congratulations or inquiries about the king's health. Failure to do so was considered a serious breach of conduct.

A prominent foreigner traveling abroad might take a letter of introduction to the king to ensure privileged treatment. For example, when a certain Hittite prince went to Ugarit, he brought with him a letter from the Hittite king:

Thus says the king to Ibirani king of Ugarit: Greetings to you!

Now Misramawa has come to live there with Akhi-sharruma. You are to treat him kindly and according to his rank . . . If you do not know him, he is the brother of Upparmawa and son of the king.[36]

Kings sometimes allowed foreigners who were administrators, commercial agents, or advisors to settle permanently in their land, even giving them estates. But this privilege was extended to few. Usually those who traveled to foreign countries were merchants, who ran the risk of being robbed and murdered for their valuable goods. Rulers entered into treaties to provide security for their citizens who had to travel. One document noted:

Ini-Teshub king of Carchemish (in Anatolia) has made this treaty with the men of Ugarit. If a man of Carchemish is killed within Ugarit, if those who killed him are arrested, they will pay threefold for the man and they will pay threefold for the goods that disappeared with him. But if those who killed him are not found, they (the people of Ugarit) will pay threefold for the life and as to the goods that disappeared with him, they will pay the capital value of so much as disappeared. And if a man of Ugarit is killed in Carchemish, compensation arrangements are the same.[37]

The treaties between rulers called for reciprocity—each ruler was responsible for the safety of the other king's subjects. Also, every ruler was held liable for any criminal offenses committed by his subjects abroad. The king took responsibility for foreigners living in his land.

Assyrian vassal kings served proudly in the Assyrian army. During the reign of Tiglath-pileser III, the body of Panamuwa I, a vassal king from Zinjirli (in Syria) who died in combat, was transported from Damascus to Assyria for a state funeral.

Death and Mourning

The death of a foreign king was officially mourned within the framework of international relations. The mourning by Hattushili III, king of the Hittites, over the death of the king of Kassite Babylon was described as follows:

> Your father and I established [a document of treaty] . . . and became good-willing brothers, we did not (become brothers) for one day only. Did we not establish contractual alliance between equals, which should last forever? We made (in this document) the following agreement: "We are only human beings. When one of us . . . [dies], then the survivor will protect his (the deceased's) sons." And while the gods kept me alive, your father died . . . according to the custom of . . . [a] brother . . . I fulfilled my duty, as I was obliged toward Your Father. I wiped . . . [away] my tears and dispatched an envoy, and to the high officials of the Land of Karduniash sent the following (written) message.[38]

This document was meant to ensure the peaceful and legal transfer of power to the heir to the throne. As today, recognition of a rightful leader of a nation was respected by other members of the international community.

11

Economy

FARMING

Mesopotamia was home to some of the oldest farming communities. By approximately 6000 BCE most staple crops known from later texts were already cultivated, the basic herd animals had been domesticated, and irrigation systems were well established, at least in northern Babylonia. The availability of profitable cereals (such as barley and wheat), irrigation, and plow agriculture were all factors that contributed to the development of large-scale farming. Despite its desertlike climate, Mesopotamia became the richest agricultural area in the ancient world. The plants grown for food in ancient Mesopotamia provided about 90 percent of the diet, and the remaining 10 percent of the food supply came from domesticated animals and their products—meat, milk, cheese, and eggs.

Barley was the most common agricultural product and was used as a means of exchange as well, with an accepted value, much like silver. In fact, wages were mostly paid in barley. Trade in grain and dates, among other goods, became the staple articles of commerce.

In early historical Mesopotamia, agricultural strategies were often directed by the urban sector in order to maximize production. This was accomplished in three ways: (1) intensive use of the ground by planting more frequently, mixing crops, and applying fertilizer; (2) expanding the area of land used for agriculture; and (3) introducing new labor sources and strategies.

Relief with *shaduf* (pump) for irrigation. The *shaduf* is an instrument consisting of a bucket on a pole. The operator stands on a brick platform, filling the bucket from a higher channel. At the extreme left, two men operate a *shaduf* to bring the water to an even higher level. The relief at the top includes the legs of the men dragging a sculpture of a bull colossus up a hill. This relief is from the palace of Sennacherib (704–681 BCE) at Kuyunjik. © BRITISH MUSEUM, LONDON.

Because of the uncertainty of the food supply due to blight, locusts, or lack of rain, Mesopotamians survived by trade, storage, and war. Law codes and legal documents constantly referred to crop loss through flooding. Swarms of locusts also presented a major threat to crops. However, the Assyrians caught and ate the locusts, which they considered a luxury food. The kings received letters from provincial administrators and astrological reports about this potential disaster.

Crops Parts of the ancient Near East generally experienced little rainfall, thereby placing great demands on plant life. Most arid land species exhibit either drought-evading or drought-resisting tendencies. Only the mountainous areas received enough rain to support forests. Overviews of the agricultural landscape were mainly irrigated fields devoted to cereal crops, which were important staples in the Mesopotamian diet. The importance of cereal cultivation underlay agricultural instructions and explanations in a Sumerian composition called "The Farmer's Instructions," which included practical advice and reminders to perform the proper rituals.[1]

Barley and emmer wheat were harvested with sickles made with flint teeth set in a wooden or bone handle. After the harvest, grain was carefully stored in granaries near the fields or transported, wherever possible on the waterways. The silos were depicted as high and cylindrical, a shape that has remained unchanged to the present day. Some had a ladder attached to enable the grain carriers to climb up and empty their sacks into the top. The amount of grain was measured by volume, not weighed. The silos rested upon a latticed wooden foundation, which provided protection against damp ground and rodent attacks.

Barley was able to withstand greater salinity and aridity than wheat, thereby ensuring that it became part of the basic staple diet. Barley provided flour and the basic ingredient in beer-brewing. Millet, which to date has not been identified at prehistoric sites, was less frequently grown. Rice was introduced in Persian times. Texts dealt mainly with essential staples produced for temple, palace, or large private estates; texts usually did not mention garden cultivation.

The vegetables most frequently mentioned were onions, garlic, leeks, turnips, lettuce, and cucumbers. Vegetables needed more frequent attention and were cultivated in separate plots, usually under the canopy provided by plantations of date palms interplanted with lower fruit trees such as apple and pomegranate. Numerous spicy and aromatic seeds were part of the Mesopotamian diet, such as cress, mustard, cumin, and coriander; others remain unidentified. Linseed was the only oil seed cultivated before 6000 BCE. The plant was used mainly to produce a fine oil, which quickly became a staple food of the Mesopotamian diet. In the Old Babylonian period commercialized production of this plant was economically important to the palace administration. Olive trees grew only in the foothills, and olive oil was manufactured locally.

The date palm was first cultivated in Lower Mesopotamia. Its position was unique, because every part of the date palm could be used. Dates, which had high nutritional value, were sometimes used as a sweetener; they could be preserved and stored. The palm sprout provided a celery-like vegetable, and an alcoholic beverage was made from the fruit. There were separate male and female plants. The Sumerians practiced artificial fertilization of the female palm. Lexical texts enumerated 150 words for various palms and their different parts. The date and the pomegranate were the most common fruits, though apples, figs, pears, and a type of plum were also known.

Timber was part of the northern landscape. The principal trees native to Mesopotamia were tamarisk, which grew to a height of several meters, poplars, willow, and a kind of pine. Several woody plants of the Near East produced gums or resins, which were used in manufacturing perfumes and incense. Mastic, an ancient form of chewing gum, was also an aromatic resin.

Animal husbandry began in the Neolithic period. The animals used by the early inhabitants of the ancient Near East **Livestock** were wild, managed, or domesticated. Remains of wild mam-

Relief with man fertilizing date palm. The man is shown climbing a ladder in order to fertilize the female tree. Ht. 63.5 cm. © BRITISH MUSEUM, LONDON.

mals and birds were discovered at various sites; such animals may have been traded between regions or eaten in difficult economic times. Dependence on wild herd animals such as the gazelle, deer, and onagers declined. Managed but not domesticated species were protected or tamed; these included fish raised in ponds, bees, and game. The animals with the temperament to be domesticated were common and widely distributed. Many species were domesticated after complex societies emerged. Throughout the history of the ancient Near East, domestic animals provided meat, dairy products, leather, wool, or hair. Pastoralists viewed animals as capital on the hoof, while hunters viewed animals as game to be redistributed.

Animals meant for temple sacrifice had to be blemish- and disease-free, and sometimes white for purity. All the domesticated animal species could be used for offerings to gods, but the sheep played an additional role in the magico-religious sphere. One of the most common ways of obtaining an omen was to present a question to the god, and then kill a sheep and examine its liver.

Sheep were the most important economically and numerically; they were domesticated the longest and present from the Mediterranean to the Indus Valley. These animals were more important for their milk products and their wool than for their meat, which was used for offerings, taking omens, gifts for weddings, and presents for access to the king. A specialist called the "animal fattener" gradually increased the rations of sheep, mostly males, to improve the flavor or fat content of the meat. Sheep adapted well to any agricultural environment. Where there was plenty of water, hence plant growth, they could be herded. In cases of little rainfall and an arid climate, they could be moved in search of plant growth.

Sheep and goats, known as "small cattle," were also kept in large flocks that belonged to the state, the temple, or private owners. When flocks were of considerable size, each animal was branded with its owner's mark. Flocks belonging to the temples were marked with the symbol of the god to whom they belonged, for example, a spade for Marduk and a star for Ishtar. If animals were not tended by a family member, they were given to shepherds, who subcontracted the actual herding to "shepherd boys." Contracts between owners and shepherds described the composition of the flocks, conditions of employment, and compensation of the shepherd, which often included a fixed share of the proceeds.[2] The size of flocks varied from four to over two hundred animals, with approximately the same number of males as females. Sheep and goats were tended for city-dwellers by shepherds assisted by their dogs to protect the herds from lions and wolves. The animals were housed in cattle pens to provide shade during the heat of the day and, even more important, to protect them against the wild beasts that attacked the flocks. Herds could be diminished by epidemics and parasitic maggots. Death caused by disease or by a lion (a smaller species than the African variety, and now extinct) was estimated at 10 percent; however, the herdsman had to account for the lost animals by presenting the skin with its wool and tendons.[3] Should death be due to the shepherd's negligence, he had to compensate the owner.[4] The shepherd usually kept all the dairy products and a fixed amount of wool as part of his pay. In Assyria, most sheep belonged to large flocks, but poorer individuals must have kept one or two, referred to as "sheep on the roof."[5]

Sheep were often herded together with goats. Goat hair was used for weaving carpets and containers. Flocks were often isolated by herdsmen to protect against the spread of disease and, perhaps, theft. As societies became more complex, animals no longer roamed to find grazing. Both isolation and segregation resulted in a reduction of the gene pool. Local animal populations showed distinctive characteristics.

Sheep were plucked until the middle of the second millennium; that is to say, the wool was pulled or combed out at the time of molt. Later shearing became the usual practice. A contract was drawn up with the herdsman at the spring shearing when the wool was weighed and the lambing season was finished.

Cows, ewes, and goats were important to the milk industry. A bas-relief from the temple at Al 'Ubaid (ca. third millennium BCE) depicted the different stages. Cows were milked at a shed made of reeds, and the milker sat behind the cow or goat. When the milk was drawn, it was placed in a large narrow-necked jar and rocked by the cowman. This regular movement was used in place of churning. When the butter had clotted, the milk was poured into another vessel through a strainer, to a wide-mouthed jar.

Animal products included meat, yoghurt, cheese, and ghee. Milk, which spoiled rapidly in hot climates, was not popular as a drink; rather, it was used in making medicines. Animals also provided wool and leather hides.

Major population centers separated herd growth from farming so that fields could be devoted to crops rather than pasture. The cuneiform texts have provided ample evidence for a system of production and redistribution of pastoral goods conducted by the two great institutions, the temple and the palace. Adams calculated that there were 2.35 million head of sheep based on the amount of wool recorded in Neo-Sumerian texts.[6] An emphasis on wool production had serious consequences for the production of meat and milk for human consumption, but the need to provide fodder distorted the agricultural economy by diverting crop lands.

Many animals were slaughtered and redistributed by state and temple. Sacrificial obligations provided stock for the major institutions and ensured the quality and availability of animals provided. Secular and sacred rubbish have been clearly identified. Evidence for slaughtering (vs. butchering) and processing of skins was found in sacred debris.

Animal husbandry developed along with inventions in agriculture. The shift to plow farming in the fifth millennium required animal traction and favored an increase of cattle. A Kassite seal (ca. 1300 BCE) showed a seeder-plow drawn by two humped oxen. A figure in the center held a bag of seed corn, which was fed into a funnel through which it passed down to a seed-drill and into the plowed furrow.[7] Cattle, like sheep, furnished leather and dairy products. Cattle were seldom sacrificed except in ceremonies of state. They played no part whatsoever in extispicy (inspection of the entrails for omens). Cattle were primarily important as draft animals, preparing the land before sowing and seeding. Cattle needed much more food than sheep and goats. They could not manage by simply grazing. Their diet included barley and reeds. When administrative officials of the Ur III period calculated the costs of cultivation, they included the oxen's barley ration as well as seed barley.

In early periods the ox was the only draft animal, but by the end of the fourth millennium the onager was used to pull wheeled vehicles. In fact, in Queen Puabi's tomb in the Royal Cemetery of Ur her sledge was drawn by onagers. The Sumerians of the Early Dynastic period used domestic asses which they crossbred with wild onagers ("donkey of the steppes") to produce a sterile offspring uniting the donkey's docility with the onager's speed and strength. This hybrid did not survive the second millennium BCE due to the arrival of the horse, which was crossed with the donkey to produce mules. Even so, mules were used only in limited ways, mainly to draw wagons, because they were more expensive than donkeys and because of the cost of crossbreeding a donkey and a horse. The donkey was the traditional beast of burden and retained that distinction even after the introduction of the horse. Donkeys were used to haul plows and carts; caravans of donkeys were used by the Assyrian merchants in Anatolia.

The horse was called "donkey of the mountain," to indicate its origins in mountainous regions. In the second millennium horses were used for drawing fighting chariots and in the first millennium for the cavalry. They were also used in ritual offerings and for ritual acts in making treaties. Horse breeding was credited to the Hurrian states, the Hittites, and later to Assyria, as documented by Hittite and Assyrian training instructions.[8] Horses were used by kings, princes, great landowners, and the army. After about 900 BCE, major centers of horse breeding were found in Armenia, northwest Iran, and the Levant. The Assyrians claimed to have taken away thousands of horses as booty during their campaigns there. White horses were considered particularly valuable and were frequently given as gifts to the temples.

Camels were not widely known in Mesopotamia until the first millennium BCE and were used mostly by nomadic Arab tribes. They were called "the donkey of the sea" or "the donkey of the south," indicating their origins. At the beginning of the first millennium BCE camel pastoralism evolved into camel caravans to expand the trade networks of nomads. In the seventh and sixth centuries BCE, Sargonic and

Neo-Babylonian monarchs launched punitive expeditions against the Arabs. In these battles a great number of camels were captured; as a result, their price plummeted in the marketplace.

The dog was one of the earliest domestic animals and served primarily to protect herds and dwellings against enemies. To date, we have been able to distinguish only two main breeds of dog: large greyhounds, which were used primarily in hunting, and a very strong breed of dog (on the order of Danes and mastiffs) suitable for herding. Greyhounds were found in Ubaid graves as early as ca. 5000 BCE. In both Mesopotamia and Anatolia, dogs were associated with healing rites, but expressions such as "vicious dog" and "dog" were derogatory terms. The house cat was kept to catch mice and rats. As mousers, cats had, as today, an important competitor in the mongoose, which also killed snakes.

The bones of wild species—lions, panthers, wolves, hyenas, foxes, wild boars, and jackals—have been found, but their numbers were reduced by hunting and habitat destruction. Armed guards stood watch to defend against robbers and wild animals in places where large-scale farming was practiced. Guards also protected flocks and herds in the farmyards. Various traps were used, such as concealed ditches in paths that led to water holes. A special kind of arrowhead, found in the Royal Cemetery of Ur, was used to stun small animals and weaken larger animals through loss of blood, thereby making them easier to capture. Some animals could be tamed as pets, among them gazelles and antelopes, which roamed the country in huge herds. The Asiatic elephant was the largest species in antiquity and inhabited riverine territories from Syria to China; today the elephant has survived only in southern and southeastern Asia. The ivory was carved by artisans.

Birds Ducks, geese, mallard, white stork, quail, and other birds were mentioned in texts, as well as the fowler or bird-keeper. A Babylonian proverb elucidated the role of the fowler and fisher:

. The fowler who had no fish, but had caught birds,
    Holding his bird net jumped into the city moat.[9]

Birds were caught primarily by nets, traps, and decoys. Birds were a source of meat and eggs; fowling played a more important role than fishing. Our knowledge of the ancient names of birds (and fish) remains inadequate. One text tried to reproduce the sounds of bird calls.[10] Ostriches still inhabited much of Africa, but their Near Eastern subspecies became extinct only in the twentieth century.

The chicken arrived in the first millennium BCE and moved west until it reached Greece (ca. 600 BCE). Chicken bones have been found in large quantities; they became a staple part of the diet during the late Persian and Hellenistic periods. Various types of wild hen, such as the francolin, were recognized as game birds as early as the second millennium. Geese, like pigeons and doves, were kept for food and sacrifices. Geese were first raised in Babylonia at the end of the third millennium, and ducks were introduced early in the second millennium. In both cases, both the meat and eggs were important.

Wild birds were kept as pets, namely, the ibis, crane, heron, and pelican; the latter was trained for fishing. The fields were home to thrushes, blackbirds, sparrows, and larks. Partridges and francolins were bred in the country. Quails were rare in ancient Mesopotamia, though they were very common in Syria. There were many birds of prey: vultures, falcons, owls, and crows. The Near East served as a series of rest stops for migrating birds as they flew over the land or water in autumn and spring.

Honey collected from wild bees was rare and expensive. The use of bees for honey and beeswax probably first began **Beekeeping** with hunting for honey in the wild hives of the Paleolithic period and evolved into full apiculture by the third millennium BCE. Beeswax was used for various purposes, including medicines and surfaces on writing boards.

The introduction of beekeeping was described on a stele found in the museum at Babylon: "I introduced the flies which collect honey, which in the time of my predecessors nobody knew nor introduced, and located them in the garden of the town Gabbarini that they might collect honey and wax; I even understood how to separate the honey from the wax by boiling; my gardeners also knew this."[11]

CANALS AND IRRIGATION

The city-states of the ancient Near East were essentially farming communities; the majority of their populations were farmers. Their political systems were based on productive local agriculture and development of large-scale irrigation. Also, some of their myths focused on the annual farming cycle and fear of destruction from flood storm, drought, and other natural disasters.

The earliest farming communities were located in rainfall zones at sites that had a variety of natural resources. Artificial watering appeared on the alluvial fans of smaller watercourses to supplement rain-fed farming (ca. 5000 BCE).

Agricultural land was best classified by its water supply, which regulated farming, the types of crops, the **Water** amount and dependability of yields, and the total area of **Management** land cultivated. Mesopotamia had two kinds of agriculture: dry farming in the north (Assyria) and irrigation farming in the south (Babylonia and Sumer).

Dry farming relied only on natural rainfall and was practiced in northern Mesopotamia. Large-scale irrigation with complex canal systems, supplemented by natural rainfall, was used in southern Mesopotamia. Barley and other cereal crops such as emmer and wheat were grown in dry farming areas. Fallow land or crop rotation was vital to the productivity of grain lands. Dry farming was characterized by extensive farming methods and a fairly mixed rural economy; a high proportion of poor and failed grain harvests could be endured. When climatic and political conditions were favorable, productivity was sufficient to support major cities and large populations. Seed-to-crop ratios were only about 1 to 5. But high total yields were possible when large-scale areas were farmed.

Irrigation was necessary for crops because the salinity of the soil was a problem early on.[12] Water was channeled to the fields from the major watercourses through branch canals and feeders, which often ran along the tops of artificial dikes.[13] The width of the primary watercourses could be 120 meters or more; the branch canals were as narrow as 1 to 1.5 meters in width and .5 to 2.25 meters in depth, with a length just under 2 kilometers. Weirs were built to raise the water level in the main stream. Bunds were constructed to protect against floods.[14] Breaches were repaired with earth and bundles of reeds. Protective quay walls of baked bricks set in bitumen were built to guard against erosion on the canal banks at critical points. To prevent scour, pebbles or stones were used to cover a canal bed (a practice recorded as early as 2400 BCE).[15] Construction and maintenance of canal systems were considered an important duty (as well as an act of piety) to be executed by Mesopotamian kings, but cleaning and dredging accumulated silt in other canals was under the jurisdiction of the local authorities.[16] The rivers and canals provided drinking water for people and animals, irrigated vegetation, and created a cool, green world along their banks.

The waters of the Tigris and Euphrates came in spring when the fields were full of standing crops. A flood would have proved disastrous at this time, so a complicated irrigation system was set up. Strongly reinforced levees were built to keep the water in the rivers. To obtain an efficient gravitational flow, the canal systems were long and well maintained.

Water was always in short supply in the growing season, and a great deal of water was lost through evaporation and seepage. The timing of watering was critical. The Mesopotamian farmer had to deal with the problem of salinity as irrigation water evaporated, slowly deteriorating the soil structure. A great deal of labor was necessary to restore fertility.

Irrigation required solving four problems: (1) supply (getting the water to land that could be cultivated); (2) storage (keeping water where needed); (3) drainage (disposal of the water when no longer needed); and (4) protection (keeping away unwanted water).

As far back as the third millennium BCE gardens or small areas were watered by hand from wells or streams, but for cereal crops the most practical system was gravity-flow irrigation. Water was brought to the fields by successively smaller branching canals or by aligning major water channels parallel to the main rivers. Two controls were essential, outlets and regulators. Outlets, or sluices, could be as small as a hole opened in the side of a canal bank to divert water into a distributary channel. Regulators were used to catch the entire main stream in order to raise the water to the appropriate level. Temporary regulators were constructed from reeds, and permanent installations were made from baked brick and bitumen.

Kitchen gardens were layered so that a variety of crops shared the same ground. The Sumerians developed tree shade **Gardens** gardening, planting their gardens close to rivers or canals in order to control irrigation. According to a myth written in Sumerian, "Inanna and Shukalletuda: The Gardener's Mortal Sin," Shukalletuda was inspired by the gods to invent the shade garden, which he planted with the *sarbatu* tree. In this way, all kinds of green plants that previously had been burned by the hot winds now thrived in the shade. The gardens were shared by palm trees and, in their shade, smaller fruit trees (citrus, pomegranate, and apple), vegetables (peas, beans, lentils, leeks, cucumbers, lettuces, and garlic), and seasonings (cumin, coriander, mustard, and watercress). Modern Iraqi date and tamarisk groves continue to follow the same practice, which originated in the Early Dynastic period— that is, date groves and fruit trees provided a double canopy for a third layer of vegetables. Water was drawn by hand from wells and ponds in pleasure gardens, as well as for small flower or vegetable plots associated with working-class private houses.

The domestication of fruit trees was different from the domestication of annual crops such as cereals, pulses, and flax. Fruit trees grew by cuttings and grafting—a much longer process than seed-planting. The first fruit crops grown were those which could be easily produced by cuttings and preserved out of season, either in brine (olives) or by drying in the sun (grapes, as raisins and currants; figs; dates). Later, when grafting was better understood, a new wave of horticultural crops was cultivated, including apple, pear, plum, and cherry.

Gardens were a status symbol to the Assyrian kings. Olive trees grew well in Assyria, but not in Babylonia. In the first millennium BCE both King Shalmaneser III (858–823 BCE) and King Sennacherib (704–681 BCE) had olive trees, called "the oil tree," planted in their parks; the descendants of these first millennium BCE trees are found near Nineveh and Nimrud today.

The Hanging Gardens of Babylon, one of the Seven Wonders of the

Ancient World, were designed by King Nebuchadnezzar II (604–562 BCE) to please his wife. These gardens were fed by an elaborate system of irrigation on raised terraces, on which trees from faraway places were planted.

Fishing   Fishing provided an important addition to the diet in early times. Fishermen caught fish mostly by using nets, either set or thrown, as well as fishing spears, harpoons, and baskets. Rods were used less frequently, because many fish were large. Fishing was done from the riverbank or from boats; sailing ships were used on the seas. Baskets were used to hold catches. Among the many types of river fish, the most common were carp. As many as fifty kinds of fish were mentioned in Sumerian documents. Unfortunately, many Sumerian and Akkadian expressions and terms for fish found in economic documents are not understood. Large amounts of salt and sometimes spices were used for preserving the fish. Turtles and turtle eggs were also eaten. After the Old Babylonian period fish and fishing were rarely mentioned. In the Neo-Babylonian city of Uruk the word for fisherman took on a new meaning: criminal!

LAND MANAGEMENT

The land was flat, and the soil lacked drainage. Problems of soil salinization have been documented from approximately 2000 BCE. Canals were often redug to reverse the process. But when irrigation was no longer possible, settlements were abandoned. The movement to northern Mesopotamia during the early second millennium BCE was probably spurred by the search for fertile, arable land.

The cultivation of most cereal crops and large-scale planting of date palms was carried out on several levels: (1) on extensive temple and palace land, either directly or farmed out; (2) on private land; and (3) in small plots allotted to city poor, nomads, and shepherds. The amount of land held by each cannot be established and probably varied according to the time period, region, and condition of the soil. Bureaucracies provided more written documentation than family or clan organizations and private persons, so our view may have nothing to do with the everyday reality. The amount of land rented by city-dwellers to private individuals or partnerships increased through time, reaching its maximum in the Neo-Babylonian period and later on. Corresponding to this development, the employment of slaves, serfs, and other menials to work the land declined.

Private Land   The farmer probably drove the plow himself, while other laborers toiled to increase plowing speed. A standard team could perhaps plow 1 *iku* or harrow 6 *iku* a day. A three-man team worked 66.75 *iku*, plowing and then harrowing three times, totaling one hundred days' work. A seed plow seems to have covered about 2 *iku* per day. During the Akkad Dynasty plots of 4 to 10 *iku* were the norm and represented the farm size needed to support a family.

The costs of farming included seed, plows, tools, and draft animals, which were expensive because oxen needed good food to work. In Mesopotamia plow oxen were fed barley during the working season—one measure of feed for every two measures of seed. The laborers also had to be fed, either in rations or by a residual share of the crop. Major irrigation works were usually performed during slack seasons.

The average price for a slave in the Old Babylonian period was approximately twenty shekels of silver, sometimes reaching a high of ninety shekels. A hired hand earned ten shekels per year. Clearly, for landowners, employing seasonal workers was cheaper than owning a slave for field work. The most common method for working the land at this time was tenant farming. The tenant received seed, animals, and tools, for which he paid a set percentage of his harvest in return.

The efficient management of a farm was based on differentiating rural occupations in irrigation zones. The peasant might own some poultry and even a sheep or goat. Domestic weaving and domestic animals were under the care of the women. Nonetheless, the household was not completely self-sufficient. The territory of the herdsman, fisherman, and fowler—the marshes, reed beds, and scrub—furnished food, fuel, and raw materials. The relationship between the farmer and the herdsman was essential. Plow oxen and beasts of burden were herded and pastured in the swamps and scrub. The animals were brought to the fields only for various forms of work, namely, plowing, treading grain, or grazing.

Large territories supported the households and administrations of the royal family and high-ranking state officials. Minor and middle-ranking officials as well as military personnel held relatively small plots which ensured a comfortable living. Low revenue assessments were usually offered to favored officials. Prosperous small landholders formed a significant part of the population. The extended family worked together to take advantage of joint cultivation. The equal division of agricultural land through successive generations could create fragmentation that was further complicated by alternating fallow lands and access to water.

Agricultural workers or tenants on the estates often became dependent upon the landlords. With a chronic shortage of manpower, an indebted farmer's downward spiral could be hastened. Old Babylonian loans recorded that the borrower was committed to work a specific number of days on the creditor's fields. Thus, the rich ensured that their crops were harvested at the optimum time so that their economic success would surely increase. At the threshing floor, when the year's harvest was ready for storage, the crop was usually divided, with one-third going to the landlord and two-thirds to the tenant.

The "farmers" in documents, law codes, revenue surveys, or land leases formed a rural subelite of those who held land and were responsible for working it. Responsibility for revenues was subcontracted to local officials. Each level of the bureaucracy received a share of the crop, from the field hand, to the local administrator, to the ruler, to the god.[17]

Institutional Estates   Records of the institutional lands of Sumer during the Third Dynasty of Ur provide the best documentation of the most efficient farming in the ancient world. The agricultural year began with the spring equinox, when half the fields were full of standing grain and half were lying fallow from the previous harvest. The spring flood waters were used to inundate the fallow in order to leach salt from the soil so the land would be ready for plowing. The harvest of different crops started about mid-April and ended in May/June, with barley and onions. Either early autumn rains or preliminary irrigation prepared the land. Fallow land was first cleared of scrub plants and reeds, and then the land was broken and evened out by dragging timber behind oxen.

The first plowing in the autumn was performed by a team of three men with four oxen. Less intensive agriculture used a two-ox team, or even donkeys, which could be worked by one man. Preparation of the land before plowing was important because the deeper the furrow, the better the crop. The plowshare was basically a point to turn over the surface, and the best wooden points were metal-tipped. Numerous plow and harrow names occur in texts, but their specific uses have not been clearly defined.

The plow team and the water supply defined the shapes of the fields. The border of each field was on a watercourse, which irrigated the field. An overview of the landscape showed a network of larger and smaller canals, with each watercourse lined by a single row of long, thin strip fields on each side with scrub land beyond the water's reach. The ideal strip field was the length plowed in a single furrow so the animals could rest, eat, drink, and be treated for harness sores.

After clod-breaking, sowing took place in October. The seed was planted in raised furrows using a seed plow worked by four men. An ordinary plow with a funnel was attached to feed the seed. Otherwise, hand drilling was employed, followed by a man with a plow. The field was then irrigated to remove salt. The Sumerian *The Farmer's Instructions* told of three waterings during the growth period, while a fourth late watering could add an extra 10 percent to the crop. Barley, the main crop, was relatively tolerant of salinity.

Both the temple and palace administrations were supported by rations of food, oil, and clothing. Both were considered households: the temple for the god and the palace for the king.

The best-documented farming organizations were those of the temple rather than those of the state. For Sumer, in the Third Dynasty of Ur, large collections of clay tablets furnished detailed information for a centralized administration of agricultural production. Similar accounts from the Neo-Babylonian period provided evidence for large-scale rent farms, that is, privatization. Records of large areas of land sales could be annulled by royal decree.

The temple was the main institution of the Early Dynastic urban economy. The temple and city were completely interdependent, with no differentiation made between sacred, secular, and economic duties. The temple included both religious priests and the secular ruler. The architectural splendor of the temples affirms the economic power of this religious elite.

The economic basis of the temple was agriculture. The temple managed its estates, working some of its own land, giving the rest as fiefs to temple employees and private citizens, and renting out some land on a sharecropping basis. The temple was economically self-sufficient, with its own granaries, mills, and bakeries as well as herds of donkeys, cattle, and sheep.

Most land not owned by temple or palace was claimed by the ruler and his family, administrators, priests, and free citizens who owned land jointly as members of a family or clan. Thus, the class structure of Early Dynastic Sumer reflected the division of land into temple, palace, and community holdings. Many free citizens were dependents of the palace, temple, or noble estate, and received gifts of land in exchange for their services. Legally the king still owned the land, but if the recipient had a son able to succeed him in performing the necessary duties, the land could become hereditary. Landless citizens included craftsmen, hired workers, sharecroppers with landowning families, and workers in service in temple estates or in the royal administration.

The temple redistributed the surpluses of its own agricultural workers, industrial workers, and craftsmen. Commercial exchanges with foreign countries promoted prosperity, technological advances, and sometimes war.

Gradually the temple's hold on the Sumerian economy loosened. Secular palaces were built as lavishly as the temples. The palace at Kish was surrounded by a thick, buttressed wall. It had more than fifty rooms, some for storage.

The Ur III dynasty operated one of the most elaborate bureaucracies of ancient times. Everything entering or leaving the palace and temple was registered; the names of the parties to each transaction were logged.

Managed systems of production and redistribution came under state control. Large numbers of animals and crops became commodities of trade, tribute, and taxes. Evidence from the third millennium BCE shows that a network linking cities, villages, and camps was constantly undergoing political and economic realignment. A profitable industry in wool and leather was closely associated with the control of state herds. Shulgi devised an elaborate schedule of monthly obligations assessed on all the major Sumerian and Akkadian provinces in order to provide for the sacrificial requirements of the Nippur temples and the maintenance of their staff.

At the top of the socioeconomic administration was the royal government with all its estates, workshops, and trade centers. The temples also had their own estates and factories, granted by the state. A class of wealthy bureaucrats arose in both the temple and state economies, their riches coming from taxes either from their provinces or on returns from their holdings. The palace storehouses fed and clothed the members of the royal family, the administrative officials, personnel of the royal household, the standing army, serfs, slaves, and other palace dependents.

Merchants grew prosperous from trade; they became the middle class. The system was based on its working classes, that is, poor citizens who became state workers, taxpayers who paid taxes by corvée labor or military service, small landowners and farmers, tenant farmers, and slaves.

Foreign trade at this time was also a royal monopoly, with royal officials importing luxury items of all sorts by land and sea: copper and tin, exotic foods, resinous plants and aromatic woods, fruit trees and herbs, ingredients for tanning, dyeing, and cleaning, ship's lumber, and even the prized tortoise shell. In return, the royal traders were able to offer the bulkier agricultural staples that Mesopotamia produced far in excess of its own needs: wool, barley, wheat, dates, dried fish, fish oil, and skins, the last both unfinished and in the form of processed leather products. Deficit balances in this trade, if any, were made good in silver, which now began to serve the three classical functions of money: as a medium of exchange, as a unit of account, and as a standard of value. Generally speaking, Sumerians recognized only centralized and communal ownership of arable land. Many imports were paid in kind by agricultural products, but silver had stipulated value and acted as cash does today.

The wealth of the great institutions gave them the opportunity to expand marginal areas too risky for the individual to undertake, and also to invest some of their surplus in creating or reclaiming new irrigated plots as well. The institutions had the economic latitude to experiment with new breeds of animals, species of plant, or technical equipment, like sickles or plows. They were able to maximize production by efficient

administration such as sheep-fattening establishments and the mathematical calculation of sowing rates.

Institutional management rarely distinguished between rent and tax.
Official documents gave an impression that the whole countryside was
subordinate—a laboring population tied to the land and the institution.
People were paid by a system of rations, attested in early Sumer. Subsistence farming and poverty were not recorded.

Wet ground was surveyed before plowing in order to establish field
boundaries, record workable land, and name or assign cultivators. In
Sumer, leases were dated after the harvest, and land surveys regulated
revenue. Sown land may have been surveyed as well. A final survey
took place before the harvest. The communal or institutional threshing
floor often served as the place for tax collection. Assessments were always made in barley.[18]

Land was often leased for two to three years; rent was paid by a percentage of the crop or "like neighboring fields."[19] A fee was levied on
the entire community to maintain the irrigation system. Special arrangements were made if tenants farmed previously uncultivated land.

The farmers of southern Mesopotamia were aware of the varying quality of their lands, which they considered in order to use their resources
most efficiently. In a land survey from the reign of King Shulgi, an official registrar described the estates as good; middling; middling with
grass; plowed, (but) grain did not grow; a bridge; good due to
reclamation ("brought out of water"); medium; flooded; poor; a canal;
wells; village; orchard; ancient mound; and a dike.[20]

During the Ur III and Old Akkadian periods, Melukkha, located in the
Indus valley, also traded with Mesopotamia. Melukkha was the source
of black wood (perhaps ebony), gold, ivory, and carnelian. These goods
either were native to Melukkha or were merely shipped via Melukkha
from more distant places.

People moved as well, even founding a "Melukkhan village" during
Shulgi's reign in greater Lagash (ca. 2060 BCE). However, there is little
evidence of a Sumerian, Akkadian, or Babylonian presence in the Indus
valley. The language of Melukkha was unintelligible to Akkadians and
Sumerians, as shown by a cylinder seal that referred to an Akkadian official as a "Melukkha translator." The growing number of artifacts
found in Oman, the United Arab Emirates, Bahrain, and southern Mesopotamia all attest to the Harappans' (from the Indus valley) ability to
cross the Arabian Sea and sail up the Arabian Gulf ca. 2300–2000 BCE.

The hallmark of Kassite material culture was an oval- or pillar-shaped
monument approximately two feet high, called a *kudurru* in Akkadian.
It recorded royal land grants and was deposited in the temple or at the
site of the grant. The landowner kept a clay-tablet copy or deposited the

Kudurru (boundary stone) marking of Nebuchadnezzar I (1126–1105 BCE), marking the king's land grant to Ritti-Marduk for military service in the inscription
(not shown). The symbols appear in six registers. The first register is the eight-
pointed star of Ishtar, the crescent of Sin and the sun-disk of Shamash. The
second register represents the shrines of Anu, Enlil, and Ea. The third register
consists of serpent daises upon which are the hoe of Marduk, the wedge of Nabu,
and an unidentified symbol. The fourth register includes an eagle-headed scepter,
a double-lion–headed mace, a horse's head on a double base with an arch, and
a bird on a rod. The fifth register shows the goddess Gula seated on a throne,
with a dog (her symbol) lying beside her, and a scorpion-man, with the legs and
feet of a bird, holding a bow and arrow. The last register includes double lightning forks supported by a bull (Adad), a tortoise, a scorpion, and a lamp on a
pedestal (the symbol of Nusku, the god of light). A snake twists along the side
of the *kudurru*. Ht. 56 cm. © BRITISH MUSEUM, LONDON.

tablet at the temple. *Kudurrus* represented a new system of social organization, a quasi-feudal policy of land grants to favored subjects of the king. Through this program more fertile land was withdrawn from the tax registers. Like the *kidinnu* privileges granted to cities, the land grants were allocated by kings to temples and faithful servants, as an act of piety or political necessity. The *kudurrus* were carved with reliefs, representing divine symbols; that is, they were signs of privileged status under divine protection. The result of both practices was to remove both individuals and cities from the tax rolls. To replace the lost revenue, the Assyrian kings built new cities, either as capitals of their empire or in strategically important regions.

Another unique legal practice of the Kassite period was the official public proclamation of land sales between private individuals. If no objection was raised by a third party, the transaction was legal and was registered in the archives. Accurate site surveys were included; one *kudurru* registered that the king himself surveyed the field before granting it.

The most striking organizational characteristic of Mesopotamian society in all periods was its economic division into the haves and have-nots, into those who held land and those dependent on the landholders. Private, literary, and legal documents (including Hammurabi's law code) portray a society in which individual rights again became an issue. A considerable portion of the populace was now legally free, attached to neither palace nor temple. The private sector of the economy—based on ownership of agricultural land and use of hired labor or slaves—flourished in Amorite-dominated Babylonia, similar to the situation under the Amorites' Semitic predecessors, the Akkadians.

In the Old Babylonian period rations had been largely replaced by the allotment of grants of land, referred to as fiefs and generally held by virtue of the performance of certain military or civil duties. Sometimes a substitute was provided to carry out some or all of the relevant duties.

The palace and temple continued to hold large plots of land worked by dependents or by others liable for civil or military duties. By far the most common system of working the land at this period was one of tenant farming. The tenant received seed, animals, and implements, for which the tenant returned a set percentage of the harvest.

THE DOMESTIC ECONOMY

Temples amassed gold, silver, and lapis lazuli, but the average Old Babylonian citizen had humbler possessions. The contents of the Babylonian larder were simple, and prices were even given, as in the opening section of the Laws of Eshnunna: **Wealth and Poverty**

1 gur barley (300 liters)	for 1 shekel (8 g) silver
3 liters best oil	for 1 shekel silver
1.2 liters vegetable oil	for 1 shekel silver
1.5 liters pig's fat	for 1 shekel silver
40 liters bitumen	for 1 shekel silver
6 minas (3 kg) wool	for 1 shekel silver
2 gur salt	for 1 shekel silver
1 gur potash	for 1 shekel silver
3 minas copper	for 1 shekel silver
2 minas worked copper	for 1 shekel silver[21]

Little is known about how these products were bought and sold, but there were references to small shops, a "street of purchases," a "gate of exchange," and traveling salesmen.[22]

Inheritance texts listed textiles, furniture, animals, and a few slaves; a bride's trousseau might include more valuable items; for example: "Bel-uballit (the bride's brother) and Gudadaditu (the bride's mother) voluntarily promised to give as dowry with Kashsha . . . one-third shekel of gold jewelry, one pair of gold earrings worth one shekel, one Akkadian bed, five chairs, one tablet, a goblet and a platter of bronze."[23]

The Third Dynasty of Ur provided the best evidence for the type of work, the number of working days, food rations, and wages. Wages were different from rations. Wages were calculated on a daily basis, and rations on a monthly basis. From the Ur III period on, the daily wage of a worker was 10 liters (about 2.5 gallons) of barley, a standard that appeared in school books and continued to be valid for two thousand years. However, actual hiring contracts showed that most people earned less than ten liters per day. Rations for male workers included two liters of bread and two liters of beer—bare subsistence level if a family was supported from these rations. Workers also received two kilograms of wool per year, barely enough to make one garment. On special occasions, such as the New Year, workers might receive extra rations of barley, meat, and oil. Middle or higher officials had a subsistence field of approximately six to thirty-six hectares (15 to 90 acres). The disappearance or flight of workers was not uncommon.

Those with old-age pensions, such as cloistered women, were provided with a minimum of nine hundred liters of barley, three kilograms of wool, twelve liters of oil, and five liters of flour annually by their adopted heirs (see Chapter 7). Sons provided their elderly fathers with a guaranteed easy living.

Once in debt, people easily became impoverished due to usurious rates of interest, usually 20 percent for silver and 12 percent for grain.[24] Additional amounts reflected penalties for late payments. When the borrower could no longer pay these usurious rates, he had to repay his debt by working for his creditor. The omen texts revealed a full range of hopes and fears: the poor hoping to become rich, the rich fearing poverty, and both rich and poor worried about interference from the palace.[25]

During the Ur III dynasty, a system of balanced accounts grew from the elaborate procedures of receipts, debits, and redistribution. Each account tablet provided a balance sheet and was part of an elaborate series of successive statements, incomes, and expenses. The period of accounting was approximately every six months or every year, with each month being thirty days; the date was not fixed.[26] Bookkeeping became an account of daily life. For example, when a female laborer died, the 187 days after her death were included both in the debit section as labor and in the credit section, theoretic and actual labor, respectively.[27]

Balanced Accounts

Males and females were treated differently in respect to free days. There was no rigid weekly schedule. Breaks occurred irregularly, depending on the work and the constitution of the workers, seldom exceeding the minimum time required for regeneration of the laborers' strength.

The merchandise listed included goods retailed by merchants on behalf of an institution, such as wool, fish, oil, wheat, figs, dates, barley, and silver. Silver (and perhaps also barley) appeared in this list to enable acquisition of items, "expenditures," that the palace estates were unable to produce. Merchants imported bitumen, gypsum, feathers, fruits, and other items. In Ur III times the merchants operated on behalf of the palace, but at other times they acted on behalf of the temple.

Agricultural products such as cereals were not mentioned in merchant dealings for the palace. The palace received large and even excessive quantities of grain from its tenants and its directly cultivated lands. Perhaps the palace stored grain against poor years and famine, though little is known about storage in early Mesopotamia in general. Grain may have functioned as currency. As such, it would be less marketable than other goods sold by merchants.

Agricultural Basis of the Economy

Farmland was valued according to the anticipated annual yield. Rents showed the owner receiving one-third to one-half of the crop. Private land leases frequently indicated who was expected to furnish the tools, animals, and seed, and who paid taxes. If the landlord paid these costs, he reduced the laborers' share to one-third or one-quarter of the crop. Also, banking firms, such as the House of Egibi in Babylon during the Neo-Babylonian and Persian periods, acted as real estate managers by renting fields for absentee landlords. The House of Murashu of Babylon, in the banking business in the last half of the fifth century BCE, rented royal lands to tenant farmers and acted as agents in converting agricultural profits into metal.

There was more fertile land available than workers to cultivate it. But land development did not produce an immediate return. Law codes and leases emphasized the duty of the tenant to keep the soil and fieldwork in good order. The individual farmer profited from intensive cultivation of less land. However, the owner profited most by cultivating the largest possible area.

The Role of Merchant Bankers

The stability of the Persian period led to the accumulation of wealth from the revenues of lands, houses, and slaves; this revenue was invested in financial and commercial operations recorded in numerous cuneiform contracts, usually found in private archives. Most of the archives were from the beginning of the Persian period (the latter part of the sixth century BCE), but these archives were often a continuation of those begun under the Neo-Babylonian kings, such as the archives of the Egibi family of Babylon and of the Ea-iluta-bani family of Borsippa, which stopped with the end of the reign of Darius I (522–486 BCE). Despite the increasing use of the Aramaic language and script throughout the Near East, the written cuneiform tradition was not extinct.

Private archives showed a large sector of the population involved in financial and commercial operations, which were often restricted to where the lenders lived. Commerce was based on a silver standard, whether for borrowing within the family or between neighbors. Some transactions put businessmen within the realm of political power or international commerce. Two archives show a wider range of transactions: those of the Egibi family, which operated throughout Babylonia and sometimes even in Iran, and that of the Murashu family of Nippur in central Babylonia, which dominated that entire region. The field of international commerce was dominated by non-Babylonian merchants.

Commercial and financial operations were modeled on promissory notes. In this type of document, the object of the transaction (precious metal or agricultural produce) was listed, then the names of the lender and the borrower; the duration of the loan; methods of reimbursement, establishing the interest to be collected; and collateral to be held by the lender. The contract ended with a list of witnesses, the scribe, the place, and the date. When the borrower repaid his debt, the promissory-note tablet was returned to him by the creditor, and usually broken to mark cancelation of the debt. If the creditor kept the tablet, he provided the debtor with a quitclaim or certificate of payment.

In general, contracts were drafted according to a formal model, from which the scribes were able to adapt the contracts to fit a variety of situations because of their knowledge of the terminology of "commercial law." Some promissory notes included a clause specifying the purpose of the transaction, "for a commercial expedition." In these capital ventures, two to five people pooled their resources to invest a certain amount of capital, depending on their respective assets. The capital was turned over to an entrepreneur to carry out commercial transactions and make a profit that would be divided pro rata, according to the initial individual investments, or according to a fixed sum paid in advance plus a bonus from surplus profits. The same format was followed in drawing up partnership contracts for commercial purposes.

The phrase "as purchase goods" refers to the purchase of goods rather than their resale. Ur III balance sheets used sil- **Currency** ver as a unit of accounting. All incoming goods were assigned values in silver by weight, which were totaled, thus providing a capital sum at the merchant's disposal—a sum for which he was responsible as well. Likewise, items bought were valued in silver; thus the merchant's account could be balanced. Was silver then used as currency or as an accounting practice for merchants? During the Old Babylonian period, payments for real estate, slaves, goods, and services were rarely paid in silver, although their prices were quoted according to a silver standard. Since Old Babylonian legal documents did not specify the quality and fineness of the silver used in payment, silver probably did not change hands in the transaction. However, in the Neo-Babylonian period, the legal texts had a rich vocabulary for describing the quality of silver given or expected. Silver was imported and taxed (in silver itself) since the Ur III period. In the Old Babylonian period the palace controlled the circulation of silver. Accumulations of silver as treasure were restricted to the palace and the temple.

Currency has four different functions: (1) as a standard of value, (2) as a medium of exchange, (3) as a means of payment, and (4) as a means for accumulating wealth.[28] Each has a role distinct from the others; that is, there is general purpose money which serves all four functions, and special purpose money which serves one function only. The use of silver was still a long way from coinage, invented in Lydia (now western Turkey). The earliest Lydian coins are dated to ca. 650 BCE. Greek coins were not found before 575 BCE and did not become popular until 550 BCE. Lydian coins found so far were made of electrum, a natural alloy of gold and silver. Coinage may have begun as a way of guaranteeing and certifying the weights of metal. The administrators who first issued such coins probably were, in effect, certifying that they would repurchase the coins at the same value.

In the annals of Sennacherib small copper "coins" were already in use in Mesopotamia at this time: "I built clay molds, poured bronze into each and made their figures perfect as in the casting of half-shekel pieces."[29] A puzzling reference by Sennacherib in 694 BCE to casting bronze colossi "like the casting of half shekels" probably referred to craftsmen handling large amounts of bronze as skillfully as if no more than half a shekel of metal was involved; however, coined money was not used until the very end of the Assyrian empire. The decisive moment was the first occasion when business was transacted in terms of small silver ingots stamped with some device such as the "head of Ishtar" or the "head of Shamash."[30] In 493 BCE Darius I issued an edict introducing silver coinage, "darics," into the Persian empire, including Babylonia. In the Seleucid period the value of silver coins depended on their weight and the ruler under whom they were struck. With the circulation of coinage, private banking thrived in Babylonia. From the late sixth century BCE onward there were several dynastic banking houses, such as the Egibi family in Babylon and the Murashu family in Nippur, who amassed huge fortunes through usurious rates of interest.

Societies that used metal as currency presented it in a specific form. In Mesopotamia silver was weighed, but some texts from the Old Akkadian period through the Old Babylonian referred the casting of precious metals into rings as a means of storing metal. The Ur III texts about casting show that the ring did not always contain the full weight of the silver that was supposed to go into it, but such objects were weighed when they were exchanged anyway. Ur III tablets indicated that silver "rings" (in the shape of a spiral coil) of uniform weight were used by the administration. Rings varied from one shekel to ten shekels, with the majority being five shekels. The rings were manufactured with one to five coils. The ring as a kind of money appeared in the Old Babylonian period, but afterwards the Old Babylonian period texts no longer recorded the use of rings as currency. Silver was measured in traditional units of weight: the mina, about 500 grams, and its subdivision, the shekel (1 mina = 60 shekels), and the talent (1 talent = 60 minas). Silver was used in the form of sheets stamped to guarantee the alloy, but also in the form of "blocks," shavings, or pieces of jewelry, rings, and bracelets.

In the early second millennium BCE, silver was the preferred currency, but barley was used as well. Other commodities, including metals such as copper, tin, bronze, and gold, available from the periphery of Mesopotamia, were all used as moneys in the sense that they at least functioned as a means of payment, with a fixed ratio established. Silver was used as a standard of accounting, although gold served this purpose later, in the Amarna age. Standardized ingots have been found at archaeological sites. Because of their heavy size and rarity, both the ingots and rings were probably not used as a means of exchange, though all the other functions of currency might apply. Silver and other metals were weighed on a scale to determine the amount, and if smaller amounts were needed, the metal block or wire was broken into smaller pieces that were then weighed. The Akkadian word for silver means "the broken thing." Other terms in Akkadian referred to broken bits of silver, and the process of breaking metals and weighing each item was widely attested before and after coinage was introduced. The most commonly found quality of silver was called "alloyed one-eighth." Silver metal was used to pay taxes, to purchase valuable property (real estate and slaves), and in certain financial operations. Texts have noted that workers were given rations of bread and beer in addition to a small amount of copper, which could be used to purchase other goods.

The actual process of weighing remains uncertain. No complete balance has been found intact; we do have actual series of weights.[31] Authorities who issued coins distrusted their value and required that the coins be weighed. Coins have been found that have shown signs of tampering—that is, coin users had a tendency to shave bits from the coins. Counterfeiting was a problem as well.

FOREIGN TRADE

Trade meant the exchange of all kinds of goods locally, between cities, and with other lands. Information about trade comes from business contracts, manifests of goods, trade letters, and references to trade of every kind in literary texts and official inscriptions. Objects from great distances have been excavated at various sites as well.

Industrial goods and goods produced by serfs or workshops in the temple or palace provided the means of exchange so that metal, stone, lumber, spices, and perfumes could be imported. Trade took place between foreign cities, trading outposts, and barbarian tribes who lacked the status, the political power, and the necessary initiative to take part in trade relations based on treaties. Foreign trade took place along the Persian Gulf and the Euphrates route into the Mediterranean littoral. Trade helped to raise the standard of living in Mesopotamia and spread the influence of Mesopotamian civilization.

Most needs of daily life were available locally: cereals, date palms, wild and domesticated animals for suste-   **Commodities** nance; animal hides, fur, or fleece for the manufacture of clothing; clay for producing pottery; soil and water for brick making; and basic woods and stone for construction were found throughout western Asia and North Africa.

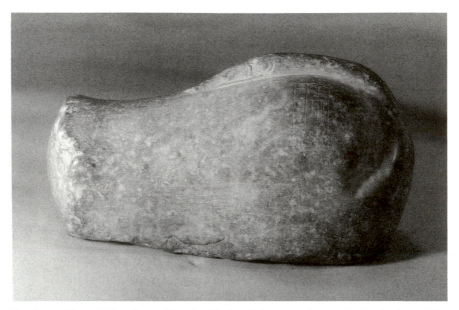

Duck weight of 10 minas. The duck's head is turned over its back. It weighs 5.371 kg, indicating that very little has been lost from the actual weight. The inscription is poorly preserved. 23.5 cm × 12.2 cm × 13 cm. © YALE BABYLONIAN COLLECTION, YALE UNIVERSITY, NEW HAVEN.

Luxury items were important for maintaining the prestige and position of the royal palaces and temples. Because of the expense and risk involved in obtaining these rare materials, their acquisition remained almost exclusively the business of kings and queens, powerful governors, and wealthy temple estates.

Over the centuries, both raw materials and finished products came to Mesopotamia from various areas, such as lapis lazuli from the Badakhshan Province in Afghanistan, reaching Mesopotamia and Egypt through a complicated network of overland routes. But many commodities arrived by sea from East Africa, the Arabian peninsula, Iran, and the Indian subcontinent.

Under Sargon the Great (2334–2279 BCE) the first major empire arose with its capital at Agade. Sargon first conquered all of southern Iraq and then followed the old trade routes up the Euphrates to gain control of two major commercial centers, Mari on the middle Euphrates and Ebla in northern Syria, both cities which were important because of their strategic position on trade routes. Mari documents recorded the distribution of wine, the drink of the rich. Ebla was the center of metal trade in the third millennium BCE.

Sargon and his successors also pushed forward along the eastward trade routes in their expansionist efforts as far east as Elam (today, southwest Iran). Military coercion increased the flow of goods to the imperial center from areas firmly under control. But merchants not under Sargon's rule engaged in limited trade.

In the late second millennium BCE, the government tightly regulated international trade. A Hittite king (ca. thirteenth century BCE) recorded the conditions under which merchants from Anatolia were permitted to trade inside Ugarit, a vassal kingdom in northern Syria. Complaints had been lodged that merchants were being given trade rights that posed a threat to the livelihood of the citizens of Ugarit. The Hittite overlord ruled that the merchants could operate in Ugarit during the summer, but not during the winter. Furthermore, Anatolian merchants were not allowed to acquire rights of residence (no green card!) or even to buy houses or land there.

International trade continued in the Assyrian empire, most often in the form of tribute (see Chapter 10) such as ivory tusks, which arrived in Assyria at the end of the eighth century BCE, after Syrian elephants had become extinct and before Assyria controlled Egypt. At the end of the eighth century BCE, the Assyrians began to play a major role east of the Zagros and may have received all their lapis lazuli as tribute from tribes in western Iran, who had received it by trade from further east. A document recorded the receipt of 730 horses from merchants—clear evidence of trade, not tribute, as horses were important for military use.

In ancient Mesopotamia, the most efficient way of transporting goods was by water, since most places in **Transportation** Mesopotamia could be reached by the Tigris and the Euphrates Rivers and through their network of rivers and canals. Ships sailed down the Persian Gulf and on the Mediterranean, and the Phoenicians might even have circumnavigated Africa. Local regions developed their own types of river craft, but seagoing ships were influenced by the fleets of the Levantine coast and, perhaps, the Aegean. When water transportation was not possible, human porters and draft animals such as donkeys and mules were used.

Wheeled vehicles were known in the ancient Near East from approximately 3500 B.C.E. However, the muddy conditions of the alluvial plains made sledges more practical. In the Royal Cemetery of Ur a sledge was drawn by a pair of cattle in Queen Puabi's tomb. Sledges transported heavy loads such as the enormous stone winged-bull colossi of Assyrian palaces. The colossi, which weighed as much as twenty tons, were also moved on rollers using poles as levers, as depicted on a bas-relief. Local trips were usually made in carts with solid wooden wheels, which are still used in the Near East today.

Overland Transport

The roads of the ancient Near East were generally unpaved, but they had to be staked out, leveled, and—in the case of those intended for wheeled transport—kept in good repair by the local authorities. The well-traveled connections had to be kept passable during the rainy season, at least for the movement of troops. Small rivulets and shallow rivers were bridged whenever possible, and larger rivers were crossed at fords or on ferryboats. The Assyrians even built pontoon bridges. Wooden bridges over raging streams and gorges had to be rebuilt constantly because of frequent destruction by floods; these bridges were supplemented by those of lighter construction meant only for pedestrians and pack animals. According to the texts, permanent bridges were built across the Euphrates in some Babylonian cities early in the second millennium BCE. Stone bridges were built in Babylon and Nineveh after 700 BCE.

There were a few great roads between important centers, but they were not roads in the modern sense—usually only tracks caused by traffic. For example, in the desert, the firmness of the soil was used to create roads, but elsewhere tracks twisted and turned to circumvent obstacles such as marshes. When the original surface had completely deteriorated through wear and tear, a new path was usually created next to the old one. As early as the thirteenth century BCE, Tukulti-Ninurta I (1244–1208 BCE) described his campaign in the mountainous regions: "I cut into their mountains with copper picks and widened their unopened paths."[32] In the mountains, building roads meant cutting through obstacles and shoring up other parts whenever possible. The earliest roads were probably built by the Urartians ca. 800 BCE.

The numerous records of the Third Dynasty of Ur added little to existing information on interregional trade routes. A messenger from the Phoenician city of Byblos was first mentioned and explained an indirect link between Egypt and southern Mesopotamia. In the third millennium BCE, smaller or medium-sized state territories were primarily involved in trade, so that most of the overland trade was subject to the shifting circumstances of foreign policy. Customs fees and duties of all kinds could be exacted, and the level of these was seldom firmly established. But the princes who controlled overland trade among the Sumerians, according to our documents, were able to conclude treaties with neighboring princes concerning the protection of trade. Such treaties dealt with permitting trade across a number of boundaries, as well as with trade between neighboring lands. The failure to keep to the terms of such a trade agreement, which normally were in the interests of all parties, could lead to war. Thus, a local ruler could not easily have refused to protect the caravans as negotiated. From time to time, merchants who asserted their claims before the king appeared in poems about the imperial kings of Akkad.

The Old Assyrian traders in Cappadocia clearly did not limit their activities to that region. They had ten trade centers in various locations. Some Cappadocian tablets told of "smugglers' road," a rugged and dangerous trail used either to avoid paying customs duties or as a shortcut.

An Old Babylonian itinerary listed the stages and length of a journey from Larsa in southern Babylonia to Emar on the Euphrates in northern Syria and the return route, which was not identical. The document did not record the purpose of the journey, which followed a long, circuitous, even unusual route with lengthy stopovers. The outbound trip lasted two months and twenty-seven days. The return to Larsa retraced the route of their outbound journey but included more detours. The entire trip lasted six months and fourteen days.

Itineraries from royal archives, such as the map of Nippur and, perhaps, the map of the world, were usually for military use. Texts referred to the same routes used for centuries for transportation of goods, the movement of troops, and the journeys of merchants or diplomatic envoys, who were often the same persons. The Akkadian term showed the wide range of activities of these agents; the Akkadian word could be translated "messenger," "envoy," "ambassador," "diplomat," "deputy," and even "merchant," depending on circumstances and contexts. Messengers and diplomats traveled by a variety of means: running on foot, on wagons or chariots pulled by asses, donkeys, or horses, and on river boats.

Routes of earlier periods continued to be used during the period of the Mari archives. The Euphrates road still continued to be heavily trafficked, connecting Syria, Mari, and Babylonia. Other routes were attested in the Mari records, such as "the great road along the near side of the Khabur," where a ferry service carried travelers and goods to the right bank.

Syro-Palestinian routes were longitudinal or transverse, varying in length and playing a major role in international trade because of their location between Anatolia to the north, Upper Mesopotamia to the east, Babylonia to the southeast, Arabia to the south, Egypt to the southwest, and the islands and coasts of the Mediterranean Sea to the west. Syria also imported raw materials and other goods from neighboring regions and exported its own products—timber, wool, olive oil, wine, dyed textiles, and artistic artifacts. A poem, looking back to the splendors of the time of Naram-Sin, referred to "mighty elephants and apes, beasts from distant lands, jostling in the great square."[33] Such exotic creatures could only have been imported by sea from India.

The Neo-Assyrian empire (ninth–seventh centuries BCE) did little to improve the roads it inherited in conquered territories. A few roads were even discontinued. But the Assyrian empire made one major change: the central government took over the management of the roads. Government maintenance brought about speedy messenger service to and from the capital and the rapid movement of troops against enemies within and without. The roads were kept in good repair, and exact information as to the terrain and distances was essential. The principal roads were called "royal roads." Official letters and legal documents referred to stations built along the royal roads, used as resting places for troops and civilian travelers and as way stations in delivering royal mail. A royal correspondent wrote, "People at the road stations pass my letters to each other and bring them to the king, my lord." A regular postal service was provided by mounted couriers, with relays at every road station. The roads were also measured with great precision, not only in "double hours" but in smaller measures from 360 meters down to 6 meters. That is, the distances on the royal roads were based on actual measurements using surveyor's cords of standard lengths. Highways were well defined and sufficiently permanent to be named as boundaries of fields in documents of land sales. Such roads were referred to as "the royal highway," or more precisely as "the royal highway to such-and-such a place," or "the highway which goes from . . . to . . ."; the names of towns were listed at each end of that section. These were clearly recognized as permanent highways, maintained by the state.

The Assyrians began to acquire and breed numerous camels in their efforts to control the Syrian and northwestern Arabian deserts and to profit from the caravan trade from Arabia. In this way, they penetrated deep into Arabia despite difficult and poorly marked desert trails.

Kings Sargon II and Sennacherib had those segments of royal roads closest to their respective capitals, Dur-Sharrukin and Nineveh, paved with stone slabs and supplied with roadside stelae as milestones. The roads were paved for a short distance outside of the cities and then quickly degenerated into a track and finally disappeared completely. This practice was subsequently discontinued until the Romans applied it, on a far greater scale, to their own imperial road network.

Travel in summer was usually undertaken at night. For security purposes, merchants usually formed joint caravans. In mountains and deserts, guides and armed escorts were hired. The track taken by a road depended on the locations of water, food supplies, mountain passes, river fords, and ferries. The rise of a new political center deflected some roads at the height of their power. In Babylonia and Assyria, the unit of road distance was called the "double hour," referring to the distance traveled in two hours' time. The double hour was based on the cubit, which was of several different sizes.

Goods could be carried on wagons drawn by oxen, on light carts drawn by donkeys, or by pack donkeys. In Babylonia, with its far-reaching network of navigable rivers and canals, wagons were used for short hauls such as transporting grain to local granaries. Farther north, in Upper Mesopotamia, and in Syria, roads were more important. Texts referred to two-wheeled, four-wheeled, and three-wheeled wagons (perhaps the third wheel was a spare). Wagons were used for loads too bulky and heavy to be carried by donkey back. The ability to carry such heavy and unwieldy loads as logs of cedar, pine, and cypress over great distances on uneven terrain implied the maintenance of ancient wagon roads. As for building mountain roads for carrying lumber, even greater engineering skill was required.

Roads suitable for wagons were few. Long-distance traffic was usually conducted by donkeys carrying packs. Donkey caravans could follow the most primitive paths and the narrowest mountain trails. As W. W. Hallo has calculated from the distances between known points in an Old Babylonian itinerary, the length of a daily stage of a caravan was between twenty-five and thirty kilometers. The load of an individual donkey, as attested by Old Assyrian texts, varied from 130 minas (65 kilograms) to 150 minas (75 kilograms).[34]

The main form of transportation continued to be the caravan, first with asses, and, after 1100 BCE, with camels. The animals traveled in single file over difficult terrain, and even the donkey drivers carried some of the goods. The goods were carried over great distances, and the caravan provided protection from occasional bandits and from wild animals. Caravans also helped control costs. Few words have been found for "caravan" in the ancient Near East; the Sumerian and Akkadian word meant "highway," "street," or "journey." The caravans were associated with particular routes, which continued to remain in approximately the same places for millennia. The mountains held few viable passes, and sufficient watering places were rarely found in the steppes. However, for camel caravans, watering stops could be spaced further apart.

Water Transport

River traffic in Mesopotamia was always heavy. Cuneiform tablets from the Old Babylonian period record the transportation of grain, cattle, fish, milk, vegetables, oil, fruit, wool, stone, bricks, leather, and people over the network of canals, for which clay "canal maps" have been found. As with river craft, not all seagoing ships were devoted to commerce. Near the end of the third millennium BCE, the Akkadian king Shar-kali-sharri sent a naval force to conquer the islands and coasts of the Persian Gulf, on which Mesopotamia was dependent for essential materials. As early as the third millennium BCE, Mesopotamian seagoing ships sailed to distant but unknown lands for raw materials, almost certainly including Harappan ports on the Arabian Sea.

Dilmun served as a port of exchange through which goods such as gold, copper, lapis lazuli, ivory, pearls (called "fish eyes"), ivory and ivory objects (such as combs, boxes, figurines, and furniture decorations), dates, and onions were traded. "Dilmun onions" were even mentioned in the economic texts dating from as early as the twenty-fourth century BCE. Timber from farther afield was transported to Lagash, Umma, and other southern cities in Mesopotamia. Dilmun has been identified with the Bahrain islands, except for the early periods of late Uruk through Early Dynastic, about 3400–2350 BCE, when the original Dilmun was located in the Eastern Province of the Kingdom of Saudi Arabia.

In the early second millennium BCE, trade was very much under royal supervision; there were checkpoints along the Euphrates, which merchants going by ship were unable to pass without a formal permit called "tablet of the king." The temple controlled the standard systems of weights and measures used in Mesopotamia. Dilmun and Melukkha had their own system, so some deliveries were entered in both forms.

Magan should be identified with Oman. In a collection of incantations, Magan was called "the home of copper."[35] Hundreds of mining and smelting sites have been discovered and studied throughout Oman and the northern United Arab Emirates. Magan was also the source of black stone (diorite or olivine-gabbro) for the many statues of Gudea of Lagash (2141–2122 BCE). Other items such as ochre, semiprecious stones, and ivory were also acquired in Magan on behalf of the Ur temple complex. During the Old Akkadian and Ur III periods, Melukkha traded with Mesopotamia. Melukkha was the source of black wood (perhaps ebony), gold, ivory, and carnelian. These goods were either native to Melukkha or were merely shipped there from more distant places.

Despite the importance of the Persian Gulf trade, there is little evidence on how their ships actually looked. Ships were referred to as the "large ship," "short ship," "wide cargo ship," and so on. Crude depictions on seals found on the island of Failaka, near the Delta, have provided us with little information other than that open-water vessels also sailed in the Persian Gulf in the Old Babylonian period.

The great inland lakes, mostly in northwestern Iran and Armenia, were particularly important for shipping. Even the seas were navigated in the ancient Near East, but mostly from coastal cities. In Babylonia, river shipping ended in Ur. From there, goods were packed on vessels that were able to navigate the bays and lagoons as far as the islands of Failaka and Bahrain. Shipping in the Persian Gulf was controlled by the Elamites, who traveled to the coast of Oman and the mouth of the Indus. The route around the Arabian peninsula and into the Red Sea was navigated ca. 3000 BCE. Some major trade centers retained their importance for long periods of time.

Because of the state of the roads, traders transported large cargoes by water routes whenever possible, especially for long-distance trade.

Lengthy journeys were undertaken in the Red Sea, Indian Ocean, and Persian Gulf in the third, second, and first millennia BCE. Maritime technology for such voyages already existed by the third and second millennia. Rudders were used to steer lighter ships and boats along the current, but heavy transport vessels and rafts were pushed with poles. In the Neo-Babylonian period a great oar at the stern took the place of the rudder. Sailboats were not suitable, and therefore uncommon, for use on the Tigris and Euphrates Rivers because the winds blew in the same direction as the currents. Water craft were sometimes towed; according to cuneiform tablets, sixteen or seventeen days were needed to tow a barge upstream 137 kilometers between Lagash and Nippur, about four times as long as needed to cover the same distance downstream. The texts recording cargoes implied that boats of small capacity were used. As far back as the Third Dynasty of Ur, boats on the canals carried from about 55 to 155 bushels of grain. At Lagash there were 125 boatmen, or one-tenth of the population of the Temple of Bau. The boatmen, including the rowers and helmsmen, were free. Male and female slaves were assigned to crews and also belonged to the individual sailors.

Sumerian texts described boat building. The boatwright constructed the shell of his vessel first, without any interior framework. The technical vocabulary was extensive, but we have not been able to identify the terms. Boat-building was a large operation, and very large boats were constructed from wood in special shipyards. These boats were probably used for long sea voyages to places such as Melukkha and Dilmun. Since the building of a boat was a considerable operation, those who required one often chose to hire. During the Neo-Assyrian period large wooden barges were depicted as being towed from riverbanks. A series of barges or boats were shown serving as the pontoons for floating bridges.

Shipwrecks were recorded in the Persian Gulf, probably along the western shores, which were shallow and full of dangerous reefs and shoals. The dangers of these commercial ventures were so great that businessmen would not enter into full partnerships with merchants. Seafarers sometimes gave silver models of their ships to their gods in gratitude for their safe return.

A merchant ship similar to one depicted in a fourteenth century Egyptian tomb was found off Ulu Burun, Turkey. The cargo was so diverse that the origin of the ship is impossible to determine. The ship was traveling the well-known counterclockwise route—from Phoenicia to Egypt by way of southern Crete. No navigation instruments were used other than sounding rods and lines. On the shipwreck at Ulu Burun there was an inventory of silver, tin, copper, and cobalt-blue glass ingots, as well as ivory, ebony logs, aromatics, and edibles such as oils, nuts, spices, and fruits for the crew.

During the first millennium BCE, the history of ships and shipping in

Skin-covered boats. This coracle was covered with skins and rowed by four oars-men. It is a detail from a Kuyunjik relief of Sennacherib (704–681 BCE). A man is fishing from an inflated goatskin. © BRITISH MUSEUM, LONDON.

the Levant belonged to Canaanite and later Phoenician ships. Assyrian kings depended on Phoenician sailors and shipwrights. A warship with a metal-covered ram protruding from the bow appeared in an eighth century BCE painting. Oars passed through small oar ports in the hull, rather than over the cap rail, to protect the rowers during war at sea. By the seventh century BCE, Phoenician warships were rowed from two lev-els, the lower rowers' oars passing through oar ports, and the upper rowers' oars passing over the cap rail. Round shields were attached in a row to the sides of an upper deck, above the heads of the upper rowers, in order to protect the soldiers on deck.

Seagoing traffic was strictly controlled. Laws dated to the second mil-lennium BCE dealt with right of way, salvage, and rates for hiring boats and paying crews. The Laws of Hammurabi even established the amount a worker could charge for caulking a boat, adding that he would have to do it over at his own expense if the boat leaked within a year.[36]

Two types of boats, the coracle and the kelek, were characteristic of Mesopotamia and have survived in identical form today. The coracle was a type of round basket, similar to those laborers used for carrying earth and bricks on top of their heads. It was called *quppu,* "round basket," in Akkadian and *quffa* in Arabic. The basket was made of plaited rushes; it was flat-bottomed, covered with skins, caulked, and not very deep. The boat was navigated by two to four men with oars. When loaded, the cargoes and gunwale cleared the water by only a few inches. The coracle sailors could cross fast-flowing rivers like the Tigris, and they traveled up and down the river carrying goods as well. The raft, called in Akkadian *kalakku* and in Arabic *kelek*, was made of the strongest reeds that grew in the marshes or, preferably, of the best wood the builder could find locally. Its buoyancy was increased by attaching inflated goatskins below its surface. The loaded rafts floated down the river with the current, with the sailors using poles to propel and steer them until they reached their destination. These rafts were particularly useful in parts of the rivers with rapids and shallows, because, despite the loss of some skins, the rafts still kept afloat. When the *kelek* reached its destination, the cargo was unloaded, the boat dismantled, the wood sold, and the goatskins deflated and loaded on donkeys to form a caravan to travel north.

Models and reliefs of canoes show that they were propelled both by paddling and by punting (moving the canoe by means of a pole pushed against the water bottom). They, too, resembled modern Mesopotamian marsh canoes and were probably constructed of wood.

Most people had to cross the network of canals, which were often too wide and too deep to ford. In such cases, people used reed floats or inflated goatskins. The goatskins were made from the skin of an animal from which the head and hoofs had been cut, thus retaining its natural shape. At first, the neck and three legs of the hide were tied tightly, enabling the swimmer to blow from time to time into the open fourth leg to keep the float buoyant. After 700 BCE larger skins were used with all four legs tightly tied. Once inflated, the people of ancient Mesopotamia could hold it, placing it under their chests, to cross without fear of drowning. Under Shamshi-Adad of Assyria, such skins were part of a soldier's issue.

The three most important of the successive capitals of Assyria, namely, Asshur, Nimrud, and Nineveh, were built alongside the Tigris, which provided a method of transportation between both ends of the central part of the Assyrian kingdom. At Nimrud a great quay wall has been traced for about 240 yards for access to the ziggurat and the palace complex. The quay way was constructed of large stone blocks rising approximately thirty-three feet above bedrock and set twenty-one feet deep below the riverbank. King Sennacherib also built a similar quay along Nineveh; in fact, one of his fifteen city gates was named "the Quay Gate." Sennacherib described using river transportation in order to bring heavy cargoes such as limestone colossi to Nineveh. The quays also provided national revenue, charging harbor dues for their use.

Old Assyrian merchant colonies have been well documented in letters, accounts, and legal documents found at sites in Anatolia. These tablets have provided us with most of our information about Asia Minor at the beginning of the second millennium BCE. To date, no tablets have been

Merchant Colonies in Anatolia

A colorful print of the city of Nimrud across the Tigris River. On the left is the ziggurat. Boats (keleks) float up and down the river, as shepherds tend their flocks. This fanciful reconstruction bears almost no resemblance to the known appearance of Assyrian buildings. 28 cm × 46.5 cm. © BRITISH MUSEUM, LONDON.

found at Asshur, their trade center. The merchants acted as middlemen in the export of textiles from Asshur and the distribution of copper and tin within Asia Minor—a practical commercial venture because the animals could only carry a given weight. Each donkey carried a load of about 90 kilograms of textiles and tin, in addition to loose tin for expenses and taxes on the trip. When the merchants left Asshur, they paid a tax of 1/120 of the value of the goods to the *limmu* official (an Assyrian official who gave his name to a year in the king's rule). To enter Kanesh, 2/65 of the value was paid to the local ruler. The cities and territories through which the caravans passed also received customs fees and duties at fixed rates. Occasional reports mentioned attacks on caravans. In the Old Assyrian period (early second millennium BCE) textual evidence recorded a trade that brought tin and textiles into Anatolia to be exchanged for silver and gold. The tin was brought to Asshur, most likely from Afghanistan. Assyrian merchants purchased the tin for reshipment (by donkey caravan) and sale at a 100 percent markup in Anatolia. Perhaps the Old Assyrian merchants imported a higher quality tin on a large scale, enriching three generations of Old Assyrian merchant families. The merchants took pride in their high social status and in their high ethical standards.

After 1850 BCE the caravan traffic between Assyria and its trade colonies in eastern Asia Minor, centered at Kanesh, was carried out with few interruptions for 100 to 120 years, as documented by thousands of records and letters from the houses of the merchant colony at Kanesh. These records described the resolution of disputes between Kanesh merchants and their counterparts at the home base at Asshur, the formation of partnerships to provide capital, the adjustment of business debts between both parties, family business such as inheritance arrangements, requests for assistance in private or business matters, and reports of taking interest and compound interest. Tablets also documented events from their journeys and distribution of goods within Anatolia.

The Assyrians lived outside the walled city of Kanesh in their own quarter, called the *kārum*, originally meaning "quay" or "wharf," where canal traffic was unloaded and business transacted; later *kārum* referred to the association of merchants, a kind of trade board, and was applied in the heart of Anatolia where there was no river or harbor. A thousand kilometer journey took approximately two months, including days of rest.

Assyrian trade was run by family firms. The head of the family lived in Asshur, and a junior member of the family would be the resident agent in the *kārum* at Kanesh. The family capitalized these ventures, but sometimes partnerships were formed to raise the necessary capital. Though Kanesh was the trade center, there were nine other merchant colonies in Anatolia. These settlements were self-governing, but under the aegis of local princes to whom they paid taxes.

The inventories of the traders before the Dark Age provide information on a large variety of luxury goods and **Role of the** necessary raw materials, apparently for the palace and tem- **Merchant** ple. There was, however, no information about what was exported. In the subsequent Old Babylonian period, the role of the merchant became more complex in the south. In Ur, during the Old Babylonian period importers brought copper from beyond the Persian Gulf; sharing the risks, responsibilities, and profits through partnerships. These texts also mentioned a merchant's organization (*kārum*, literally, "wharf") with its own legal status and location outside the city limits.

After the Dark Age passed, the circumstances of the merchants at Mari became the norm throughout the ancient Near East. Trade relations have been detailed in the Mari texts, which linked international trade in the Persian Gulf with Dilmun via the Euphrates, and Aleppo and the Orontes valley to the Mediterranean. Mari was also an entrepôt on the tin trade route between inner Asia and the Mediterranean. Tin was essential in manufacturing bronze. Mari trade was carried out differently from that at Ur and Kanesh; caravans received royal protection on their journeys.

The traders were royal envoys as well, bringing valuable gifts from one ruler to the next. Treaties guaranteed their safety and limited their private entrepreneurial activities. The risks were great, and merchants were often attacked or murdered. Soon after the Amarna period we have little information about trade and traders until the end of the Babylonian empire. We should not assume that trade relations ended in that millennium, especially since trade flourished in the subsequent period when Aramaeans and Arab tribes controlled the extensive caravan traffic in the triangle between the Mediterranean, the Red Sea, and the Persian Gulf, as well as routes leading deep into central Asia. An inscription from Sargon II documented expanded foreign trade; he was the first ruler who compelled Egypt to open trade relations with his country.

Besides merchants involved in large-scale trade, there were plenty who operated on a small scale, similar to shopkeepers or peddlers. These merchants sold to individuals, as there was reference to "a merchant's leather bag for weights." Dishonest practices by retail merchants were alluded to as "who, as he holds the balance, indulges in cheating, by substituting weights." As for peddlers, the "firewood man" was noted in Assyria and a "salt man" in Babylonia—both could be house-to-house small traders.[37]

Temples and private persons advanced silver for commercial trade ventures. The merchants would repay the loan in commodities. The lender of the silver would expect to benefit by a favorable price for the commodities at the time of repayment, or by the payment of interest, or both.

CRAFTS AND LABOR

Sumerian and Akkadian had a word meaning "specialist," which included specific artisans, artists, and scholars—that is, people with specialized learning or skill. The terms for many craftsmen were pre-Sumerian and belonged to substrate languages. Knowledge of crafts was learned by oral teaching, apprenticeship, and writing, in the case of scribes. Crafts were often taught within families or clans. The Laws of Hammurabi decreed that an adopted son could not be reclaimed by his own parents if he had been taught a craft.[38] Apprenticeship was long, as much as eight years for a house builder and four for a seal cutter. Sometimes the craftsmen were slaves, but only wealthy families could afford to have their slaves trained. Half of the surviving apprenticeship contracts were written on behalf of the powerful Egibi family.

The earliest records of jewelers' workshops were from the Ur III period. An archive from Ur recorded the business of a large workshop divided into eight departments: metalworkers, goldsmiths, stonecutters, blacksmiths, leather workers, felters, carpenters, and reed workers. The texts contained deliveries of material to these craftsmen and orders for certain types of objects.

In the Old Babylonian period, "guilds" of brewers, smiths, and other trades were organized under an administrator, as part of the palace or temple organization. Important craftsmen, such as brewers, smiths, and weavers, achieved some kind of independence within and among the organizations. The overseers of these artisans achieved social status and power, and they were well compensated. But the supervisor of the musicians was much poorer because he had little to sell or hire. Guilds, as known from medieval times, could not function as independent bodies because of the difficulty of acquiring raw materials.

Beginning with the early Neo-Babylonian period, the names of professions became family names (similar to the present-day Smith, Weaver, Miller, etc.), suggesting that craftsmen enjoyed status in the preceding period. Most were scribes, but there were also carpenters, metalworkers, and goldsmiths. Their ancestors' names could be traced back to the Kassite period. Texts also referred to the "city" of the tanners and the "city" of the metalworkers, that is, special quarters to which certain crafts were limited or in which they were concentrated for convenience.

Ancient material culture was often changing, with new styles arising due to a central authority or to technical ad-   **The Crafts** vances. Technical advances did not always lead to better art; sometimes they led inferior art to be mass-produced. Whether the styles were local or foreign in origin, an innovation had to be locally accepted. The court style naturally inspired derivative art for ordinary people. The Kassite cylinder seals show how the craftsmen indulged the needs of different parts of society. Four styles were in use at the same time, two for the rich and two for the poor.

Artists adapted works from their own heritage, thus reviving ancient forms. A plaque from Sippar, depicting a statue of the god Shamash, noted in the accompanying text that the statue was made as an imitation of an ancient portrait. Ancient objects were often preserved for long periods of time; for example, the stele of Naram-Sin was publicly displayed for more than a thousand years. Artists may also have been influenced by antiquities found in the ground. A letter described looking for beads in the ground, most likely at ancient sites.

Tradition was most likely transmitted through older people, clay models, and perhaps books of patterns, though none have been found. The same motif recurred on objects as dissimilar as a cylinder seal and a bas-relief. Quality terms applied to artifacts referred mainly to their cost. Metal objects were evaluated by weighing them, but a premium of one-tenth to one-third was sometimes added for workmanship. The premium was greater for smaller objects. In antiquity, this pricing is understandable, since large works were commissioned by the temple or ruler who wanted them. Larger works of art would have no market value except as scrap.

Archaeologists have been able to identify crucibles, equipment used for filtering and distillation, and even drip bottles. Also, mortars and pestles, strainers, and mills have been found—items that could be used in either home or "office." Some Mesopotamian technology can be traced back to prehistory, as shown by vocabulary for such items and the craftsmen who used them.

In the first millennium BCE, Assyrians were familiar with acids, producing compounds such as sulfuric acid. Babylonian chemists were familiar with acids, sodas, silicates, limes, metals, and metallic oxides. There were even references to using sulfur to produce a flame, but we do not know how the sulfur was lit.

Carpentry

Wood, regardless of quality, was used for building bridges, wagons, ships, and occasionally houses. The Babylonian lexical lists of wood objects were longer than those for objects made from copper, clay, or leather. Since wood survived only in the desert, often as carbonized remains, our knowledge of woodworking must be drawn almost entirely from the numerous ancient texts, which survived in abundance for all of Mesopotamia and northern Syria. The range of skill of woodworking required trained craftsmen.

We do not know if carpenters were asked to build simple, single-story homes or parts of them such as the roof, the door frame, or the doors. Little is known about their tools. Carpenters were certainly employed for building temples and palaces, which involved all kinds of cypress, cedar, beech, and other imported woods. The great tree trunks from Syria and other forested regions were floated down river on rafts and used to make palace doors.

Pottery and Clay Goods

The most common craft was pottery made from clay. Utensils included pots, drinking vessels, plates, and bowls, their shapes still found today. The potter also made large jars for storing goods, ovens, and even coffins (in the latter he competed with the carpenter and basketmaker). Some pottery was formed by hand and manufactured by punching a central hole into a lump of clay and adding pieces of clay as pellets, slabs, or coils. Some vessels were pressed in a mold, and others were shaped on a slow wheel (ca. 4500 BCE) or on a fast wheel (ca. 2000 BCE) to create thin-walled vessels with spouts, handles, covers, and even reliefs. We do not know what these potter's wheels looked like and how they functioned. There is no Akkadian word for "potter's wheel." The potter's wheel was instrumental in mass-producing large quantities of pottery in order to supply the needs of the major cities. Containers of fired clay were needed as offerings to the gods and kings and to store oil, wine, grain, and so on.

The Near East contained the raw materials needed by potters, namely, clay, water, fuel, and iron-rich pigments. The chemical composition of clays used to make pots varied, but their sources have often been identified by scientific analysis. The absence of oxygen in the kiln chamber changed the color of the clay from red to gray or black.

There were various kinds of pottery ovens, like the simple hearth in which a stack of dried vessels was covered with brush, straw, or dung cakes to form a continuously renewable dome of fuel over the pots. Other pottery ovens included a trench dug to house the wares and fuel and a C-shaped retaining wall built as a container and windbreak for the firing. All these kiln types are still in use today. More-developed kilns have been recognized at some excavation sites. Generally they were cylinders built of fired brick, about two meters in interior diameter and two meters above the ground. A pre-Sumerian word for "potter" appears in Sumerian and as cognates in other Semitic languages.

Potters may have specialized in particular types of pottery. Painted ware as well as enameled and glazed ceramic ware appeared, primarily in Assyria, with old motifs revised. The development of glazed pottery came during the Neo-Assyrian and Neo-Babylonian periods, suggesting craft communication with glass and metal workers. Inscribed pottery was widespread throughout the history of Mesopotamia, ranging in size from small vessels to ones holding up to 250 liters. Whether pottery was made by men or by women assisted by children remains uncertain. Women may have decorated pots, but men may have worked with apprentices on a full-time basis. Manufacture and decoration were characteristic of different regions and periods, so pottery has been used for dating. Pottery has also provided information as to trading activities and cultural influences.

The greatest number of miniature sculptures were made from clay. Terra-cottas were rarely made individually; usually clay forms were used to produce them, and then they were fired. For three-dimensional figures, two forms were needed. Terra-cotta figurines were often painted and in later periods overlaid with colorful glazes.

Mud and clay were necessary for the monumental building projects for which hundreds of thousands of bricks were used. Nevertheless, the profession of "brick maker" was seldom attested. After the mud was prepared, it was put into a wooden form and removed after each brick had dried. After sun-drying, some bricks were baked in small ovens and then smoothed and polished. Thousands of workers were recruited for making bricks and building monuments. Supervisors made certain that a given number of bricks were stamped and inscribed. Later in Assyria and Nebuchadnezzar's Babylon, brick reliefs were created from embossed, often colorfully glazed bricks. The glazed brick walls of the Ishtar Gate and Processional Way at Babylon were made of blue, turquoise,

The Sargon Vase. A glass vase of light green and two vertical lug handles bears the inscription, "Palace of Sargon (II), King of Assyria" (721–705 BCE). The lion incised is associated with Sargon. Ht. 8.8 cm, diam. 5.7 cm. © BRITISH MUSEUM, LONDON.

green, yellow, white, and black glazed bricks, providing evidence of ceramic mass production. The glazing substance was frequently artificial lapis lazuli. Asphalt was used to cover bricks used in foundation walls and courts.

Glass Making and Glazes

According to cuneiform records, glass was produced in Sumerian times, but it has not been found at sites predating 1500 BCE. In the fourth and third millennia BCE, the ancient chemists experimented with chem-

Relief of a woman spinning yarn. She is holding a spindle and possibly wool in her hands. She is sitting on a low lion-footed stool with a lion-footed table in front of her. A servant stands behind fanning her mistress. Ht. 9.3 cm. © LOUVRE MUSEUM, PARIS.

icals such as lime soda and silicates (namely, quartzite sand) in combination with mineral substances in vivid colors. From these operations, various forms of glass making evolved: glazes, frits, and glass of many compositions, some more durable than others, opaque and translucent glass, and, in some cases, molds. Glass was commonly used to manufacture containers, beads, small figurines, or component parts of statues.

When hot, glass is extremely malleable; it can be rolled into sheets, drawn into tubes, rods, or threads, cut with shears, or pressed into molds. When the glass is ready to be formed into objects, it must be worked quickly, since the cooling glass changes quickly from a highly viscous liquid to a solid.

Textiles

Spinning and weaving of flax and wool were predominantly women's work. Weavers, following a period of apprenticeship, specialized in particular types of work, such as weaving linen or colored textiles. Female weavers were frequently mentioned. Many kinds of materials were woven, both coarse and fine, and with colors and bleaches. Both male and female washers, called fullers, were considered skilled workers.

Textiles were produced on looms. The first, and probably earliest, was a ground loom, with stakes in the ground to keep the warps stretched tightly and the loom secured. The ground loom was favored by nomads because of its portability and ease of assembly. The second basic loom was the warp-weighted loom, which has been documented in the ancient Near East by the presence of ceramic weights and from illustrations on seals and in paintings. Numbers of large beads with a single hole may be identified as drop-spindles used for spinning, and those with a circular groove may have served as bobbins for weaving tapestries. Among grave goods were found slim bone knives used by carpet weavers.

Color in ancient textiles was produced from natural dyestuffs derived from animal, plant, or mineral matter. The Syrians and Phoenicians produced purple cloth, as purple snails were found only off the Phoenician coast. The most famous and costly dye of antiquity was a purple extracted from a gland in seal mollusks. Other natural colors such as red, yellow, blue, black, and purple have all been described.

Sack makers and the rug tyer were textile professions. The production of rugs and tapestries was well attested at Old Babylonian Mari and Nuzi, although the technique of tying carpets was probably developed later, after 1500 BCE. Rugs provided warmth and decoration on a wall or floor and could be used in both nomadic and sedentary environments. There is little material evidence for the presence of carpets before the eighth century BCE.

Clothing was probably sewed by women. It was not considered a skilled craft as evidenced by the lack of an Akkadian word for the tailor, embroiderer, and producer of artificially fringed hems. But in later texts, words for the repair tailor occurred. Since extremely artistic and ornate vestments were created for kings, statues of gods, high priests, and others, sewing and embroidery would have demanded great skill. Neo-Babylonian texts mentioned tailors of mourning garments. Statues and reliefs provide a great deal of information on garments (see Chapter 7).

Many ancient techniques involving textiles are still in use today: felt for insulating material for roofing; rope for suspending, securing, binding, and lifting; linen for warm weather; wool for winter; and bales of cotton, bags of flour or coffee beans, or potato sacks for packaging.

Basketry

Basket making was related to weaving, since various products could be made by either process. For example, the sails of a boat could be made from woven fibers or thick canvas. The basket maker also made round hampers, boxes, and even seats using ropelike fibers from the largest reeds. Like crude boats, the cheapest coffins were made of woven reeds.

Reeds were especially important in treeless areas; reeds grew in abundance along the waterways and in the marshes and thickets. They were used for making baskets of all kinds, the shafts of arrows, spears, fences, doors, reed furniture, mats, boat building, and shelters for humans and animals in the countryside. In the construction of public works, such as ziggurats, layers of reed mats were laid at intervals between the layers of bricks. Reed mats were used for roofs; their carbonized remains are still frequently preserved.

Leather Work

All kinds of animal skins were worn by people and were used to carry water and other liquids. The hair was removed from the hide by using oak apples, tree bark, alum, fats, oils, and other substances. The hide was first treated and soaked in prescribed liquids and then rubbed with fats and oils, at which point the hide was considered tanned. The tanner was not aware of the effectiveness of each of the individual processes, so he used them all. Manure was used to soften the leather. The leather was even dyed, but we do not know how.

The leather worker provided sandals, boots, and other types of shoes. Leather was particularly important in military equipment. Leather straps and insets were needed mainly for helmets, shields, and armor, which also were made in part from bronze or iron. In the first millennium BCE, quivers were made from leather. Leather was even used for war chariots and bridles.

Stone Sculpture

Some of the best-known objects of Assyrian art were the bas-reliefs from the walls of the palaces in Nimrud, Nineveh, and Dur-Sharrukin. The early reliefs actually converted wall painting into stone. There were ritual, ceremonial, and mythological scenes centered on the king in addition to scenes of hunting and war. At first each slab was treated as an individual entity, but later a series of slabs was used to tell a running story.

In bas-reliefs little attention was given to perspective. Every item was carved as though the artist were standing in front of it, so that buildings never receded into a three-quarters view and soldiers scaling ladders in the assault and capture of a town were never represented in profile. Human figures were portrayed according to their rank or importance, with kings larger than courtiers, who were larger than ordinary people. The head was usually portrayed in profile, and the upper part of the body was shown full frontal or at a slight angle. But the Assyrian beard, which was square, was shown head-on even though its wearer was in profile. Like the head, the pelvis and legs were shown in profile, with the feet one behind the other in the same plane. The arms were always

shown. At the beginning of the Neo-Assyrian Dynasty, the people were
larger than life, the details clear and well proportioned, but the landscape
was often disregarded. The north was indicated by the vine, with twist-
ing branches forming a decorative pattern. The south was indicated by
a few common trees, such as date palms, dwarf palms, and conifers. By
the end of the Neo-Assyrian period, the human figures were carved on
a smaller scale. Battle scenes were portrayed, with chariots, horses, and
fighters tangled among the dead and the wounded.

Certain conventions were followed. For example, galloping horses
were drawn with legs extended. The artist suggested the required number of persons or horses, up to four, by carving one or more lines exactly
following the outline of the principal figure. As for the sculptural treatment of the bull-colossi that guarded the palace gates, the spectator was
assumed to look at the bull-colossi either facing him or sideways. In
order to achieve a two-dimensional aspect for the four feet, but to cor-
respond with the three-dimensional view of the forequarters, an extra
front foot was added for a total of five feet. The reliefs, like the frescoes,
were never colored completely. Only certain features were highlighted,
such as beards, ornaments and garments with red or blue. Assyrian
sculpture in the round was mainly life-sized stone statues of gods and
kings. The figures stood stiffly at attention, the body shown by regular
curves.

The quarrying of hard stones made large-scale building projects possible. Stone was quarried as near as possible to the construction site.
After quarrying, the blocks were cut roughly to size or shape to facilitate
handling and transportation. The stone was transported to the construction site using boats, wooden rollers, sledges, and ropes, and various
draft animals such as oxen and donkeys. At the construction site, ramps
made of wood, earth, and bricks were used to build walls or to erect
colossal statues or obelisks. Blocks or sculptures were also moved by
human labor. Massive building projects required both unskilled and
skilled laborers, such as stonemasons or wood workers, whose marks
have sometimes been preserved on worked blocks or on the background
of carved reliefs.

Artisans involved with stone included the "stoneworker" and "picture
carver." Finished sculptures, including relief carvings and statues in the
round, were very often painted to make them appear more lifelike. For
the same reason, eyes were frequently inlaid with other materials, such
as shell and lapis lazuli, set in bitumen. There were a great many lists
of magical stones from Babylonia and Assyria, the lists beginning with
lapis lazuli.

The earliest painting on built walls is dated to the Neolithic era.
Throughout historical times, the interior walls of houses, temples, and
palaces were often decorated with painted patterns or scenes with figures

applied over layers of fine white mud plaster. Paint was made from finely ground minerals, mixed with water and an adhesive, often gelatine or glue, gum, or albumen (eggwhite). Carbon, azurite, ochre (iron oxide), and malachite were used to create pigments of black, blue, brown or red, and green. Artificial pigments have been found. Variations and muted shades, though rarely used, could be made by mixing the primary materials. Paints were applied to surfaces with brushes made of pieces of fibrous wood bruised at one end to separate the fibers and form bristles. Beeswax was also used as a binding medium and as a protective coating on the surfaces of paintings.

Seals and Sealing

Seals were used from the beginning of writing. When rolled over a lump of clay, the seal marked the authentication of a contracting party or witness. Cylinder seals were usually made from colorful, hard stones, such as green and red jaspers, dark green serpentines, transparent quartz, hematite, and lapis lazuli. The color of the seal was often associated with the fate of its owner. Individuals could also own and use more than one seal, either concurrently or sequentially. Different seals often marked changes in the status of an official; or a new seal could be used to mark service under successive monarchs.

Royal seals have been identified by a carved inscription citing a royal name. Seals were given by the king to various high-ranking administrative officials. Some kings owned a number of seals, which officials were permitted to use. Sometimes the kings had personal, dynastic, and heirloom seals.

There were seals belonging to the gods, and statues of the gods were sometimes depicted wearing seals. Gods wrote letters to kings and sealed them to authenticate them. Divine seals were also used to seal important documents such as treaties.

Seals were worn hanging from pins or suspended at the wrist. In fact, the Sumerian word for "wrist" was literally "seal holder." In the Royal Cemetery at Ur, Queen Puabi was buried in full regalia, wearing crossed gold pins with lapis lazuli heads, and hanging from one of the pins was her lapis lazuli cylinder seal. In the second millennium BCE, seals usually hung from a loop and were worn around the neck.

Seals were used as gifts to the gods, funeral offerings to the dead, and personal possessions taken to the graves of their owners. Women even wore their husband's seals to the grave and vice versa.[39]

Metal Work

Excavations have provided information about the workshops of metal workers, bronze foundries, vase factories, and armament production. Records of the institutional metal workshops recorded the weight of

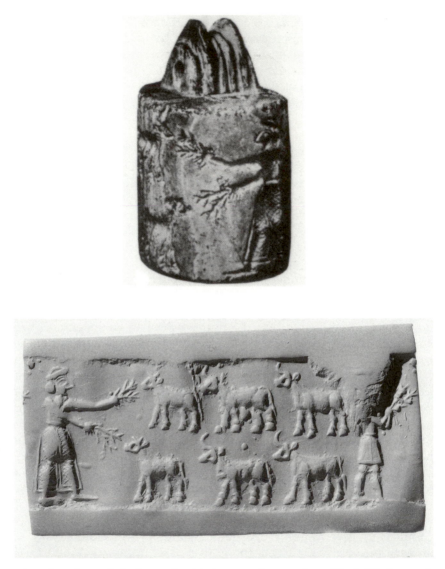

Seal and sealing. Cylinder seal with loop at the top from Uruk IV shows the king with a netted skirt; the attendant behind the king has branches to supplement the king's offerings to two rows of animals. Ht. 63 mm (seal 46 mm), Diameter 37 mm. © YALE BABYLONIAN COLLECTION, YALE UNIVERSITY, NEW HAVEN. See B. Buchanan, *Early Near Eastern Seals in the Yale Babylonian Collection* (New Haven and London: Yale University Press, 1981), no. 134.

metal items that were melted down and remade. On urban sites collections of weapons, tools, and scrap were often found.

In the Bronze Age, the metalworker was a specialist whose products helped to transform society by their effect on agriculture, warfare, and transportation. Anatolia has the richest copper ore deposits in the whole Near East. Though copper was already known as early as the Neolithic period, the technology developed during the fourth millennium BCE. Native copper could be found in numerous deposits in a belt of mineralization extending across southeastern Anatolia into northern Iraq. In the early third millennium BCE the Sumerians suddenly switched to the Persian Gulf trade for copper. Considerable amounts of copper were involved in this trade. A text from Ur, dated to the reign of Rim-Sin of Larsa (1822–1763 BCE), recorded the receipt of copper in Dilmun (presumably from Magan), which weighed, according to the standard of Ur, 18,333 kilograms. One-third of this copper was earmarked for delivery to Ea-nasir of Ur, a merchant who had close connections with the Dilmun and Magan copper trade.[40]

The metals known and used in the ancient Near East were copper, tin, bronze (an artificial alloy of copper and tin), gold, silver, electrum (a natural alloy of gold and silver), lead, iron, and steel (an artificial alloy of iron and carbon). Metals such as arsenic and zinc were usually used as materials alloyed with copper to produce arsenical copper and brass, respectively. Only copper, lead and silver-bearing ores were mined prior to about 1000 BCE. Tin and gold presented special problems. Mineral tin and gold were both panned, and some pans believed to have been used for this purpose have been found at Early Bronze Age Troy and in Grave 20 at Asshur. Also, the mineral ores of gold and tin were deposited in quartz veins running through granite rock. The similarity in their geological history may suggest a possible historical connection between tin and gold, with the two metals first being used at about the same time.

The texts often referred to copper refining operations as the "washing" of copper. The copper ingots came in an impure state requiring as many as three washings. As much as one-third of the metal was lost in a refining operation.[41] Copper technology involved melting and smelting. Melting involved heating copper metal until it became a liquid that could be poured and cast in open molds requiring suitable crucibles. Smelting involved heating copper ores with charcoal to remove all oxides, carbonates, or sulfides from the copper. Copper can be shaped and hardened by hammering, but repeated hammering makes the copper brittle enough to crack. When heated, its malleability is restored. By the fourth millennium BCE, advanced processes were used which included "lost wax," a process in which the shape was first sculpted in wax, then enclosed in a clay mold until the wax melted, thus producing a hollow mold in the desired shape.

The Iron Age began ca. 1200 BCE, though miscellaneous pieces of iron have been found in archaeological contexts as far back as the fifth millennium BCE. Once serious ironwork began, the technology soon followed. The early history of iron metallurgy was traditionally viewed as a monopoly on the secrets of working with iron. The Hittites used iron metallurgy in their military successes, particularly against the Egyptians at the battle of Qadesh in Syria (ca. 1275 BCE). When the Hittite empire fell at the end of the Bronze Age, control over the use of iron and iron technology fell to the Philistines. Iron became the metal of choice for the common man.

The most general word for a metal artisan was "metalworker," but more frequently "smith" was used. In addition, the "goldsmith" processed silver and other metals for jewelry and valuable items. Later the "ironsmith" or "blacksmith" worked primarily in the production of weapons. At the beginning of the second millennium BCE, iron with nickel content was known in eastern Asia Minor, and iron was considered more valuable than gold. However, large-scale use of iron began when the Hittites succeeded in smelting iron ore and applying appropriate alloys. Iron technology is more complex than the processes for smelting copper and making bronze. Forging could produce wrought iron, which is almost free of carbon, making it more malleable. Wrought iron can be made to absorb more carbon by reheating it in a furnace in contact with carboniferous materials. To give the resultant metal its maximum hardness, it has to be suddenly cooled by quenching it in water or oil in order to become steel. Iron came into widespread use when iron metallurgists had mastered these processes. Bronze continued to be used for many practical items, such as utensils, tools, and nails.

The use of arsenical ores exposed prehistoric smiths to chronic arsenic poisoning, with symptoms including muscular atrophy and loss of reflexes. Serious health hazards may explain a widespread theme in mythology in which the smith-god was a cripple. Classical literature referred to the Greek smith-god Hephaestus and his Roman counterpart Vulcan, who were described as lame, a characteristic shared by smith-gods from Scandinavia to West Africa.[42]

Archaeological evidence for metal workshops has been rare. Only two early second millennium BCE shops are known, one in the *kārum* at Kanesh and another in the kingdom of Eshnunna (today inside modern Baghdad). Archaeologists found the equipment of the coppersmith: clay molds, crucibles, and clay pipes which would be connected to bellows.[43]

Statues and bronze surface panels made by metalworkers have survived. Bronze was used for artistic works, particularly for larger sculptures, because gold and silver were too expensive. Between 650 and 600 BCE, the kingdom of Urartu was a center of metal artwork where new techniques were continuously developed.

The statue of Napir-Asu, queen of Elam, in its present mutilated condition, weighs nearly two tons. When the statue was made in the second millennium BCE, numerous crucibles, all heated simultaneously to the same temperature, would have been needed when the molten metal was poured. The statue was cast in two sections—front and back—and then soldered together and filed for smoothness. Though the statue was very thick, more metal was poured inside to make it sufficiently solid. Spreading the metal evenly inside was not completely successful. When Susa was plundered, the shoulder and the left arm were knocked off by a blow from a club. The technical skill shown in this statue, reliefs and jewelry achieved a degree of excellence that was unsurpassed until the end of the nineteenth century in western Europe.

Jewelry

Jewelry was usually made from very thin leaf metal and set with brightly colored stones. Necklaces were made from semiprecious stones, gold beads, and shapes such as leaves. Bracelets were spiral-shaped or circular, sometimes with an animal's head at the end, or with a single or double rosette. Earrings were crafted in the shape of rings, bunches of grapes, or cones partly covered with a granulated pattern of animal or human heads.

Jewelry was made from agate, jasper, carnelian, rock crystals, and other semiprecious stones. The Mesopotamian's fascination with colored and precious stones gave rise to a technology based on fire, like metalwork and pottery. The scarcity of imported precious stones gave rise to the manufacture of artificial stones. Quartz pebbles were painted with mineral ores of blue and green. With the application of heat, they became permanent vitreous colored glazes. Carnelian was similarly treated—it could be decorated with red mineral dyes or bleached by alkaline substances placed on it. Precious stones, such as emeralds, were found only in the later periods, and then rarely.

Jewelers usually worked on larger objects, such as statuettes, ceremonial weapons, vessels made of precious metals, and furniture that was gold-leafed or inlaid with precious materials. Jewelers manufactured jewelry either for human use or for statues of the gods. The profession was passed down from father to son. Although jewelers' quarters existed in some cities, the craftsmen were not organized in guilds. No jeweler's workshop has been found, but a jeweler's hoard dated to the Old Babylonian period was uncovered at Larsa. The deposit was a jar containing bronze tweezers, a small anvil, gravers, a smoothing stone, and sixty-seven small weights, in addition to beads of agate, lapis lazuli, carnelian, and hematite and pieces of jewelry in silver, electrum, and gold, clearly intended for melting down and reworking. Artifacts from the Royal Cemetery revealed that various metalworking techniques were in use by

Jewelry from the Royal Cemetery at Ur: (a) lapis and gold choker, (b) lapis and gold leaf necklace, and (c) gold hoop earrings. © BRITISH MUSEUM, LONDON.

this time in Mesopotamia, including the earliest known examples of granulation, fine hammered work, cloisonné, repoussé, chasing, engraving, and filigree. Cemetery burials included gold diadems, lobed earrings with fine granulation, beaded necklaces, and decorative pins.

Small animal figurines often combined precious metals and stones. Two statues found in the Great Death Pit at Ur were excellent examples of this technique. Each is a goat standing on its hind legs and resting its forelegs on a plant before it. The plant, the goat's legs, and the face were made of gold. The goat's horns were of lapis lazuli, and the fleece on its upper back consisted of individual locks, each carved of lapis lazuli. Inlays of the eyes, eyebrows, and beard of the goat were also of lapis. Its belly was silver, with shell used for detailing.

Numerous texts from the palace archives of Mari dealt with goldsmiths. Among them was a letter from the priestess Bakhlatum to Iliiddinam, a jeweler, complaining of a four-year delay in making her necklace and ornamented garment even though the jeweler had been paid in advance. The Mari archives also described the composition of jewelry items:

> 1 necklace of flat speckled chalcedony beads including: 34 flat speckled chalcedony beads, [and] 35 gold fluted beads, in groups of five.
>
> 1 necklace of flat speckled chalcedony beads including: 39 flat speckled chalcedony beads, [with] 41 fluted beads in a group that make up the hanging device . . .
>
> 1 necklace with rounded lapis lazuli beads including: 28 rounded lapis lazuli beads, [and] 29 fluted beads for its clasp.
>
> 1 necklace of flat lapis lazuli beads including: 13 flat lapis lazuli beads, and 14 fluted beads in groups.
>
> Seven large necklaces with hanging rock crystal beads, their clasps are in gold
>
> 1 belt in lapis lazuli, with 14 rows.[44]

Ivory Work

Many luxury items were imported or seized as booty, in particular, ivories made by Phoenician and Syrian craftsmen in the early first millennium BCE. Ivory from the hippopotamus and elephant was carved with either scenes of figures or plant motifs. Ivory was also used to make small objects, such as boxes, handles, spoons, and combs. Ivory plaques were carved in relief or openwork, often dyed, inlaid with other materials, or overlaid with gold leaf, and then inserted into or joined with

The Royal Cemetery of Ur: the "Ram in a Thicket" is one of a pair found in the great Death Pit in the Royal Cemetery at Ur (ca. 2500 BCE). Each ram is standing on its hind legs and resting its forelegs on a plant before it. The ram's head and legs are covered in gold leaf, its twisted horns and shoulder fleece of individual locks are lapis lazuli, and its body fleece is shell. Inlays of the eyes, eyebrows, and beard of the goat were also of lapis. Its belly was silver, with shell used for detailing. The tree, branches and flowers are all gold leaf. Ht. 45.7 cm. © BRITISH MUSEUM, LONDON.

parts of wooden furniture for decoration. Many of the subjects depicted on the walls of Assyrian palaces were repeated on the ivory carvings of the period, such as battle scenes, divine animals or genies, and gods flanking the "sacred tree." Animal and human figures of ivory also were carved in the round, in the Assyrian style.

Ivory, shell, mother-of-pearl, bone, and lapis lazuli were used extensively for inlaid decoration of gaming boards, wall plaques, boxes, and musical instruments. Shells, including ostrich eggshell, tortoise shell, and marine and freshwater shell, were used for cosmetic implements or for inlay. Mother-of-pearl, the material that lines the shell of the pearl oyster and the pearl mussel, was particularly sought for jewelry or inlay.

Selling Songs

The selling of songs (sacred and secular), a minor trade, was always popular but poorly paid. Among the catalogues of titles is a collection of song titles, such as "He appears, the god of fire, the Lord of battles," "Your love is like the scent of cedar wood, oh my Lord," "Come to the king's garden: it is full of cedar trees," "Oh, gardener of the garden of desires," and "In the streets, I saw two harlots."[45]

Modern music theory has roots in ancient Mesopotamia. Seven-tone and eight-tone musical scales, including our standard modern major scale, were used as early as the Old Babylonian period (ca. 1800 BCE). Music theory and practice spread to the Levant and ancient Greece by the first millennium BCE. Pythagoras claimed that he learned his mathematics and music in the Near East, and he probably did. The style in which music was performed remains unknown. Wind, percussion, and stringed instruments were known.

Throughout the history of Mesopotamia, the importance of the private and institutional sectors varied. The temples **The Private** and the palaces were the principal patrons of the crafts. **Sector** There were craftsmen employed as part of the work force of the great institutions, but independent workers were also hired as needed. In the Isin craft archive, the craftsmen labored part-time in the workshop. This may have reflected a general trend toward contracting services out during the Old Babylonian period. A few slaves performed all kinds of crafts, but the slaves were unable to compete with free labor. Craftsmen owned slaves to assist them.

The status of free artisans varied throughout history. Unlike slaves, who received only rations, artisans received payment. In the Old Babylonian period their compensation was regulated by the Laws of Hammurabi, which listed payment for textile workers, leather workers, reed workers, and others.[46] The same craftsman could make both ordinary objects and works of art. Metalworkers and jewelers sometimes worked with more than one kind of metal. A group of proverbs described specialists who had disgraced their professions. For example, "A disgraced smith becomes a man of the sickle." [47]

The activities of the private sector remain undocumented. We do not know whether crafts were organized as guilds outside of the temple or palace. Some crafts had a patron deity, such as the brick god Kulla, who may have held the group together through common worship. Trades passed from father to son, so that a family connection tended to concentrate members of the same craft in one part of a city. Some crafts such as textile work could be done at home. Texts mention craft quarters named after trades, such as the wards of goldsmiths, bleachers, and potters, a craft quarter at Mari, the street of the bakers in Jerusalem (Jeremiah 37:21), and the "gate of the foundry workers" at Asshur. Craft quarters have been identified at various sites. At Nineveh a craft quarter was earmarked for metalworking, later for stoneworking, then for making pottery, and finally as a cemetery; this section never became residential again. Crafts could be performed within the city or outside of it, in the latter case because workshops were either noisy or smelly or because the necessary resources were obtained more easily outside.

In the Old Babylonian period the Diqdiqqeh area northeast of Ur produced many terra-cotta plaques, as shown by the discovery of molds, unfinished seals, and artists' trial pieces. There is, however, little archaeological evidence of buildings. Perhaps the craftsmen worked in reed booths which could not be preserved in the climate of Mesopotamia.

The only apprenticeship agreements found were for a singer and a cook recorded in a scribal form-book from Old Babylonian Isin, but during the Neo-Babylonian period contracts of employment were routinely drawn up.[48]

Institutional Sector   The institutions not only provided capital for investment but also time and freedom from economic pressures for craftsmen to experiment and produce new inventions.

Though crafts were usually taught orally, manuals such as *The Farmer's Instructions* as well as works on horse-training, glass making, cooking and beer brewing were composed, and the technical terminology of the craftsmen was recorded.[49] Colophons to these manuals have noted, "Let the initiate show the initiate; the non-initiate shall not see it. It belongs, to the tabooed things of the great gods."[50]

In the Akkadian period a state workshop was organized under the direction of one of the highest officials in the palace in order to supervise the massive royal decoration of the temples. The administration was concerned with the supply and control of valuable materials. In archives documenting the decoration of the Temple of Enlil at Nippur in the Old Akkadian period, gold was weighed by the overseers, released to the goldsmiths to be made into artifacts, and then received and checked again by the overseers. During the reign of Esarhaddon, there were state workshops located in the royal arsenals built in major cities. When the capital moved to Nineveh, the building was no longer used to prepare armaments for campaigns; most of the workshops were turned into stores or living quarters.

An Ur III archive from the temple at Ur showed that a number of different crafts were responsible to a single administrative officer. Labor was recruited and supervised. For example, texts recorded the amounts produced by potters, listing the exact time needed to make each type of pot.[51] This was also true for other crafts, such as the textile industry, in which types and grades of cloth were precisely listed and recorded together with the workdays required. Materials were regularly recycled in palaces and temples. The temple supplied raw materials which were kept in a special storehouse for manufacture; finished goods were distributed to their destinations. Furnaces were designated specifically for the recycling of metal into assayed ingots which would be redistributed as needed; both archaeological and textual sources have confirmed this process.

The Ur craft archive listed raw materials and finished goods, both balanced by records of labor. Some daily accounts showed that the same craftsmen came to work regularly, though occasionally they were recorded as "sick" or just absent. The rations issued to state employees in the Ur III period consisted mostly of grain, wool or cloth, and oil, but other commodities were sometimes included.[52] The texts clearly differentiated between workers according to age and sex. The level of remuneration was correlated with the kinds of service performed, so that foremen of labor teams, or workers on better-quality cloth, received more pay. Long-term workers, whether freemen or slaves, received rations on a monthly basis.[53] The wool ration issued to temple employees of the third millennium BCE implied that these workers were expected to spin and weave their own garments. For example, 600 tons of wool were turned over to a factory at Lagash, where over 6,000 workers toiled, the majority being women and children.[54] After the Ur III period, there was less evidence for large-scale centrally controlled production.

In Lagash both the workers of the Ur III period and the royal subjects of the Pre-Sargonic Dynasty performed state service by turn, a month at a time. When they were officially called to duty, they were described as "serving (their) turn," for which they received rations. When employed outside their formal term, they were described as "sitting out (their) turn." Off-duty, they were free agents and received wages, against which they borrowed. These workers often worked during the winter months on jobs such as dike repairing and canal clearing. They were probably Ur III city residents, because texts have described their absence from work as not having left the city.[55]

The balance of power between the institutions and the private sector has been difficult to document. A formal transfer of power from temples to palace took place between 2500 and 1500 BCE. The most obvious example was Shulgi's "nationalization" of the temples. That is, the major temples of Lagash and other cities were placed under the supervision of secular officials to administer the state economy. Hammurabi continued this practice with the state usurpation of local institutions. Temples were assigned accountants by the state.

The workshop received and delivered partly made items; for example, furniture would be sent to another workshop to be inlaid with valuable materials. Workshops under state control performed work for manufacturing magnificent religious emblems whose dedications often gave their name to the year of the king's reign. Workshops made all kinds of objects, such as bags, baskets, shoes, furniture, weapons, musical instruments, chariots, and, especially, doors.

Mari officials had difficulty in finding the right staff, suggesting a shortage of craft skills. Despite the long distance involved, a chariot builder was requested from Ekallatum. The search for artisans took place throughout the kingdom, even among nomads and deported people. The artisans might work inside the palace, or outside under the authority of a central office. In the palace, the artisans were given apprentices, their own accommodation, garments, and rations. They were also employed for life.

Most of the specialists who appeared in the Amarna correspondence were not craftsmen but intellectuals, such as physicians and exorcists. People were impressed by foreign gods and rituals. A letter from the king of Mitanni described sending a statue to Egypt so that its magical powers might help the pharaoh. The statue was a loan, not a gift.

As in all patronage, the taste and interest of top officials influenced the quality of the art produced. A letter to Sargon II asked for his opinion on the details—hands, elbows, and drapery—of a sculpture. The Neo-Assyrian kings were particularly concerned with the progress of their colossal metal sculptures and were interested in the technical processes used in their kingdoms and abroad. Monumental inscriptions often accompanied major sculptures. A Neo-Assyrian letter requested that the king send the exact text of an inscription to be engraved. Other correspondence from the Neo-Assyrian period dealt with details such as date of delivery and artisans on strike: "the men are not pleased, and consequently will not do the King's work. . . . All the stonemasons have spoken discontentedly, saying, 'He (foreman) oppresses us, for no one has paid us for the months of Siwan and Tammuz.' Let my lord give orders and pay them, for they are very threatening."[56]

Specialists were exchanged by kings. During the first millennium BCE, prisoners were taken to work in state labor gangs. However, kings also carefully selected political leaders and craftsmen for deportation. After the surrender of Jerusalem, Nebuchadnezzar II carried away "all the princes, and all the mighty men of valor . . . and all the craftsmen and smiths: none remained, except for the poorest sort of people of the land" (2 Kings 24:14).

12

The Legacy of Ancient Mesopotamia

The people of ancient Mesopotamia have left behind a legacy of inventions and institutions. Their contributions to human culture began approximately twenty-five hundred years before the flowering of classical Greek civilization (fifth through fourth centuries BCE).

The most important contribution was writing, dated to ca. 3100 BCE. The people of ancient Mesopotamia were the first to develop writing, which was triggered by economic necessity. Memory was no longer sufficient for complicated bookkeeping. Once developed, writing soon evolved from numbers and pictograms of accounting to a script that was fully able to represent the Sumerian language and later Akkadian. Other writing systems soon followed. Mesopotamia's writing system influenced Egyptian hieroglyphics, proto-Elamite from Iran (which remains undeciphered), the Indus valley script from Pakistan and India (also undeciphered), Minoan Linear A from Crete (still undeciphered), Hittite hieroglyphics (used in central Asiatic Turkey), and Chinese writing. Each nation gave its own unique stamp to a writing system that originated in Mesopotamia. Sumerian was the first written language in the ancient world. In the eighteenth century BCE, Akkadian replaced Sumerian as the language of diplomacy, and then in the eighth century BCE Aramaic replaced Akkadian.

The Sumerians were the first in known history to develop an epic literature with heroic tales. The earliest literary texts found to date are from Ebla, Abu Salabikh, and Fara (ca. 2400 BCE). In some, even the authors were identified, and divine inspiration was acknowledged. The

Babylonians and Assyrians continued to study Sumerian literature and language throughout their history. Even though Sumerian eventually became a dead language, numerous Sumerian texts existed with interlinear translations into Akkadian.

Other literary compositions included myths, epics, prayers, hymns, laments, rituals and incantations, omens, essays, wisdom literature, and historiography. Sumerian literary forms and motifs influenced the writings of the ancient world, for example, the story of the Tower of Babel (referring to a ziggurat) and the Flood story. Personal and state correspondence was also recorded on clay. Economic documents such as sales, deeds, marriage settlements, adoption contracts, inheritance documents, loan agreements, receipts, contracts, court decisions, and wage memos were recorded.

The Amorites, a Semitic people much derided by the Sumerians for their uncivilized ways, brought an end to Sumerian civilization. The Amorites, usually known as the Babylonians because their capital was the city of Babylon, became the custodians of Sumerian culture and civilization. Except for the language, the Babylonian educational system, religion, mythology, and literature were almost identical to those of the Sumerians.

The ancient Mesopotamians tried to understand the world around them. To this end, they made lists of animals, plants, minerals, manufactured objects, and so on, as early as the third millennium BCE. The Sumerian lists were initially monolingual, but each country or people added a column in its own language, as, for example, the Akkadians. The Sumerian-Akkadian lists added a third and even a fourth column, such as Hittite, Hurrian, and Ugaritic. Aramaic took the place of Akkadian in the ancient Near East; however, no list with Aramaic has yet been found. A few very late copies of lists had Greek transcriptions. Homonyms, synonyms, and explanations were added. However, the Greeks showed little interest in other languages, so lexicography waited until the Renaissance to develop.

By the Old Babylonian period, mathematics appeared fully developed. There were tables for multiplying and dividing and for calculating squares and square roots, cubes and cube roots, reciprocals, exponential functions, and so forth. Approximations of reciprocals of irregular numbers were examined. In addition to table texts, there were problem texts, both algebraic/geometric problems and practical problems such as excavating or enlarging canals, military engineering, earthmoving, and so forth. Babylonian mathematics was mainly algebraic; the people of ancient Mesopotamia never took the next step of formulating a theorem. Geometrical concepts played a small role in Babylonian mathematics, mostly by the use of formulas for various shapes. However, the scribes used the Pythagorean formula more than a thousand years before Pythagoras as well as such geometrical principles as similarity.

Initially Babylonian astronomy was crude and based largely on observation. By the Seleucid period (ca. fourth century BCE) true mathematical astronomy was developed, with sophisticated theories comparable in all respects to contemporary classical Greek systems. The Greeks confirmed that their astronomical tradition should be attributed to the Babylonians.

Accurate astronomical observation was necessary to achieve regularity in the lunar calendar, which had to be aligned with the solar calendar in an agrarian society. At first an extra month was added once every three years. By the eighth century BCE a regular intercalation of seven months every nineteen years had been established. Approximately four hundred years later mathematical calculations were used to establish the Metonic Cycle, which was used as the basis of later Jewish and Christian calendars. The Greek astronomer Ptolemy, who lived in Alexandria in the second century CE, indicated that lists of eclipses dating back to Nabu-nasir's reign (747 BCE) were available to him.

The modern signs of the zodiac first appeared on cuneiform texts in the middle of the first millennium BCE, though the tradition of the zodiacal constellations can be assigned an earlier date. There is evidence that the first personal horoscopes also originated in Babylonia at the same time as astrology. As with mathematics, the roots of astronomy and astrology lay in Babylonia; this knowledge transmitted through Arab sources, which dominated the ancient world and western Europe until Newton's time.

Ancient technology included the manufacture of glass, the brewing of beer, the early use of copper, the late spread of iron, vaulting and other building techniques, and so on. The technical vocabulary was rich. Recipes for the manufacture of glass, beer, perfumes, and bronze were unusual, but even they did not always reveal the technology used. Common knowledge and practice were often not recorded. Further information comes from economic archives, letters, and archaeological investigation. Among the chemical apparatuses uncovered were crucibles, vessels for filtering, equipment for distillation and extraction, drip bottles, and so forth.

Caution must be exercised at all times, since many facets of Babylonian technology have their roots in prehistory. For example, written sources attest to the importance of the wool industry; however, the arts of bleaching, spinning, fulling, dyeing, and weaving were fully developed by the fourth millennium. Two of the oldest industries were those of the potter and metalworker. The potter's wheel was already widely used before 4000 BCE. We know even less about early metal, since it was melted down and reused.

Notes

CHAPTER 1

1. H.W.F. Saggs, *The Might That Was Assyria* (London: Sidgwick and Jackson, 1984), 291.

2. Time-Life Books, eds., *Sumer: Cities of Eden, Lost Civilizations* series (Alexandria, VA: Time-Life Books, 1993), 20.

3. See Saggs 1984: 274.

4. L. Depuydt, "Ptolemy's Royal Canon and Babylonian Chronology," *Journal of Cuneiform Studies* 47 (1995): 99–117.

CHAPTER 2

1. See William W. Hallo and William Kelly Simpson, *The Ancient Near East: A History*, 2d ed. (New York: Harcourt Brace College Publishers, 1998), 21–23.

CHAPTER 3

1. See Hallo and Simpson 1998: 32–51 for a critical study of the Sumerian King List.

2. Professor Hallo suggested that the transfer of kingship did not indicate that dynasties were successive (private communication).

3. J. N. Postgate, *Early Mesopotamia: Society and Economy at the Dawn of History* (New York: Routledge, 1992), '29, n. 1.

4. See Hallo and Simpson 1998: 23 figure 4.

5. Professor Hallo suggested that Sargon was the first in a series of rulers.

Events from Naram-sin and Shar-kali-sharri were telescoped and attributed to Sargon as first king of his dynasty (private communication).

6. See W. W. Hallo, *Early Mesopotamian Royal Titles: A Philologic and Historical Analysis*, American Oriental Series 43 (New Haven, CT: American Oriental Society, 1957).

7. S. N. Kramer, *The Sumerians: Their History, Culture and Character* (Chicago: University of Chicago Press, 1963), 64.

8. Ibid., 65.

9. Ibid., 63.

10. Michael Roaf, *Cultural Atlas of Mesopotamia and the Ancient Near East* (New York: Facts on File, 1990), 99; see Thorkild Jacobsen, *The Sumerian King List* (Chicago: University of Chicago, 1939).

11. After Kramer 1963: 68.

12. Th. Jacobsen, "Sumer," in Arthur Cotterell, ed., *The Penguin Encyclopedia of Ancient Civilizations* (London: Penguin Books, 1980), 82.

13. Hallo and Simpson 1998: 68–69.

14. Joan Oates, *Babylon*, 1979, rev. ed. (London: Thames and Hudson, 1986), 52; see Th. Jacobsen, *The Harps That Once . . . : Sumerian Poetry in Translation* (New Haven, CT: Yale University Press, 1987), 200.

15. After Hallo and Simpson, 1998: 83.

16. L. W. King, *Babylonian Boundary Stones* (London, 1912), no. 6 *apud* Oates 1986: 105; D. J. Wiseman, *Cambridge Ancient History*, 3rd ed., vol. 2 (London: Cambridge University Press, 1975), 2, 455.

17. A. K. Grayson, *Assyrian and Babylonian Chronicles* (London: J. J. Augustin, 1975), 189 *apud* Oates 1986: 106.

18. Roaf 1990: 182.

19. Ibid., 181.

20. Oates 1986: 119.

21. Saggs 1984: 113.

22. Roaf 1990: 198.

23. H. Tadmor, "The Inscriptions of Nabunaid: Historical Arrangement," *Assyriological Studies* 16 (1965): 351–63 *apud* Oates 1986: 132.

CHAPTER 4

1. After M. Civil, "The Sumerian Flood Story," in *Atra-hasis: The Babylonian Story of the Flood*, ed. W. G. Lambert and A. R. Millard (Oxford: Clarendon Press, 1969), 168 *apud* Postgate 1992: 51.

2. C.B.F. Walker, *Cuneiform* (London: British Museum Publications, 1987), 27.

3. H.W.F. Saggs, *Everyday Life in Babylonia and Assyria* (New York: G.P. Putnam's Sons, 1965), 78.

4. See B. Landsberger, "Scribal Concepts of Education," in *City Invincible: Urbanization and Cultural Development in the Near East*, ed. C. H. Kraeling and R. McAdams (Chicago: University of Chicago Press, 1960), 94–123.

5. See S. N. Kramer, *History Begins at Sumer: Twenty-Seven "Firsts" in Man's Recorded History* (New York: Doubleday, 1959), 8–11; Kramer 1963: 237–40.

6. Kramer 1963: 241–43.

7. Kramer 1959: 12–16; 1963: 244–45.

8. Kramer 1963: 246–48.

9. Georges Roux, *Ancient Iraq* 3rd ed. (Harmondsworth, Eng.: Penguin Books, 1992), 356; L. Waterman, *Royal Correspondence of the Assyrian Empire*, vol. 4 (Ann Arbor, MI: University of Michigan Press, 1930–1936), 213, no. 6; E. Chiera, *They Wrote on Clay: The Babylonian Tablets Speak Today*, ed. G. G. Cameron (Chicago: University of Chicago Press, 1938), 174.

10. After J. M. Sasson, "Some Comments on Archive Keeping at Mari," *Iraq* 34 (1972): 55–67 *apud* Postgate 1992: 60.

11. Stanley M. Burstein, *The Babyloniaca of Berossus* (Malibu: Undena Publications, 1978), 21–22.

12. H. Hunger, *Babylonische und Assyrische Kolophone*, Altes Orient und Altes Testament 2 (Neukirchener-Vluyn: Verlag Butzon and Bercker Kevelaer, 1968), 53–54, no. 136.

13. Benjamin R. Foster, *Before the Muses: An Anthology of Akkadian Literature*, 2nd ed., 2 vols. (Bethesda, MD: CDL Press, 1996), 127; W. Farber, *Texte aus der Umwelt des Alten Testaments*, II/2 (Gütersloh: Gütersloher Verlagshaus Gerd Mohn, 1982), 256.

14. W. W. Hallo and J.J.A. van Dijk, *The Exaltation of Inanna*, Yale Near Eastern Researches 3 (New Haven, CT: Yale University Press, 1968), 29.

15. Foster 1996: 326–27.

16. See Kramer 1963: 225.

17. After Å. Sjöberg, "The Old Babylonian Eduba," *Jacobsen Festschrift*, Assyriological Studies 20 (Chicago: University of Chicago Press, 1975), 159, and Kramer 1963: 236.

18. Foster 1996: 102; Karl Hecker, *Texte aus der Umwelt des Alten Testaments*, II/5 (Gütersloh: Gütersloher Verlagshaus Gerd Mohn, 1982), 747–50.

19. Foster 1996: 159; Hecker 1982: 752.

20. After Th. Jacobsen, "The Historian and the Sumerian Gods," *Journal of the American Oriental Society* 114 (1994): 151–53.

21. Foster 1996: 159; Erika Reiner, "An Assyrian Elegy," in *Your Thwarts in Pieces, Your Mooring Rope Cut: Poetry from Babylonia and Assyria* (Ann Arbor, MI: Horace H. Rackham School of Graduate Studies at University of Michigan, 1985), 85–93; Foster 1996: 890; Hecker 1982: 780–81.

22. Foster 1996: 313; R. Labat, *Les Religions du Proche-Orient Asiatique* (Paris: Fayard-Denoël, 1970), 328–41.

23. Foster 1996: 313; Labat 1970: 328–41.

24. After A. Leo Oppenheim, *Letters from Mesopotamia: Official, Business, and Private Letters on Clay Tablets from Two Millennia* (Chicago: University of Chicago Press, 1967), 96–97; G. Dossin, "Correspondance de Šamši-Adad et de ses fils," *Archives Royales de Mari* I (Paris: Imprimerie Nationale, 1950), no. 6.

25. My translation of Dossin, *Archives Royales de Mari* I: 108.

26. A. L. Oppenheim, *The Interpretation of Dreams in the Ancient Near East*, Transactions of the American Philosophical Society, New Series 46/3 (Philadelphia: American Philosophical Society, 1956), 276.

27. Oppenheim 1967: 166; R. F. Harper, *Assyrian and Babylonian Literature, Selected Translations* (Century Bookbinding, 1901, reprint 1980), no. 353.

CHAPTER 5

1. Herodotus, *History* II.84 and I.197 *apud* H.W.F. Saggs, *The Greatness That Was Babylon: A Sketch of the Ancient Civilization of the Tigris-Euphrates Valley* (New York: New American Library, Mentor Books, 1962), 460.

2. H.W.F. Saggs, *Civilization Before Greece and Rome* (New Haven, CT: Yale University Press, 1989), 263.

3. Oates 1986: 182; E. K. Ritter, "Magical-Expert (=Āšipu) and Physician (=Asû)," *Assyriological Studies* 16 (1965): 308, 315, 320.

4. Roux 1992: 370; A. Finet, "Les Médecins au royaume de Mari," *Annuaire de l'Institut de Philologie et d'Histoire Orientales et Slaves, Bruxelles* 15 (1954–1957), 123–44.

5. Saggs 1989: 260.

6. Saggs 1962: 435.

7. Oates 1986: 181.

8. Ibid.

9. Saggs 1989: 260–61.

10. Saggs 1962: 193; Oppenheim, 1956.

11. O. Neugebauer and A. Sachs, *Mathematical Cuneiform Texts*, American Oriental Society 29 (New Haven, CT: American Oriental Society and the American Schools of Oriental Research, 1945), 91.

12. After D. D. Luckenbill, *Ancient Records of Assyria and Babylonia*, vol. 1 (Chicago: University of Chicago Press, 1927), 189.

13. Luckenbill 1927, vol. 2: 177.

CHAPTER 6

1. W. W. Hallo, "Antediluvian Cities," *Journal of Cuneiform Studies* 23 (1970), 57–67.

2. Saggs 1989: 120–21; Luckenbill 1927, vol. 2: 195.

3. See Saggs 1962: 183.

4. Martha T. Roth, *Law Collections from Mesopotamia and Asia Minor* (Atlanta: Scholars Press, 1995), 85, Laws of Hammurabi, ix. 28–45.

5. M. Bayliss, "The Cult of Dead Kin in Assyria and Babylonia," *Iraq* 35 (1973): 120 *apud* Postgate 1992: 83.

6. F. A. Hole, "Assessing the Past Through Anthropological Archaeology," *Civilizations of the Ancient Near East*, [hereafter cited as *CANE*], ed. Jack M. Sasson, vol. 4 (New York: Scribner, 1995), 2723.

7. J. Cooper, *The Curse of Agade* (Baltimore: Johns Hopkins University Press, 1983), 31 *apud* G. M. Schwartz, "Pastoral Nomadism in Ancient Western Asia," *CANE*, vol. 1 (1995), 250.

8. Schwartz 1995: 250 [*CANE*].

9. After G. Buccellati, *The Amorites of the Ur III Period* (Naples: 1966), 92 *apud* Postgate 1992: 83.

10. After M. Civil, "Šu-Sin's Historical Inscriptions: Collection B," *Journal of Cuneiform Studies* 21 (1967): 31 *apud* Postgate 1992: 84.

11. J.-M. Durand, "Fourmis blanches et fourmis noires," *Contribution à l'histoire*

de l'Iran: Mélanges offerts à Jean Perrot I (Paris: Editions Recherche sur les civilisations, 1990), 101–8 *apud* Postgate 1992: 85.

12. Schwartz 1995: 250 [*CANE*].

13. Roth 1995: 102–5, CH § 115–19. Note that Roth uses LH § rather than CH; I will follow the convention of CH used by most text editions.

14. Ibid., 76–77; Laws of Hammurabi, Prologue, i, 27–49.

CHAPTER 7

1. Georges Contenau, *Everyday Life in Babylon and Assyria*, translated by K. R. Maxwell-Hyslop and A. R. Maxwell-Hyslop (New York: St. Martin's Press, 1954), 27.

2. Roth 1995: 125 CH §229–§230.

3. E. Simpson, "Furniture in Ancient Western Asia," *CANE*, vol. 3 (1995), 1654.

4. See Saggs 1984: 158.

5. M. Stol, "Private Life in Ancient Mesopotamia," *CANE*, vol. 1 (1995), 488.

6. Ibid.; see also *Chicago Assyrian Dictionary*, vol. 17/3, Š, ed. Erica Reiner et al., s.v. *šīru*, 118b.

7. S. Greengus, "Legal and Social Institutions of Ancient Mesopotamia," *CANE*, vol. 1 (1995), 478.

8. Stol 1995: 488 [*CANE*].

9. V. Donbaz and N. Yoffee, *Old Babylonian Texts from Kish Conserved in the Istanbul Archaeological Museums*, Bibliotheca Mesopotamica 17 (Malibu: Undena Publications, 1986), 58–89, §G and §H *apud* Postgate 1992: 93.

10. Saggs 1984: 137.

11. Jeremy Black and Anthony Green, *Gods, Demons and Symbols of Ancient Mesopotamia: An Illustrated Dictionary* (Austin, TX:University of Texas Press, 1992), 30.

12. Ibid., 115–16.

13. Ibid., 147–48.

14. Z. Bahrani, "Jewelry and Personal Arts in Ancient Western Asia," *CANE*, vol. 3 (1995), 1640.

15. Black and Green 1992: 115–16.

16. R. D. Biggs, "Medicine, Surgery, and Public Health in Ancient Mesopotamia," *CANE*, vol. 3 (1995), 1917.

17. Saggs 1984: 139.

18. Ibid., 1984: 138–39.

19. Foster 1996: 890; Reiner, 1985: 85–93.

20. Stol 1995: 491 [*CANE*].

21. Ibid., 492.

22. My translation; see also Postgate 1992: 93 for a translation of G. Boyer, *Textes juridiques*, Archives royales de Mari, vol. 8 (Paris: Imprimerie Nationale, 1958), no. 1.

23. My translation; G. Dossin, *Textes cunéiformes du Louvre*, vol. 18 (Paris: P. Geuthner, 1934), no. 111; see *The Ancient Near Eastern Texts Relating to the Old Testament* [hereafter cited as *ANET*³], 3rd ed., with supplement, ed. J.B. Pritchard (Princeton: Princeton University Press, 1969), 629.

24. Wolfram von Soden, *The Ancient Orient: An Introduction to the Study of the Ancient Near East*, translated by Donald G. Schley (Grand Rapids, MI: William B. Eerdmans, 1994), 74; G. Wilhelm, *Grundzüge der Geschichte und Kultur der Hurriter* (Darmstadt: Wissenschaftliche Buchgesellschaft, 1982), 66.

25. See Saggs 1984: 146.

26. My translation; see Roth 1995: 63 Laws of Eshnunna §§ 27–28.

27. See Postgate 1992: 103.

28. S. Greengus, "The Old Babylonian Marriage Contract," *Journal of the American Oriental Society* 89 (1969): 516 *apud* Postgate 1992: 103.

29. Stol 1995: 488 [*CANE*].

30. Ibid., 489.

31. Ibid., 489–90.

32. Roth 1995: 111 CH §157.

33. After Roth 1995: 169 MAL §41.

34. Saggs 1984: 144.

35. W. G. Lambert, *Babylonian Wisdom Literature* (Oxford: Clarendon Press, 1960), 226–27, 230, lines 1–7; see Saggs 1984: 144.

36. See Saggs 1984: 144.

37. Stol 1995: 490 [*CANE*].

38. Roth 1995: 160, MAL §20.

39. Ibid., 110 MAL §153; Saggs 1984: 144–45.

40. Roth 1995: 158, MAL §15.

41. W. G. Lambert, "The Theology of Death," in *Death in Mesopotamia*, Mesopotamia 8, Papers read at the XXVIe Rencontre assyriologique internationale, ed. Bendt Alster (Copenhagen: Akademisk Forlag, 1980), 56. See also W. G. Lambert and A. R. Millard, *Babylonian Literary Texts*, Cuneiform Texts from Babylonian Tablets in the British Museum 46 (London: Trustees of the British Museum, 1965), 7–10, 13–26, 29–32.

42. Scurlock 1995: 1893 [*CANE*].

43. Maureen G. Kovacs, *The Epic of Gilgamesh* (Stanford, CA: Stanford University Press, 1989), 70.

44. My translation; "The Poem of the Righteous Sufferer," Tablet II, lines 114–15.

45. Scurlock 1995: 1884 [*CANE*].

46. Ibid., 1888.

47. Lambert 1980: 59.

48. Foster 1996: 402, lines 4–12.

49. Stol 1995: 487 [*CANE*].

50. See, for example, Roth 1995: 176, Middle Assyrian Laws B §1.

51. Stol 1995: 497 [*CANE*].

52. E. C. Stone, *Nippur Neighborhoods*, Studies in Ancient Oriental Civilization, vol. 44 (Chicago: University of Chicago Press, 1987).

53. E. Prang, "Das Archiv von Imgua," *Zeitschrift für Assyriologie* 66 (1976): 3–7 *apud* Postgate 1992: 97.

54. E. Leichty, "Feet of Clay," in *Sjöberg Festschrift*, Occasional Publications of the Samuel Noah Kramer Fund, vol. 11 (Philadelphia: University Museum, 1989), 349–56 *apud* Postgate 1992: 98.

55. Stol 1995: 490 [*CANE*].

56. Postgate 1992: 90.

57. See Stol 1995: 490 [*CANE*].

58. Ibid., 486.

59. See Roth 1995: 173: MAL §33 and §46.

60. Saggs 1984: 154.

61. Jacobsen 1987: 17.

62. D. Wolkstein and S. N. Kramer, *Inanna: Queen of Heaven and Earth* (New York: Harper and Row, 1983), 53.

63. L. Delaporte, ed., *Textes de l'époque d'Ur*, Mission de Chaldée: Inventaire des tablettes de Tello conservées au Musée Impérial Ottomon, vol. 4 (Paris: E. Leroux, 1912), no. 7248; see H. Limet, "The Cuisine of Ancient Sumer," *Biblical Archaeologist* 50 (1987): 134.

64. J. M. Renfrew, "Vegetables in the Ancient Near Eastern Diet," in *CANE*, vol. 1, 199.

65. See Limet 1987: 137.

66. See Saggs 1962: 178.

67. E. Gordon, *Sumerian Proverbs: Glimpses of Everyday Life in Ancient Mesopotamia* (Philadelphia: University Museum, 1959), 144, and 291–92, no. 1.191.

68. Ibid., 68–69, and 459, no. 1.55.

69. J. Bottéro, *Textes Culinaires de Mari* (Winona Lake, IN: Eisenbrauns, 1995).

70. Ibid., 13–14.

71. Ibid., 13–14.

CHAPTER 8

1. After *ANET*³, 560.

2. Foster 1996: 793.

3. Ibid., 796.

4. Ibid., 801.

5. Ibid., 802.

CHAPTER 9

1. See, for example, J. J. Stamm, *Die Akkadische Namengebung* (Darmstadt, Germany: Wissenschaftliche Buchgesellschaft, 1968).

2. After Foster 1996: 313, Tablet II, lines 36–38.

3. W. G. Lambert, "Myth and Mythmaking in Sumer and Akkad," *CANE*, vol. 3 (1995), 1828.

4. Ibid., 1829.

5. Jacobsen, "Sumer," in Cotterell 1980: 90.

6. Thorkild Jacobsen, *The Treasures of Darkness: A History of Mesopotamian Religion* (New Haven, CT: Yale University Press, 1976), 85.

7. Erica Reiner, *Astral Magic in Babylonia*, Transactions of the American Philosophical Society, vol. 8, part 4 (Philadelphia: American Philosophical Society, 1995), 21; A. Livingstone, *Mystical and Mythological Explanatory Works of Assyrian and Babylonian Scholars* (Oxford: Clarendon Press, 1986), 82–87.

8. Jacobsen 1976: 155; *Cuneiform Texts from Babylonian Tablets*, XXXVIII, pl. 17, line 95, and pl. 30, line 23.

9. Jacobsen 1976: 160; E. Ebeling, *Keilinschriften aus Assur religiösen Inhalts*, Deutsche Orientgesellschaftliche Veröffentlichungen 28 and 34 (Leipzig, 1915–23), no. 423, ii. 23.

10. Jacobsen 1976: 160; Lambert 1960: 104, lines 135–41.

11. Jacobsen 1976: 231; E. Ebeling and F. Köcher, *Literarische Keilschrifttexte aus Assur* (Berlin, 1953), no. 73 obv. 8–9, 13 and 7.

12. Jacobsen 1976: 232; W. von Soden, "Gibt es ein Zeugnis dafür dass die Babylonier an die Wiederauferstehung Marduks geglaubt haben," *Zeitschrift für Assyriologie* 51 (1955): 130ff.

13. Jacobsen 1976: 97; H. Frankfort et al., *Before Philosophy* (Baltimore, MD: Pelican Books, 1949, rpt. 1968), 153.

14. Jacobsen 1976: 122; C. J. Gadd et al., *Ur Excavation* I (Oxford: Oxford University Press, 1927), no. 300, lines 1–11.

15. Hallo and van Dijk, 1968: 14 I. 1 *apud* Jacobsen 1976: 141.

16. Oppenheim 1977: 207.

17. W. F. Leemans, *Ishtar of Lagaba and Her Dress* (Leiden: E.J. Brill, 1952), 1–2 *apud* Postgate 1992: 119.

18. Oppenheim 1977: 286–87.

19. Ibid., 183ff.

20. Oates 1986: 175; *ANET*³: 343–45; F. Thureau-Dangin, *Rituels accadiens* (Paris: E. Leroux, 1921), 62ff., 74ff.

21. Oppenheim 1977: 271.

22. Jean Bottéro, *Mesopotamia: Writing, Reasoning and the Gods*, translated by Zainab Bahrani and Marc van de Mieroop (Chicago: University of Chicago Press, 1992), 227; see J. Bottéro, *Mythes et rites de Babylone* (Paris: Librarie H. Champion, 1985), 209f.

23. Postgate 1992: 135; M. van de Mieroop, "Gifts and Tithes to the Temples in Ur," *Sjöberg Festschrift*, 1989: 347–401.

24. R. Marcel Sigrist, *Les sattukku dans l'Ešumeša durant la période d'Isin et Larsa*, Bibliotheca Mesopotamica 11 (Malibu: Undena Publications, 1984), 160 *apud* Postgate 1992: 127.

25. After D. Charpin, *Le Clergé d'Ur au siècle d'Hammurabi XIXe-XVIIIe siècles av. J.-C.* (Geneva: Librarie Droz, 1986), 322–25 *apud* Postgate 1992: 125.

26. Postgate 1992: 131; E. C. Stone, "The Social Role of the Nadītu Women in Old Babylonian Nippur," *Journal of the Economic and Social History of the Orient* 25 (1982): 55–56.

27. Roth 1995: 117–120.

28. A. Kuhrt, "Ancient Mesopotamia in Classical Greek and Hellenistic Thought," *CANE*, vol. 1 (1995), 59.

29. Oates 1986: 176.

30. Jacobsen 1976: 122.

31. Ibid., 126; H. de Genouillac, *La trouvaille de Drehem* (Paris 1911), no. 16.

32. Von Soden 1994: 200; cf. G. Meier, ed., *Die assyrische Beschwörungssammlung Maqlû*, Archiv für Orientforschung, Beihehft 2 (Berlin: Selbstverlag, 1937).

33. Roth 1995: 81 §2; see also ibid., 18 §13, 172–73 §47, 145–46 §7.

34. W. Farber, "Witchcraft, Magic, and Divination in Ancient Mesopotamia," *CANE*, vol. 3 (1995), 1906.

35. Saggs 1984: 218.

36. S. Parpola, *Letters from Assyrian and Babylonian Scholars*, State Archives of Assyria 10 (1993), no. 160 *apud* Reiner 1995: 65.

37. See Oppenheim, 1956; also A. L. Oppenheim, "New Fragments of the Assyrian Dream Book," *Iraq* 31 (1969): 153–65.

38. G. Buccellati, "Ethics and Piety in the Ancient Near East," *CANE*, vol. 3 (1995), 1693; V. K. Shileiko, *Izvestiya Rossiyskoy Akademii Istorii Material'noy Kul'tury*, vol. 3 (1924).

39. Reiner 1995: 1; cf. Foster 1996: 569.

40. Reiner 1995:18; E. Ebeling, and F. Köcher, *Literarische Keilschrifttexte aus Assur* (Berlin: Akademie-Verlag, 1953), 58.

41. Reiner 1995: 4.

42. Ibid., 114.

43. Ibid., 63; see also A. L. Oppenheim, "Divination and Celestial Observation in the Last Assyrian Empire," *Centaurus* 14 (1969): 97–135.

44. H. Hunger, *Astrological Reports to Assyrian Kings*, State Archives of Assyria 8 (Helsinki: Helsinki University Press, 1992); Reiner 1995: 64.

45. Reiner 1995: 16; Ebeling and Köcher, 1953: 29d ii 1ff.

46. After Farber 1995: 1896 [*CANE*]; Foster 1996: 833.

47. Farber 1995: 1897 [*CANE*].

48. Reiner 1995: 119; R. Borger, *Die Inschriften Asarhaddons Koenigs von Assyrien*, Archiv für Orientforschung 9 (Osnabrück: Biblio-Verlag, 1967): 61 §27 Episode 22, A vi 15–16.

49. Reiner 1995: 120; E. Reiner et al., eds., *The Assyrian Dictionary* (Chicago: Oriental Institute, 1956), K, 449.

50. Reiner 1995: 135; W. Mayer, *Untersuchungen zur Formensprache der babylonischen "Gebetsbeschwörungen,"* Studia Pohl, Series Maior 5 (Rome: Biblical Institute Press, 1976), 531, rev 19'.

51. See Foster 1996: 636 for translation and bibliography.

52. Reiner 1995: 136–37; Franz Köcher, *Die babylonisch-assyrische Medizin in Texten und Untersuchungen* (Berlin: de Gruyter, 1963), 228, 229, 323.

53. Reiner 1995: 23; Mayer 1976: 392.

54. After Foster 1996: 869; Farber 1995: 1901 [*CANE*].

55. Oates 1986: 177; O. R. Gurney, "Babylonian Prophylactic Figures and Their Ritual," *Annals of Archaeology and Anthropology* 22 (1935), 31–96.

56. Reiner 1995: 122; Köcher 1963: 194 vii 4.

57. See A. L. Oppenheim, *Glass and Glassmaking in Ancient Mesopotamia* (Corning, NY: Corning Museum of Glass, 1970).

58. Reiner 1995: 127.

59. Ibid., 126; Köcher 1963: 351–52.

60. J. C. Vanderkam, "Prophecy and Apocalyptics in the Ancient Near East," *CANE*, vol. 3 (1995), 2091–94.

61. After *ANET³*: 606.

62. Oppenheim 1977: 226.

CHAPTER 10

1. Lambert 1960: 281–82.

2. Postgate 1992: 150.

3. After Charpin 1986: 275–76 *apud* Postgate 1992: 261.

4. F. Thureau-Dangin, "Notes assyriologiques: XVI: Un jugement sous le règne de Samsu-iluna," *Revue d'Assyriologie et d'Archéologie Orientale* 9 (1912): 21–24 *apud* Postgate 1992: 279.

5. After M. Schorr, *Urkunden des altbabylonischen Zivil- und Prozessrechts*, Vorderasiatische Bibliothek 5 (Leipzig, 1913), no. 280 *apud* Postgate 1992: 279.

6. Th. Jacobsen, "An Ancient Mesopotamian Trial for Homicide," in *Towards the Image of Tammuz* (Cambridge, MA: Harvard University Press, 1970), 193 *apud* von Soden 1994: 142.

7. My translation; see Roth 1995: 82.

8. A. Walther, *Das altbabylonische Gerichtswesen*, Leipziger Semitistische Studien 6 (Leipzig, 1917), 177–78 *apud* Postgate 1992: 282.

9. See Postgate 1992: 278; see also Walther 1917: 100.

10. Bottéro 1992: 180; F. R. Kraus, *Königliche Verfügungen in altbabylonischer Zeit* (Leiden: E. J. Brill, 1984), 180, 182.

11. Postgate 1992: 284; see J. Krecher, "Kauf.A.I," *Reallexikon der Assyriologie* 5 (1980): 494–95.

12. My translation; CH col. xxvb: 3–19.

13. Bottéro 1992: 168; A. Ungnad, "Datenlisten," *Reallexikon der Assyriologie* 2 (1938): 179.

14. My translation; CH col. xxvb: 59–85.

15. Oates 1986: 75; D. O. Edzard, "The Old Babylonian Period," in *The Near East: The Early Civilizations*, ed. J. Bottéro, E. Cassin, and J. Vercoutter (London: Weidenfeld and Nicolson, 1967), 221.

16. Luckenbill 1927, vol. 2: 80–81.

17. S. Dalley, "Ancient Mesopotamian Military Organization," *CANE*, vol. 1 (1995), 422.

18. U. Jeyes, "Death and Divination in the Old Babylonian Period," in *Death in Mesopotamia*, Mesopotamia 8: Papers read at the XXVIe Rencontre assyriologique internationale, ed. Bendt Alster (Copenhagen: Akademisk Forlag, 1980), 109.

19. A. Kirk Grayson, "Assyrian Rule of Conquered Territory in Ancient Western Asia," *CANE*, vol. 2 (1995), 961.

20. Ungnad 1938: 141 *apud* Postgate 1992: 242.

21. C. Wilcke, "Ein Gebet an den Mondgott vom 3. IV. des Jahres Ammiditana 33," *Zeitschrift für Assyriologie* 73 (1983): 54–56 *apud* Postgate 1992: 242.

22. After Roth 1995: 88.

23. Dalley 1995: 418 [*CANE*].

24. Ibid.

25. Oates 1986: 70.

26. I. J. Gelb, "Prisoners of War in Early Mesopotamia," *Journal of Near Eastern Studies* 32 (1973): 71–72 *apud* Postgate 1992: 254.

27. A. Westenholz, "*Berūtum, Damtum*, and the Old Akkadian KI.GAL: Burial of Dead Enemies in Ancient Mesopotamia," *Archiv für Orientforschung* 23 (1970): 27–31 *apud* Postgate 1992: 254.

28. Postgate 1992: 256; see Civil 1967: 36.

29. D.J. Wiseman, "Murder in Mesopotamia," *Iraq* 36 (1974): 249; D. J. Wiseman, "The Vassal-Treaties of Esarhaddon," *Iraq* 20 (1958): 3ff.

30. Wiseman 1974: 249.

31. For a complete version of this text see *ANET*³: 534–41.

32. P. Villard, "Un roi de Mari à Ugarit," *Ugaritforschungen* 18 (Neukirchen-Vluyn, 1986), 387–412 *apud* Postgate 1992: 258.

33. After Luckenbill 1927, vol. 2: 44.

34. After Saggs 1984: 129.

35. Saggs 1989: 183.

36. J. Nougayrol, *Le palais royal d'Ugarit*, vol. 4 (Paris: Imprimiere Nationale, 1956), 193, no. 17.423.

37. Saggs 1989: 192–93.

38. P. Artzi, "Mourning in International Relations," 1980: 162–63.

CHAPTER 11

1. M. Civil, *The Farmer's Instructions: A Sumerian Agricultural Manual*, Aula Orientalis-Supplementa 5 (Barcelona: Editorial AUSA, 1994).

2. J. J. Finkelstein, "An Old Babylonian Herding Contract and Genesis 31: 38f.," *Journal of the American Oriental Society* 88 (1968): 30–36; see CH §261–67; Roth 1995: 129–30.

3. R. P. Dougherty, *Records from Erech, Time of Nabonidus (555–538 BCE)*, Yale Oriental Series 6 (New Haven, CT.: Yale University Press, 1920), no. 155; F. R. Kraus, *Staatliche Viehhaltung im Altbabylonischen Lande Larsa*, Mededelingen der Koninklije Akademie van Wetenschappen, afdeeling letterkunde. Nieuwe Reeks 29/V (Amsterdam, 1966), 132; Finkelstein 1968: 34 *apud* Postgate 1992: 160; J. N. Postgate and S. Payne, "Some Old Babylonian Shepherds and Their Flocks," *Journal of Semitic Studies* 20 (1975): 6; CH §266, see Roth 1995:130.

4. CH §267; Roth 1995: 130.

5. Saggs 1984: 168.

6. B. Hesse, "Animal Husbandry and Human Diet in the Ancient Near East," *CANE*, vol. 1 (1995), 212; R. McC. Adams, *Heartland of Cities: Surveys of Ancient Settlement and Land Use on the Central Floodplain of the Euphrates* (Chicago: University of Chicago Press, 1981), 148.

7. Oates 1986: 193, figure 132.

8. See A. Kammenhuber, *Hippologia hethitica* (Wiesbaden: O. Harrassowitz, 1961); E. Ebeling, *Bruchstücke einer mittelassyrischen Vorschriftensammlung für die Akklimatisierung und Trainierung von Wagenferden* (Berlin, 1951).

9. Lambert 1960: 216–17, lines 42–43.

10. W. G. Lambert, "The Birdcall Text," *Anatolian Studies* 20 (1970): 111ff.

11. Oates 1986: 195; M. Levey, *Chemistry and Chemical Technology in Ancient Mesopotamia* (New York: Elsevier, 1959), 94–95.

12. Th. Jacobsen, *Salinity and Irrigation Agriculture in Antiquity*, Bibliotheca Mesopotamica 14 (Malibu: Undena, 1981), 5–8; R. Mc.C. Adams, *Land Behind Baghdad* (Chicago: University of Chicago Press, 1965), 7–12; see K. R. Nemet-Nejat, *Cuneiform Mathematical Texts as a Reflection of Everyday Life in Mesopotamia*, American Oriental Society 75 (New Haven, CT: American Oriental Society, 1993), 42–43.

13. P. Steinkeller, "Notes on the Irrigation System in Third Millennium Southern Babylonia," *Bulletin on Sumerian Agriculture* 4 (1988): 74.

14. W. Pemberton, J. N. Postgate, and R. F. Smyth, "Canals and Bunds, Ancient

and Modern," *Bulletin on Sumerian Agriculture* 4 (1988): 207–21; Steinkeller 1988: 73–74.

15. Jacobsen 1981: 62–63.

16. J. Renger, "Rivers, Watercourses and Irrigation Ditches," *Bulletin on Sumerian Agriculture* 5 (1990): 38–39; R. C. Hunt, "Hydraulic Management in Southern Mesopotamia in Sumerian Times," *Bulletin on Sumerian Agriculture* 4 (1988): 196–202.

17. See CH §§45–47 and §§60–63.

18. K. R. Nemet-Nejat, *Late Babylonian Field Plans in the British Museum*, Studia Pohl, Series Maior 11 (Rome: Pontifical Biblical Institute, 1982).

19. Postgate 1992: 185; see H.P.H. Petschow, "Die §§45 und 46 des Codex Hammurapi. Ein Beitrag zum altbabylonischen Bodenpachtrecht und zum Problem: Was ist der Codex Hammurapi?" *Zeitschrift für Assyriologie* 74 (1984): 190–93.

20. See Postgate 1992: 176.

21. R. Yaron, *The Laws of Eshnunna* (Jerusalem, Magnes Press, Hebrew University 1969), 20–21, lines 8–17.

22. Postgate 1992: 192; see B. Landsberger, "Akkadisch-hebräische Wortgleichungen," in *Hebräische Wortforschung*, Supplement to Vetus Testamentum 16 (Leiden: E. J. Brill, 1967), 176–204.

23. M. T. Roth, *Babylonian Marriage Agreements 7th–3rd Centuries BC*, Alter Orient und Altes Testament 222 (Neukirchen-Vluyn: Neukirchener Verlag, 1989), nos. 26, 92–95, lines 15–22.

24. Nemet-Nejat 1993: 60–61.

25. Oppenheim 1964: 87–88.

26. For example, H. J. Nissen, P. Damerow, and R. K. Englund, *Archaic Bookkeeping: Writing and Techniques of Economic Administration in the Ancient Near East*, translated by Paul Larsen (Chicago: University of Chicago Press, 1993), chap. 9; D. C. Snell, *Ledgers and Prices: Early Mesopotamian Merchant Accounts*, Yale Near Eastern Researches 8 (New Haven, CT: 1982).

27. Nissen, Damerow, and Englund 1993: 88.

28. D. C. Snell, "Methods of Exchange and Coinage in Ancient Western Asia," *CANE*, vol. 3 (1995), 1487; Postgate 1992: 203.

29. Oates, 1979: 187; cf. Reiner et al. 1956-: s.v. *ze'pu*; Luckenbill 1927, vol. 2: 176.

30. Oppenheim 1964: 87.

31. M. A. Powell, "Sumerian Numeration and Metrology," Ph.D. diss., University of Minnesota, 1973, 167–207 and 237–43.

32. Saggs 1984: 196.

33. Saggs 1989: 139.

34. W. W. Hallo, "The Road to Emar," *Journal of Cuneiform Studies* 18 (1964): 57–88.

35. Potts 1995: 1454 [*CANE*]; see the so-called Lipshur litanies.

36. Roth 1995: 125–26, CH §234 and §235.

37. Saggs 1984: 173.

38. Roth 1995: 119, CH §§188–89.

39. P.R.S. Moorey, "What Do We Know about the People Buried in the Royal Cemetery (of Ur)?" *Expedition* 20 (1977–78): 24–40; W. W. Hallo, "For Love Is

Strong as Death," Comparative Studies in Honor of Yochanan Muffs, *Journal of the Ancient Near Eastern Society* 6 (1964): 45–50.

40. H. H. Figulla, *Letters and Documents of the Old Babylonian Period*, Ur Excavations Texts 5 (London: Trustees of the Two Museums, 1953), 796.

41. For example, *Archives Royal de Mari* 24, no. 106.

42. Saggs 1989: 200–201.

43. T. Özgüç, *Kültepe-Kaniš II* (Ankara: Türk Tarih Kurumu Basimev, 1986), 39–51 *apud* Postgate 1992: 228–29; see P.R.S. Moorey, *Ancient Mesopotamian Materials and Industries: The Archaeological Evidence* (New York: Oxford University Press, 1994), 216–301; P.R.S. Moorey, *Metals and Metalwork, Glazed Materials and Glass*, International Series 237 (Oxford: British Archaeological Reports, 1985).

44. *Archives Royal de Mari* 21, no. 247; *apud* Bahrani 1995: 1642 [*CANE*].

45. After Contenau 1954: 100.

46. Roth 1995: 131, CH §274.

47. D. Mathews, "Artisans and Artists in Ancient Western Asia," *CANE*, vol. 1 (1995), 459.

48. C. Wilcke, "Die Inschriften der 7. und 8. Kampagnen (1983 und 1984)," in *Isin-Išān Bahriyāt III*, ed. B. Hrouda (Munich: Verlag der Bayerischen Akademie der Wissenschaften, 1987), 104–6 *apud* Postgate 1992: 231.

49. A. W. Sjöberg, "Der Examenstext A," *Zeitschrift für Assyriologie* 64 (1975): 137–76.

50. Saggs 1962: 471.

51. P. Steinkeller, *Third Millennium Legal and Administrative Texts in the Iraq Museum, Baghdad* (Winona Lake, IN: Eisenbrauns, 1992), Texts 26 and 32.

52. H. Waetzoldt, "Compensation of Craft Workers and Officials in the Ur III Period," in *Labor in the Ancient Near East*, American Oriental Series 68, ed. M. A. Powell (New Haven, CT: American Oriental Society, 1987), 118–41.

53. Ibid., 119–21.

54. H. Waetzoldt, *Untersuchungen zur neusumerischen Textilindustrie* (Rome, 1972).

55. Postgate 1992: 237.

56. Translation by J. M. Sasson of G. Dossin, *Archives royales de Mari* 10, no. 109.

Glossary

Absolute dating. Exact dating uses a fixed point in time for dating according to calendar years, for example, 1545 BCE, 135 CE.

Achaemenid rule. After King Cyrus I entered Babylon in 539 BCE, Mesopotamia fell under Persian rule. The Persian period extended from 539 BCE to Alexander the Great (330–323 BCE) from Macedon. Generally, the Persian kings made few changes. Cyrus I created a large administrative unit that included Babylonia, the Syrian coast, and ancient Israel.

Agglutinative. Languages in which verbs or nouns are expressed by a fixed syllable or root that can be modified by long chains of prefixes and postfixes, signifying specific grammatical elements.

Alluvial plain. A flat stretch of land where a river has deposited fertile soil.

Almanacs. Predictions for the coming year for the length of each month, the rising and setting of each planet, the zodiacal positions of the planets, eclipses, equinoxes, and the movements of Sirius.

Amorites. The ancient Mesopotamians distinguished between the urbanized Akkadians and the unassimilated Semites, calling the latter Amorites and their homeland Amurru. The Amorites originally came to Mesopotamia as soldiers and workers in the second millennium BCE and eventually became politically dominant. Their language, called Amorite, a West Semitic dialect, deferred to the Akkadian language of the country.

Amulet. An object believed to have both magical and protective powers.

Amulets brought luck or prevented evil. They were either worn by a person or set in a location so that they could produce the necessary magical effect.

An/Anu. The sky god, whose name meant "sky," was originally chief god of the pantheon. (For the gods, the Sumerian name, listed first, is followed by the Akkadian equivalent.)

Apodosis. See **Protasis**.

Apotropaic figures. Representations of beneficent gods and demons, natural and fantastic animals.

Arabs. People who spoke Arabic and came from north of the Arabian peninsula. They were nomads. South Arabians, a related group, used the camel as a means of transportation to open new trade routes and eventually develop a profitable trade between Egypt and the Mediterranean. Classical Greek authors wrote of the fortunes made from the incense and spice trade, which the South Arabians monopolized.

Aramaeans. A Semitic-speaking people who came from the Syrian desert in the second half of the second millennium BCE, first as invaders and later as settlers in Syria and along the Euphrates. In Syria the Aramaeans formed a number of petty kingdoms; from northern Syria they steadily penetrated into the remaining states of the Hittite empire until they finally took hold of them. The Aramaeans were wealthy traders in the area extending from the Persian Gulf to the Mediterranean. Because of the range of their trading enterprises, the Aramaeans eventually spread their language, Aramaic, so that it became the lingua franca of the ancient Near East by the sixth century BCE.

Archive. All records amassed at the time a particular task was carried out by an institution or person.

Assur. Patron god of Assyria and head of the Assyrian pantheon.

Astrolabe. A device that combined mythology with observational astronomy. According to mythology, there were three main stations of the sky under the aegis of three great gods: Anu (the head of the pantheon), Ea (the god of wisdom), and Enlil (the god of wind). This concept provided the framework for organizing the positions of major constellations, stars, and planets according to different months. The information was arranged either in three columns or in three concentric circles, which in turn were divided into twelve sectors. The three columns or concentric circles represented the three stations. A column or the twelve sectors symbolized the twelve months of the year and the heliacal rising of each star in its respective month.

Astronomical diaries. Monthly or yearly records of astronomical observations concerning the moon, the planets, solstices and equinoxes, Sirius, meteors, comets, etc. Also included was information about the weather, the prices of commodities, the river level, and historical events.

Bedouin. The term bedouin, borrowed from Arabic, is used today to refer only to camel-nomads, who cross the desert by dromedary.

Berossus. A priest of Marduk in Babylon ca. third century BCE, who narrated ancient Mesopotamian cultural traditions and history in *Babylonaica* at the request of Antiochus I. His work is known only in part through quotations in works by later Greek writers.

Bioarchaeology. The study of organic remains from the past. By using various methods of recovery and analysis, bioarchaeology provides botanical and zoological information.

Camel-nomad/camel nomadism. See **Bedouin.**

Canaanites. According to Israelite tradition, which has been confirmed by archaeology, they were the indigenous peoples of ancient Israel and part of Syria.

Cella. A term borrowed from Greek architecture to refer to the inner sanctuary of a temple. A statue of the god was placed here along with other cult furnishings.

Chaldeans. The Chaldeans entered southern Babylonia ca. 1000 BCE, settling in the swampland along the lower courses of the Tigris and Euphrates Rivers. The tribal territories were not well marked, and the political power of each sheikh depended on his personality and prestige. Their tribal organization was composed of houses, each under the leadership of a sheikh who sometimes referred to himself as king. The Chaldeans probably spoke Babylonian, and most had Babylonian names. The last Chaldean dynasty was established by Nabopolassar (625–605 BCE).

Cilicia/Cilicians. A Neo-Hittite center located in Asia Minor. The Neo-Hittite states continued the traditions of the Hittite empire, using Hittite hieroglyphs to write their language. Tiglath-pileser III (744–727 BCE) made Cilicia an Assyrian province.

Cimmerians. In 714 BCE, fierce warriors from southern Russia descended on Urartu from the north. At the same time, the Assyrians under Sargon II (721–705 BCE) also mounted a campaign against the southern parts of Urartu. Urartu fell. The alliances made proved useless. Approximately 695 BCE, the Cimmerians moved further west, conquered Phrygia, and burned it to the ground.

Citadel city. A military stronghold built to safeguard the population of the city, often by building a second line of walls. The small mounds of the early settlements were used as raised platforms upon which temples and palaces were constructed and even separated from the rest of the city by fortifications. New fortifications were erected to enclose a larger, lower town. With the advent of the Neo-Assyrian empire, the temple and palace became a single complex built on high citadel mounds, walled off from the rest of the city. In this way, a city within a city was created from which ordinary citizens were excluded.

City. Characterized socially by a complex economic structure and allegiances based on the urban community rather than the tribe. The city was distinguished physically by public buildings and a strong wall to protect the people from invasion; citizens felt great loyalty to their city.

City-state. An administrative unit that included several cities.

Colophon. Literary texts had a space reserved in the last column for information that a modern book provides on its title and imprint pages. The colophon could include any of the following data: the title of the work (that is, the shortened first line of the work), the number of tablets in the series, the catch line or beginning of the next tablet, the name of the owner, the name of the scribe, the date of the work, comments on the original which the scribe had copied, and an invocation or curses against any unauthorized person removing the tablet.

Cult. Religious acts of worship which included prayers, processions, sacrifice, adoration of divine images, gestures, and genuflections. Such rituals could be performed in temples, shrines, etc., depending on the believers. The cult might include theology (philosophical and rational explanations for faith) and mythology (allegorical or metaphoric narrative to explain elements of the faith).

Cultural assemblage. Household goods, tools, weapons, and buildings of ancient cultures, which are organized by archaeologists according to their similarities.

Dendrochronology. Dates dead timber by counting the rings of wood produced by trees each year. These circles of growth vary in size due to both climatic changes and the age of the tree. Trees of the same species in the same area usually show the same pattern of growth. Long master sequences have been developed for each species back from the present and for trees actually used in the past.

Determinative. A sign used either before or after a word to indicate the category of objects to which the word belongs, for example, wood, deity, human being (male or female), river, place, etc.

Divination. Various methods used to predict events.

Diviner. A specialist who solicited omens from the gods and interpreted the signs. A diviner (literally, "examiner") communicated with divine forces through extispicy, hepatoscopy, lecanomancy, and libanomancy. Diviners usually worked for the king, either directly as palace scholars or indirectly as a part of the government or the army.

Dry farming. Agriculture that relied only on natural rainfall.

Dynasty. Royal succession became an institution of society. Kings were no longer elected for specific needs such as leadership in times of war. Kings claimed to rule by divine right, which remained in the family and passed to brothers or sons.

Elam. Located in southwest Iran, it served as a link between Mesopotamia and more distant parts of Iran. Its capital was Susa. The language, Elamite, cannot be related to any other language and is only partly understood. It is written in a variant form of Sumerian.

Enki/Ea. The god of the fresh waters and a benefactor of mankind. He was the source of all secret magical knowledge.

Enlil. "Lord wind," initially as the national god of Sumer, held the Tablets of Destiny. He was also a benefactor of mankind.

Ephemerides. The most important texts dealing with mathematical astronomy can be dated from 300 BCE to the beginning of the Christian era. These texts record the daily and monthly positions of the moon and the planets (Venus, Mercury, Saturn, Jupiter, and Mars). Procedure texts augment this information with rules for calculating the Ephemerides.

Equinox. The sun and moon cross the celestial equator twice a year, at which time the length of night and day are approximately the same.

Ereshkigal. Queen of the Netherworld.

Ethnoarchaeology. A discipline developed by archaeologists in order to study contemporaneous cultures to understand their material culture, for example, buildings, tools, and settlements.

Exorcist. A member of the priesthood, the exorcist used various procedures, such as oral formulas, manual rituals, and prayers, to avoid evil happenings.

Extispicy. A type of divination based on examination of the intestines of animals slaughtered for the purpose of foretelling future events. The favorable and unfavorable features, discolorations, and markings have been compiled.

Faience. A composite material of powdered quartz with a vitreous alkaline glaze.

False value. A method for solving first and second degree equations by which the unknown is provisionally designated by 1 in order to find the coefficients.

Frit. A substance used in making glazes or glass.

Full, fulling. Increasing the weight and volume of cloth by shrinking, beating, and pressing it.

Gilgamesh. King of Uruk "after the Flood." A series of adventures were written about this hero, who tried to find immortality but failed.

Glaze. Application to a surface of powdered quartz and alkali by high firing.

Goal year texts. Compilations made from the diaries of previous years for the purpose of predicting astronomical events in the coming year, which is called the goal year.

Haruspex. The diviner who read the liver omens in order to predict the future.

Hemerology, pl. hemerologies. List of auspicious and inauspicious days for undertaking certain activities according to the order of the calendar.

Hepatoscopy. A type of divination in which the liver (perhaps together with the gall bladder) of a sacrificed animal was examined to predict the future.

Hittites. The Hittites, known from both Egyptian and Biblical sources, inhabited a kingdom in what is today Asia Minor (eastern Turkey) and Syria. The kingdom of "Hatti" became one of the major powers in the Near East in the second millennium BCE. The capital city was Khattusha (about one thousand miles east of Ankara in Turkey). The people spoke Hittite, an Indo-European language similar to Greek and Latin. They wrote Hittite in the cuneiform of the Akkadians. The Hittites were important as a channel for the spread of Mesopotamian ideas (via the Hurrians) to Asia Minor and then on to Greece. The Hittites developed iron technology.

Homophony. The practice of using several signs to represent the same sound.

Hurrians. The place of origin of this people remains uncertain, but it may have been in Armenia or further north. By the middle of the second millennium BCE they founded the mighty Hurrian kingdom of **Mitanni**. According to linguistic evidence, Mitanni was home to two peoples, Hurrians as the majority and Indo-Aryans as a small but significant minority. The Hurrian language is related only to Urartian. The Hurrians transmitted Mesopotamian ideas and culture to the Hittites and even as far as Greece. The Indo-Aryans are credited with introducing the horse, particularly in warfare, to the ancient Near East. Almost everything we know about Mitanni comes from foreign sources.

Ideograph/ideogram. A symbol used in writing to represent a word or semantic range of words.

Inanna/Ishtar. She embodied the roles of different goddesses and was called "Lady of myriad offices" (Jacobsen 1976: 141). By the second millennium BCE, Ishtar became the best known and most widely worshiped Babylonian deity, and the name Ishtar came to be the generic word for "goddess." Inanna was the Morning Star and Evening Star. She was also the goddess of love and sexuality as well as patron goddess of the harlot and the alehouse.

Incipit. The title of a text, which is usually the first line.

Incubation. A practice used to induce dream messages by spending the night in a sanctuary.

Jezirah (Arabic, "island"). Steppe zone south of the foothills of the Taurus Mountains, in the northwestern part of Mesopotamia in the area spanning the 250 miles that separate the Euphrates and Tigris Rivers.

Josephus. A Jewish historian who wrote in Greek in the first century CE. When he was governor of Galilee, he was captured by the Romans, who spared his life. In 70 CE Josephus moved to Rome, where he became a citizen. He wrote *Jewish Antiquities* and *Jewish War*.

Kassites. The origin of the Kassites is unknown. They first appeared in Babylonia as agricultural workers, but by the end of the seventeenth century BCE, their social status grew. The number and order of the early Kassite kings is uncertain. The first king identified as ruling in Babylon was Agum II. The Kassites ruled peacefully for more than four hundred years (ca. 1595–1158)—longer than any other dynasty. They restored the Babylonian empire to glory after the Hittites sacked Babylon in 1595 BCE. The Kassites followed the social and religious customs of the Babylonians and used the Akkadian language. The scribes of the Kassite period tried to compose authoritative versions of texts.

Kidenas. A Babylonian astronomer (ca. 375 BCE) who calculated the length of the solar year with marginal error.

Kudurru. Akkadian word for a Kassite oval or pillar-shaped monument approximately two feet high. It is a record of royal land grants. The *kudurru* was deposited in the temple or at the place of the grant. The landowner kept a clay-tablet copy or deposited the tablet at the temple. The text gave details about the plot of land and any taxes and duties due. A list of witnesses was included. Elaborate curses were invoked against anyone who tampered with the monument or deprived the owner of his land. A standard *kudurru* had symbols of the gods sculpted on the top or on one side, perhaps to enhance the curse formulas directed at an illiterate audience.

Lecanomancy. A form of operational divination in which the diviner provides the deity with the chance of directly affecting communication by the spreading of oil.

Levant. The coast and surrounding area of the eastern Mediterranean. It is synonymous with the area otherwise designated as Syro-Palestine. Levant (French, "rising") is said of the sun.

Libanomancy. A form of operational divination in which the diviner provides the deity with the chance of communicating by affecting the observation of smoke from incense.

Limmu **lists**. A date list in which each year after the first year of a king's rule was named after an Assyrian official, a practice dating to the first millennium BCE.

Marduk (Akkadian, "son of the storm"). Patron god of Babylon and head of the Babylonian pantheon.

Medes. A people who entered northwest Iran at the end of the second millennium BCE. Though influenced by the cultural developments in Assyria, the Medes played a key role in the overthrow of Assyria.

Mitanni. See **Hurrians**.

Mul-Apin. A three-tablet series named after the first entry, meaning "plow-star" or Andromeda. This series included a list of stars arranged in three parallel "roads," with the middle one following the equator, as well as references to the planets, to complexities of the calendar, and to observations of Venus' disappearance and reappearance behind the sun.

Mythopoeic. Pertaining to the creation of myth.

Namburbû. A form of exorcism. Rituals of undoing.

Nanna/Sin. The full moon, the crescents, and the new moon. The terms were also used for the gods associated with the moon.

Nergal. King of the netherworld.

Neti. Gatekeeper of the netherworld.

Ninkhursaga. As "Lady of the stony ground" or "Lady of the foothills," she originally was the numinous power in the alluvial stony ground. She was the goddess of birth for pregnant animals. She also acted as midwife to the gods.

Ninurta. "Lord Plow" represented the humid thunderstorm of spring, which made the soil easy to plow.

Nomads/nomadism. Shepherds who migrated with their herds through areas not generally used for agriculture. Nomads belonged to social groups larger than the family, such as tribes or clans.

Numina (plural of Latin *numen*). Early humans regarded the supernatural forces controlling their world as mysterious and impersonal. For them, storms, rivers, lakes, marshes, mountains, sun, wind, and fire were all living beings.

Obsidian. Dark, volcanic glass with hard flintlike edges used to create tools and weapons.

Occupation level. At an archaeological site, the principle of stratigraphy is applied—early deposits lie beneath later ones. By examining materials that indicate human activities, such as cultural assemblages, buildings, and organic remains, human occupational levels are determined.

Omen. A large group of omens revealed a predetermined situation that could be avoided by magical means. Omens were solicited and unsolicited. The omens involved two types of divine revelation given to individuals: (1) a warning about a specific danger predicted by an observable event, or (2) a notification of a propitious development in the future. Omens were the main way in which Mesopotamian gods communicated their intentions and decisions.

Paleography. Study of the changes in the ancient writing scripts through time.

Pastoralists/pastoralism. Sheep or goat herders whose lifestyle is basically nomadic. They live off their animals' products, but occasionally they also plant crops at a base.

Persian period. The Persian period refers to Mesunder Achaemenid rule (539–333 BCE) and includes among its rulers Cyrus II, Cambyses II, Darius (I, II, III), Xerxes and Attaxerxes (I, II, III).

Phoenicians. The Canaanites were their ancestors. The Phoenicians emerged ca. 1100 BCE. Because of various folk migrations, they were confined to the coast from modern Lebanon to northern Israel. Phoenicia was considered a string of coastal cities rather than a nation. The Phoenicians were mariners and traders who helped spread Near Eastern civilization and culture to the western Mediterranean and transmitted the alphabet to the Greeks, which the Greeks called "Phoenician things."

Phrygia/Phrygians. Gordion, the capital of Phrygia, is located in Anatolia. Archaeological expeditions have provided extensive evidence of settlements from the Early Bronze Age into the Roman period. The first Phrygians immigrated to Asia Minor from Macedon and Thrace after the Trojan War (ca. twelfth century BCE). The Phrygians appeared with the migration of several new population groups in Asia Minor after the collapse of the Hittite empire ca. 1200 BCE.

— **Phylactery, pl. phylacteries.** Objects similar to amulets and charms which were worn or "tied on" as a sign of piety.

Pictogram/pictograph. In the earliest stage of writing the signs are drawings of the objects they represent.

Place-value notation. A system in which the magnitude of a very limited number of symbols is determined by position, with the higher values on the left and the lower values on the right. Also called positional number system.

Polos. A shadow clock or an ancient device used to tell time. A hollow hemisphere with a needle fixed at the center; its shadow was cast on the walls, which were marked at intervals.

Polyphony. The principle of assigning one sign several values.

Positional number system. See **place-value notation.**

Prebends. Allocations of redistributed offerings received by the temple and given to temple staff. The prebends or temple offices could be sold, rented, or inherited. The temple prebend was sometimes subdivided so that individuals held office as little as one day a year. The nominal character of these offices was further emphasized by the right of an individual to hold more than one office at a time.

Protasis. The conditional clause (protasis) which stated the proposition or "case." The apodosis explained the prediction. For example, "If (in his dream) one gives him a seal (protasis): he will have a son (apodosis)."

Ptolemy (Claudius Ptolemaeus, 127–48 CE). A second century CE Greek geographer from Alexandria. Ptolemy added to one of his books a list of the kings of Babylon and Persia, the Near Eastern segment dated from Nabonassar (747 BCE) through Cleopatra VII (30 BCE). This list, called *Ptolemy's Canon*, gives both the length of each king's reign and some of the outstanding astronomical events. Because of Ptolemy's Canon, these chronologies can be converted into Christian era dates. Through the years, scholars continued working on Ptolemy's Canon to include Byzantine rulers up to the fifteenth century CE.

Radiocarbon dating. Absolute dates can be established by radiocarbon or carbon-14 dating, which was discovered by Willard Libby of the University of Chicago. Radiocarbon dating measures the decay of the radioactive isotope carbon-14 in organic material in order to determine the age of anything that contained carbon and then died. The age of a plant or animal can be calculated from the amount of radiocarbon remaining in the sample. The isotope carbon-14, present in minute amounts, decays at a steady rate, expressed in terms of a half-life of 5,730 years. The method can be used anywhere to date organic material as far back as 50,000–80,000 years.

Relative dating. Approximate dating in which artifacts (such as pottery, tools, jewelry, household objects, etc.), buildings, skeletal remains, layers of soil deposits, and even societies are deemed relatively earlier, later, or even contemporary by organizing them into sequences based on cumulative information. The date cannot be stated precisely in calendar years.

River Ordeal. Cases were brought before the divine judges of the river when evidence and testimony were in dispute. Immersion in the "Divine River" brought a verdict of guilt (drowning) or innocence (survival).

Sedentists/sedentism. Settled peoples such as farmers and townspeople.

Seleucids (Seleucid period). This hybrid civilization represented native Mesopotamian, Syrian (or Aramaean), and Greek cultures. The Seleucid era began with Seleucid era year 1 = 311 BCE.

Semi-nomad/semi-nomadism. See **transhumant/transhumancy**.

Series. A group of related thematically texts compiled and edited in ancient times into a standard work. The title was taken from the first line of the work. The series, in turn, was divided into sections called "tablets."

Seven Counselors. Seven divine sages sent by Ea before the Flood to teach mankind the arts of civilization—the crafts. They angered Ea, the god of wisdom, who banished the Seven Counselors forever. After the Flood, certain great men were called sages, but they were never accorded divine status.

Sexagesimal system. A mathematical system that uses 60 as its base.

Stele, pl. stelae. An upright stone or pillar with an inscription and/or design. It serves as a marker, monument, etc.

Steppe. A semi-arid plain that may be covered by seasonal grasses in spring. The steppe in western Asia is found in the Jezirah.

Stratigraphy. Stratigraphy, the study of strata or layers of occupational debris, lying one above the other, provides a relative chronology from the bottom, or earliest, to the top, or most recent.

Substrate/substratum. A language that has influenced a more dominant language in vocabulary, grammar, and syntax in a given geographical area.

Syntax. The study of word combinations and sentence structure.

Tablets of Destiny. The fates of men and gods were recorded here, so whoever held the Tablets of Destiny ruled the universe.

Tell (Arabic, "hill"). A mound of heaped-up layers of continuous human occupation and abandonment formed over a long period of time.

Transhumant/transhumancy. The terms semi-nomads (semi-Bedouins) and transhumants refer to nomadic tribes or clans who farmed and raised animals on the outskirts of settlements.

Trepanation. Removal of part of the scalp and a piece of the skull bone. Trepanations were performed when the skull was fractured or to relieve headaches or epilepsy.

Tribute. A kind of tax paid by a territory that had already been conquered either by force or by diplomacy.

Urartu. Located in the mountainous area of eastern Turkey and mentioned in the Bible. Urartu was the Assyrian name for Armenia and its mountain called Ararat. It was known for its exquisite metalwork. Its language is a later form of Hurrian.

Utu/Shamash. A god whose Sumerian and Akkadian names mean "sun." He was entrusted with the responsibility of dispensing justice to both gods and men.

Venus tablets. The Babylonian "Venus" tablets record the appearance and disappearance of Venus during the twenty-one years of the reign of King Ammi-saduqa (1646–1626 BCE), a ruler of the First Dynasty of Babylon. The tablets provide enough information for modern astronomers to calculate several alternative dates of three likely Venus cycles. Therefore, three chronologies, called high, middle, and low chronologies, have arisen for Babylonia during the second millennium BCE. The tablets have been recopied through time and possibly changed in the process; the Venus tablets available to us today date

to the seventh century BCE, raising questions about the accuracy of
the data.

Water clock. All information we have on water clocks is indirect. There
are no drawings in the mathematical texts. Water clocks were either
cylindrical or prismatic. Time was calculated by filling a vessel of a
given height with water to a marked line and then letting the water
escape through a hole in the bottom of a water clock. To date, only
one extant artifact from the ancient Near East has been identified as
connected with the measurement of time using water: it is a bowl
with a central hole in the base, similar to European clock bowls,
which offer a more practical method for measuring small intervals
of time. When placed on the surface of water in another receptacle,
these bowls sink in a very short time due to the weight of the bowl
and the size of the hole. A set of these bowls could be used in conjunction with the water clock to measure short and long portions of
time.

Xenophon (ca. 428 BCE–354 BCE). A Greek historian who in his youth
was a follower of Socrates. He wrote on a variety of subjects, including hunting, horsemanship, estate management, and finance. He
also wrote two major historical texts: *Hellenica*, which covers Greek
history from 411 to 362 BCE, and *Anabasis*, based on his adventures
with 10,000 mercenary soldiers led by Cyrus the Younger against his
brother, Artaxerxes II, who became emperor after their father's
death.

Ziggurat. Mesopotamian monumental building with stepped tower with
progressively receding stories. At the top was the shrine of a specific
god, which could be reached by ramps and staircases.

Selected Bibliography

Black, Jeremy, and Anthony Green. 1992. *Gods, Demons and Symbols of Ancient Mesopotamia: An Illustrated Dictionary*. Austin, TX: University of Texas Press.

Bottéro, Jean. 1992. *Mesopotamia: Writing, Reasoning and the Gods*. Translated by Zainab Bahrani and Marc van de Mieroop. Chicago: University of Chicago Press.

Burstein, Stanley M. 1978. *The Babyloniaca of Berossus*. Sources from the Ancient Near East 1/5. Malibu: Undena Publications.

Collon, Dominique. 1995. *Ancient Near Eastern Art*. Berkeley and Los Angeles: University of California Press.

Contenau, Georges. 1954. *Everyday Life in Babylon and Assyria*. Translated by K. R. Maxwell-Hyslop and A. R. Maxwell-Hyslop. New York: St. Martin's Press.

Cotterell, Arthur, ed. 1980. *The Penguin Encyclopedia of Ancient Civilizations*. London: Penguin Books.

Dalley, Stephanie. [1989] 1992. *Myths from Mesopotamia: Creation, the Flood, Gilgamesh and Others*. Reprint. New York: Oxford University Press.

Diakonoff, I. M., ed. 1991. *Early Antiquity*. Translated by Alexander Kijanov. Chicago: University of Chicago Press.

Edwards, I.E.S., C. J. Gadd, and N.G.L. Hammond, eds. 1970. *The Cambridge Ancient History*. 3rd ed. Vol. 1, Part 1, *Prolegomena and Prehistory*. Cambridge: Cambridge University Press.

———. 1971. *The Cambridge Ancient History*. 3rd ed. Vol. 1, Part 2, *Early History of the Middle East*. Cambridge: Cambridge University Press.

Edwards, I.E.S., C. J. Gadd, N.G.L. Hammond, and E. Sollberger, eds. 1973. *The Cambridge Ancient History*, 3rd ed. Vol. II, Part 1, *History of the Middle East and the Aegean Region ca. 1800–1380 BCE*. Cambridge: Cambridge University Press.

———. 1975. *The Cambridge Ancient History*, 3rd ed. Vol. 2, Part 2, *The History of the Middle East and the Aegean Region ca. 1380–1000 BCE*. Cambridge: Cambridge University Press.

Foster, Benjamin R. 1996. *Before the Muses: An Anthology of Akkadian Literature*. 2nd ed. 2 vols. Bethesda, MD: CDL Press.

Hallo, William W. 1992. "Sumerian Literature." In *Anchor Bible Dictionary*, Vol. 6. Edited by David Noel Freedman. New York: Doubleday.

———. 1996. *Origins: The Ancient Near Eastern Background of Some Modern Western Institutions* (Studies in the History and Culture of the Ancient Near East 6). Leiden: E. J. Brill.

Hallo, William W., and William Kelly Simpson. 1998. *The Ancient Near East: A History*, 2nd ed. New York: Harcourt Brace College Publishers.

Hunger, Hermann, F. Richard Stephenson, and Christopher B.F. Walker. 1985. *Halley's Comet in History*. London: British Museum Publications.

Jacobsen, Thorkild. 1946. "Mesopotamia." In *The Intellectual Adventure of the Ancient Man*, by H. Frankfort et al. Chicago: University of Chicago Press.

———. 1976. *The Treasures of Darkness: A History of Mesopotamian Religion*. New Haven, CT: Yale University Press.

James, Peter. 1993. *Centuries of Darkness: A Challenge to the Conventional Chronology of Old World Archaeology*. In collaboration with I. J. Thorpe, Nikos Kokkinos, Robert Morkot, and John Frankish. New Brunswick, NJ: Rutgers University Press.

Knapp, A. Bernard. 1988. *The History and Culture of Ancient Western Asia and Egypt*. Illinois: Dorsey Press.

Kramer, S. N. 1959. *History Begins at Sumer: Twenty-Seven "Firsts" in Man's Recorded History*. New York: Doubleday.

———. 1963. *The Sumerians: Their History, Culture and Character*. Chicago: University of Chicago Press.

Leick, Gwendolyn. 1988. *A Dictionary of Ancient Near Eastern Architecture*. New York: Routledge.

McCall, Henrietta. 1990. *Mesopotamian Myths*. Legendary Past Series. Austin, TX: University of Texas Press.

McIntosh, Jane. 1986. *The Practical Archaeologist: How We Know What We Know about the Past*. London: Facts on File, Paul Press.

McMillon, Bill. 1991. *The Archaeology Handbook: A Field Manual and Resource Guide*. New York: John Wiley and Sons.

Nissen, Hans J. 1988. *The Early History of the Ancient Near East 9000–2000 B.C.* Translated by Elizabeth Lutzeier, with Kenneth J. Northcott. Chicago: University of Chicago Press.

Oates, Joan. [1979] 1986. *Babylon*. 1979. Rev. ed. London: Thames and Hudson.

Oppenheim, A. Leo. [1964] 1977. *Ancient Mesopotamia: Portrait of a Dead Civilization*. Revised by Erica Reiner. Chicago: University of Chicago Press.

———. 1967. *Letters from Mesopotamia: Official, Business, and Private Letters on Clay Tablets from Two Millennia*. Chicago: University of Chicago Press.

Postgate, J. N. 1992. *Early Mesopotamia: Society and Economy at the Dawn of History*. New York: Routledge.

Pritchard, J. B., ed. 1969. *The Ancient Near Eastern Texts Relating to the Old Testament*. 3rd ed. With supplement. Princeton: Princeton University Press. [*ANET³*]

Reiner, Erica. 1985. *Your Thwarts in Pieces, Your Mooring Rope Cut: Poetry from Babylonia and Assyria*. Ann Arbor, MI: University of Michigan.

———. 1995. *Astral Magic in Babylonia*. Transactions of the American Philosophical Society, vol. 8, part 4. Philadelphia: American Philosophical Society.

Renfrew, Colin. 1991. *Archaeology: Theories, Methods, and Practice*. New York: Thames and Hudson.

Roaf, Michael. 1990. *Cultural Atlas of Mesopotamia and the Ancient Near East*. New York: Facts on File.

Roth, Martha T. 1995. *Law Collections from Mesopotamia and Asia Minor*. Atlanta: Scholars Press.

Roux, Georges. [1964] 1992. *Ancient Iraq*. Middlesex, Eng.: Penguin Books. 3rd ed. Harmondsworth, Eng.: Penguin Books, 1992.

Saggs, H.W.F. 1962. *The Greatness That Was Babylon: A Sketch of the Ancient Civilization of the Tigris-Euphrates Valley*. New York: New American Library, Mentor Books.

———. 1965. *Everyday Life in Babylonia and Assyria*. New York: G. P. Putnam's Sons.

———. 1984. *The Might That Was Assyria*. London: Sidgwick and Jackson.

———. 1989. *Civilization Before Greece and Rome*. New Haven, CT: Yale University Press.

Sasson, Jack M., ed. 1995. *Civilizations of the Ancient Near East*, 4 vols. New York: Charles Scribner's Sons. [*CANE*]

Time-Life Books, eds. 1993. *Sumer: Cities of Eden*. Lost Civilizations series. Alexandria, VA: Time-Life Books.

———. 1995. *Mesopotamia: The Mighty Kings*. Lost Civilizations series. Alexandria, VA: Time-Life Books.

von Soden, Wolfram. [1985] 1994. *The Ancient Orient: An Introduction to the Study of the Ancient Near East*. Translated by Donald G. Schley. Grand Rapids, MI: William B. Eerdmans.

Walker, C.B.F. 1987. *Cuneiform*. London: British Museum Publications.

Ward, William A., and Martha S. Joukowsky, eds. 1989. *The Crisis Years: The Twelfth Century BCE from Beyond the Danube to the Tigris*. Iowa: Kendall/Hunt.

Index

Page numbers in *italics* refer to illustrations.

About the Author

KAREN RHEA NEMET-NEJAT was the first woman to receive her Ph.D. in Ancient Near Eastern/East Languages, History and Cultures at Columbia University. She is the author of a forthcoming *Catalogue of the Babylonian Collections at Yale, Cuneiform Mathematical Texts as a Reflection of Everyday Life in Mesopotamia,* and *Late Babylonian Field Plans in the British Museum.* She is currently working on her fifth book. She has also taught at University of Connecticut at Stamford and has held two fellowships at Yale.

DATE DUE